PEOPLE AND ISSUES IN
LATIN AMERICAN HISTORY

The Colonial Experience

PEOPLE AND ISSUES IN LATIN AMERICAN HISTORY

THE COLONIAL EXPERIENCE

Second Edition

Sources and Interpretations

Edited by
LEWIS HANKE and
JANE M. RAUSCH
University of Massachusetts, Amherst

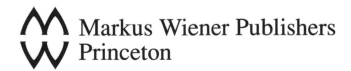 Markus Wiener Publishers
Princeton

Second updated and expanded edition.

© Copyright 2000 by Lewis Hanke and Jane M. Rausch.

For information write to: Markus Wiener Publishers
231 Nassau Street, Princeton, NJ 08542

Library of Congress Cataloging-in-Publication Data

People and issues in Latin American history. The colonial experience—sources and interpretations / edited by Lewis Hanke and Jane M. Rausch.—2nd ed.
    Includes bibliographical references.
    ISBN 1-55876-234-5 (pb: alk. paper)
    1. Latin America—History—To 1830.
    I. Hanke, Lewis.   II. Rausch, Jane M., 1940-
F1412.P383 2000
980—dc21   99-089843

The photographs in the text are reproduced courtesy of the following sources: Library of Congress; University of California Library, Berkeley; The Peabody Museum, Harvard University; Instituto Nacional de Anthropologia e Historia, Mexico; Bayerische Staatsbibliothek, Munich.

Printed in the United States of America on acid-free paper.

CONTENTS

SECTION VI: *António Vieira and the Crises of Seventeenth-Century Brazil*   229

SECTION VII: *The Development of Society*   277

PREFACE TO THE SECOND EDITION

In 1967 when Lewis Hanke published *History of Latin American Civilization: Sources and Interpretations*, a two-volume reader designed to serve as the principal text for survey courses, his purpose was "to present a reasonable selection of sources on and interpretations of some of the important events and topics in the history of Latin America." The books were an instant success. Scores of professors adopted them for their classes, prompting Little, Brown and Company to bring out a revised second edition in 1973 and a one-volume abridged version in 1974. Unfortunately, despite their popularity, all versions of the text went out of print within a decade, and no new reader of similar design appeared to take its place.

People and Issues In Latin American History: The Colonial Experience was and is an attempt to salvage and update the first volume of Hanke's valuable text. In the first edition published by Markus Wiener in 1990, I integrated sections selected from the 1973 and 1974 editions, leaving them mostly intact and adding only one new unit. For the second edition, however, I have thoroughly revised and expanded the materials in order to better reflect the new publications and fresh ideas that have marked research in the colonial era over the last three decades.

Unlike the companion volume, *People and Issues in Latin American History— The National Era* (2nd. ed. New York: Markus Wiener, 1998), in which five of the eight sections focus on representative personalities rather than issues, *The Colonial Experience* remains faithful to Hanke's original design by highlighting nine important topics debated by historians. Nevertheless, within these pages students will meet Bartolomé de Las Casas, the stout defender of the Indians in sixteenth-century Spanish America, and Antonio Vieira, his seventeenth-century counterpart in Brazil. They will critically examine Columbus's role in the Iberian conquest of America, and encounter Isabel Moctezuma, a "pioneer of mestizaje;" Juan Garrido, a black conquistador; Francisco de Toledo, Viceroy of Peru; Johan Maurits, the humanist Dutch governor of Recife; Sor Juana de la Cruz, "Supreme Poet of the Seventeenth Century Spanish World;" Tupac Amaru, the leader of the last Inca rebellion in Peru; and the German savant and scientist, Alexander von Humboldt. Finally, they will read about the nameless men and women—Spanish, Portuguese, Indian, and African—whose collective stories make the history of three hundred years ago more comprehensible to our twentieth-century mentalities.

Lewis Hanke firmly believed that "Latin American history offers exciting and fruitful ideas for college students to encounter as part of their general education." "Latin American history," he wrote, "should not be looked upon as a 'crisis' subject, but as the unfolding story of a culture, a civilization both interesting and worthy of attention in itself." It is my hope that this revised volume will remain faithful to this objective and provide North American undergraduates with a "window" on a fascinating world that will enable them to learn about other people, other cultures, and other points of view.

Jane M. Rausch
Amherst, January 2000

Christopher Columbus. There are numerous portraits of Columbus, but none are regarded as definitive. This woodcut engraving by Tobias Stimmer was the first one published that is believed to be somewhat accurate. It is a copy of a portrait once owned by Paolo Giovvio in 1550 (now lost) which Stimmer completed in Basel, Switzerland, in 1575. As Martin Lunenfeld explains, "The picture shows Columbus dressed in a Spanish tabard, a red cloak then worn by sailors, while the frame depicts two figures standing on world globes, one a European and the other an Amerindian." (Source: 1492: Discovery, Invasion, Encounter, p. 101)

SECTION I

Columbus and the
Transit of Civilization

THE INFLUENCE OF EUROPE

Why have so little effort and imagination been spent on determining what ideas, institutions, values, and ways of life the Spanish and Portuguese carried to America during their more than three centuries of colonial rule? More particularly, why has such minor attention usually been given in Latin American history courses to the European scene, the background from which the conquerors and colonists came?

One answer can be given easily: there is simply too much material on Spanish and Portuguese history, and what interest historians have displayed in the subject has been too narrowly focused on the specific ethnic, cultural, and institutional elements the mother countries transplanted across the Atlantic from 1492 on. Charles Julian Bishko of the University of Virginia, who has been a major figure in enlarging our views of Iberian background studies, would emphasize the period from 711 C.E., when the Arabs first swept into the Iberian peninsula, until the death of Philip II in 1598, which marks the end of "the basic epoch of the discovery, conquest, and colonization of the Spanish and Portuguese Indies." But he also states: "Broadly speaking from the chronological standpoint, the background stretches from the first human habitation of the peninsula right down to present-day Spanish and Portuguese influence upon Latin America."[1] Given the size of the task, is it any wonder that Latin Americanists, pressed to cover a large New World history in a short time, have tended to devote scant attention to the Old? Fortunately for students who wish to pursue Iberian background studies further, there is a valuable one-volume survey that for the first time provides a solid basis of readings in English.[2]

Another explanation of the special problem faced by Iberian background studies

---

1. Charles Julian Bishko, "The Iberian Background of Latin American History: Recent Progress and Continuing Problems," *Hispanic American Historical Review* 36 (1965): 50–80. The quotations from this article appear on pp. 53–55.
2. H. B. Johnson, Jr., ed., *From Reconquest to Empire: The Iberian Background of Latin American History* (New York: Knopf, 1970).

1

is the influence that present politics sometimes exert on the writing of history. Since the sixteenth century, arguments have been loud and bitter on the correct interpretation of the role of Portugal and Spain in the New World. Grand generalizations still flourish.[3] For some, these Iberian nations redeemed a wilderness of savages and brought them into a Christian, Western way of life; for others the institutions and ways of life brought from Europe were largely destructive and were almost wholly responsible for all the ills Latin America has suffered from 1492 to today. The publication of thousands of works prompted by the 1992 quincentennial anniversary of Columbus's first voyage failed to produce consensus on the legacy of the Euro-American encounter and demonstrated once again how the historical study of these important and enduring influences has been hampered by the passion and dogmatism engendered all too often by political considerations.[4]

THE IBERIAN BACKGROUND

We must remember that conquest and colonization was not a simple process, for it varied somewhat from region to region. Moreover, early modern Europe in the era of the Renaissance and Reformation carried medieval elements as well as more modern ideas into an already populated continent whose cultures had been evolving for centuries with few outside contacts. There were also differences between the history and life styles of the Portuguese and Spanish peoples, even though they shared the same peninsula, cherished the same faith, and had much in common. Less has been written on the Portuguese background, but Professor Stuart B. Schwartz provides a succinct and interesting overview (Reading 1).

Conquest has dominated Spanish history from remote time. Following earlier invasions of Phoenicians, Greeks, and Carthaginians, the Romans controlled the Iberian Peninsula from 201 B.C.E. to the early fifth century and imposed their language and institutions on the native peoples. They left a strong Latin heritage, before falling in turn before the onslaught of a Germanic people, the Visigoths. In 711 Muslims from North Africa invaded the peninsula and decisively defeated Roderic, the last Gothic king. Within a few years all of Spain except for a few remote northern regions fell into Muslim hands. The peninsula was not completely retaken by Christian forces until the fall of Granada in 1492.

For seven centuries Iberia was the economic and intellectual showplace of the Mediterranean world, for the Muslims introduced new irrigation systems, new crops

---

3. See Lewis Hanke's "A Modest Proposal for a Moratorium on Grand Generalizations: Some Thoughts on the Black Legend," *Hispanic American Historical Review* 51 (1971): 112–27. For a rebuttal see Benjamin Keen's article, ibid., pp. 336–55.

4. David Block, "Quincentennial Publishing: An Ocean of Print," *Latin American Research Review* 29:3 (1994): 101–28.

such as sugar, saffron, cotton, silk, and citrus fruits, new industries as well as the science and learning of the Arab world. At the same time, as Derek W. Lomax points out, this period was marked by the "Reconquest"—the long struggle by Christian kings and nobles to expel the Muslims that made the "Middle Ages" of Iberia unique from the rest of Western Europe. Reconquest also set a pattern for the conquest of the New World where "independent conquistadors, sometimes with and other without specific authorization from the crown, put into practice the negotiating and fighting techniques their ancestors evolved over centuries."5 (Reading 2).

The marriage of Ferdinand of Aragon and Isabella of Castile in 1469 was the crucial event of Iberian history between the mid-fifteenth century and the fall of Granada since it paved the way for the unification of three quarters of the peninsula under a vigorous monarchy. The Portuguese recognition of Isabella's claim to the Castilian throne by the Treaty of Alcaçovas in 1479 granted to the Catholic sovereigns control of the Canary Islands in exchange for Spanish acknowledgment of Portuguese rule of Madeira, the Azores and Cape Verde—the other known Atlantic islands. Spanish settlement of the Canaries, as described by Felipe Fernández-Arnesto (Reading 3), was an important prelude for the subsequent conquest of America.

CHRISTOPHER COLUMBUS: MAN AND MYTH

Perhaps no event was more momentous for subsequent global history than Columbus's first voyage to America in 1492. Setting off from Palos, Spain on August 3 with three small ships, the Genoese mariner was looking for a sea route to Asia, and on landing on October 12 on an island in the Bahamas which he named San Salvador, Columbus believed that he had reached Cathay (China) and Xipango (Japan). His letter to Ferdinand and Isabella which summarized the trip and its results was intended to prove that he had succeeded in his mission and to encourage the funding of a second voyage to reap the wealth that he believed was guaranteed. Scholars have subsequently subjected this letter to tortured scrutiny endeavoring to discover what Columbus was truly thinking, but despite their sometimes laborious explications, the Admiral's genuine wonder over the marvelous environment and peoples that he saw for the first time is evident to the most uninformed reader (Reading 4).

The myths surrounding Columbus make it difficult to put his accomplishments into their proper context. Too often he has been depicted as "a perfect hero in advance of his times," but really he was a product of his times, strongly influenced

5. Marvin Lunenfeld, ed., *1492: Discovery, Invasion, Encounter* (Lexington: D. C. Heath, 1991), p. 23.

by the powerful religious and economic currents of the fifteenth century. For example, in pursuit of wealth, he established a slave trade in Caribbean natives, but at the same time he hoped they would be converted to Christianity, and he planned to use some of his profits to recapture Jerusalem from the Muslims in fulfillment of Christian prophecy. Neither a "simple hero" nor an "unredeemable villain," Columbus was a complex human being who exemplified the virtues and the flaws of Europeans of his era,[6] and ultimately, as John Noble Wilford concludes, "His place in history can only be judged in relation to the place accorded America in history over the last five centuries." (Reading 5)

FROM HEMISPHERE TO HEMISPHERE

Columbus's 1492 voyage initiated a biological, botanical, cultural, and political interchange between the two hemispheres which continues to this day. In Reading 6 William and Carla Phillips explain that the effect of the discovery on Europe was largely positive. Once it was understood that America was not part of Asia but a whole new continent, the expansion of geographical horizons was accompanied by new ways of viewing the world that contributed significantly to intellectual progress. In the course of defining New World peoples, Spaniards had to redefine themselves as well, and their quickly won colonial empire at first strengthened the monarchy at home and ultimately led to its downfall. Inflation generated by the great expansion of trade contributed to the so-called "Price Revolution" in Western Europe and to the development of banking and credit in the sixteenth century, while the global migration of plants and animals continues to this day.

Until recently few questioned that the impact on the New World was equally fortuitous, but awareness of Eurocentric connotations of "Discovery" and "Conquest" has led many twentieth-century scholars to assert that the events of 1492 were an "unmitigated disaster" for the native peoples of America. They point out that the arrival of the Europeans cut short the development of brilliant native civilizations and initiated a process of ecological devastation. Moreover, the brutal exploitation of the natives and the introduction of new diseases for which they had no immunity led to perhaps the greatest demographic catastrophe in recorded history, a topic discussed by Alfred W. Crosby (Reading 7).

6. William D. Phillips, Jr., "Columbus, Christopher," in Barbara A. Tenenbaum, ed., *Encyclopedia of Latin American History and Culture* (New York: Charles Scribner's Sons, 1996), p. 225.

A FINAL QUESTION

Why were some Iberian customs, ideas, and institutions accepted or modified in America and others rejected? As anthropologist George Foster emphasizes, Spanish forms of material culture and techniques were welcomed by the indigenous people when they saw them as useful, and when there were no indigenous counterparts or where Spanish forms represented a significant extension of their indigenous forms. But in the broad field of folk culture—dietary patterns, superstitions, folk medicine, folklore, and music—"Spanish traits found themselves in competition with indigenous traits, and often with no clear advantage."[7]

Indian populations under colonial pressure retained powers of selective choice, accepting certain European subsistence activities, and rejecting others. In Peru, these patterns of selective choice were governed, on the whole, by environmental limitations and by antecedent Indian needs and habits. Most interesting are these latter. Once a European food plant, for instance, had weathered the transportation to an American climate, that import was doomed to failure unless it found Indian acceptance. Examples in Peru during the sixteenth century were European squashes and gourds and beans; rice, and gardening vegetables; grapes and orchard fruits; barley and rye. If cultivated, these species were grown only for European use, and never came to dominate Indian subsistence. On the other hand, Indians accepted and exploited horse- and cattle-breeding, pigs, sheep, and goats, as well as cats; chickens; sugarcane, mustard, garlic, and alfalfa. In the absence of specially intense pressures, therefore, the Indian communities could pick and choose among the new subsistence activities. Their choices were governed by certain simple considerations. They were not interested in European species that closely resembled their own or provided analogous satisfactions. European squashes illustrate the point: a plant food insufficiently distinguished from Indian varieties. Indians were also disinclined to cultivate plants from which few by-products were available, or which required large amounts of land: orchards and vineyards are examples. They also refused species whose cultivation cannot be grown by the traditional, easy-going communal methods of Andean corn-agriculture. The Indians long avoided these crops, even in favorable climatic and geographical conditions.

But horses and cattle, unlike the native livestock (llama, alpaca, vicuña), could be used as draft animals, and their hides and fats were useful by-prod-

7. George M. Foster, *Culture and Conquest: America's Spanish Heritage* (Chicago: Quadrangle Books, 1960), p. 229.

ucts. The Indians accepted them, even at the expense of giving over arable land to alfalfa and other fodder crops. Sugarcane, to take another case, yielded a prized sweetening, a welcome addition to Indian diet, as well as fuel from the discarded fiber. Mustard and garlic finally, competed successfully as condiments with Indian peppers, and entailed no basic changes in the methods of agriculture.[8]

It also appears that "cultural crystallization" took place in the early years of the conquest: "The early decades in America were decades of decision, a time when new adjustments and colonial cultures were roughed out and the basic outlines set."[9]

The readings in this section will indicate some important and constant flow of ideas and materials back and forth across the Atlantic Ocean between the Iberian motherlands and their American colonies. Much more research must be undertaken, but enough is known to suggest the extent of this reciprocity in the history of Latin America.

8. George Kubler, *Mexican Architecture of the Sixteenth Century*, vol. 2 (New Haven: Yale University Press, 1948), p. 419.
9. Foster, *Culture and Conquest*, p. 234.

THE IBERIAN BACKGROUND

1. Brazil's Portuguese Heritage Should Not Be Forgotten

STUART B. SCHWARTZ

Professor Schwartz of Yale University is a representative of the vigorous school of Brazilianists that has been developing since the 1960s to bring fresh ideas and research power to the study of Portuguese colonial history. Owing much to the inspiration and example of such *grandes figuras* as Charles R. Boxer, they have contributed their own insights and balanced views to the complicated and relatively unstudied history of colonial Brazil and other topics in the story of the widely scattered Portuguese empire. Here we have an excellent example of Schwartz's interpretive work, which focuses on the social and cultural heritage transferred to Brazil "not by the government of Portugal, but by the Portuguese people."

There is a famous painting by Maria Margarida entitled *"Tres Meninas da Mesma Rua,"* which is often reproduced in books on Brazil. This painting symbolically depicts three beautiful girls representing each of the three major racial components of Brazilian society: Indian, Negro and white. Anthropologists and other social scientists, perhaps lured by the exotic, have ardently courted the first two young ladies in the sense that much attention has been given to the Indian and Negro elements in Brazilian society. The white girl, however, has been neglected. This is especially true of the Portuguese element of Brazil which is obviously so crucial for an understanding of Brazil's past and present. Monograph after monograph can be found on almost all facets of the Negro and Indian contributions to Brazilian culture but information on the Portuguese remains scarce. . . .

The Portuguese heritage of Brazil can be examined on two different levels. One is the administrative, official aspect which amounts to the history of Portuguese

From "The Uncourted Menina: Brazil's Portuguese Heritage," by Stuart B. Schwartz, *Luso-Brazilian Review* 2 (Summer 1965): 67–81, passim. © 1965 by the Regents of the University of Wisconsin. Reprinted by permission.

colonial control of Brazil. The other is the social and cultural heritage transferred not by the government of Portugal, but by the Portuguese people. The two are at many points difficult to separate, but it is the social and cultural tradition which will be discussed here. What were the characteristics of the Portuguese colonizers? What aspects of Brazilian life are the result of Lusitanian influence? These are the primary questions. Almost everyone who writes on Brazil agrees that the common denominator of Brazilian culture is basically Portuguese. There remains to be studied, however, what these elements are, what changes they underwent, and how they were integrated into Brazilian culture.

Certainly, the starting point of an examination of Brazil's cultural debt to Portugal must be a discussion of the development and character of the Portuguese people. The Portuguese at the time of the conquest of Brazil were not a racially homogeneous group and their culture was a result of a variety of contacts and developments. The original Lusitanians had, through contact with Phoenicians, Romans, French and English knights, Moors, Jews, and Negroes, acquired a complex of traditions and values which formed the basis of Portuguese society. In a sense the Portuguese were a people of mixed cultural and racial heritage, a fact that would be important in their settlement of Brazil. . . .

The Portuguese have been called a mixture of dreamers and of men of action who do not lack a practical side to their nature. They can be extremely pragmatic and adaptable when faced with a problem that calls for a practical solution. This plasticity and adaptability has been considered by some to be the basic key to the success of Portugal in creating a lasting civilization in Brazil. As an active dreamer, the Portuguese, if given an ideal, is capable of great efforts through determined and persistent action involving self-denial, sacrifice, and courage. When, however, the task is mediocre and does not arouse his interest, he lacks initiative. . . . It was the stimulation of his imagination and interest for the glory of conquest and battle, the lure of wealth, and the service of religion which motivated the Portuguese in the age of Discovery.

The heart is the measure of all things for the Portuguese and he is basically human, amorous, and affectionate. The pleasures of the Lusitanian tend to be organic rather than intellectual and the Portuguese have a robust humor that can lead them to "Breughel-like frolicking." Violence and unnecessary suffering are avoided, as is the case in the Portuguese-style bullfight, or *tourada*, in which the bull is not killed. If outraged or dishonored, however, the Portuguese is capable of extreme and sudden violence. As will be shown below, this is especially true when the chastity of the female members of his family is concerned or when his own personal honor is at stake. The Portuguese has a strong belief in miracles and in the stroke of luck, as is evidenced by the popularity of the lottery in Portugal and as has been shown in the past by the cult of Sebastianism. This belief in miraculous solutions appears to have been inherited by the Brazilians, who have developed a "Deus é brasileiro" attitude toward their problems. This attitude has been reinforced, however, by Brazil's own peculiar history, especially in view of its economic cycles and boom-bust-boom experience.

The Portuguese, like his Iberian relatives, is an individualist who places great emphasis on personal relationships. He avoids impersonal, secondary relations and prefers to act within the broad ties of the family, often reinforcing these relations with the *compadrio* system. The "autarchy of the individual" and the emphasis on personality are constants of his nature which he will only renounce for a greater good. The result has often been either anarchy or extreme centralization tending toward dictatorship.

An aspect of Portuguese character which the people of Portugal like to claim as theirs alone is that of *saudade*. *Saudade* is an untranslatable word which seems to be a combination of sentimentality, homesickness, and nostalgia. This *saudade,* this sadness of character, is a current which runs deeply throughout Portuguese literature. At times it can become fatalistic and even morbid. The soul-rending *fado* heard in Lisbon originated as an expression of the *saudade* of the Portuguese colonizer in Brazil for his homeland. This longing for Europe, for the metropolis, which characterized many Portuguese in Brazil during the colonial period, has been viewed as one of the worst aspects of the Portuguese heritage of Brazil, for its result was the *mazombismo* of Brazil which depreciated things Brazilian and looked toward Europe, first Portugal and then France, for a model. No less a friend of the Portuguese than Gilberto Freyre has said, "since the end of the sixteenth century the Portuguese has lived parasitically on a past whose splendour he exaggerates." *Saudade*, however, in its less malignant aspects, is soft and sentimental—which is quite understandable when it is remembered that for the Portuguese the heart is the measure of all.

The penchant of the Portuguese for display and ostentation has been noted by many writers. Though there might be little to eat at home, there was always an air of pomp and gentry. . . . It seems, however, that this ostentation was not a matter of personal luxury and comfort but rather of imagination. Jorge Dias has noted that the Portuguese have the hardest beds in Europe, while the streets are filled with automobiles. Poor people who lack the least comfort in their home appear in the street in elegant dress. A similar situation was noted in colonial Brazil and still exists today in rural areas, where women whose dress at home may be ragged appear at mass in finery to which all attention is given. This "Sunday best" is known in Brazil as *traje domingueiro* or *roupa de ver-a-Deus*. Gilberto Freyre, using Thorstein Veblen's term, has called this ostentation "conspicuous waste," and has noted that in the colonial period women who had so many jewels they could not wear them all at the same time often put them on the slaves who followed their mistresses to church.

Coupled with the ostentation of the Portuguese has been his attitude toward work. There existed, during the period of conquest, a depreciation of manual labor. Peasants, although they labored hard, shared the *fidalgo* ideal with the nobility. This attitude was found among the Spaniards as well. The Iberian hoped to get rich quickly, perhaps to own land, but not to labor. Work was for the slave. In fact, in Portugal the verb "to work," *trabalhar*, was often replaced with *mourejar*, "to work like a Moor." Perhaps this attitude of antipathy to manual labor was due to the fact that work indicates the submission of the individual will to an external force, and the Iberian with his emphasis on the individual could not condone this. The result in Brazil was a "bandeirante spirit" in which all energy was devoted to the quick profit. Even in agriculture the emphasis was on the large profit, and at times the Portuguese government had to legislate to force plantation owners to grow food crops. The result of this attitude was the development in Brazil of a "gentleman complex" which depreciated manual labor and emphasized non-functional education as a sign of breeding to be coupled with wealth. Even among the Brazilian lower classes the idea of the quick fortune is pervasive, and men in the Amazon often desert farming in hopes of a rapidly amassed fortune in rubber-hunting. In the mind of the Portuguese productive activity has had much less value than contemplation and love, and a dignified idleness always seemed more noble than the "insane struggle for the daily bread."

The most important aspect of Portuguese character, or at least the most often discussed, is his adaptability. The Portuguese lacks the flame and orthodoxy of the Castilian; rather, he is a compromiser without immutable prejudices who has been able to adapt to climates, occupations, cultures, and races in an exceptional manner. The quality of flexibility and tolerance of other races led in Brazil to miscegenation of an unprecedented extent. This miscegenation and the adaptation of the Portuguese to his new environment has been the basis on which Gilberto Freyre has advocated a new field of study, "Lusotropicalism," or the study of Portuguese integration in the tropics.

Much has been written on the capacity of the Portuguese people to mix with other races. As has been noted earlier, they are themselves a mixed race in which Semitic and Negro elements are important. Some writers, like Freyre, have attributed the race mixing in Brazil to Portugal's contact with the Moors, the concept of the *moura encantada* as the ideal and epitome of sex and beauty for the Portuguese being transferred to the darker-skinned Indians. This ideal, plus the social plasticity of the colonizer in which no firm racial lines were drawn, has often been cited as the prime reason for the success of miscegenation in Brazil. It has been pointed out, however, that the scarcity of women may have had much to do with the extent of racial mixing, and in instances of colonization in Brazil in which the colonist was accompanied by his wife, as in Santa Catarina, much less miscegenation took place.

Slavery, of course, played a role in the process of race mixture in Brazil.

Whatever the cause, miscegenation did take place in Brazil. Slavery was certainly a cause, but slavery, says Freyre, was inevitable. The result of lasting importance was the creation of a psychological and cultural unity of the Brazilian people. An author less convinced of the benefits of race mixture, especially through illegal unions, has noted the characteristics of the *mestiços* or *mulatos* as, "emotional imbalance, inner discord, insecurity, instability, resentment, marginalism, laziness, melancholy," and a constant search for a father-image. . . .

The family in Brazil has been considered the most important institution in the history of the nation and has played a dominant role in the course of Brazil's history. The Brazilian colonial family has often been thought of as that patriarchal institution depicted in the works of Gilberto Freyre which describe the sugar region of the Northeast. The colonial family seen as patriarchal, extended, multifunctional, and of "towering dominance" has been questioned to some extent, since in Brazil variation between groups in the social strata is enormous. The ecological and economic conditions in Brazil did play a part in the continuance of the extended family, as did the weakness of the colonial government. . . .

The prescribed roles of men and women in both the Brazilian and the Portuguese family are based on the virility/virginity complexes. The woman is expected to lead a secluded life, never appearing in public unless properly accompanied. Freyre has laid this tradition to Moorish antecedents. After marriage the woman is expected to be mother and housekeeper, not a companion to her husband. Virginity is a primary requisite before marriage, and should the bride be found lacking in this respect the groom has proper grounds for annulment of the marriage. Any extra-marital relations on the part of the woman are considered grounds for separation. It is common, however, for a husband to kill both the unfaithful wife and her lover and then claim temporary insanity. This is expected and accepted community behavior.

In contrast to the female role in the upper-class Brazilian family is the virility complex of the male, which encourages sexual contact at an early age, ridicules male chastity, and considers extra-marital sexual relations permissible. With the home, however, the male is expected to act as guardian and protector. The males of the family are also expected to be avengers of the family's honor, especially that of its female members. This attitude in Brazil has been reinforced by immigration from Portugal, Spain, and southern Italy. Thus far, the above description can be applied to both Brazilian and Portuguese upper-class families.

The lower-class Brazilian family places much less emphasis on the virginity/virility complex. Marriage is far less stable, and extended kinship groups are not viewed as of great importance. These facts tend to substantiate Willems' thesis that the patriarchal, extended family lessens in importance as one descends the social scale. A similar situation might be expected in Portugal, but such is not the case. The

Portuguese lower-class rural families are based on property, which acts as an adhesive force, holding the family together and reinforcing traditional attitudes. . . . The rural Brazilian family is weak, for it can offer little, and its children tend to leave the paternal home to seek better-paying jobs. It is significant to note that the Brazilian-type rural family is to be found in Alentejo among migratory workers. Here is a case of economic conditions affecting traditional patterns.

Another difference between lower-class Brazilian and Portuguese rural families derives from the tendency of the Portuguese to live in villages or small communities, which act as factors of control and stabilization through community pressure. The more dispersed nature of many of Brazil's rural families means a lessening of community pressure and more individuality and plasticity in family structure. Willems in his studies has shown that the original Portuguese family structure did not remain unchanged in Brazil but was altered to meet ecological, human, and economic conditions, and due to these new changes new structural organizations developed.

The patriarchal family usually attributed in its origins to Portugal must undergo some review, since it has been discovered that in some regions the patriarchal family is not as dominant an institution as had been thought. . . . In parts of the Algarve, the women are the members of the family who take an active part in community life. In Brazil, similar developments can be noted which seem to be exceptions to the patriarchal generalization. Women in São Paulo of land-holding but not of planter-class families often raise their own produce and sell it, keeping the profits themselves. Occasionally, these women engage in speculative loans. These economic activities indicate a degree of independence not usually associated with the Brazilian woman. In both Portugal and Brazil the role of the patriarchal family must be studied further, for it would seem that important exceptions to it do exist. . . .

It is in the everyday life of the Brazilian, especially the rural Brazilian, that the Portuguese heritage is to be seen. The language of Brazil is Portuguese and the style of life of the Brazilian reflects the Portuguese heritage in a hundred ways. For example, the *mutirão,* or mutual work party, although found among Africans and Indians, can be seen in Alentejo, Beira, and Minho. The festivities in Brazil following a *mutirao* are found only in Portuguese origins. Here is but one more example of the duration of the Lusitanian element in Brazil.

The aspect of the Portuguese heritage of Brazil which is most apparent in everyday life and is probably easiest to study is that of the popular folk traditions of Brazilian society. Certainly, the administrative actions of the metropolis during the colonial period played an important role in the formation of Brazilian society just as the Church did in conjunction with the Jesuit Order. But it is the popular rather than the official traditions to which I am referring. . . . Folk tales and folk songs, as well as *louvores populares* to the Virgin, can serve as a basis for tracing the transmission of Portuguese popular cultural elements to Brazil, especially since much work has been done on both sides of the Atlantic in collecting these songs and stories. Théo Brandão in his *Trovas Populares de Alagoas* noted the adaptation of Portuguese *trovas* to Brazilian conditions with modifications due to environment, local expressions, and structural changes. . . . Also, it seems that the custom of the *desafio,* the improvisation of verses by two contending balladeers so clearly explained by Euclides da Cunha in *Os Sertões,* is a Lusitanian custom. . . . From infancy, the Brazilian child is exposed to the Portuguese heritage of his nation. The Brazilian's first games and playthings and even the bogey-men used to frighten him are of Lusitanian origin. The Papão and the Cuca, two such mythical creatures, can be traced directly to Portugal. . . . Even the *lobisomen,* or werewolves, do not stem from any Indian forest spirit but are to be found in Portuguese folk traditions.

The extent to which the Lusitanian folk tradition is dominant in Brazil varies greatly within the diverse cultural regions of the nation. The influence of other cultural elements dilutes the strength of Portuguese cultural tradition while enriching it at the same time. Aside from the obvious cultural differences of non-Portuguese immigrants, other traditions continue to exist, but usually within the basic Portuguese framework. For example, in Rio Grande do Sul the Hispanic influences of the La Plata area are strong, while in the Amazon the economic and cultural patterns show heavy Indian influence. In other areas, particularly the old sugar-producing regions of Bahia and Pernambuco, the cultural heritage of the Negro is evident. Brazilian culture is not Portuguese culture transplanted, but without this element it would be much different than it is.

Certainly, one of the most enduring aspects of Portuguese cultural heritage in Brazil is that of Catholicism: that special brand of Catholicism characteristic of Portugal. The agony-torn Christs of Spain and the soaring Gothic Spanish cathedrals are lacking in Portuguese Catholicism, which was and is a humanistic form of Christianity with anthropomorphic tendencies, often giving special importance to saints associated with love and agricultural fertility. It was the body of Catholic thought which had been softened by long contact with the Moors but which had left a place for saints of the Reconquest. This last aspect can be seen in Brazil in the existence of Sebastianism mixed with other elements in the messianic movements of the Northeast. Religion in Portugal and then in Brazil served a social as well as a spiritual function.

The parallelism and the cultural borrowing of Brazilian Catholicism from its Portuguese antecedents is extensive. The importance of shrines, pilgrimages, and the ceremony of the blessing, all so important in Brazilian Catholicism, stem from the Catholic traditions of Portugal. In both countries the June cycle of the three major saints—St. Anthony, St. John, and St. Peter—is a high point of the religious calendar, even though in Brazil June is a winter not a summer month as it is in

Portugal. In Brazil and Portugal St. Anthony is a *santo pândego* or *santo folião,* a patron of revelry, a forgiver of human weakness, and a noted matchmaker to whom ribald songs are often sung. Also, saints' images are often treated like human beings and are punished or rewarded as their case may merit. It has been noted that Portuguese seamen who have prayed for a favorable wind and fail to receive it lash the saint's effigy to the mast and flog it. In Brazil a non-compliant saint's image may be put uncomfortably near a fire or even pounded to dust in a mortar.

The list of particularly Lusitanian features of Brazilian religion, especially in its folk manifestations, could be extended to great lengths. The impact of the Portuguese form of Catholicism on Brazilian religious and social life is undeniable. It must be remembered, however, that contact of Portugal with Brazil was a historical process extending over at least three centuries, and that the element of change is a part of this process. . . .To continue the analogy made at the beginning of this paper, the third *menina* deserves to be courted, for she comes from a fine old family which has left her a rich inheritance.

2. Spain During the Reconquest

DEREK W. LOMAX

After 711 the Muslims controlled nearly all of Iberia, but a few Christian realms survived in the least productive lands to the far north, and from these remnants grew the kingdoms of León, Castile, Aragon, and Portugal. The Reconquest began as a struggle of Christian kings and nobles to regain their lost lands and serfs, but early in the ninth century when the tomb of St. James, supposedly found in northwest Spain, became the center of the famous pilgrimage of Santiago de Compostela and gave Spain a warrior patron saint, it took on the character of a crusade.

Seven centuries of fighting left an indelible mark on Spanish history and culture. In this reading a seasoned hispanist, Derek W. Lomax, suggests that between 1050 and 1250 Spain transferred from the Islamic culture which was passing its zenith to become part of western Christendom, and argues that after the fall of Granada in 1492, no other European society was prepared as well as Spain to conquer and administer the populous areas of the New World.

It is hardly surprising that a process lasting seven centuries should have given rise to innumerable differences of interpretation, especially since terms like Reconquest, Holy War and Crusades have been used with considerable ambivalence, since some periods have been but little studied and since source material is generally patchy. However it is already possible to indicate the main lines of development and some of the problems yet to be solved.

If one defines the Reconquest as the transfer of political power over the Peninsula from Muslim to Christian hands, then it is clear that this really occurred between 718 and 1492. What is also clear is that most of the characteristics of this transfer already existed by the time of Alfonso III [866–911], rather than being inventions of the eleventh century. The chronicles of his reign show that the policy of reconquering the whole of Spain had already been formulated and adopted, that one motive for this policy was the desire to recover the heritage which the Muslims had allegedly usurped from the rightful successors of the Visigothic [Germanic tribal] monarchy, and that the other motives included religious hatred of the enemy: the Christians were already fighting against the Muslims, not only as "usurpers" but

From *The Reconquest of Spain* by Derek W. Lomax (New York: Longman Inc. 1978), pp. 173–78 passim. Reprinted by permission.

also as "infidels." On the other hand, there is simply no earlier evidence for deciding how far this religious motivation and the adoption of this policy preceded their formulation in the texts of Alfonso III's reign. There is a similar lack of evidence about such questions for 910–1035; and in both periods the safest course is to suspend judgment rather than to argue from the silence of our scanty texts. In contrast, the whole tradition of Frankish [Germanic tribal] military involvement is fairly well documented from Charlemagne down to the reconquest of Granada; it was by no means a novelty in the age of Alfonso VI [1065–1109].

What then was new in the eleventh century? With the collapse of the caliphate, there ended any chance of a powerful independent monarchy among the Spanish Muslims, and the balance of political power tipped decisively away from them and towards the Christians, although the reasons for this decisive change are still obscure. On the Christian side, there now appeared for the first time, not foreign expeditionaries nor the concept of the Holy War—both had existed for centuries—but the idea of the Crusade, that is, a Holy War entered into for religious motives (among others, no doubt), authorized by the Church and conferring on its participants a specific juridical status, no matter whether they were French, English or Spanish. And, of course, Frankish expeditions increased in frequency, size, recruiting-areas and effectiveness . . . most of them went to the Ebro valley and provided essential assistance in its reconquest. . . .

One must discount the view that the peaceful co-existence of the ordinary people was occasionally disturbed by warfare provoked by the religious and political establishment; it would be truer to say that the kings made occasional ineffectual attempts to limit the endless warfare enjoyed by their subjects. This was natural enough: as in medieval Russia, though to a lesser extent, the ease with which peasants could acquire land and freedom on an open frontier meant that it was difficult for the civil and military authorities to control them. Consequently, they were left within the framework of frontier townships and militias to do very much as they liked, and what they liked was plundering Muslim villages. The concepts of Reconquest and Crusade may have originated among the leaders of Christendom; the practice of permanent warfare against the Muslims was a creation of the people. And, despite the gaps in our evidence, it seems clear that even these concepts of Reconquest, Holy War and Crusade became widely diffused and accepted among the lower levels of society. . . .

Even with what is known now, however, it ought to be possible to reach some tentative conclusions. The Reconquest was a lengthy process and a continuous one in the sense that fighting rarely stopped for long, but it was not, as is often implied, a slow, steady and gradual one. The Christians did not advance steadily, step-by-step; they took great leaps forward, to the Duero [River], the Tagus [River], the Guadalquivir [River] and the south coast, and after each leap they waited for centuries to consolidate their position before making the next one. Rather than gradual, the Reconquest was spasmodic; it proceeded not by townships but by great regions such as Aragón, New Castile, or Andalusia, and one of its results was to emphasize the importance of such regions as the basic units of Spanish national life.

Other results have aroused more polemical discussion. Sánchez Albornoz has argued that the Muslim Conquest diverted Spain from its natural development as a European country and that though the Reconquest corrected this diversion, its slowness placed Spain several centuries behind Europe on the path of prgress. Though this theory does not define Europe or progress, it implicitly identifies both with France, and on its own terms is unanswerable. Not even Spain, where most things are possible, can be as French as France—but this is not the fault of Tariq [Muslim general] or Pelayo [Germanic Christian warrior].

Other historians argue that Spanish civilization reached its zenith in the tenth century and then declined because its Muslim rulers were replaced by Christians; but this is hardly supported by the history of civilization in neighbouring Morocco, where no Reconquest occurred. The case of Spain is more complex and unusual than, for example, the decline of Italy in the seventeenth century or the rise of England in the nineteenth; for between 1050 and 1250 Spain *transferred* from one culture, the Islamic, which was passing its zenith, to another, western Christendom, which was rising. Her exceptional case cannot therefore be measured by the simper standards of Morocco or France, for unlike them she has mixed two cultures, the Islamic and the Latin Christian, in a process which has here been called the Muslim Conquest and the Reconquest.

The mixture was strongest between 1000 and 1250 when political forces reinforced nobler motives making for religious toleration. Spain was then a land of several religions, and not until 1492 did it adopt the European pattern of uniformity which before 1250 would have been disastrous for the Christians as it proved for the Almoravids and Almohads [North African Muslim groups]. Under a regime of religious pluralism this society was intellectually very productive. The science of ancient Greece and medieval Persia and India was translated into Arabic in Syria, imported into Spain by the scholars of Ummayad Córdoba, augmented by Spanish scholars like Averroes and then translated into Latin by Christian scholars who spread the knowledge to the rest of Europe. Astronomy, physics, medicine, optics, mathematics, alchemy and magic suddenly burst upon a world which had known little beyond Bede and Isidore [of Seville]. So too did stories from Asian bazaars, new types of mysticism, new legends about the after-life and new philosophical theories. Thanks to the translators, both Spanish and foreign, doctors throughout Europe learned new cures for diseases, merchants and administrators could calculate accounts with positioned Hindu numbers and overseas discoverers could rely on tables of the stars for the voyages to Africa, Asia and America. It was the

Reconquest which provided suitable positions for these translations, for only in reconquered territory did Christians have the opportunity and interest to make them. None were made in Muslim Africa, where all educated men read Arabic, and even in Sicily such translations were fewer and dependent on capricious royal patronage.

In Spain these translations crowned a political, economic, social and cultural revolution as profound as any in medieval Europe. This had been achieved because the Christians had learnt several lessons in the twelfth century. The first and most important was the value of unity: realizing that their former quarrels had led to defeat at the hands of the Almohads, the Christians collaborated with each other after 1224 and, in their turn, exploited Muslim disunity. Secondly, recognizing the ineffectiveness of foreign crusaders and of the international military Orders, they learned to rely on themselves alone and to create their own Orders of Santiago, Calatrava and Alcántara. Thirdly, the resettlement of the south with Christians ensured that the next African invasion would face not merely Christian garrisons in a Muslim country but a solid line of Christian cities, prosperous and belligerent, with their own militias and castles. The social revolution which this implied led briefly to a wide distribution of property in Andalusia; but this did not last. Emigration from north to south probably impoverished the northern nobels, driving them into rebellion, whilst southern land was so cheap that noble families could buy up farms and amass great estates, and whenever the monarchy was weak they enriched themselves, and rewarded their vassals, at the expense of crown, Church and cities.

Indeed, they were almost forced to do so by the nature of Spanish society. For though capable leaders' unity, self-reliance and resettlement all helped to achieve the Reconquest, the most important factor was probably the willingness of Christian Spaniards to transform their society for this purpose. This transformation was extremely thorough. Late medieval Castile became essentially a society organized for war, a dynamic military machine which would function well so long as it had more lands to conquer. It might be disconcerted by military defeats, but it could survive them. What threw it into complete confusion was the end of the attempt at conquest, and when the kings stopped leading their armies against Granada they implicitly invited their barons to find a new role which could only be that of fighting each other. Just as the English barons of Edward III or Henry V united to plunder the French, so the Castillian barons would unite under Alfonso XI [1312–1350] to plunder Granada, the France of Castile; but, just as peace with France led to civil wars within England under Richard II and Henry VI, so peace with the Muslims led to civil wars within Castile under Fernando IV [1295–1312] and Juan II [1406–1454]. Fernando and Isabel [Ferdinand and Isabella] could cure one crises in 1481 simply by setting the war-machine to work once more, to conquer Granada; but after 1492, there was no more Muslim territory to be conquered inside Spain. The machine was running out of land, and more crises loomed ahead.

It might of course have been sent against the Maghrib [in North Africa], and raids were made on Melilla (1497), Oran (1509) and Algiers (1510), and perhaps it might have conquered Morocco. Or it might have been turned back against northern Europe, with incalculable effects on the sixteenth-century religious wars. However, in thanksgiving for the fall of Granada, Isabel equipped Columbus's exploratory expedition and in 1492 his discover of America opened up a virtually limitless stretch of conquerable territory. Castillian society rose to the occasion. Within fifty years it conquered most areas from Texas to Argentina and established the framework of political, religious, social and economic life within which they would henceforth live.

No other European society could have done this at that date. Explorers from England, for example, discovered Nova Scotia in 1497, but no permanent English setttlement was made in America until the seventeeth century. Only Spain was able to conquer, administer, Christianize and Europeanize the populous areas of the New World precisely because during the previous seven centuries her society had been constructed for the purpose of conquering, administering, Christianizing and Europeanizing the inhabitants of al-Andalus [Muslim Spain]. Thus if the Reconquest is important in Old World history because it is the primary example of the reversal of an Islamic conquest and because it fostered the transfer of Greek and Asian culture to western Europe, in the general sweep of world history it is vital because it prepared the rapid conquest and Europeanization of Latin America and thereby spared it most of the religious and imperialist wars which would henceforth afflict almost all the rest of mankind.

3. The Conquest of the Canary Islands

FELIPE FERNANDEZ-ARMESTO

The Western Hemisphere was not the first site of European overseas colonization. In the early fifteenth century the Portuguese claimed and began to settle Madeira, the Azores, and Cape Verde—islands in the Atlantic which Portuguese sea captains had encountered as they were exploring possible routes along the North African coast. To head off the Portuguese, Ferdinand and Isabella took the island of Gran Canary during the war of succession between the two countries in 1475. They conquered Palma in 1490 and Tenerife in 1493 so that by the end of the century the whole archipelago was in their hands.

The Spanish used swords, cannon, muskets, horses, and dogs to defeat the Stone Age Canary islanders. After they introduced sugar cane, grapes, and wheat, the colony was soon a profitable venture, but as Felipe Fernández-Arnesto, a Professor of Modern History at Oxford University, notes, the practice of enslaving the natives was troubling the Catholic Sovereigns who regarded them as royal vassals to be converted to Christianity. In the Canaries, as well as the New World, the ethical issues arising from their need to reconcile expansion with evangelism was a problem that would beset Spanish monarchs for the next two hundred years.

In the Treaty of Alcaçovas of 1479, Ferdinand and Isabella expressly reserved to Castile the conquest of the stretch of coast opposite the Canary Islands, where their subjects established a garrison at Santa Cruz de la Mar Pequeña, and continued to make raids and attempts at conquest in a sporadic and individual fashion. In 1492 the monarchs commissioned the conquistador Alonso de Lugo to organize these efforts, but the vastness of the area and the strength of resistance confined him to raiding and the maintenance of coastal footholds. The fall of Granada in 1492 released energies for assaults elsewhere on the mainland. In 1495 the Pope confirmed Castile's rights—for although these had long been assumed, pontifical clarification was useful in the face of conflicting Portugues claims—and in 1497 a major successful expedition, which conserved many elements of organization and personnel from the time of the Granada war, seized Melilla for the monarchs. But the same years saw the rise of the Barbary corsairs and, correspondingly, the diffi-

From *Ferdinand and Isabella* by Felipe Fernández-Arnesto (New York: Taplinger Publishing Co., 1975), pp. 146–61, passim.

culties of making more than local North African conquests increased. In that area of expansion Ferdinand and Isabella were limited to a coastal, military presence and could not establish settled colonies.

But already before the completion of the Reconquest, when Castileian expansion overseas could be launched in earnest like the ships that bore it, settlers from Andalucia had begun the colonization of the Canary Islands. . . .

The decisive phase came with the reign of Ferdinand and Isabella who completed the conquest of the Canary Islands, encouraged their "peopling" with colonists by means of fiscal exemptions, and imposed a policy of land-and-water-sharing, which encouraged sugar production. Madeiran and Valencian personnel were deliberately introduced to run the irrigation and refining industries. Genoese capitalists were brought in with sufficient money concentrations to set up the waterways and mills, and Negro slaves imported to supplement the indigenous and colonial labour-force. As well as sugar, corn was cultivated on dry lands by poorer settlers; and other Spanish crops like grapes, quince and saffron were introduced and nurtured in a garden economy of the Andalucian type, which grew up in the hinter-lands of the growing townships. Cattle, pigs and sheep were imported to supplement the goats, while Castilian co-operative pastoral methods were promoted. The indices of the rapidity and extent of change are clear. Before the monarchs' reign, sugar was unknown on Gran Canaria; but within a few years Bernáldez could call it "a land of many canes." A clergyman who visited La Laguna in 1497, within a year of its foundation found "only two or three shanties"—but by the end of the reign it had some 6,000 inhabitants. To a great extent, the architect of the new kind of colonial economy was Alonso Fernández de Lugo, who had served in the conquest of Gran Canaria and took command for the wards in Tenerife and La Palma: he seems to have realized that because of the distribution of rainfall in the Archipelago, the western islands could be adapted for sugar-farming in a way that had not been possible in the early conquests. He introduced the sugar-cane in 1484, as soon as the conquest of Gran Canaria was completed, and risked controversy and unpopularity during his governorship of Tenerife by favouring foreign technicians and capitalists.

For the monarchs particularly desired that the soil of the Indies should be divided among the colonists, and a new agronomy introduced, just as was being effected by their command at the same time in the Canary Islands. They repeated the same policy, based on land grants and fiscal exemptions, for encouraging immigration, as had been used in the Canaries. Lastly, the elements of the new agronomy were not to be cultivated to the exclusion of the pastoral sector, which the monarchs were determined to favour in their new as in their old realms. Within a few years, as in the Canaries, the labour force of the new colonies was expanded by the importation of Negroes though the paganism and indiscipline of black slaves so perturbed the early governors, and the Portuguese monopoly of the trade was so strong, that the supply was only intermittent under the Catholic monarchs. Isabella was personally opposed to the employment of Negroes because she was afraid that their pagan practices would impede Spanish efforts to evangelize the Indians. Even though after her death Ferdinand removed all restrictions on the trade in blacks, the labour force of the New World colonies remained far more heavily dependent on indigenous sources than did that of the Canary Islands; as Columbus insisted, "The Indians are the wealth of Hispaniola—for they perform all labour of men and beasts.". . .

To exacerbate the efforts of their relative remoteness, the methods of finance employed in the conquests of the Canaries and the New World displayed ominous features for the future of royal government there. In the Canary Islands from 1477, the monarchs had placed the burden of financing the conquests on the royal exchequer {treasury}, and indeed the first expeditions relied heavily on public finance: the methods of finance and recruiting of these earlier days were largely borrowed from the *Reconquista* {Reconquest}. But as the conquest wore on and more expeditions were dispatched, private sources of finance and means of recruiting tended increasingly to displace public ones. Instead of wages, the *conquistadores* would receive the promise of *repartimiento* or a share of the soil; instead of the yield from the sale of indulgences or the direct use of the royal fifth to meet the expenses of war, fifths yet uncollected were pledged as rewards to conquerers who could raise the necessary finance elsewhere. In other words, the conquest of the islands was begun with the financial arrangements of the *Reconquista*, and terminated with those of the conquest of the New World. . .

In many ways the crucial similarity between the Canarians and Indians was that they were naked: that was the first fact Columbus noticed about the Indians and the first which Europeans had observed about the Canarians; indeed for every European observer of primitive peoples till well into the sixteenth century, clothes were the measure of difference between primitivism and civilization; conformity of dress was a sign of conformity of manners. The promotion of European *couture* was a major preoccupation of the proselytizers of the Moors and the Spanish settlers among the Indians. Beatriz de Bobadilla, heiress of the isle of Gomera and enslaver of its people, argued before Ferdinand and Isabella that the Gomerans could not be considered truly Christian on the ground that "they go about naked." Hieronymus Münzer at about the same time displayed the same state of mind when he wrote of the Canarians. "They all used to go naked, but now use clothes like us." Then he added, very characteristically of his epic, "Oh, what doctrine and diligence can do, that can turn beasts in human shape into civilized men!" But in terms of the two cultural traditions of which men in the late Middle Ages disposed—that of Christianity and that of classical antiquity—social nakedness had a profound significance: it evoked in the context of the first idea of primitive innocence, in that of the second, the legend of the age of gold.

Both these concepts were of great importance in the formation of European ideas about Canary Islanders and Indians. Accounts of the Canary Islanders influenced notions of the age of gold; Peter Martyr and his correspondents thought the Indians a model of sylvan innocence. Of both peoples, it was thought that their uncorrupt state peculiarly fitted them to hear the gospel and helped to create the widespread impression that the existing and often harsh juridical norms for the treatment of pagans were unsuited to them. . . .

In 1477, however, a new factor intervened which acted as a catalyst around which the prevailing doctrine on savages' rights was altered. In October of that year, Ferdinand and Issabella took the conquest of the three still unsubdued Canary Islands under their own wing, out of the hands of the local seigneurs and private adventurers, whose efforts had been so unproductive in the preceding years. On the question of whether the islanders should be enslaved, the Catholic monarchs upheld the cautious doctrines of Pope Eugenius and the missionaries. In 1477, their liberation of "certain Canarians who are Christians and others who are on the road to conversion" on the grounds that "it would be a source of bad example and give cause why none should wish to be converted," may be compared with the aim expressed by Eugenius forty-three years previously when he spoke of the danger of pagans being deterred from joining the faith. No doubt the monarchs' attitude was not uncoloured by the exigencies of power: enslavement would have involved a change in the natives' status from royal vassals to personal chattels, whereas the monarchs' aim was as far as possible to exclude intermediate lordship from the institutions by which they ruled their monarchy (or at least to limit it where it existed already). In this respect, their ordinances against enslavement of the Canary Islanders were motivated in a way akin to those by which they protected the Indians of the New World. Columbus's first plans for enslaving the Indians aroused the monarchs' immediate disapproval. " What does he think he is doing with my vassals?" Isabella is traditionally said to have asked. They commissioned a "junta of theologians" to examine the proposed enslavement, and when they pronounced unfavourably, ordered Fonseca to have the slaves liberated and their owners compensated. This was almost a re-enactment of their reaction to the enslavement of the Gomerans in 1489.

It was equally in the interests of extending their own power that the monarchs insisted on their right to make war against the savages. This was made clear by their attitude to the bulls of indulgence for the conversion of the Canarians, promulgated by Sixtus IV in 1478. The Pope, continuing the traditions of peaceful evangilization and apparently sharing the common opinion that to make war on the islanders was unlawful, designated the funds expressly for the conversion of the natives and the erection of religious houses. By an insidious abuse of language, however, the monarchs' writs on this subject described the bulls as "for the said conversion and conquest" or with equivalent phrases. Antonio Rumeu de Rmas has recently shown that this early case of "double-think" caused a rift between the monarchs and some of their clergy, in which opponents of the use of violence actually attempted to suspend the collection of funds. At the end of the day, the success of the monarchs' policy brought their expansionist and evangelistic aims into perfect harmony: it would be but a short step now to Alexander VI's bulls on the New World, where the duty of evangelization would be seen as making the Castilian conquest just. This was an important moment in the elaboration of the cannonistic doctrine of just war: conversion had never in itself been generally considered sufficient pretext (though it had been advocated by individuals) up to that time.

In the remainder of the monarchs' reign one final development was still to come. Most clerics and religious continued to espouse exclusively peaceful methods of conversion. And Ferdinand and Isabella were not ill-disposed towards attempts along those lines, provided obedience to themselves was among the objects to which the missionaries sought to persuade their congregations: for instance, the mission of Fray Antón de Quesada, whom the monarchs dispatched to Tenerife in 1485, involved a brief both to convert the natives and reduce them to royal authority. Meanwhile, peaceful conversion revived in peninsular Spain when Granada was conquered and proselytization of the new community began. The tenacity of the pacific point of view about conversion during these wars led to the separation in doctrine of a war of conversion from a war waged in order to subject the heathen and so render by peaceful means possible conversion. This was not a point contrary to existing doctrines but merely a question which earlier jurists had left in doubt. Under this new doctrinal distinction, Ferdinand and Isabella were free to make war on the Indians and Canarians as on rebel subjects, theoretically without prejudice to the question of peaceful conversion. . . .

CHRISTOPHER COLUMBUS: MAN AND MYTH

4. *"I have found many islands, inhabited by numberless people"*

CHRISTOPHER COLUMBUS

Columbus's letter describing his first voyage to the New World was addressed to Luis de Santangel, the manager of King Ferdinand's household accounts who had been instrumental in convincing Queen Isabella to support the endeavor as a relatively cheap gamble with potentially great reward. The letter, written on February 16, 1493, summarized the trip and its results, but there is general agreement among scholars that much of it was fabrication—"a tissue of exaggerations, misconceptions, and outright lies." Columbus deliberately inflated the evidence to support his main contention that he had found lands of boundless wealth, but his unbridled optimism and wonder over the marvels he had found and observed was genuine. If the letter's historicity is doubtful, its literary success was unparalleled. Within a few years it went through eight editions in the original Spanish, was paraphrased in Italian verse and translated into a Latin version that was read all over Europe. In the view of Emir Rodriguez Monegal, "America as a literary and poetic subject was invented by this hyperbolic Genoese."*

Sir, forasmuch as I know that you will take pleasure in the great triumph with which Our Lord has crowned my voyage, I write this to you from which you will learn how, in twenty[1] days I reached the Indies with the fleet which the most illustrious King and Queen, our lords, gave to me. And there I found very many islands filled with people without number, and of them all have I taken possession for Their Highnesses, by proclamation and with the royal standard displayed, and nobody objected. To the first island which I found I gave the name *Sant Salvador*, in recog-

From *Journals and Other Documents on the Life and Voyages of Christopher Columbus* by Samuel Eliot Morison (Avon, Conn.: The Heritage Press, 1963).

*Emir Rodriguez Monegal, *The Borzoi Anthology of Latin American Literaure: From the Time of Columbus to the Twentieth Century,* 2 vols. (New York: Knopf, 1988), 1:5.

1. *Veinte.* Probably a misprint for *treinta*, or xxxiii. The actual time, as the postcript states, was thirty-three days.

nition of His Heavenly Majesty, who marvelously hath given all this; the Indians call it *Guanahani*. To the second I gave the name *Isla de Santa María de Concepción;* to the third, *Ferrandina;* to the fourth, *La Isla Bella;*[2] to the fifth, *La Isla Juana*; and so to each one I gave a new name.

When I reached Juana, I followed its coast to the westward, and I found it to be so long that I thought it must be the mainland, the province of Catayo[3] And since I found neither towns nor cities along the coast, but only small villages, with the people of which I could not have speech because they all fled forthwith, I went forward on the same course, thinking that I should not fail to find great cities and towns. And, at the end of many leagues, seeing that there was no change and that the coast was bearing me northward, which was contrary to my desire since winter was already beginning and I proposed to go thence to the south, and as moreover the wind was favorable, I determined not to wait for a change of weather and backtracked to a certain harbor already noted,[4] and thence I sent two men upcountry to learn if there were a king or great cities. They traveled for three days and found an infinite number of small villages and people without number, but nothing of importance, hence they returned.

I understood sufficiently from other Indians, whom I had already taken, that continually[5] this land was an island, and so I followed its coast eastward 107 leagues up to where it ended. And from that cape I saw toward the east another island, distant 18 leagues from the former, to which I at once gave the name *La Spañola*. And I went there and followed its northern part, as I had in the case of Juana, to the eastward for 178 great leagues in a straight line. As Juana, so all the others are very fertile[6] to an excessive degree, and this one especially. In it there are many harbors on the sea coast, beyond comparison with others which I know in Christendom, and numerous rivers, good and large, which is marvelous. Its lands are lofty and in it there are many sierras and very high mountains, to which the island *Centrefrei*[7] is not comparable. All are most beautiful, of a thousand shapes, and all accessible, and filled with trees of a thousand kinds and tall, and they seem to touch the sky; and I am told that they never lose their foliage, which I can believe, for I saw them as green and beautiful as they are in Spain in May, and some of them were flowering, some with fruit, and some in another condition, according to their quality. And there

2. Misprint for Isabela, the name he gave to Crooked Island.
3. I.e., a province of China.
4. Puerto Gibrara.
5. *continuamente*. Not clear whether he meant that the Indians told him continually that Cuba was an island, or that it was one continual island.
6. *fortissimas*. Probably a printer's error for *fertilissimas,* and 178 is a misprint for 188 leagues, as stated later in the Letter.
7. Misprint for Tenerife.

were singing the nightingale and other little birds of a thousand kinds in the month of November, there where I went. There are palm trees of six or eight kinds, which are a wonder to behold because of their beautiful variety, and so are the other trees and fruits and plants; therein are marvelous pine groves, and extensive meadow country; and there is honey, and there are many kinds of birds and a great variety of fruits. Upcountry there are many mines of metals, and the population is innumerable. *La Spañola* is marvelous, the sierras and the mountains and the plains and the meadows and the lands are so beautiful and rich for planting and sowing, and for livestock of every sort, and for building towns and villages. The harbors of the sea here are such as you could not believe it without seeing them; and so the rivers, many and great, and good streams, the most of which bear gold. And the trees and fruits and plants have great differences from those of La Juana, in this [island] there are many spices and great mines of gold and of other metals.

The people of this island and of all the other islands which I have found and seen, or have not seen, all go naked, men and women, as their mothers bore them, except that some women cover one place only with the leaf of a plant or with a net of cotton which they make for that purpose. They have no iron or steel or weapons, nor are they capable of using them, although they are well-built people of handsome stature, because they are wondrous timid. They have no other arms than arms of canes, [cut] when they are in seed time, to the ends of which they fix a sharp little stick; and they dare not make use of these for oftentimes it has happened that I have sent ashore two or three men to some town to have speech, and people without number have come out to them, and as soon as they saw them coming, they fled; even a father would not stay for his son; and this not because wrong has been done to anyone; on the contrary, at every point where I have been and have been able to have speech, I have given them of all that I had, such as cloth and many other things, without receiving anything for it; but they are like that, timid beyond cure. It is true that after they have been reassured and have lost this fear, they are so artless and so free with all they possess, that no one would believe it without having seen it. Of anything they have, if you ask them for it, they never say no; rather they invite the person to share it, and show as much love as if they were giving their hearts; and whether the thing be of value or of small price, at once they are content with whatever little thing of whatever kind may be given to them. I forbade that they should be given things so worthless as pieces of broken crockery and broken glass, and lace points, although when they were able to get them, they thought they had the best jewel in the world, thus it was learned that a sailor for a lace point received gold to the weight of two and a half castellanos, and others much more for other things which were worth much less; yea, for new blancas,[8] for them they would give all

8. A copper coin worth half a maravedi, about a third of a cent.

that they had, although it might be two or three castellanos' weight of gold or an arroba or two of spun cotton; they even took pieces of the broken hoops of the wine casks and, like animals, gave what they had, so that it seemed to me to be wrong and I forbade it, and I gave them a thousand good, pleasing things which I had brought, in order that they might be fond of us, and furthermore might become Christians and be inclined to the love and service of Their Highnesses and of the whole Castilian nation, and try to help us and to give us of the things which they have in abundance and which are necessary to us. And they know neither sect nor idolatry, with the exception that all believe that the source of all power and goodness is in the sky, and they believe very firmly that I, with these ships and people, came from the sky, and in this belief they everywhere received me, after they have overcome their fear. And this does not result from their being ignorant (for they are of a very keen intelligence and men who navigate all those seas, so that it is wondrous the good account they give of everything), but because they have never seen people clothed or ships like ours.

And as soon as I arrived in the Indies, in the first island which I found, I took by force some of them in order that they might learn [Castilian] and give me information of what they had in those parts; it so worked out that they soon understood us, and we them, either by speech or signs, and they have been very serviceable. I still have them with me, and they are still of the opinion that I come from the sky, in spite of all the intercourse which they have had with me, and they were the first to announce this wherever I went, and the others went running from house to house and to the neighboring towns with loud cries of, "Come! Come! See the people from the sky!" They all came, men and women alike, as soon as they had confidence in us, so that not one, big or little, remained behind, and all brought something to eat and drink, which they gave with marvelous love. In all the islands they have very many *canoas* like rowing *fustes*, some bigger and some smaller, and some are bigger than a *fusta* of eighteen benches. They are not so beamy, because they are made of a single log, but a *fusta* could not keep up with them by rowing, since they make incredible speed, and in these they navigate all those islands, which are innumerable, and carry their merchandise. Some of these canoes I have seen with seventy and eighty men on board, each with his oar.

In all these islands, I saw no great diversity in the appearance of the people or in their manners and language, but they all understand one another, which is a very singular thing, on account of which I hope that Their Highnesses will determine upon their conversion to our holy faith, toward which they are much inclined.

I have already said how I went 107 leagues in a straight line from west to east along the coast of the island Juana, and as a result of that voyage I can say that this island is larger than England and Scotland together, for, beyond these 107 leagues, there remain to the westward two provinces where I have not been, one of which they call Avan,[9] and there the people are born with tails. Those provinces cannot have a length of less than 50 or 60 leagues, as I could understand from those Indians whom I retain and who know all the islands. The other, *Española*, in circuit is greater than all Spain, from *Colonya* by the coast to *Fuenteravia* in Vizcaya, since I went along one side 188 great leagues in a straight line from west to east.[10] It is desirable land and, once seen, is never to be relinquished; and in it, although of all I have taken possession for their Highnesses and all are more richly supplied than I know or could tell, I hold them all for their Highnesses, which they may dispose of as absolutely as of the realms of Castile. In this *Española,*in the most convenient place and in the best district for the gold mines and for all trade both with this continent and with that over there belonging to the Grand Khan, where there will be great trade and profit, I have taken possession of a large town to which I gave the name *La Villa de Navidad*, and in it I have built a fort and defenses, which already, at this moment, will be all complete, and I have left in it enough people for such a purpose, with arms and artillery and provisions for more than a year, and a *fusta*, and a master of the sea in all [maritime] arts to build others, and great friendship with the king of that land, to such an extent that he took pride in calling me and treating me as brother; and even if he were to change his mind and offer insult to these people, neither he nor his people know the use of arms and they go naked as I have already said, and are the most timid people in the world, so that merely the people whom I have left there could destroy all that land; and the island is without danger for their persons, if they know how to behave themselves.

In all these islands, it appears, all the men are content with one woman, but to their *Maioral,* or king, they give up to twenty. It appears to me that the women work more than the men. I have been unable to learn whether they hold private property, but it appeared true to me that all took a share in anything that one had, especially in victuals.

In these islands I have so far found no human monstrosities, as many expected, on the contrary, among all these people good looks are esteemed;[11] nor are they Negroes, as in Guinea, but with flowing hair, and they are not born where there is

9. *Auau* in the original Spanish edition, *Avan* in the 1497 Spanish edition. *Anan* in the Latin translation. Columbus meant *Avan*, the Arawak word for a Cuban region from which *Havana* is derived. Tailed men was one of the most popular yarns of Sir John Mandeville. Columbus and his men frequently inquired about such creatures and were "yessed" by the Indians, who probably thought they were talking about monkeys, not Cubans.

10. I.e., from Collioure, a port in the Gulf of Lyons that then belonged to Aragon, around the entire Spanish Peninsula to Fuenterrabia, the frontier town on the Bay of Biscay. Like his other estimates of land distances, this was greatly exaggerated.

11. *Mas antes es toda gente de muy lindo acatamiento.* The meaning is somewhat obscure; the Latin translator of the Letter thought that Columbus meant that the people were reverential.

excessive force in the solar rays; it is true that the sun there has great strength, although it is distant from the Equator twenty-six degrees.[12] In these islands, where there are high mountains, the cold this winter was severe, but they endure it through habit and with the help of food which they eat with many and excessively hot spices. Thus I have neither found monsters nor had report of any, except in an island[13] which is the second at the entrance to the Indies, which is inhabited by a people who are regarded in all the islands as very ferocious and who eat human flesh; they have many canoes with which they range all the islands of India and pillage and take as much as they can; they are no more malformed than the others, except that they have the custom of wearing their hair long like women, and they use bows and arrows of the same stems of cane with a little piece of wood at the tip for want of iron, which they have not. They are ferocious toward these other people, who are exceedingly great cowards, but I make no more account of them than of the rest. These are those who have intercourse with the women of *Matremomio,*[14] which is the first island met on the way from Spain to the Indies, in which there is not one man. These women use no feminine exercises, but bows and arrows of cane, like the abovesaid; and they arm and cover themselves with plates of copper, of which they have plenty. In another island, which they assure me is larger than *Española,* the people have no hair. In this there is countless gold, and from it and from the other islands I bring with me *Indios*[15] as evidence.

In conclusion, to speak only of that which has been accomplished on this voyage, which was so hasty, Their Highnesses can see that I shall give them as much gold as they want if Their Highnesses will render me a little help; besides spice and cotton, as much as Their Highnesses shall command; and gum mastic, as much as they shall order shipped, and which, up to now, has been found only in Greece, in the island of Chios, and the Seignory[16] sell it for what it pleases; and aloe wood, as much as they shall order shipped, and slaves, as many as they shall order, who will be idolaters.[17] And I believe that I have found rhubarb and cinnamon, and I shall find

12. *Veinte e seis,* a radical revision downward of the Admiral's two inaccurate calculations that the north coast of Cuba was in lat. 42° N and that of Hispaniola 34° N. Actually 21° and 20° are correct.

13. The Latin edition names this island *Charis,* i.e., *Caire,* the Carib name for Dominica. Note that the Admiral's captive Indians had given him the position of this island and that he steered for it on his Second Voyage.

14. Thus in both Spanish editions, *Mateunin* in the Latin, *Matinino* in the Journal for 15 January 1493. The French named it Martinique.

15. The first appearance in print of this name that Columbus gave to the natives of America.

16. The government of Genoa. Columbus as a young man had made a voyage or two to Chios.

17. I.e., the slave trade will be legitimate if not in Christians.

a thousand other things of value, which the people whom I have left there will have discovered, for I tarried nowhere, provided the wind allowed me to sail, except in the town of Navidad, where I stayed [to have it] secured and well seated. And the truth is I should have done much more if the vessels had served me as the occasion required.[18]

This is enough. And the Eternal God, Our Lord, Who gives to all those who walk in His way victory over things which appear impossible; and this was notably one. For, although men have talked or have written of these lands, all was conjecture, without getting a look at it, but amounted only to this, that those who heard for the most part listened and judged it more a fable than that there was anything in it, however, small.[19]

So, since our Redeemer has given this triumph to our most illustrious King and Queen, and to their renowned realms, in so great a matter, for this all Christendom ought to feel joyful and make great celebrations and give solemn thanks to the Holy Trinity with many solemn prayers for the great exaltation which it will have, in the turning of so many peoples to our holy faith, and afterward for material benefits, since not only Spain but all Christians will hence have refreshment and profit. This is exactly what has been done, though in brief.

Done on board the caravel off the Canary Islands,[20] on the fifteenth of February, year 1493.

At your service.
THE ADMIRAL.

Additional Note,[21] Which Came within the Letter.

After having written this, and being in the Sea of Castile, there rose up on me so great a wind south and southwest,[22] that I was obliged to ease the ships.[23] But I ran hither today into this port of Lisbon, which was the greatest wonder in the world, and whence I decided to write to their Highnesses. In all the Indies I have always

18. An oblique reference to the *Pinta*, or to the loss of the *Santa María*.
19. He probably had in mind *The Book of Ser Marco Polo*, which most of the learned in Europe regarded as fabulous.
20. So in both Spanish editions; doubtless a misprint, as the *Niña* was already off Santa María of the Azores on the fifteenth, and Columbus knew perfectly well that he had been there before he sent the letter off. The Latin editions omit this line. See Señor Sanz's discussion in *La Carte de Colón* (folio, 1956) 25-8.
21. *Anima* (modern *nema*): a paper wraped around a letter after its conclusion, and to which the seal is affixed.
22. *Sueste:* a misprint for *sudoeste*, as may be seen from the Journal.
23. Plural in both Spanish editions.

found weather as in May; I went thither in thirty-three days and would have returned in twenty-eight but for these tempests which detained me twenty-three days, beating about in this sea. Here all the seafarers say that never has there been so bad a winter or so many losses of ships.

Done the fourteenth[24] day of March.

This letter Columbus sent to the Keeper of the Privy Purse[25] about the islands discovered in the Indies. Contained in another for their Highnesses.

24. *Quatorze*: a misprint for *quatro*, for the *Niña* entered the Tagus on the 4th.
25. *El Escribano de Ración*, Luís de Santangel, Columbus's friend. The Latin editions name the recipient Gabriel (or Rafael) Sanxis, meaning Gabriel Sánchez, Treasurer of Aragon. It is probable that Columbus addressed another copy of the letter to him.

5. His Place in History

JOHN NOBLE WILFORD

The 1492 quincentennial inspired a number of biographies of Columbus. Some were translations, and some were new editions of past publications, but others offered new interpretations that broaden understanding of the man and his times. *The Mysterious History of Columbus* falls into the latter category. Written by John Noble Wilford, a science correspondent for *The New York Times* and former Pulitzer Prize winner, the book is a biography of the great navigator that sifts through myth and history, hagiography and fanatical debunking to present a textured portrait of a man who seems more elusive the more he is celebrated. In the section reprinted here, Wilford explains why North Americans were so eager to seize on Columbus as a hero and discusses why and how the rhetoric of Columbus scholarship has changed in the last three decades of the twentieth century.

Columbus's reputation in history has followed a curious course. His obsession, obstinacy, and navigational skill had carried Europe across the ocean. "The Admiral was the first to open the gates of that ocean which had been closed for so many thousands of years before," Las Casas wrote in the middle of the sixteenth century. "He it was who gave the light by which all others might see how to discover."

Yet, in the century after 1492, Columbus was anything but the stellar figure in history that he was to become. Vespucci by being a more perceptive interpreter of the New World and a more engaging writer, had already robbed Columbus of prominence on the map. His star also tended to be eclipsed by conquering explorers like Cortés, and Pizarro, who cut a more glamorous swath (Bernal Díaz, chronicler of the conquest of Mexico by Cortés, contributed with passages evoking the romances of chivalry) and by other mariners, like Da Gama, who actually reached the Indies, and Magellan, whose expedition of circumnavigation was the first to confirm by experience the world's sphericity—and also left no doubt about the magnitude of

From *The Mysterious History of Columbus* by John Noble Wilford (New York: Vintage Books, 1991), pp. 247–49, 258–65, passim. Copyright © 1991 by John Noble Wilford Reprinted by permission of Alfred A. Knopf, a Division of Random House, Inc.

Columbus's error in thinking he had reached Asia. His immediate reputation was diminished by his failures as a colonial administrator and the protracted lawsuit in which doubts were cast on the singularity of his plan for sailing west to the Indies. Humphrey Gilbert, the navigator who in 1583 established the first British colony in North America, at St. John's, Newfoundland, wrote: "Christopher Columbus of famous memory was not only derided and generally mocked, even here in England, but afterward became a laughing-stock of the Spaniards themselves."

Many books of general history in the first decades of the sixteenth century either scarcely mentioned Columbus or ignored him altogether. J.H. Elliott, the British historian, finds that writers of that time "showed little interest in his personality and career, and some of them could not even get his Christian name right." Responsibility for the neglect has been attributed in part to Peter Martyr. His letters made much of the years of discovery but gave only passing notice to Columbus himself (though acknowledging his fortitude and courage), and, with the poverty of available documentation about the man, there were few alternative sources of information; Oviedo, Las Casas, and his son Hernando had yet to publish their histories. Another explanation has been offered by Henry Harrisse. "The fact is," he writes, "that Columbus was very far from being in his lifetime the important personage he now is; and his writings, which then commanded neither respect nor attention, were probably thrown into the waste-basket as soon as received."

In his history published in 1552, Francisco López de Gomara devoted more attention to the exploits of Cortés and Pizarro, who obtained more gold and glory for Spain and had the good fortune to conquer not an assortment of islands but splendid empires like the Aztecs of Mexico and Incas of Peru. Still, Gomara reflected an awareness then growing among Europeans as to the significance of what Columbus had done. In a ringing assessment that would be repeated time and again, Gomara wrote: "The greatest event since the creation of the world (excluding the incarnation and death of Him who created it) is the discovery of the Indies."

On the strength of this realization, Columbus emerged from the shadows, reincarnated not so much as a man and historical figure as he was as a myth and symbol. He came to epitomize the explorer and discoverer, the man of vision and audacity, the hero who overcame opposition and adversity to change history. By the end of the sixteenth century, English explorers and writers acknowledged the primacy and inspiration of Columbus. "Had they not Columbus to stirre them up," Richard Hakluyt wrote in 1598. He was celebrated in poetry and plays, especially by the Italians. Even Spain was coming around. In a popular play, *El Nuevo Mundo descubierto por Cristóbal Colón,* Lope de Vega in 1614 portrayed Columbus as a dreamer up against the stolid forces of entrenched tradition, a man of singular purpose who triumphed, the embodiment of that spirit driving humans to explore and discover.

Nowhere were people more receptive to this image of Columbus than in the British colonies of North America, beginning in the late seventeenth century . . . .

It is not hard to understand the appeal of Columbus as a totem for the new republic and the former subjects of George III. Columbus had found the way of escape from Old World tyranny. He was the solitary individual who challenged the unknown sea, as triumphant Americans contemplated the dangers and promise of their own wilderness frontier. He had been opposed by kings, and (in his mind and according to the accounts of his son, which were the primary source of the Columbus legend in those days) was ultimately betrayed by royal perfidy. But as a consequence of his vision and audacity, there was now a land free from kings, a vast continent for new beginnings. In Columbus the new nation without its own history and mythology found a hero from the distant past, one seemingly free of any taint from association with the European colonial powers. The Columbus symbolism gave Americans an instant mythology and a unique place in history, and their adoption of Columbus magnified his own place in history . . . .

In 1892 and 1893, Columbus the man and the symbol was treated to a year-long commemoration throughout the United States. To the beat of brass bands and a chorus of self-congratulation, Americans hailed the man who had crossed uncharted seas as they had now leaped a wide and wild continent. Antonin Dvorák composed his symphony *From the New World* as an evocation of the sweep and promise of the beckoning American landscape. President Benjamin Harrison proclaimed: "Columbus stood in his age as the pioneer of progress and enlightenment." In New York, the ethnic hero was commemorated with a statue atop a column of Italian marble placed at the corner of Central Park that was renamed Columbus Circle; the money for it was raised by Italian immigrants, who had joined the Irish in search of an identity with the larger American community. There was a nighttime parade and fireworks from the Brooklyn Bridge re-creating Niagara Falls . . . .

The grandest of all the celebrations, the World's Columbian Exposition in Chicago, was billed as "the jubilee of mankind." It was so grand and ambitious, in fact, that the opening had to be delayed until 1893. President Grover Cleveland threw the switch on that new invention, electricity, to set in motion the many machines and architectural marvels by which the United States advertised itself as an emerging giant among the nations. Columbus was now the symbol of the American success. The invocation was a prayer of thanksgiving for "that most momentous of all voyages by which Columbus lifted the veil that hid the New World from the old and opened the gateway of the future of mankind." Clearly, the exposition was more than a commemoration of the past; it was also the exclamation of a future that self-confident Americans were eager to shape and enjoy . . . .

Early in the twentieth century, a few researchers like Henry Vignaud approached new materials from the archives with an increasingly critical eye and exposed contradictions, lacunae, and suspected fictions in the familiar story passed down from Hernando Columbus, Oviedo, Las Casas, and other contemporary accounts. Parts of the story unraveled. No one could be so sure anymore when and how Columbus arrived at his idea, what his real objective was, or what manner of man he was–an inspired but rational genius, a lucky adventurer clouded by mysticism, a man of the Renaissance or from the Middle Ages. But doubt and skepticism about the real Columbus seldom found expression in popular discourse. In textbooks, statuary, and Columbus Day rhetoric, the estimate of the man changed little from that of Edward Channing in 1905, who concluded in his *History of the United States:* "No man has done more to change the course of human history than Christopher Columbus."

Drawing on the accumulating documents and his own seafaring expertise, Samuel Eliot Morison in 1942 rescued Columbus from mythology and portrayed the man as what he had been first and foremost: an inspired mariner of the fifteenth century. Morison's biography, *Admiral of the Ocean Sea,* is written with verve and authority. His Columbus is no saint, but he could sail a ship and possessed the will and courage to go where no one had presumably gone before. His Columbus deserves the fame he has been accorded. His Columbus was a satisfying exemplar of the humble individual who through heroic exertions could change history. But Morison chose to stress the one aspect of Columbus—his skill as a mariner, demonstrated in four daring voyages—that has been beyond serious dispute.

The world was changing, though, and so was Columbus's reputation in history. World war and relentless strife, tyranny and greed, widespread poverty amid plenty, and economic expansion that ravages nature without necessarily satisfying basic human needs—modern life was making disbelievers of many who once worshipped at the altar of progress. If they now doubted progress, they also came to question Columbus, who had been the icon of progress. The idol had been the measure of the worshippers, but now there were atheists all around. In the years since World War II, nearly all of the colonies of the major empires won their independence and, like the United States in its early days, began to view world history from their own anti-colonial perspective. And in their view, the Age of Discovery initiated by Columbus was not the bright dawning of a glorious epoch in history, but an invasion, a conquest, and the end of their own peculiar histories. To them Columbus was no hero, no symbol of progress, but the avatar of oppression.

With critics chipping away at the pedestal on which Columbus has stood for so long in history, the hero is tottering and at risk of falling in a crumbling heap. The Columbus who symbolized new beginnings and progress seems anachronistic, diminished and cast aside by the iconoclasm, pessimism, and cynicism in vogue. The Columbus of 1992 is post-colonial and demythologized Columbus. He has been stripped of the symbolic cloak of optimism and exposed as a human being whose flaws were many and of reverberating consequence. The imagery imposed on him is now more apt to be that of pessimism concerning the human condition. Another Columbus for another age. Such, it seems, is the fate of great figures in history.

"A funny thing happened on the way to the quincentennial observation of America's 'discovery,'" historian Garry Wills writes in *The New York Review of Books* in 1990. "Columbus got mugged. This time the Indians were waiting for him. He comes now with an apologetic air—but not, for some, sufficiently apologetic . . . . He comes to be dishonored."

The rhetoric of Columbus scholarship has changed, more concerned as it is with exploring and assessing the man and his motives and filled with reproof instead of adulation. The Columbus whom Winsor had limned a century ago to widespread disapproval is now in fashion.

Francis Jennings, a historian at the Newberry Library in Chicago, reflects the increasingly critical approach in a book, published in 1975, examining the European incursion in America more from the standpoint of the native Americans. The title is revealing: *The Invasion of America: Indians, Colonialism, and the Cant of Conquest.* Another influential book is *The Columbian Exchange,* in which Alfred W. Crosby, a historian at the University of Texas at Austin, examines the biological consequences of the discovery—the exchange of plants and animals between continents, the spread of devastating disease, the eventual globalization of biology. Historians are increasingly addressing consequences as well as actions. In deference to Indian sensitivities and the obvious fact that, strictly speaking, America had been discovered thousands of years before, scholars eschew the words "discovery" and "discoverer" in their discourse. They speak of the "encounter" or the "contact." Typically, a research group at the University of Florida is named the Institute for Early Contact Period Studies.

In public forums, the atmosphere is even more emotionally charged. Columbus is tarred as the precursor of exploitation and conquest. Kirkpatrick Sale, in *The Conquest of Paradise,* argues that Columbus was a grasping fortune-hunter whose legacy was the destruction of the native population and the rape of the land that continues to this day. Descendants of the native Americans and the African slaves brought to the New world, as well as those who sympathize with their causes, are understandably reluctant to celebrate Columbus and the 500th anniversary of his landfall. In Madrid, a group known as the Association of Indian Cultures has threatened to sabotage celebratory ceremonies in Spain and throughout Latin America. Basque separatists in 1986 murdered Admiral Cristóbal Colón, a descendant of the explorer. In politically troubled Haiti, demonstrators descended from African slaves tossed a statue of Columbus into the bay. In the United States, leaders of Indian organizations condemned Columbus as a pirate or worse; Russell Means of the

American Indian Movement said that Columbus "makes Hitler look like a juvenile delinquent." Vernon Bellecourt, another leader of the movement, called for "militant demonstrations" against celebrants in 1992 "to blow out the candles on their birthday cake."

A sense of guilt has spread among others. The governing board of the National Council of Churches, a predominantly Protestant organization, resolved that, in consideration of "genocide, slavery, 'ecocide' and exploitation" that followed Columbus, the quincentenary should be a time of penitence rather than jubilation. The National Conference of Catholic Bishops, though acknowledging the "harsh and painful" treatment of indigenous Americans, cautioned that "the effort to portray the history of the encounter as a totally negative experience in which only violence and exploitation of the native peoples were present is not an accurate interpretation of the past."

In 1986, after four years of impassioned debate, the United Nations abandoned its attempt to plan a quincentennial celebration. Spain had made the proposal, and the United States, Canada, and a number of Latin American countries had supported it. But opposition came from many quarters. The Scandinavians argued that it ignored the exploits of Leif Eriksson. Ireland touted St. Brendan as the discoverer. Most African and some Asian states opposed any celebration that, in effect, glorified the colonial past. And some American states, where African and Indian blood runs thick, expressed strong reservations about honoring Columbus.

Once again, Columbus has become a symbol, this time of exploitation and imperialism. Garry Wills observes that the "issues that ramify out from the revolt against European imperialism are everywhere evident around us—in the feminist and minority questioning of 'dead white males' as the arbiters of our culture. The battles over a standard or core curriculum are simply this same war fought on slightly different grounds. So is the political struggle over one official language for the United States." In reviewing *The Conquest of Paradise,* Wills points out that the author "is on to something when he makes Columbus the deadest whitest male now offered for our detestation, If any historical figure can appropriately be loaded up with all the heresies of our time—Eurocentrism, phallocentrism, imperialism, elitism, and all-bad-things-generally-ism—Columbus is the man."

It was time that the encounter was viewed not only from the European standpoint, but from that of the indigenous Americans. It was time that the sanitized storybook version of Europeans bringing civilization and Christianity to America was replaced with a more clear-eyed recognition of the evils and atrocities committed in wresting a land from its original inhabitants. It was time that Columbus was judged by the evidence of his actions and words, not by the legend that had been embedded in our imaginations. But are we burdening him with more guilt than any one man should have to shoulder? Surely we have not finally established Columbus's place in history. It would be interesting to know how he will be characterized in 2092. For it seems that Columbus's destiny is to serve as a barometer of our self-confidence and complacency, our hopes and aspirations, our faith in progress and the capacity of humans to create a more just society.

Herbert Butterfield compained of the tendency of many historians to look in the past for "roots" and "anticipations" of their own time, and to single out and praise only those personalities who turned out to have been successful in fighting for causes and values esteemed in the historian's contemporary society. He called this the Whig interpretation of history—"the theory that we study the past for the sake of the present." Some historians can be said to be guilty of this in both building the image of Columbus and, in more recent times, tarnishing it almost beyond recognition. They should, instead, strive to reconstruct the person who really was, insofar as the record allows, and the times as they really were—and leave to others, who are never in short supply, the task of measuring the person for the hero's cloak.

Here is a summary of what can be said. Columbus was, as far as we can tell, a man from Genoa who grew up in a family of wool-weavers and then went to sea. He found his way to Portugal, where exploration of the sea was a dynamic of the age and the search for a new route to the Indies was an economic and religious imperative. There he became obsessed with an idea of sailing across the sea to reach the Indies. He was ambitious for fame and wealth and, quite likely, to serve as God's messenger to the world and restore the holy Sepulcher to Christendom. Some of his ancestors may have been Jewish, but he was a devout Christian who sailed for the crown of Spain. Through single-minded persistence and the charisma to make friends in high places, he prevailed on Ferdinand and Isabella to back his bold scheme. He was not the only European to believe the world was round, but he seems to have been the first to stake his life on it.

He was a consummate mariner, everyone seemed to agree. As Cuneo, who sailed with him, said: "By a simple look at the night sky, he would know what route to follow or what weather to expect; he took the helm and once the storm was over, he would hoist the sails, while the others were asleep." And he found a new world. Though he probably never realized it, and certainly never admitted it, he made a discovery that would change the world. If there had not been an America to find, he would probably have sailed to his death and certainly to oblivion. He could never have made the Indies, which lay far beyond where his miscalculations had placed them. He was wrong, but lucky. No explorer succeeds without some luck. But his skill and fortune deserted him on land. He wa an inept administrator of the colony he established at La Isabela, ruling by the gibbet, antagonizing his own men to insurrection, and goading the Tainos into bloody rebellion. At the first opportunity, he captured Tainos and shipped them to Spain as slaves, a practice not without precedent in Europe or even among the people of pre-Columbian America.

His geographic interpretations were muddled by preconceptions and a blind reliance on venerated church teachings. His was not an open mind. He sought confirmation of received wisdom rather than new knowledge. Enthralled by the proximity of what he believed was the earthly paradise, he failed to appreciate that he had reached the South American continent. Yet he persevered, often wracked with the pain of arthritis and fevers, completing four epic voyages that showed the way to countless others. As he approached death, his mind was consumed with self-pity, mysticism, and a desperate desire to seize Jerusalem in preparation for Judgment Day.

Here is now Columbus himself, in his Letter to Santángel in February 1493, judged the meaning of his life and achievement:

> . . . the eternal God, Our Lord, Who gives to all those who walk in His way victory over things which appear impossible, and this was notably one. For although men have talked or have written of these lands, all was conjecture, without getting a look at it, but amounted only to this, that those who heard for the most part listened and judged it more a fable than that there was anything in it, however small.
>
> So, since our Redeemer has given this victory . . . for this all Christendom ought to feel joyful and make great celebrations and give solemn thanks to the Holy Trinity with many solemn prayers for the great exaltation which it will have, in the turning of so many peoples to our holy faith, and afterwards for material benefits.

But how are we to judge the historical Columbus, the man and not the legend? Was he a great man?

No. If greatness is measured by one's stature among contemporaries. Justin Winsor said a century ago: "The really great man is superior to his age, and anticipates its future." We will never know whether the course of history might have been any different if Columbus had been a kinder, more generous man, like Las Casas. But, then, Las Casas himself went to the Caribbean, like so many others, with every intention of exploiting it for personal gain. Or if he had been more like Captain James Cook—stern, unyielding, a peerless mariner, but also a commanding spirit, intellectually curious and hospitable to the sciences, devoted completely to the mission of exploration and discovery. But Cook lived in a different time, about three centuries later. To argue that Columbus was acting in the accepted manner of his time is to concede that he was not superior to his age. To contend (with ample supporting evidence) that, even if Columbus had set a better example, others who followed would eventually have corrupted his effort, is to beg the question. Moreover, the only example Columbus set was one of pettiness, self-aggrandizement, and a lack of magnanimity. He could not find in himself the generosity to share any credit for his accomplishments. Whatever his original objective, his lust for gold drove him from island to island and, it seems, to the verge of paranoia. And the only future he could anticipate was wealth for himself and his heirs and the chimera of imminent end of the world.

Yes, if greatness derives from the audacity of his undertaking, its surprising revelation, and the magnitude of its impact on subsequent history. Columbus did cross the uncharted Atlantic Ocean, no mean feat. He did find new lands and people, and he returned to tell of it so that others could follow, opening the way to intercontinental travel and expansion. True, if he had never sailed, other mariners would eventually have raised the American coast, as the Portuguese did in reaching Brazil by accident in 1500. But it was Columbus who had the idea, ill-conceived though it was in many respects, and pursued the idea with uncommon persistence, undeterred by the doubters and scoffers. As it was put in the apocryphal story, Columbus showed the world how to stand an egg on its end.

Whether he was a great man or merely an agent of a great accomplishment, the issue is his standing in history. And that, Butterfield notwithstanding, depends on posterity's changing evaluation—Whitman's "ever-shifting guesses"—of him and the consequence of Europe's discovery of America. His reputation is inextricably linked to America. Ultimately, Columbus's place in history can only be judged in relation to the place accorded America in history over the last five centuries.

FROM HEMISPHERE TO HEMISPHERE

6. The Effect of the American Conquests on Europe

WILLIAM D. PHILLIPS, JR., AND CARLA RAHN PHILLIPS

The effect of America on Europe has been less thoroughly investigated than the transit of civilization westward across the Atlantic. The most immediate and dramatic effect was to be seen in Seville, the Andalusian port town that was converted into a thriving international metropolis. The discovery of America doubled its population within fifty years to make it the largest city in Spain, but beyond this immediate impact, as William and Carla Phillips point out, it took the Spaniards nearly a century and other Europeans even longer to assimilate the reality of the New World and its peoples. Both the Phillips are professors of history at the University of Minnesota, and the section reprinted below is taken from their fine study, *The Worlds of Christopher Columbus.*

Europe and the rest of the Old World felt much less dramatic effects from the clash of civilizations begun by Columbus. In exchange for the devastating diseases introduced to the New World, the Old World evidently contracted only syphilis, a venereal disease. Syphilis spread with epidemic fury in the aftermath of Columbus's first return voyage in 1493, largely through sexual contact but also through the skin by contact with the lesions of victims of the disease in its active phase. Transmitted to Italy by 1493, and elsewhere in Europe almost as quickly, syphilis seems to have made its way to India, and even to China as early as 1505. Its rapid progress shows, ironically, that the trading networks of the Old World were fairly efficient links, even before the voyages of exploration greatly expanded their scope.

Despite the advent of syphilis and other immediate results of the voyages, it is widely acknowledged that Europeans did not fully comprehend the reality of the New World until nearly a century after Columbus's first voyage. At the root of this lingering incomprehension lay a European view of the universe that had not known the New World and its peoples existed and consequently had not allowed for them

From *The Worlds of Christopher Columbus* by William D. Phillips, Jr., and Carla Rahn Phillips (New York: Cambridge University Press, 1992), pp. 256–60, 269–72. Reprinted with the permission of Cambridge University Press.

in its systems of law, religion, and intellectual outlook. Educated individuals at the court of Charles V might realize the magnitude of the discovery—Francisco López de Gómara, secretary to the conqueror Cortés, called it *"the greatest event since the creation of the world"*—but ordinary Spaniards and others had trouble knowing just what it meant. Without having seen the New World for themselves, they could not absorb it into their consciousness.

The precise geographical location of the New World in America, and its vast extent, became known to Iberian mariners through a series of extraordinary voyages. The dozen or so expeditions that sailed across the Atlantic during Columbus's lifetime were followed by others, fanning out along the coasts as the explorers gained confidence in unfamiliar waters. As one piece after another of the coastline was explored, they were mapped and studied in Seville. In many ways the crucial voyage was the circumnavigation of the globe begun in 1519 by Ferdinand Magellan, a Portuguese in Spanish service, and completed after Magellan's death by the Basque Juan Sebastián del Cano in 1522. During the years when Cortés conquered Mexico, Magellan's voyage proved just how far Mexico was from Asia. Another vast ocean separated the lands Columbus had found from the ones he had sought. In 1529 another Portuguese working for Spain, the cartographer Diego Ribero, produced a remarkable map of the world, summarizing the knowledge gained by Iberian exploration in the previous thirty-five years. On Ribero's beautiful "Carta universal," all of Africa, the eastern coastline of North America, and nearly the full coastline of South America were fairly accurately mapped. India, Asia, and the Pacific were less accurate, and many areas were left blank. The relationship between "New Spain" (Nueva España), recently conquered by Cortés, and Asia remained unknown, even in official circles.

Outside Iberia, even officials did not have access to detailed maps of the lands beyond the seas, in part because those maps were often considered state secrets. Moreover, when monarchs presented maps to one another as ceremonial gifts, the geographical features were not necessarily represented accurately. A map was a political statement in the rivalry among nations; geographical features might be sized to indicate their importance rather than their true configurations. Only slowly and incrementally did the shape of the real world become known. If Ribero illustrated what was known in 1529, the small globe made by Caspar Vopell Medebach in 1543 showed how much was still not known, at least in northern Europe. One realizes with a jolt that Medebach placed Mexico ("Messigo") and other Spanish colonies on the same land mass with China. In other words, he conceived the Americas as a huge peninsula attached to Asia, rather than as two separate continents, thousands of miles east of Japan.

To assimilate the reality of the New World and its peoples took Spaniards nearly a century, and other Europeans even longer. At first many writers compared the

Indians of the New World to figures from classical Greek and Roman mythology, as if they represented an unspoiled and nobler version of the European past. Only gradually did they recognize that the peoples of the New World were very different from the peoples of the Old World, even if they held certain traits in common. To govern and Christianize them, which Spain recognized as a clear duty resulting from the conquest, Spaniards first had to understand them. This led bureaucrats, clerics, and other intelligent observers to study various aspects of New World cultures. Some aspects the Spaniards found uninteresting, such as many varieties of Amerindian art. Other aspects they found profoundly offensive, such as human sacrifice, cannibalism, homosexuality, bestiality, and other sexual practices. What really interested them were New World systems of government, land tenure, taxation, and social organization. At least among the major New World empires, bureaucratic and societal organization had a familiar shape, which the Spaniards could compare and contrast with their own ways of doing things. Knowledge about government and society had an obvious practical value, as Spain created a bureaucratic structure to govern its growing empire.

In the course of defining New World peoples, Spaniards had to define themselves as well and to reexamine their role within God's universal plan for mankind. Because the New World peoples were clearly part of creation, they had a place in God's plan, which could only be ascertained by studying them in relation to the other human groups on earth. The first observer to put all the pieces together was José de Acosta. His *Natural and Moral History of the Indies,* published in 1590, examined a wide range of evidence about the New World's peoples, defining them as capable of receiving God's grace, and civilized in some ways. In other ways, he found them less advanced than Europeans or Asians. For example, many of the native inhabitants did not live in large civilizations but in small tribal groups, which appeared disorganized and therefore barbarous to European observers. Acosta's scale of gradation from barbarism to civilization reinforced the European notion of progress in human affairs and imposed a duty on the Spanish conquerors to help the New World's peoples progress toward civilization and acknowledge of God. The Spanish quest to understand the reality of the New World ultimately strengthened some of their own beliefs, even as the moral issues raised by the conquest cast others into doubt. Overall, in approaching an understanding of the New World and its peoples, Spaniards and other Europeans experienced a renewed sense of the worth of Christian civilization and its place in God's design.

Spain's colonial empire in the Americas strengthened the monarchy at home in a variety of ways. For one, the expanded need for trained administrators created an array of lucrative jobs. As a result, ambitious nobles and commoners found an acceptable outlet for their energy overseas, relieving some of the pressures within Spanish society. This safety valve contributed to the relative social peace in Spain during the sixteenth and seventeenth centuries, a time in which nearly every other country in Europe was beset by social and political unrest, and some were beset by widespread rebellion and even regicide.

Moreover, tax revenues from the New World provided additional funds for Spain's ambitious European foreign policy, serving to extend the reach, if not the grasp, of Spanish ambitions. In the late sixteenth and early seventeenth centuries, Spain championed the Catholic Reformation and fought nearly continual wars to defend the lands inherited by Charles V and his successors. Although revenues from the American empire generally provided only about 11 percent of the annual income of the Spanish crown, and never more than 20 percent, New World revenues provided the crucial margin that made such high expenditures thinkable, if not always affordable. Ultimately, the overextension of its resources would cause the downfall of Spanish power in Europe, and many historians have blamed the empire and its windfall of wealth for luring Spanish monarchs into disaster. For over a century, however, New World wealth helped to bring Spain to the pinnacle of power at home and abroad. Even when that power faded in Europe, the overseas empire remained in Spanish hands, reminder of past glories that would last into the nineteenth century.

INCURSIONS INTO THE IBERIAN EMPIRES

Other countries felt the lure of the New World as well, attracted by the vast wealth filtering through Spain. By the late sixteenth century, France, England, and Spain's own rebellious subjects in the Netherlands were trying to break into the Spanish Empire, refusing to accept Spanish claims to a monopoly on trade with its colonies. These incursions into the Americas—"piracy" when they were forbidden by their home governments, and "privateering" when they were not—put great pressure on Spanish defenses. At least part of the overextension that brought about the end of Spanish hegemony was due to the need to defend the colonies against foreign attackers and interlopers.

By an extraordinary effort during the late sixteenth and seventeenth centuries, Spain managed to keep intruders out of the heart of its empire, from the mainland of Mexico and Central America to the tip of Tierra del Fuego. Except for a few toeholds on the coasts and on Caribbean islands, would-be rivals were pushed northward beyond the effective limits of Spanish authority, settling along the eastern coast of North America and only slowly pushing their way inland in their own colonial adventures.

Elsewhere, European rivals encroached on the Portuguese trading empire in Africa, Asia, and Brazil. Through the sixteenth century, Portugal concentrated its efforts on seaborne trade with Asia and Africa, on the other side of the world from the Spanish Empire in the Americas. Even while Portugal and Spain shared a monarch, between 1580 and 1640, their two empires remained legally separate. Nonetheless, Spain's enemies also attacked the Portuguese empire from the late sixteenth century on, and Portuguese and Spanish forces were combined to fight Dutch incursions into Brazil in the 1630s. Portugal managed to oust the Dutch from Brazil in the mid-1650s, in the midst of its rebellion against Spain, but it could not avoid losing control of its far-flung empire in Asia. Ironically, as the Iberian phase of expansion reached its limits, Columbus's goal finally came to pass. After two decades of effort, Spain conquered the Philippine Islands in 1565 and established a trading colony in Manila, with access to the rich markets of Asia. Thereafter, Spanish galleons carried Mexican and Peruvian silver from Acapulco across the Pacific to Manila and returned with the Asian silks and spices eagerly sought by the wealthy Spanish colonial elite. What Columbus had vainly attempted in the Caribbean was eventually realized in the South China Sea. By 1650 European expansion overseas included the Dutch, the French, and the English, as well as the Portuguese and the Spanish, encompassing ever-wider areas within a global trading network . . . .

Europeans also adopted American foods, some more readily than others. Sailors in Spanish fleets as early as Columbus's first return voyage became accustomed to eating sweet potatoes and cassava bread on their homeward voyages, as well as to more exotic items such as sea turtle, which they compared in taste and texture to the veal they knew at home. In broader terms, however, the most important New world foods introduced to Europe were undoubtedly potatoes and maize.

Potatoes, introduced to Europe by Spaniards before the mid-sixteenth century, could grow in wet, cold climates where it was difficult to produce a reliable wheat harvest year after hear. They eventually flourished not only in the British Isles, Poland, Germany, Russia, and other northern European countries but also in the cold, wet regions of northern Spain, in parts of France, and elsewhere in southern Europe. This is not to say they were adopted overnight. Profound social and economic changes, such as changes in traditional diets, generally take decades or even centuries to develop. Many European peasants resisted the potato at first. Learned men had determined that it was related to the poisonous nightshade plant, and, indeed, its uncooked eyes are toxic to humans. The strange shapes and colors in which some potatoes grew also caused suspicion among a cautious and ignorant peasantry. Only gradually did the merits of the potato as a food crop overcome the reluctance of ordinary people to try it. Potatoes produced a high yield on small plots of land. Where its culture spread, the potato multiplied the available food supply enormously and may have encouraged young couples to marry and establish families earlier than time-honored custom allowed. This had far-reaching implications for the expansion of the European population in the eighteenth century, the beginning of sustained population growth in Europe.

Maize had a similar career. A crop of almost magical reproductive qualities, it could produce high yields on lands that discouraged other crops. Columbus himself took it to Spain, and by the time of his third voyage he was able to say that there was much of it growing in Castile. The Spanish and Portuguese introduced maize to Africa and Asia as well in the sixteenth century, but it took several centuries to become an important staple of the human diet, mostly for the poor. By the eighteenth century it had gained a permanent place around the globe as a food for human beings and for livestock. In regions where wheat and other grains had always been scarce, maize—like the potato—allowed the expansion of the human population on limited amounts of land, a development that has been a distinctly mixed blessing for the modern world.

Several other crops, less important than staples in human consumption, became very important to the development of the European economy. Coffee and sugar, Old World crops of debatable nutritional value, and tobacco and cocoa, New World crops of similarly questionable merit, share the distinction of contributing to the store of wealth in Europe and to the eventual rise of mass markets and industrialization. Sugar, long considered to have medicinal value, was priced beyond the reach of ordinary consumers in the Middle Ages. Its availability began to increase and its price to fall when it was introduced to the Atlantic island and grown on large plantations with coerced labor. Transplanted to the New World and grown commercially by slave labor, it became cheap enough to figure in the diet of quite poor people by the seventeenth century. Coffee, also reserved for the rich in former centuries, developed into an important cash crop in the New World and in Asia, with a price low enough to attract a mass market. Tobacco, a New World crop to begin with, soon found an audience of dedicated addicts in Europe. The hysteria of booming tobacco prices in Europe in the early seventeenth century encouraged a heavy investment in its production in the New World for the international market. And New World cocoa became a fashionable drink in Europe at all levels of society. The mass market for these products in Europe fueled the expansion of trade and trading profits in the seventeenth and eighteenth centuries, in the same way that the seaborne spice trade with Asia had expanded profits in the sixteenth century.

Long distance trade, which had relied in past centuries on the high profits made from mostly low-bulk luxury goods, began to rely instead on the profits from a high volume of low-priced goods. Trade could expand in both volume and extent in a manner undreamed of in the fifteenth century. Increased agricultural production and productivity in Europe also played an important role in the expanding economy of the late seventeenth and eighteenth centuries. Overall, the combination of agricultural progress and expanding markets and profits from trade helped to lay the basis for the Industrial Revolution in Europe from the mid-eighteenth century on. The voyages of Columbus and the plants and animals exchanged in the wake of the historic contact he initiated played a crucial role in the process that led to the modern world economy, characterized by interdependent global trade.

INFLATION AND THE MONEY SUPPLY

Money and credit arrangements underlay the great expansion of trade, and here too the discovery of the New World contributed importantly to their development. Spaniards brought back gold, pearls, jewels, and—above all—silver form their American colonies, starting in the fifteenth century and reaching a peak in the early seventeenth. Altogether it has been estimated that between 1500 and 1650 some 181 tons of gold and 16,000 tons of silver arrived in Europe from the Spanish colonies. And that is only the amount legally registered, from which the crown extracted a hefty tax. Smuggling added an unknown quantity to the total of precious metals imported from the New World. Many historians think that the amount smuggled was no more than 10 percent in the sixteenth century but rose much higher in the seventeenth century.

Viewed in one way, gold and silver are themselves commodities, which are produced by investment in land, labor, and capital and can be exchanged for other commodities, such as food and manufactured products. Viewed in another way, their use as money makes gold and silver the intermediaries of exchanges, setting the value of goods in the marketplace. The value of those goods, defined by their price in silver or gold, is affected not just by market demand but also by the amount of money in circulation. A restricted money supply tends to hold prices down; an expanded money supply allows them to rise more easily if market demand increases. Europe on the eve of its overseas exploration is thought to have had a limited supply of money, which internal silver mines could only partially ease. The rise in population that began about 1450 increased market demand for food, manufactured goods, labor, and nearly everything else. Consequently, prices tended to rise, but with a limited money supply they did not rise as high and as fast as they might have done otherwise.

A scholarly argument much in vogue until a few decades ago held that the enormous flow of New World bullion into Europe was primarily responsible for the great rise in prices that occurred in the sixteenth century. Recently scholars have provided a much more detailed explanation. When large amounts of gold and silver began arriving in Spain in the mid-sixteenth century, the increased money supply allowed prices to rise. Eventually, a large part of the imported bullion flowed out of Spain to pay the costs of trade and empire. The effects of bullion imports therefore spread all over Europe, increasing the supply of money, allowing prices to rise, and affecting local economies in a variety of other ways.

Some scholars have judged the European price rise of the sixteenth century to be so large and influential that they have called it a "Price Revolution." Others have questioned the effects and even the existence of dramatic price rises in particular areas. In Spain, prices rose fivefold in about one hundred years, not a dramatic rise compared to hyperinflation in certain periods and places in the twentieth century but disturbing and probably without precedent in the sixteenth century. Yet even in the case of Spain, the effects of the price rise are still debated by scholars. Did it mean that the economy was growing, or did the bullion simply allow prices to rise without promoting growth? Were the common people better off because of rising wages or worse off because of rising prices? What did inflation mean for the overall shape of the Spanish economy? We know that Spain's political power in Europe declined in the seventeenth century. What role, if any, did inflation play in the decline? Similar questions arise as historians try to sort out the effects of inflation elsewhere in Europe, and the debates are not likely to be settled soon. What most agree upon is that bullion from the New World expanded the money supply and fueled international trade and warfare, both of which had important consequences in Europe and the wider world. Much of the New World bullion eventually found its way to Asia, to pay for trade goods and the cost of maintaining overseas empires. Historians are still trying to attach figures to these flows of bullion on a worldwide scale and to assess their effect on the growth of a global marketplace.

BANKING AND CREDIT

In another way as well, the aftermath of Columbus's voyages contributed to the evolution of world trade. Credit and banking arrangements in medieval Europe assumed a fairly short time to complete a cycle of trade and clear merchants' account books of outstanding debts and credits. To finance trading voyages, a medieval merchant might borrow money to buy goods, or he might join with partners to share the risks and potential profits. For example, several merchants might invest in sending a ship carrying Venetian cloth to Alexandria in Egypt, where spices could be bought for the return voyage. Even in peacetime, such ventures were risky and could go wrong at several points. Spreading the risk became the prime goal of cautious merchants. Larger groups of associates might come together as insurance underwriters, each one signing up to guarantee the safe arrival of a fraction of the cargo that a trading vessel carried, in return for a fee paid by the owner of the goods. Should the cargo suffer damage or loss at sea, the underwriters would reimburse the owner. Should the cargo arrive without mishap, the insurance fee contributed to the profits of the insurers. Within a few weeks or months, all the parties concerned would know the outcome of the voyage and would be able to total their profits or losses on the venture, clearing the books and freeing their money to be used for other purposes, perhaps to finance another voyage.

The scope and the scale of long-distance trade changed greatly in the wake of European voyages of exploration. As regular trade to Asia and America developed in the sixteenth century, the lines of credit and exchange had to be lengthened to accommodate the greater distances and times involved. A merchant who borrowed money for a shipment of goods to the Spanish colonies might not know the outcome of the voyage for several years. In the sixteenth century, typical fleets for the Indies sailed in spring or summer, stayed the winter to trade and acquire goods for the return voyage, and returned the following year. Delays or danger from one's markets, because merchants had to predict changes in prices and demand that occurred thousands of miles away and took months or years to develop. The difficulties of the Asian trade were, if anything, even greater, although the potential profits were sometimes greater as well. As first the Portuguese and then other European merchants risked their livelihoods on long-distance trade to Asia, they were forced to develop some flexible methods of doing business and better ways of borrowing money and establishing credit over the long term. Maritime insurance, banks, sophisticated partnership contracts, and varied methods of ownership all evolved to spread the increased risks of global trade.

7. The Disastrous Effects of European Diseases in the New World

ALFRED W. CROSBY

Alfred W. Crosby, a professor of American Studies and Geography at the University of Texas at Austin, was one of the first to suggest that the introduction of plants and animals to the New World was not entirely peaceful nor beneficial. In his book *The Columbian Exchange: Biological and Cultural Consequences of 1492* (Westport, Conn.: Greenwood Press, 1972) he pointed out that a variety of plants indigenous to the New World were pushed aside by vegetation such as "Kentucky" bluegrass, daisies, and dandelions, while domestic animals and the Amerindians themselves were crowded by vast numbers of wild, imported horses, dogs, pigs, and steers. Still greater was the human cost, for in the essay reprinted below Crosby argues that the rapidity of Spanish conquests in America was due to an unseen but "formidable ally"—the spread of deadly European diseases for which the Amerindians had no biological immunity.

The most sensational military conquests in all history are probably those of the Spanish conquistadores over the Aztec and Incan empires. Cortés and Pizarro toppled the highest civilizations of the New World in a few months each. A few hundred Spaniards defeated populations containing thousands of dedicated warriors, armed with a wide assembly of weapons from the stone and early metal ages. Societies which had created huge empires through generations of fierce fighting collapsed at the touch of the Castilian.

After four hundred years the Spanish feat still seems incredible. Many explanations suggest themselves: the advantage of steel over stone, of cannon and firearms over bows and arrows and slings; the terrorizing effect of horses on foot-soldiers who had never seen such beasts before; the lack of unity in the Aztec and Incan empires; the prophecies in Indian mythology about the arrival of white gods.

For all of that, one might have expected the highly organized, militaristic societies of Mexico and the Andean highlands to survive at least the initial contact with European societies. Thousands of Indian warriors, even if confused and frightened and wielding only obsidian-studded war clubs, should have been able to repel at least the first few hundred Spaniards to arrive.

From "Conquistador y Pestilencia: The First New World Pandemic and the Fall of the Great Indian Empires" by Alfred W. Crosby, *Hispanic American Historical Review*, 47:2 (May 1967): 321–37, passim. Reprinted by permission of Duke University Press.

The Spaniard had a formidable ally to which neither he nor the historian has given sufficient credit—disease. The arrival of Columbus in the New World brought about one of the greatest population disasters in history. After the Spanish conquest an Indian of Yucatán wrote of his people in the happier days before the advent of the Spaniard:

There was then no sickness; they had no aching bones; they had then no high fever; they had then no smallpox; they had then no burning chest; they had then no abdominal pain; they had then no consumption; they had then no headache. At that time the course of humanity was orderly. The foreigners made it otherwise when they arrived here.

It would be easy to attribute this lamentation to the nostalgia that the conquered always feel for the time before the conqueror appeared, but the statement is probably in part true. During the millennia before the European brought together the compass and the three-masted vessel to revolutionize world history, men at sea moved slowly, seldom over long distances, and across the great oceans hardly at all. Men lived at least in the same continents where their great-grandfather had lived and rarely caused violent and rapid changes in the delicate balance between themselves and their environments. Diseases tended to be endemic rather than epidemic. . . .

Migration of man and his maladies is the chief cause of epidemics. And when migration takes place, those creatures who have been longest in isolation suffer most, for their genetic material has been least tempered by the variety of world diseases. Among the major subdivisions of the species *homo sapiens* the American Indian probably had the dangerous privilege of longest isolation from the rest of mankind. The Indians appear to have lived, died, and bred without extra-American contacts for generation after generation, developing unique cultures and working out tolerances for a limited, native American selection of pathological micro-life. Medical historians guess that few of the first rank killers among the diseases are native to the Americas. (A possible exception is syphilis. It may be true, as Gonzalo Fernández Oviedo maintained four hundred years ago, that syphilis should not be called *mal francés* or *mal de Nápoles,* but *mal de las Indias.*)

When the isolation of the Americas was broken, and Columbus brought the two halves of this planet together, the American Indian met for the first time his most hideous enemy—not the white man or his black servant, but the invisible killers which these men brought in their blood and breath. The fatal diseases of the Old World killed more effectively in the New, and comparatively benign diseases of the Old World turned killers in the New. There is little exaggeration in the statement of a German missionary in 1699 that "the Indians die so easily that the bare look and smell of a Spaniard causes them to give up the ghost." The process is still going on in the twentieth century, as the last jungle tribes of South America lose their shield of isolation.

The most spectacular period of mortality among the American Indians occurred during the first century of contact with the Europeans and Africans. Almost all contemporary historians of the early settlements from Bartolomé de las Casas to William Bradford of Plymouth Plantation were awed by the ravages of epidemic disease among the native populations of America. We know that the most deadly of the early epidemics in the New World were those of the eruptive fevers—smallpox, measles, plague, typhus, etc. The first to arrive and the deadliest, said contemporaries, was smallpox.

At this point the reader should be forewarned against too easy credulity. Even today smallpox is occasionally misdiagnosed as influenza, pneumonia, measles, scarlet fever, syphilis, or chicken pox, for example. Four hundred years ago such mistakes were even more common, and writers of the accounts upon which we must base our examination of the early history of smallpox in America did not have any special interest in accurate diagnosis. The early historians were much more likely to cast their eyes skywards and comment on the sinfulness that had called down such obvious evidences of God's wrath as epidemics than to describe in any detail the diseases involved. It should also be noted that conditions which facilitate the spread of one disease will usually encourage the spread of others, and that "very rarely is there a pure epidemic of a single malady." Pneumonia and pleurisy, for instance, often follow after smallpox, smothering those whom it has weakened. . . .

Smallpox has been so successfully controlled by vaccination and quarantine in the industrialized nations of the twentieth century that few North Americans of Europeans have ever seen it. But it is an old companion of humanity, and for most of the last millennium it was among the commonest diseases in Europe. With reason it was long thought one of the most infectious of maladies. Smallpox is usually communicated through the air by means of droplets or dust particles, and its virus enters the new host through the respiratory tract. There are many cases of hospital visitors who have contracted the disease simply by breathing for a moment the air of a room in which someone lies ill with the pox.

Where smallpox has been endemic, it has been a steady, dependable killer, taking every year from three to ten percent of those who die. Where it has struck isolated groups, the death rate has been awesome. Analysis of figures for some twenty outbreaks shows that the case mortality among an unvaccinated population is about thirty percent. Presumably, in people who have had no contact whatever with smallpox, the disease will infect nearly every single individual it touches. When in 1707 smallpox first appeared in Iceland, it is said that in two years 18,000 out of the island's 50,000 inhabitants died of it.

The first people of the New World to meet the white and black races and their diseases were Indians of the Taino culture who spoke the Arawak language and lived on the islands of the Greater Antilles and the Bahamas. On the very first day of landfall in 1492 Columbus noted that the Tainos "are very unskilled with arms. . ." and "could all be subjected and made to do all that one wishes." These Tainos lived long enough to provide the Spaniard with his first generation of slaves in America, and Old World disease with its first beachhead in the New World.

Oviedo, one of the earliest historians of the Americas, estimated that a million Indians lived on Santo Domingo when the European arrived to plant his first permanent colony in the New World. "Of all those," Oviedo wrote, "and of all those born afterwards, there are not now believed to be at the present time in this year of 1548 five hundred persons, children and adults, who are natives and are the progeny or lineage of those first."

The destruction of the Tainos has been largely blamed on the Spanish cruelty, not only by the later Protestant historians of the "Black Legend" school but also by such contemporary Spanish writers as Oviedo and Bartolomé de las Casas. Without doubt the early Spaniard brutally exploited the Indians. But it was obviously not in order to kill them off, for the early colonist had to deal with a chronic labor shortage and needed the Indians. Disease would seem to be a more logical explanation for the disappearance of the Tainos, because they, like other Indians, had little immunity to Old World diseases. At the same time, one may concede that the effects of Spanish exploitation undoubtedly weakened their resistance to disease.

Yet it is interesting to note that there is no record of any massive smallpox epidemic among the Indians of the Antilles for a quarter of a century after the first voyage of Columbus. Indians apparently suffered a steady decline in numbers, which was probably due to extreme overwork, other diseases, and a general lack of will to live after their whole culture had been shattered by alien invasion. How can the evident absence of smallpox be explained, if the American Indian was so susceptible, and if ships carrying Europeans and Africans from the pestilential Old World were constantly arriving in Santo Domingo? The answer lies in the nature of the disease. It is a deadly malady but it lasts only a brief time in each patient. After an incubation period of twelve days or so, the patient suffers from a high fever and vomiting followed three or four days later by the characteristic skin eruptions. For those who do not die, these pustules dry up in a week or ten days, and form scabs, which soon fall off, leaving the disfiguring pocks that give the disease its name. The whole process takes a month or less, and after that time the patient is either dead or immune, at least for a period of years. Also there is no non-human carrier of smallpox, such as the flea of typhus or the mosquito of malaria; it must pass from man to man. Nor are there any long-term human carriers of smallpox, as, for instance, with typhoid and syphilis. It is not an over-simplification to say that one either has smallpox and can transmit it, or one has not and cannot transmit it.

Consider that, except for children, most Europeans and their slaves had had smallpox and were at least partially immune, and that few but adults sailed from Europe to America in the first decades after discovery. Consider that the voyage was one of several weeks, so that, even if an immigrant or sailor contracted smallpox on the day of embarkation, he would most likely be dead or rid of its virus before he arrived in Santo Domingo. Consider that moist heat and strong sunlight, characteristic of a tropical sea voyage, are particularly deadly to the smallpox virus. The lack of any rapid means of crossing the Atlantic in the sixteenth century delayed the delivery of the Old World's worst gift to the New.

It was delayed; that was all. An especially fast passage from Spain to the New World; the presence on a vessel of several nonimmune persons who could transmit the disease from one to the other until arrival in the Indies; the presence of smallpox scabs, in which the virus can live for weeks, accidentally packed into a bale of textiles—by any of these means smallpox could have been brought to Spanish America.

In December 1518 or January 1516 a disease identified as smallpox appeared among the Indians of Santo Domingo, brought, said Las Casas, from Castile. It touched few Spaniards, and none of them died, but it devasted the Indians. The Spaniards reported that it killed one-third to one-half of the Indians. Las Casas, never one to understate the appalling, said that it left no more than one thousand alive "of that immensity of people that was on this island and which we have seen with our own eyes.". . .

Thus began the first recorded pandemic in the New World, which was "in all likelihood the most severe single loss of aboriginal population that ever occurred." In a matter of days after smallpox appeared in Santo Domingo, it leaped the channel to Puerto Rico. Before long, Tainos were dying a hideous and unfamiliar death in all the islands of the Greater Antilles. Crushed by a quarter-century of exploitation, they now performed their last function on earth; to act as a reserve of pestilence in the New World from which the conquistador drew invisible biological allies for his assault on the mainland. . . .

The melodrama of Cortés and the conquest of Mexico need no retelling. After occupying Tenochtitlán and defeating the army of his rival, Narváez, he and his troops had to fight their way out of the city to sanctuary in Tlaxcala. Even as the Spanish withdrew, an ally more formidable than Tlaxcala appeared. Years later Francisco de Aguilar, once, a follower of Cortés and now a Dominican friar, recalled the terrible retreat of the *Noche Triste*. "When the Christians were exhausted from war," he wrote, "God saw fit to send the Indians smallpox, and there was a great pestilence in the city. . . ."

With the men of Narváez had come a Negro sick with smallpox, "and he infected the household in Cempoala where he was quartered, and it spread from one

Indian to another, and they, being so numerous and eating and sleeping together, quickly infected the whole country." The Mexicans had never seen smallpox before and did not have even the European's meager knowledge of how to deal with it. The old soldier-chronicler, Bernal Díaz del Castillo, called the Negro "a very black dose" for Mexico, "for it was because of him that the whole country was stricken, with a great many deaths."

Probably, several diseases were at work. Shortly after the retreat from Tenochtitlán Bernal Díaz, immune to smallpox like most of the Spaniards, "was very sick with fever and was vomiting blood." The Aztec sources mention the racking cough of those who had smallpox, which suggests a respiratory complication such as pneumonia or a streptococcal infection, both common among smallpox victims. Great numbers of the Cakchiquel people of Guatemala were felled by a devastating epidemic in 1520 and 1521, having as its most prominent symptom fearsome nosebleeds. Whatever this disease was, it may have been present in central Mexico along with the pox.

The triumphant Aztecs had not expected the Spaniards to return after their expulsion from Tenochtitlán. The sixty days during which the epidemic lasted in the city, however, gave Cortés and his troops a desperately needed respite to reorganize and prepare a counterattack. When the epidemic subsided, the siege of the Aztec capital began. Had there been no epidemic, the Aztecs, their war-making potential unimpaired and their warriors fired with victory, could have pursued the Spaniards, and Cortés might have ended his life spread-eagled beneath the obsidian blade of a priest of Huitzilopochtli. Clearly the epidemic sapped the endurance of Tenochtitlán to survive the Spanish assault. As it was, the siege went on for seventy-five days, until the deaths within the city from combat, starvation, and disease—probably not smallpox now—numbered many thousands. When the city fell "the streets, squares, houses, and courts were filled with bodies, so that it was almost impossible to pass. Even Cortés was sick from the stench in his nostrils." . . .

If we attempt to describe the first coming of Old World disease to the areas south of Panama, we shall have to deal with ambiguity, equivocation, and simple guesswork, for eruptive fever, now operating from continental bases, apparently outstripped the Spaniards and sped south from the isthmus into the Incan Empire before Pizarro's invasion. Long before the invasion, the Inca, Huayna Capac was aware that the Spaniards—"monstrous marine animals, bearded men who moved upon the sea in large houses—were pushing down the coast from Panama. Such is the communicability of smallpox and the other eruptive fevers that any Indian who received news of the Spaniards could also have easily received the infection of the European diseases. The biologically defenseless Indians made vastly more efficient carriers of such pestilence than the Spaniards.

Our evidence for the first post-Columbian epidemic in Incan lands is entirely hearsay, because the Incan people had no system of writing. Therefore, we must depend on secondary accounts by Spaniards and by mestizos or Indians born after the conquest, accounts based on Indian memory and written years and even decades after the epidemic of the 1520s. The few accounts we have of the great epidemic are associated with the death of Huayna Capac. He spent the last years of his life campaigning against the people of what is today northern Peru and Ecuador. There, in the province of Quito, he first received news of an epidemic raging in his empire, and there he himself was stricken. Huayna Capac and his captains died with shocking rapidity, "their faces being covered with scabs."

Of what did the Inca and his captains die? One of the most generally reliable of our sources, that of Garcilaso de la Vega, describes Huayna Capac's death as the result of "a trembling chill. . . , which the Indians call *chucchu,* and a fever, called by the Indians *rupu. . . .*" We dare not, four hundred years later, unequivocally state that the disease was not one native to the Americas. Most accounts call it smallpox, or suggest that it was either smallpox or measles. Smallpox seems the best guess because the epidemic struck in that period when the Spaniards, operating from bases where smallpox was killing multitudes, were first coasting along the shores of Incan lands.

The impact of the smallpox pandemic on the Aztec and Incan Empires is easy for us of the twentieth century to underestimate. We have so long been hypnotized by the derring-do of the conquistador that we have overlooked the importance of his biological allies. Because of the achievements of medical science in our day we find it hard to accept statements from the conquest period that the pandemic killed one-third to one-half of the populations struck by it. Toribio Motolinía claimed that in most provinces of Mexico "more than one half of the population died; in others the proportion was little less." "They died in heaps," he said, "like bedbugs."

The proportion may be exaggerated, but perhaps not as much as we might think. The Mexicans had no natural resistance to the disease at all. Other diseases were probably operating quietly and efficiently behind the screen of smallpox. Add too the factors of food shortage and the lack of even minimal care for the sick: Motolinía wrote: "Many others died of starvation, because as they were all taken sick at once, they could not care for each other, nor was there anyone to give them bread or anything else." We shall never be certain what the death rate was, but, from all evidence, it must have been immense. . . .

In Peru the epidemic of the 1520s was a stunning blow to the very nerve center of Incan society, throwing that society into a self-destructive convulsion. The government of the Incan Empire was an absolute autocracy with a demigod, the Child of the Sun, as its emperor. The loss of the emperor could do enormous damage to the whole society, as Pizarro proved by his capture of Atahualpa. Presumably the damage was greater if the Inca were much esteemed, as was Huayna Capac. When he died, said Cieza de León, the mourning "was such that the lamentation and shrieks rose to the skies, causing the birds to fall to the ground. The news traveled far and wide, and nowhere did it not evoke great sorrow." Pedro Pizarro, one of the first to record what the Indians told of the last days before the conquests, judged that had "this Huayna Capac been alive when we Spaniards entered this land, it would have ben impossible for us to win it, for he was much beloved by all his vassals."

Not only the Inca but many others in key positions in Incan society died in the epidemic. The general Mihcnaca Mayta and many other military leaders, the governors Apu Hilaquito and Auqui Tupac (uncle and brother to the Inca), the Inca's sister, Mama Coca, and many others of the royal family all perished of the disease. The deaths of these important persons must have robbed the empire of much resiliency. Most ominous loss of all was the Inca's son and heir Ninan Cuyoche.

In an autocracy no problem is more dangerous or more chronic than that of succession. One crude but workable solution is to have the autocrat, himself, choose his successor. The Inca named one of his sons, Ninan Cuyoche, as next wearer of "the fringe" or crown, on the condition that the *calpa*, a ceremony of divination, show this to be an auspicious choice. The first *calpa*, indicated that the gods did not favor Ninan Cuyoche, the second that Huascar was no better candidate. The high nobles returned to the Inca for another choice and found him dead. Suddenly a terrible gap had opened in Incan society: the autocrat had died, and there was no one to take his place. One of the nobles moved to close the gap. "Take care of the body," he said, "for I go to Tumipampa to give the fringe to Ninan Cuyoche." But it was too late. When he arrived at Tumipampa, he found that Ninan Cuyoche had also succumbed to smallpox pestilence.

Among the several varying accounts of the Inca's death the one just related best fits the thesis of this paper. And while these accounts my differ on many points, they all agree that confusion over the succession followed the unexpected death of Huayna Capac. War broke out between Huascar and Atahualpa, a war which devastated the empire and prepared the way for a quick Spanish conquest. "Had the land not been divided between Huascar and Atahualpa," Pedro Pizarro wrote, "we would not have been able to enter or win the land unless we could gather a thousand Spaniards for the task, and at that time it was impossible to get together even five hundred Spaniards. . . ."

The psychological effect of epidemic disease is enormous, especially of an unknown disfiguring disease which strikes swiftly. Within a few days smallpox can transform a healthy man into a pustulated, oozing horror, whom his closest relatives can barely recognize. The impact can be sensed in the following terse, stoic account, drawn from Indian testimony, of Tenochtitlán during the epidemic.

It was [the month of] Tepeilhuitl when it began, and it spread over the people as great destruction. Some it quite covered [with pustules] on all parts—their faces, their heads, their breasts, etc. There was a great havoc. Very many died of it. They could not walk, they only lay in their resting places and beds. They could not move; they could not stir; they could not change position, nor lie on one side, nor face down, nor on their backs. And if they stirred, much did they cry out. Great was its [smallpox'] destruction. Covered, mantled with pustules, very many people died of them.

. . . For those who survived, the horror was only diminished, for smallpox is a disease which marks its victims for the rest of their lives. The Spanish recalled that the Indians who survived, having scratched themselves, "were left in such a condition that they frightened the others with the many deep pits on their faces, hands, and bodies." "And on some, "an Indian said, "the pustules were widely separated; they suffered not greatly, neither did many [of them] die. Yet many people were marred by them on their faces; one's face or nose was pitted." Some lost their sight—a fairly common aftereffect of smallpox.

The contrast between the Indians' extreme susceptibility to the new disease and the Spaniards' almost universal immunity, acquired in Spain and reinforced in pestilential Cuba, must have deeply impressed the native Americans. The Indian, of course, soon realized that there was little relationship between Cortés and Quetzalcóatl, and that the Spaniards had all the vices and weaknesses of ordinary men, but he must have kept a lingering suspicion that the Spaniards were some kind of supermen. Their steel swords and arqebuses, their marvelously agile galleys, and above all, their horses could only be the tools and servants of supermen. And their invulnerability to the pox—surely this was a shield of the gods themselves!

One can only imagine the psychological impact of smallpox on the Incan peoples. It must have been less than in Mexico, because the disease and the Spaniards did not arrive simultaneously, but epidemic disease is terrifying under any circumstances and must have shaken the confidence of the Incan people that they still enjoyed the esteem of their gods. Then came the long ferocious civil war, confusing a people accustomed to the autocracy of the true Child of the Sun. And then the final disaster, the coming of the Spaniards.

The Mayan peoples, probably the most sensitive and brilliant of all American aborigines, expressed more poignantly than any other Indians the overwhelming effect of epidemic. Some disease struck into Guatemala in 1520 and 1521, clearing the way for the invasion shortly thereafter by Pedro de Alvarado, one of Cortés' captains. It was apparently not smallpox, for the accounts do not mention pustules but emphasize nosebleeds, cough, and illness of the bladder as the prominent symptoms. It may have been influenza; whatever it was, the Cakchiquel Mayas who kept a chronicle of the tragedy for their posterity, were helpless to deal with it. Their words speak for all the Indians touched by Old World disease in the sixteenth century:

> Great was the stench of the dead. After our fathers and grandfathers succumbed, half of the people fled to the fields. The dogs and vultures devoured the bodies. The mortality was terrible. Your grandfathers died, and with them died the son of the king and his brothers and kinsmen. So it was that we became orphans, oh, my sons! So we became when we were young. All of us were thus. We were born to die!

SECTION II

Was Inca Rule Tyrannical?

EUROPEAN REACTIONS TO INDIAN CIVILIZATIONS

Spaniards were amazed by the strange people they found in the New World, and over the years, as they strove to conquer and Christianize the Indians, they devoted much attention to the many native languages, religions, and cultures. The kind of culture the Indians had attained became part of the verbal battles over their "rationality." Bartolomé de Las Casas, the sixteenth-century Protector of the Indians, attempted in a long treatise, *Apologetic History*, to prove that the Indians were eminently rational beings with such "excellent, most subtle and natural intelligence" that they satisfied all the requirements laid down by Aristotle for the good life.[1] Besides these obviously political reactions, others looked at Indian achievements in art through professional eyes. Albrecht Dürer, the outstanding German painter and engraver of the time, visited the first exhibition of aboriginal Mexican art in Europe that took place in Brussels before Emperor Charles V in 1520. Dürer recorded his surprise and delight in his diary on first examining the gold and silver objects wrought by the Indians and dispatched by Hernando Cortés to illustrate the greatness of his conquests: "All the days of my life I have seen nothing that rejoiced my heart so much as these things, for I saw amongst them wonderful works of art, and I marveled at the subtle ingenuity of men in foreign lands."[2] Cortés also sent an Aztec ballet troop to Spain a few years later, which greatly impressed Charles and his imperial court. As described by Friar Diego Valadés, in his *Rhetorica Christiana* (Perusia, 1579), the first book published in Europe by a native-born Mexican: "Their dances are very worthy of mention, since despite such a multitude they sing in the most perfect unison and move in perfect synchronism, whatever the shifts of measure and melody. The invincible emperor Charles V could not believe the report of so great a number of dancers and their rhythmic perfection until he witnessed

---

1. For more information on this treatise, see Lewis Hanke, *Aristotle and the American Indians* (Bloomington: Indiana University Press, 1970).
2. Robert Stevenson, *Music in Aztec and Inca Territory* (Berkeley, 1968), p. 88.

Francisco de Toledo, Viceroy of Peru (1569–1581). One of the best ways to study the nature of Spanish rule in America would be to examine closely the objectives and accomplishments of this notable viceroy who established Spanish power in Peru. To this end he elaborated laws to regulate pratically all aspects of colonial life, executed the Inca Tupac Amaru, concentrated Indians in communities and harnessed their labor for agriculture and mining. He was also concerned to prove that Spanish rule was recognized as just and that Inca rule had been unjust (Reading 4).

their performance at Valladolid, where he and a number of his principal courtiers were enthralled by their demonstration an entire morning."[3]

WAS INCA RULE JUST?

Art and music were all very well, but what really interested the sixteenth-century Spaniards was to establish without question the justice of their rule in the New World and the tyranny of the native governments. Questions on the just title of Spain to the Indies were raised in the early days of discovery, and they continued as the Spaniards toppled the Maya and Aztec empires. As the conquest moved to the high Andean regions in Peru, the arguments over the kind of civilization created by the Indians there became more acute and more political. The youthful conquistador Pedro de Cieza de León admired Inca achievements (Reading 1), while the oldest · survivor of the conquest in Peru, one Mancio Sierra de Leguízamo, solemnly swore on his deathbed in 1589 that not only were the Incas wise rulers but that the invading Spaniards had corrupted an ideal Indian society (Reading 2).[4] The Inca Garcilaso de la Vega, the son of an Inca princess and a Spanish captain, wrote nostalgically of the civilization his maternal ancestors had created and his paternal kin had destroyed (Reading 3).

Viceroy Francisco de Toledo on his arrival in Peru in 1569 discovered so much uncertainty over the comparative merits of Inca and Spanish rule that he launched a frontal attack on the Inca system (Reading 4).

LATER ECHOES OF THE ARGUMENT

Inca government and Inca history continued to play a political role long after Viceroy Toledo returned to Spain in 1581. As we will see in Section VIII, José Gabriel Tupac Amaru attempted to utilize the glory of his Inca ancestors to help him during the revolt in Peru in the 1780s, though his aim was to capture Spanish institutions, not to destroy or displace them by others. During the wars for independence in Argentina in the early nineteenth century General José de San Martín and Manuel

3. Ibid., p. 89. In 1528 Cortez took with him to Spain a troupe of native entertainers, including some jugglers from Tlaxcala who performed "in a manner never seen or heard in Spain." Also brought along to impress the court were male and female dwarfs, hunchbacks, and native prestidigitators. See Howard F. Cline, "Hernando Cortés and the Aztec Indians in New Spain," *Quarterly Journal of the Library of Congress* 26 (1969): 70–90.

4. A number of other wills on behalf of Indians by conquistadors testify to the influence of Las Casas's demand that restitution be paid to despoiled Indians. See Guillermo Lohmann Villena, "La restitución por conquistadores y encomenderos: un aspecto de la incidencia lascasiana en el Perú," in *Estudios Lascasianos: IV Centenario de la muerte de fray Bartolomé de las Casas, 1466–1966* (Seville, 1966), pp. 21–89.

Belgrano supported the idea of an "Inca Monarchy" to supplant that of Spain, and even had propagandistic handbills printed in the Indian languages Aymara and Quechua for distribution among native caciques to arouse sympathy for the revolutionists against Spain.[5] In northern South America, far from Cuzco and other ancient centers of Inca strength, the opponents of Spain continued to invoke the splendors of the Indian past to aid their campaigns. The Liberator Simón Bolívar and his generals "were tiresomely extolled as the final 'avengers' of the fallen Incan Empire."[6]

A century later in Peru, during the early years of President Augusto B. Leguía's administration in the 1920s, Fredrick Pike states: "An increasing number of Peruvian intellectuals turned their attention to Inca history, folklore, and archaeology. In Lima the Society of the Golden Arrow was formed, the purpose of its members being to study the glories of the Inca past . . . Leguía himself joined in, and liked to be referred to as Viracocha, the white-skinned, culture-bearing deity."[7] Though Leguía did not pursue these Inca interests, other Peruvians such as José Carlos Mariátegui and Victor Raúl Haya de la Torre did; some of the roots of the APRA (Alianza Peruana Revolucionaria Americana) political party are sunk in the Inca past. In the years between the two world wars Italian fascism found Inca "communism" a useful tool, and the Bolivian revolution of 1952 is said to have been prepared for by renewed interest in Inca studies.[8]

Scholarly attention to all aspects of Inca history has grown during the last half century, though it has not produced a consensus. Philip Ainsworth Means, a pioneer student of Inca history in the United States, agreed with the highly favorable accounts of the sixteenth-century Spaniards and concluded: "Such was the unique civilization which Spanish culture, bringing with it Christianity and money culture, was destined to overwhelm and change beyond recognition . . . The greatest, the fundamental and the universal source of evil brought into Peru by the Spaniards was the money-complex whence arose all the endless misery which has weighed down the Andean peoples ever since the money-less empire of the Incas was shattered."[9]

Later writers, influenced by the swirling currents of discussion in Europe on the proper functions of the state, have characterized Inca culture as "socialistic."[10] A

5. Harry Bernstein, *Modern and Contemporary Latin America* (Philadelphia: Lippincott, 1952), p. 199.

6. David Bushnell, *The Santander Regime in Gran Colombia* (Newark: University of Delaware Press, 1954), p. 175.

7. Fredrick B. Pike, *The Modern History of Peru* (London: Weidenfeld & Nicholson, 1967), chap. 8.

8. Benedetto Giacalone, *Comunismo Incaico-araucania-Florida-Colombiano* (Genoa: Bozzi, 1936), and Charles Arnade, "The U.S. and the Ultimate Roots of the Bolivian Revolution," *Historia* (Río Piedras), n.s., vol. 1 (1962), no. 1, pp. 35–50.

9. P.A. Means, *Fall of the Inca Empire* (New York: Scribners, 1932), p. 12.

10. Louis Baudin, *A Socialist Empire: The Incas of Peru* (Princeton, 1961).

more evaluative note was struck by the late Swiss anthropologist, Alfred Métraux, who objected to attempts to force the Inca system to conform "to a modern formula: a socialistic, a totalitarian, or a welfare state" (Reading 5). Though "romantic attitudes and unfounded prejudices, glib exaggerations and superficial generalizations have provided the basis for either uncritical exaltation or contemptuous denigration of Peru aborigines and their historical feats," as Professor Pike declares,[11] a new realism is being brought to bear upon the Inca past. The young Swedish scholar Ake Wedin has challenged previous interpretations of Inca chronology,[12] and John V. Murra has also denounced the practice of classifying the Inca system using terms applied to European and political history.[13] He refuses to employ the labels "socialistic, " feudal," "totalitarian," or the concepts implicit in "commoner," "nobleman," or "lumpenproletariat." Another author to survey the interpretations of Inca rule reaches this conclusion: "The old sources of knowledge of Inca culture . . . indicate that one cannot speak of an Inca communistic order, nor of a collectivistic system, or a socialist centralization of land tenure. The property tax of 66%, the personal service or *prestación*, the compulsory change of residence, and the impossibility of overcoming social barriers because of the static order of social class, show very clearly that the Incas and their form of the state cannot serve as a model for our times."[14]

The study of Inca culture, however, holds rich rewards, because one may learn more about a remarkable civilization the Spaniards encountered and may see how cultural history has been manipulated for varied purposes.

A FINAL THOUGHT

One of the conclusions to be drawn from these conflicting interpretations of Indian culture is that "virtue lies in the eye of the beholder." Benjamin Keen's stimulating volume on the ways Aztec civilization has been viewed demonstrates that

11. Pike, *Modern History of Peru*, chap. 1.

12. Ake Wedin, *La cronología de la historia incaica: Estudio crítico* (Madrid: Instituto Ibero-Americano de Gotemburgo, 1963). See also his monographs, *El sistema decimal en el imperio incaico: Estudio sobre estructura política* (Madrid: Instituto Ibero-Americano de Gotemburgo, 1965), and *El concepto de lo incaico y las fuentes: Estudio crítico*, Studia Historica Gothoburgensia, 7 (Uppsala: Scandinavian University Books, 1966).

13. John V. Murra, "On Inca Political Structure," *Systems of Political Control and Bureaucracy in Human Societies, Proceedings of the 1958 Annual Spring Meeting of the American Ethnological Society*, ed. Verne F. Ray (Seattle, 1958), p. 30. See also his "Social, Structural and Economic Themes in Andean Ethnohistory," *American Anthropologist* 34, no. 2 (1961): 47–59.

14. Horst Nachtigall, "El estado estamental de los incas peruanos," *América Indígena* 24, no. 2 (1964): 93–110.

Inca culture was not the only one to provoke a variety of reactions.[15] Keen cites a dramatic example in the work of the late George Vaillant, one of the leading American archaeologists of this century. Writing in the dark and uncertain years just before World War II, Vaillant reflected in this way on the meaning of the Aztec way of life for his own time:

> The civilization of the Indian may not offer a direct inspiration to us modern individualists, yet we have profited from their labor in our food plants and the wealth produced by our neighbor republics to the south. In this world, torn with hate and war, adrift without an anchor or a compass with which to chart our course, we may well consider their example. The Indians worked together for their common good, and no sacrifice was too great for their corporate well-being. Man's strength lay in the physical and spiritual welfare of the tribe, and the individual was honored only inasmuch as he contributed to that communal good. The Indian civilization may have been powerless to resist the culture of the western world, but it did not consume itself, as we are doing, in the expression of military power.[16]

Keen's comment on the above statement is pertinent: "That Vaillant, who knew the sources of Aztec society so well, should have shut his eyes so tightly to the abundant evidence of social cleavages and tensions within it testifies to the power of emotive factors in the way we view the past. Vaillant's radiant vision of Aztec civilization undoubtedly reflects his profound discontent with the state of the world in which he lived, a discontent that may have contributed to his tragic death by suicide . . . shortly after the publication of the *Aztecs of Mexico*."[17] Many other examples of this type can be found. Therefore as we read about Indian cultures we should first of all try to understand the perspective from which the author develops his interpretation.

It is unfortunate that Indians left few written records of their views of Spanish culture. We know that many fled away to the hills to escape the invaders, which is one response. Others we are told committed suicide or faded away as they came to realize the gulf between their culture and that of the invaders. Still others sought to make the best of the situation by making alliances with the Spanish and manipulating the colonial political and economic institutions to their own advantage.[18]

One of the rare testimonies on Indian views is found in the official history of Antonio de Herrera, who reports that one day a Spaniard in Peru inquired of "a discreet Indian" what he considered the most significant contributions of the Spaniards to their life. The reply must have surprised the Spaniard, for the discreet Indian said not a word about the Christian religion, education, or plants. Instead he emphasized the importance of chicken eggs, horses, and candles: "The eggs because they are abundant and fresh everyday, and good for old and young whether cooked or not; horses because they allow one to travel without fatigue and relieve men of burden bearing; and candles because with their light one may live a part of the night."[19]

The most valuable document by a Peruvian Indian on Andean life before Pizarro came from the pen of Guaman Poma de Ayala, who in about 1615 wrote what he called "a letter" to the King of Spain. This 1,200 page work, illustrated by the author with 400 drawings, is a unique source: "It was mostly a cry of anguish, a petition to the all-powerful King overseas to look at what his men were doing in America, to look at what they had destroyed. . . But it also is a constructive document; most of it is devoted to plans for a "buen gobierno," a good government Poma thought could still be devised by combining revived Inca social and economic organization with Christianity and some beneficial aspects of European technology, such as growing grapes and making wine."[20]

Poma never achieved his dream of presenting his manuscript to Philip III. But it somehow was saved and finally printed. A new critical edition of *Nueva Corónica y Buen Gobierno*, with indexes, translations of the material in Quechua, and a transcription of the entire manuscript, came out in 1980 in Mexico, edited by J. V. Murra and Rolena Adorno, but for English readers Poma's work will be most accessible through Rolena Adorno's monograph, *Guaman Poma: Writing and Resistance in Colonial Peru* (Austin: University of Texas Press, 1986).

15. Benjamin Keen, *The Aztec Image* (New Brunswick: Rutgers University Press, 1971).

16. George C. Vaillant, *The Aztecs of Mexico* (New York, 1941), pp. 280–81.

17. Keen, *The Aztec Image*, p. 493.

18. Steve J. Stern, "The Rise and Fall of Indian-White Alliances: A Regional View of 'Conquest' History," *Hispanic American Historical Review* 61:3 (August, 1981): 461–91.

19. Antonio de Herrera y Tordesilla, *Historia general de los hechos de los castellanos en las islas y tierra firme del mar océano*, ed. Antonio de Ballesteros and Angel Altolaguirre, vol. 2 (Madrid, 1934), pp. 34–35.

20. John V. Murra, "Guaman Poma de Ayala: A Seventeenth-Century Indian's Account of Andean Civilization," *Natural History* 70, no. 7 (1961): 35.

FAVORABLE ASSESSMENTS

1. How the Incas Achieved So Much

PEDRO CIEZA DE LEÓN

This chronicler went to America as a boy of 13, became one of the youngest conquistadors on record, and gathered information as he participated in the conquest from northern South America to southern Peru. He kept a diary of his many experiences and on his return to Spain in 1550 published *Crónica del Perú* (Sevilla, 1553), a remarkably accurate and detailed work. A second work, *Senorio de los Incas,* was not published until 1880 and is considered an indispensable work on Inca society.

Cieza de León was a friend and admirer of Las Casas, as his recently discovered will shows, and did not hesitate to criticize his fellow conquistadors harshly, but by the middle of the sixteenth century he felt Spanish government was just: "I remember that when I was in the province of Jauja a few years ago the Indians told me with great contentment and happiness these are happy, good times, similar to those of Inca Tupac Yupanqui. . . . Certainly, all of us who are Christians should rejoice and give thanks for this to our Lord God, that in such vast areas and lands, so far from our Spain and all Europe, there should be such justice and such good government."*

One of the things most to be envied these rulers is how well they knew to conquer such vast lands and, with their forethought, bring them to the flourishing state in which the Spaniards found them when they discovered this new kingdom. Proof of this is the many times I recall hearing these same Spaniards say, when we were in some indomitable region outside these kingdoms, "Take my word for it, if the Incas had been here it would have been a different story." In a word, the Incas did not make their conquests any way just for the sake of being served and collecting tribute. In this respect they were far ahead of us, for with the order they introduced

---

*Bailey W. Diffie, *Latin-American Civilization: Colonial Period* (New York: Octagon Books, 1967), p. 311.

From *The Incas of Pedro de Cieza de León* by Pedro de Cieza de León, trans. Harriet de Onis, ed. with intro. by Victor W. von Hagen, pp. 158–61. Copyright 1959 by the University of Oklahoma Press. Reprinted by permission.

the people throve and multiplied, and arid regions were made fertile and bountiful, in the ways and goodly manner that will be told.

They always tried to do things by fair means and not by foul at the beginning; afterward, certain of the Incas meted out severe punishments in many places, but they all tell that they first used great benevolence and friendliness to win these people over to their service. They set out from Cuzco with their men and weapons, and traveled in careful manner until they were close to the place they were going and planned to conquer. There they carefully sized up the situation to learn the strength of the enemy, the support they might have, and from what direction help might come, and by what road. When they had so informed themselves, they tried in every possible way to prevent them from receiving succor, either by rich gifts or by blocking the way. Aside from this, they built fortifications on hills or slopes with high, long stockades, each with its own gate, so that if one were lost, they could retire to the next, and so on to the topmost. And they sent out scouts of their confederates to spy out the land and learn the paths and find out whether they were waiting for them, and where the most food was. And when they knew the route by which the enemy was approaching and the force in which they were coming, they sent ahead messengers to say that the Inca wanted them to be his kin and allies, and, therefore, to come out to welcome him and receive him in their province with good cheer and light heart, and swear him fealty as the others had done. And so they would do this willingly, he sent gifts to the native rulers.

In this way, and with other good methods they employed they entered many lands without war, and the soldiers who accompanied the Inca were ordered to do no damage or harm, or robbery or violence. If there was a shortage of food in the province, he ordered supplies brought in from other regions so that those newly won to his service would not find his rule and acquaintance irksome, and that knowing and hating him would be one. If in any of these provinces there were no flocks, he instantly ordered that they be given thousands of head, ordering that they tend them well so that they would multiply and supply them with wool for their clothing, and not venture to kill or eat any of the young during the years and time he fixed. And if there were flocks, but they lacked some other thing, he did the same. If they were living in hills and wooded places, he made them understand with courteous words that they should build their villages and houses in the level parts of the sierras and hillsides; and as many of them were not skilled in the cultivation of the land, he had them taught how they should do it, urging them to build irrigation canals and water their fields from them.

They knew how to provide for everything so well that when one of the Incas entered a province in friendship, in a little while it seemed a different place and the natives obeyed him, agreeing that his representatives should dwell there, and also the *mitimaes*. In many others, where they entered by war and force of arms, they ordered that the crops and houses of the enemy be spared, the Inca saying, "These will soon be ours like those we already possess." As this was known to all, they tried to make the war as mild as possible even though fierce battles were waged in many places, because, in spite of everything, the inhabitants of them wanted to preserve their ancient liberty and not give up their customs and religion for others that were alien. But in the end the Incas always came out victorious, and when they had vanquished the others, they did not do them further harm, but released those they had taken prisoner, if there were any, and restored the booty, and put them back in possession of their property and rule, exhorting them not to be foolish and try to compete with his royal majesty nor abandon his friendship, but to be his friends as their neighbors were. And saying this, he gave them a number of beautiful women and fine pieces of wool or gold.

With these gifts and kindly words he won the good will of all to such a degree that those who had fled to the mountains returned to their homes, and all laid down their arms, and the one who most often had sight of the Inca was considered blessed and happy.

They never deprived the native chieftains of their rule. They were all ordered to worship the sun as God, but they were not prohibited from observing their own religions and customs. However, they were ordered to be ruled by the laws and customs which prevailed in Cuzco, and all were to speak the general language.

And when the Inca had appointed a governor with a garrison of soldiers, he went on, and if the provinces were large, he at once ordered a temple built to the sun and women assigned to it as in the others, and palaces built for the Inca, and the amount of tribute to be paid fixed, without ever making this burdensome or offending the people in any way, but building them in the ways of their polity, and teaching them to wear long clothing and live in their settlements in orderly manner. And if they lacked for anything, they were provided with it, and taught how to plant and cultivate. So well was this done that we know of many places where there had been no flocks that had them in abundance from the time the Incas subdued them, and others where there had been no corn that later had more than they could use. Those who had lived like savages, poorly clad and barefoot, after they acknowledged this ruler wore shirts and ribbons and blankets, and their women likewise, and other good things; so much so that there will always be memory of all this. In the Collao and other regions they ordered *mitimaes* to go to the highlands of the Andes to plant corn and cocoa and other fruits and roots, the necessary number from all the settlements. And these and their wives always lived in the place there they planted their crops, and harvested so much of what I have described that there was no lack, for these regions produced so much that there was no village, however small, that did not receive something from these *mitimaes*.

2. Spaniards Corrupted an Ideal Indian Society

MANCIO SIERRA DE LEGUIZAMO

Spanish soldiers often developed mixed feelings about their labors during the conquest and afterward. Because Las Casas and other Indian defenders denounced the cruelty of their fellowmen, it was not uncommon to find conquistadors leaving money in their wills to benefit Indians in order "to make restitution." One of the best known of these doubters of the justice of Spanish rule was Mancio Sierra de Leguizamo, who had participated actively in wars against the Indians for many years. He had become famous throughout Peru for having won as booty the celebrated gold image of the sun in Cuzco.* It is possible that as the conquistador lay dying in 1589 some zealous, pro-Indian ecclesiastic actually composed his moving last will and testament and threatened him with hell fire if he did not sign the document.

Before beginning my will, I declare that for many years I have wished for the opportunity to advise his Catholic Majesty, King Philip, our Lord—seeing how Catholic and very Christian he is and how zealous in the services of our Lord God—of what is necessary for the relief of my soul because of the large part I played in the discovery, conquest, and settlement of these Kingdoms when we took them away from those who were Inca Lords and possessed and ruled them as their own, putting them under the royal crown. His Catholic Majesty should understand that the said Incas had these kingdoms governed in such a manner that in all of them there was not a single thief, nor man of vice, nor idle man, nor any adulterous or bad woman; nor were people of loose morals permitted among them. Men had honorable and useful occupations; uncultivated lands, mines, pastures, hunting grounds, woods, and all kind of employments were so managed and distributed that each person knew and held his own estate and no one else took possession of it or deprived him of it; nor was there any litigation over it. Military enter-

---

*James Lockhart, *Men of Cajamarca* (Austin: University of Texas Press, 1972), p. 469. He claimed this, but apparently fibbed.

From "Testamento de Mancio Sierra de Leguizamo," *Revista del Archivo Histórico del Cuzco* 4 (1953): 91–102, passim.

prises, although they were frequent, did not obstruct commercial matters, and the latter did not impede farming nor anything else; in everything from the most important to the most trifling, there was order and methodical arrangement. The Incas, as well as their governors and captains, were respected and feared by their subjects as persons of great capacity and leadership; and since we found that they were the ones who had the strength and authority to offer resistance, we had to deprive them of their power and goods by force of arms in order to subdue and oppress them for the service of our Lord God and in order to take away their land and put it under the royal crown. Our Lord God having permitted it, it was possible for us to subjugate this kingdom with such a multitude of people and riches, and those who had been lords we made servants, as is well known. . . .

His Majesty should understand that my motive in making this declaration is to unburden my conscience of guilt for having destroyed by our bad example people of such good conduct as were these natives, both men and women, and so little given to crime or excess. An Indian who had 100,000 pesos in gold and silver in his house would leave it open and put a broom or small stick across the doorway as a sign that the owner was not there; with this, according to their custom, no one could go inside nor take anything from within. When they say that we had doors and keys in our houses, they thought that this was due to fear that they would kill us, but they did not believe that anyone would take or steal the property of another; and thus when they saw that among us there were thieves and men who incited their wives and daughters to sin, they regarded us with disdain. These natives have become so dissolute with their offenses against God because of the bad example we have given them in everything that their former extreme of doing no evil has been transformed, so that today they do little or no good. . . . In addition, those who were kings and lords, wealthy and obeyed, have come to such a low estate that they and their descendants are the poorest men in the kingdom. Moreover, we Spaniards even want to force them to serve as bearers, to clean and sweep our houses, to carry refuse to the dung-heaps, and to perform even lowlier tasks. And to avoid such tasks, these Inca Lords have started to learn shoe-making and similar trades, taking advantage of an ordinance of the Viceroy, D. Francisco de Toledo, that natives who served the public did not have to perform personal service, for Toledo's ordinance has greater influence than their being free men. Many things of this nature are permitted, which His Majesty would do well to realize and correct for the relief of his conscience and those of us who were discoverers and settlers and caused these ills. I can do no more than to inform his Catholic Majesty of these conditions, and with this I beg God to absolve me of my guilt, which I myself confess I am moved to speak because I am the last survivor of all the discoverers and conquerors since, as is well known, there is no other left in this kingdom or outside of it.

3. "The Incas Had Attained to a High State of Perfection. No Thoughtful Man Can Fail to Admire So Noble and Provident a Government"

GARCILASO DE LA VEGA

This famous mestizo was born in Cuzco of a Spanish captain and an Inca princess in 1539. He went to Spain in 1560 and there embarked on a literary career. He had learned much about Inca history as a boy in his mother's house, for his father had taken a Spanish lady as wife and married off Garcilaso's mother to a Spanish soldier. His account of the culture of his maternal ancestors, the Royal Commentaries, was only one of his notable contributions to Spanish prose, but it became the most widely read and translated source of pre-Conquest Inca life. It was an honest picture, for he does not hide the misery of the masses, but for Garcilaso, Inca rule was perfect, a "Paradise Lost," and he is generally considered an apologist for the Incas.

HOW THEY DIVIDED THE LAND AMONGST THE VASSALS

As soon as the Ynca had conquered any kingdom or province, and established his Government amongst the inhabitants according to his laws and idolatrous customs, he ordered that the cultivated land capable of yielding maize should be extended. For this purpose he caused irrigation channels to be constructed, which were most admirable, as may be seen to this day; both those that have been destroyed, the ruins of which are yet visible, and those still in working order. The engineers led the irrigation channels in directions required by the lands to be watered; for it must be known that the greater part of this land is barren as regards corn-yielding soil, and, for this reason, they endeavoured to increase its fertility as much as possible. As the land is under the torrid zone it requires irrigation. The Yncas supplied the water with great ingenuity, and no maize crop was sown without being also sup-

From *First Part of the Royal Commentaries* by Garcilaso de la Vega, trans. Clements R. Markham (London: The Hakluyt Society, 1st series, nos. 41, 45, 1869–1871), no. 45, pp. 3–29, passim.

plied with water. They also constructed channels to irrigate the pasture land, when the autumn withheld its rains, for they took care to fertilise the pastures as well as the arable land, as they possessed immense flocks. These channels for the pastures were destroyed as soon as the Spaniards came into the country, but the ruins may be seen to this day. . . .

THE ARRANGEMENT THEY ADOPTED FOR TILLING THE LAND, AND OF THE FESTIVAL THEY HELD WHEN THEY CULTIVATED THE LAND OF THE YNCA AND THE SUN

They also established a regular order in the tilling and the cultivating of the land. They first tilled the fields of the Sun; then of the widows, orphans, aged, and sick, for all these persons were classed as poor, and, as such, the Ynca ordered that their fields should be tilled for them. In each village, or in each ward, if the village was large, there were men deputed to look after the lands of persons who were classed as poor. These deputies were named *Llactacamayu,* which means "officers of the village." They superintended the ploughing, sowing, and harvesting; and at such times they went up into towers the night before, that were built for the purpose, and after blowing through a trumpet or shell to secure attention, cried with a loud voice that on such a day such and such lands of the poor would be tilled, warning those, whose duty it might be, to repair thither. The inhabitants of each district were thus apprised on what lands they were to give assistance, which were those of their relations or nearest neighbors. Each one was expected to bring food for himself of what he had in his house, for those who were unable to work were not required to find food for those who could. It was said that their own misery sufficed for the aged, sick, widows, and orphans, without looking after that of the neighbours. If the disabled had no seed, it was provided from the stores, of which we shall speak presently. The lands of soldiers who were employed in the wars were also tilled in this way, like those of widows and orphans; and while the husbands were serving in the wars, their wives were looked up as widows during their absence. Great care was taken of the children of those who were killed in the war, until such time as they were married.

After the lands of the poor and distressed had been tilled, the people worked on their own lands, the neighbours assisting each other. They then tilled the fields of the Curaca, which were the last that received attention in

each village or district. In the time of Huayna Ccapac, an Indian superinten-
dent, in the province of Chachapoyas, was hanged because he caused the
land of a Curaca, who was a relative of his, to be tilled before that of a
widow. He was punished as a breaker of the rules established by the Ynca
for the tilling of the land, and the gallows were set up on the land of the
Curaca. The Yncas ordered that the lands of their vassals should take precedence of their own, because they said that from the prosperity of his subjects
was derived their faithful service to the King; for if they were poor and in
need, they would not be able to serve well either in peace or war.

The last fields that were cultivated were those of the King. All the people
tilled the lands of the Ynca and of the Sun in common, and they went to them
with great joy and satisfaction, dressed in the clothes which they wore on
their grandest festivals. These garments were covered with plates of gold
and silver, and the people also wore plumes of feathers on their heads. When
they ploughed (which was the labour they most enjoyed) they sang many
songs, composed in praise of the Yncas, and they went through their work
with joy and gladness, because it was in the service of their God and of their
King.

Hard by the city of Cuzco, on the slopes of the hill where the fortress
stands, there was a terrace covering many *fanegas* of ground, and it will be
there still, if it has not been covered with houses. It was called the
Collcampata. The suburb which contains it, takes its name from the terrace,
and this terrace was the special and principal jewel, so to speak, belonging
to the Sun; for it was the first land that was dedicated to that deity throughout the whole empire of the Yncas. This land was cultivated by persons of
the blood royal, and none but Yncas and Pallas could work on it. The work
was performed with great rejoicing, especially the ploughing, when the
Yncas came forth in their richest clothes. All the songs that were sung in
praise of the Sun and of their Kings, were composed with reference to the
meaning of the word *Haylli,* which in the general language of Peru means
"triumph." Thus they were said to triumph over the earth by ploughing it,
and turning it up so that it might yield fruit. In these songs they inserted
graceful references to discreet lovers and to valiant soldiers, all bearing on
the triumph over the land that they were tilling. The refrain of each couplet
was the word *Haylli,* repeated as often as was necessary to complete the
compass which the Indians made; for they ploughed the land backwards and
forwards so as to break it up more thoroughly. . . .

The songs of the Indians and their tune appearing good to the master of the choir of the cathedral church of Cuzco, he composed a chaunt, in the year 1551 or 1552, for the feast of the most holy sacrament, very like the *Haylli*. Eight mestizo boys, school-fellows of mine, came forth dressed as Indians, each with a plough in his hand, to represent the song of *Haylli* in the procession, an the whole choir joined them in the refrain of the couplets, which pleased the Spaniards, and caused great joy to the Indians to see the Spaniards solemnizing the festival of our Lord God, whom they called Pachacamac, with the native songs and dances. . . .

THE TRIBUTE THAT THEY GAVE TO THE YNCAS, WITH AN ACCOUNT OF THE GRANARIES

Now that the method the Yncas had of dividing the land has been described, and how it was cultivated by the vassals, it will be well to explain the nature of the tribute they paid to their kings. Their tribute was to cultivate the lands of the Sun and of the Ynca, to gather in the harvests, and to store them in granaries which were kept in each village. One of the chief crops was the *uchu*, which the Spaniards call *axi*, and for another name pepper.

The granaries, called *pirua*, were built of clay mixed with straw. In the time of the Yncas they were constructed with great care. The blocks of clay were of a size conformable to the height of the wall where they were placed, and were cast in different sizes in a mould. They made the granaries of sizes according to the required measurement, some larger than others, to hold from fifty to two hundred *fanegas*. Each granary was measured so as to be of the required size. It had four walls, and there was a passage down the middle, leading from one granary to another, so that they could be emptied or filled at pleasure. But they did not move them from where they were once placed. In order to empty a granary, they had small windows in front, in eight squares, opening so as to give a measurement of the quantity of grain that was poured out, and thus they knew the number of *fanegas* that had been taken out and the quantity remaining without having to measure it further. Thus they could easily tell, by the size of the granaries, the quantity of maize in each depôt, and by the windows they knew how much had been taken out and how much was left in each granary. I saw some of these granaries, which remained from the time of the Yncas, and they were among the best, for they were in the house of the virgins of the Sun, and were built for the use of those women. When I saw them, the convent had become the house of the sons of Pedro del Barco, who were my school-fellows.

The crops of the Sun and those of the Ynca were shut up in places apart, though in the same depôt. The seeds for sowing were given by the Lord of the land, who was the Sun or the King; and in the same way for the sustenance of the Indians who worked, that they might be maintained each out of his own estate, when they tilled and cultivated their lands; so that the Indians had only to give personal labour as their tribute. The vassals paid nothing to the Ynca from their own crops. . . .

THE VASSALS WERE SUPPLIED WITH CLOTHES. NO BEGGING WAS ALLOWED

As there were regulations for the supply of clothing, in abundance to the soldiers; so also the wool was given to the Curacas and vassals generally every two years, to enable them to make clothes for themselves and their families; and it was the duty of the Decurions to see that the people were clothed. The Indians, and even the Curacas, had few Llamas; while the Sun and the Yncas possessed innumerable flocks. The Indians said that when the Spaniards first came to the country there was scarcely sufficient pasture for the flocks, and I have heard my father and his contemporaries relate the great excesses and waste committed by some Spaniards among these flocks. . . . In the warm country cotton was distributed from the royal estates for clothing for the Indians and their families. Thus they had all that was required for human life, both in clothes, shoes, and food; and no one could be called poor, or require to seek alms. For all had as much as they would have required if they had been rich, but they were as poor as possible in unnecessary things, having nothing more than they required. Father Acosta, speaking of Peru says briefly and compendiously what we have related with so much prolixity. At the end of the fifteenth chapter of the sixth book he has these words: "The sheep were shorn at the proper season, and each person was given wool to spin and weave into cloth for his wife and children. Visits were made to see if this was done, and the idle were punished. The wool that was over was put into the storehouses; which were full of it, and of all other things necessary for human life, when the Spaniards arrived. No thoughtful man can fail to admire so noble and provident a Government. For, without being religious or Christians, the Indians attained to a high state of perfection in providing all that was necessary, and plentifully sustaining their houses of religion, as well as those of their King and Lord. . . . "

In the following chapter, speaking of the occupations of the Indians, he . . . says what follows, copied word for word: "Another thing which the Indians of Peru practised was to teach each boy all the arts which it was necessary a man should know to sustain human life. For, among these people, they had no special tradesmen, as we have, such as tailors, shoemakers, or weavers; but each man learnt all, so that he could himself make all that he required. All men knew how to weave and make clothes, so that when the Ynca gave them wool, it was as good as giving them clothes. All could till and manure the land, without hiring labourers. All knew how to build houses. And the women knew all these arts also, practising them with great diligence, and helping their husbands. Other occupations, which were not connected with ordinary wants, had their special artizans. Such as silversmiths, painters, potters, boatmen, accountants and musicians. Even in the ordinary labours of weaving, tilling, and building, there were masters for special work, who served the Lords. But among the common people, as has been said, each could do all that was necessary in his household without having to pay another, and it is the same at the present day. . . . In truth, these people were neither covetous nor wasteful, but were contented to pass their lives in great moderation, so that surely if their mode of living had been adopted from choice, and not from habit, we must have confessed that it was a very perfect state of existence. Nor were the seeds wanting for the reception of the doctrine of the Holy Gospel, which is so hostile to pride, avarice, and waste. But the preachers do not always make their acts agree with the doctrine they preach to the Indians." A little further on he says: "It was an inviolable law that no one should change the peculiar dress of his province, even if he moved to another; and the Yncas held this rule to be very conducive to good government. The custom is still observed, although not so strictly as it was then." So far the Father Acosta. The Indians wonder much at the way the Spaniards change the fashion of their dress every year, and attribute it to pride and presumption.

The custom of never seeking alms was still observed in my day; and up to the time when I left Peru, in 1560, throughout all the parts that I travelled over, I never saw an Indian, man or woman, begging. I only knew one old woman in Cuzco, named Isabel, who begged, and her habit was more to go jesting from house to house, like a gipsy, then to seek alms from necessity. The Indians quarrelled with her, and spat on the ground, which is a sign of contempt and abhorrence; so that she never begged of the Indians, but only of the Spaniards; and as, even in my time, there was no regular money in the country, they gave her maize as alms, which was what she wanted. . . .

The Yncas, in their administration, did not forget the travellers, but along all the royal roads they ordered houses for travellers to be built, called *corpahuasi,* where they were given food and all things necessary for their journeys from the royal stores kept in each village. If they fell ill, they were attended with great care and kindness; so that they had everything as if they had been in their own houses. It is true that they did not travel for their own pleasure or amusement, nor on their own business, for no such thing was known; but by order of the King or of the Curacas, who sent them from one part to another, or by direction of captains or officials, either of war or peace. These travellers were carefully looked after, but any who travelled without just cause, were punished as vagabonds.

THE SPANISH JUSTIFICATION FOR CONQUEST

4. Viceroy Francisco de Toledo's Attack on Inca Rule

LEWIS HANKE

Francisco de Toledo proved to be one of the most energetic administrators Spain ever sent to America. Of all the campaigns to justify Spain's right to rule the New World, his was the most public, the most determined. His principal action was to commission one of his trusted advisers, Pedro Sarmiento de Gamboa, to compile a history that would prove that the Inca system had been tyrannical and a "rule by force, with deaths, robberies, and rapine without the will and election of the natives." Thus the Spanish conquest was eminently just, for the conquistadors had "liberated"—to use a modern term—the Indians from cruel and despotic oppressors.

Once Toledo had demolished the Inca claim to rule Peru, he proceeded to draw up a notable series of laws on practically all aspects of life in the colony that firmly established Spanish power and tightly controlled both Indians and Spaniards.

The best example of the effect produced by Fray Bartolomé de Las Casas' theoretical writings concerning the just title Spain held to America occurred in Peru during the rule of Viceroy Francisco de Toledo, wise law-giver, energetic administrator, and greatest viceroy Spain ever sent to Peru, who laid the basis for Spanish rule there during the years 1569–1582. Before his coming, Peru had had a most turbulent and bloody history, and Toledo arrived with one great aim—to establish without question in his territory the position of the King of Spain. One of his earliest acts was to execute the Inca, Lord Tupac Amaru, the Indian leader who refused to accept Spanish rule. Presently, with a view to establishing Spain's judicial title to Peru, he undertook an extensive historical investigation which attempted to demonstrate the unjust nature of the Inca regime and thus demolish the doctrines of Las Casas. . . .

From "Viceroy Francisco de Toledo and the Just Titles of Spain to the Inca Empire" by Lewis Hanke, *The Americas* 2 (July 1946): 3–19, passim. Reprinted by permission of the Academy of American Franciscan History.

The Viceroy was impelled to this task by what he considered the pernicious influence of Las Casas. Even before Toledo's arrival in Peru, in fact in the instructions given to him by the king on January 28, 1568, he had been warned against free-speaking friars. The king had understood that "the ecclesiastics, who have resided and reside in those parts on the pretext of protecting the Indians have wished to busy themselves concerning the justice and the lordship of the Indies and in other matters which lead them into much scandal, particularly when they treat these subjects in pulpits and public places." Therefore, he warned Toledo to take care to prevent such occurrences by conferring with the provincials and superiors of these ecclesiastics, for in no wise should such scandals be permitted. So serious did Toledo consider this problem that early in his career as viceroy he conferred with the high ecclesiastical authorities of Peru to determine whether the newly established Inquisition could not be utilized, not to smoke out heretics but to impose silence "on preachers and confessors in this realm who hold contrary opinions on jurisdictional matters and on security of conscience.". . .

The Viceroy took three positive steps to combat these theories. First, he inspired the composition of a treatise against Las Casas; second, he embarked upon an investigation of the justice of Inca rule by collecting the so-called *Informaciones*; and finally, he arranged for the preparation of a "true history" of Peru's past by Pedro Sarmiento de Gamboa. This section will discuss the treatise.

The treatise is in the form of an anonymous letter dated at the Valley of Yucay on March 16, 1571, and is entitled "Defense of the Legitimacy of the Rule of the Kings of Spain in the Indies, in Opposition to Friar Bartolomé de Las Casas." The author, who appears to be rendering a formal opinion to Viceroy Toledo, has been identified by some as Polo de Ondegardo, one of Toledo's principal jurists, by others as Pedro Sarmiento de Gamboa, another one of Toledo's principal officers, but perhaps was neither. For at one point, after referring to himself he mentions "many other friars" as though he were one himself and the impression that the author is a friar is strengthened when in closing he states that he was happy to give an opinion "on a matter so appropriate to my profession." If the author were an ecclesiastic, he may have been the Viceroy's chaplain, the Franciscan Pedro Gutiérrez.

At any rate this treatise was a frontal attack on the theories of Las Casas who, the author points out, although he was never in Peru and therefore could know nothing first hand of conditions there, has stirred up all the trouble. The author states that the Indies were given to Spain as a reward for her eight centuries of warfare against the Moslems and insists that the Incas were tyrants in Peru "which fact, Your Excellency is now making abundantly clear with great authority in the investigation you are making." . . .

Much harm will come if the just title of the king of Spain is not clarified, continues the author. Christian government and justice will be hindered, conversion will lag, and other Christian princes will use the excuse of ill treatment of the Indians to try to take over part of all of the Indies. Moreover, and this is a curious sidelight on the times, some Spaniards have married Indian women of the Inca family in order to be in line to rule by the hereditary right if the Incas should return to power, as will happen, warned the author, "if this indiscreet and mistaken Bishop has his way." Finally, Lutheran, English, and French heretics will use the beclouded title of Spain as an excuse to rob Spaniards in the Indies, to harry the land, to ascend rivers and disseminate their heresies in all the empire.

The author then proceeds to state certain basic propositions, such as, that the Incas were modern tyrants, that before Topa Inga conquered the land there was no general overlord, that the Pope made the king of Spain lord over them and that, since they had no natural or legitimate lord, the king of Spain became their ruler. The author combats the idea put forward by Las Casas that the Incas had been received voluntarily as lords, and the charge that, whereas the Spaniards levy taxes and send money abroad, the Incas levied none and spent what money they had in Peru.

In a final burst, the author expresses his amazement at those who "under the guise of zealousness try to give these Indians titles and things which did not belong to them, because God didn't choose to give them nor is it appropriate . . . for they are minors who must be governed. . . . It has been a most delicate subtlety of the Devil to select as his instrument an ecclesiastic and apparently a person of zeal, but deceived and ill-speaking and of little discretion, as may be seen by the publication of his books, and by the disturbances he created in Peru when Blasco Núñez came." . . .

THE "INFORMACIONES" OF VICEROY FRANCISCO DE TOLEDO

The *Informaciones* consisted of a formal inquiry, by order of the Viceroy, into the ancient history of the Incas, the conquests of Tupac Yupanqui the last Inca ruler, the institution of the *Curacas,* the Inca religious beliefs and practices, and their sacrifices, nature, and customs. Information was taken down, by means of translators, from two hundred Indians at eleven different points in Peru during the period November, 1570–March, 1572, while Viceroy Toledo was making a general inspection of Peru at the beginning of his rule there, much in the same way the Inca rulers began their administration by first formally surveying their realms. The complete record of this inquiry has only recently been made available by the Argentine historian. Roberto Levillier.

Few episodes in the colonial history of Peru have been interpreted so variously by modern historians as this inquiry. Clements Markham, José de la Riva-Agüero, Horacio Urteaga, and Philip A. Means believe that Toledo organized this as a public spectacle to present the Incas as monsters of cruelty, to falsify their history and customs in order to make certain of Spain's title. They state that senile, servile "yes-men" were chosen as witnesses, and that if a witness happened to tell an unpalatable truth his answer was changed by the interpreter from "no" to "yes," or "yes" to "no," as the occasion required. In short, that it was intended to blacken the Incas. . . .

Levillier rejects this conclusion vehemently. He points out that not one of these writers had available all the *Informaciones,* and insists that the inquiry was an honest and important investigation which constitutes one of the most trustworthy sources available for a reconstruction of the events and of the spirit of the prodigious Inca community republic.

These inquiries make curious and interesting reading. The records tell us, for example, that on March 13, 1571, there were examined at Cuzco these witnesses: Don Francisco Antigualpa, Governor of Los Andesuyos, aged eighty years; Don Joan Llamoca, Principal of Los Lurinsoras, aged sixty years; Don Joan Caquya, Principal of Los Lurinsoras, aged fifty-five years; Don Lucas Chico, Cacique of Urcos, aged seventy years; Don Bautista Gualpuracana, Curaca of Cachec, aged seventy-five years; and Don Lope Martín Cuntimaycta, Curaca of Yucay, aged sixty years. Among the questions put them there were these:

1. Is it true that the first Inca, he who was called Mango Capac, tyrannically subjugated the Indians living around Cuzco by force of arms and despoiled them of their lands, killing them, warring against them, and otherwise maltreating them? And did all the rest of the Incas do likewise, until the fourth, called Maita Capac, who completed the

conquest?

2. Is it true that the Indians never recognized voluntarily these Incas as their lords, and only obeyed them through fear of great cruelties inflicted against them?

3. Is it true that neither you nor your ancestors ever elected the Incas as your lords, but that they supported their tyrannical position by force of arms and the inculcation of fear?

Practically all the questions were of this yes-or-no character, and there were evidently more yes- than no-men in the group interrogated, for the answers all tended to establish that the whole history of the Incas, from 565 A.D. when Manco Capac founded the dynasty until 1533 when Francisco Pizarro won Peru for Spain, was but a succession of tyrannical and brutal overlords who ruled despotically. It was thereupon an easy transition for the interrogators to elicit that the Spanish invasion was thus a deliverance and greatly to the advantage of the Indians, who were now to be Christianized by the ecclesiastics and protected by the Crown. Another set of questions put to a different set of witnesses drew information that the Incas sacrificed to their gods and idols the most beautiful children to be found, that the Incas realized the laziness of their subjects and kept them at work, even if it had no real value, and that some of the Indians were cannibals.

Although Levillier has published all these *Informaciones* in a bulky volume and attacked the "campaign" theory vigorously in an extensive and detailed analysis, it is probable that we can never be quite certain that the last word has been said on this controversy. For the purposes of this present study it is enough to know Toledo's motive in instituting the inquiry. As his secretary, Alvaro Ruiz de Nabamuel, declared, "He had seen how badly the rights of the King of Spain to the Indies were treated in Spain and in the Indies, and how unreasonable and dangerous it was to attribute to these Incas the true lordship of these kingdoms."

Viceroy Toledo summed up his own view on the meaning of the inquiry when he transmitted to the King a summary of the *Informaciones* with a letter dated March 1, 1572, in which he declared:

1. Your Majesty is the legitimate ruler of this kingdom and the Incas are tyrannical usurpers.

2. Your Majesty may assign at will the *Cacicazgos* as you see fit,

and this action would be one of the most important steps you could take for the spiritual and temporal rule of the Indians.

3. Your Majesty may therefore, bestow the lands of Peru upon Spaniards and ignore the scruples of those who have claimed the Incas are the legitimate rulers.

4. Moreover, all mines and minerals, as well as the property of the Incas, belong to Your Majesty.

5. As legitimate ruler, Your Majesty rightly exercises jurisdiction over the Indians and, given their weak reason and rude understanding, Your Majesty must devise laws for their conservation and require them to obey these ordinances.

Toledo closes this letter with the earnest hope that "such a variety of opinion on matters of great importance will cease," and the King, his ministers and inhabitants of Peru will no longer have their consciences so disturbed and confused as in the past whenever some ignorant person dares to open his mouth and cry to high heaven.

The "HISTORIA INDICA" OF PEDRO SARMIENTO DE GAMBOA

The inquiry into Inca history and Indian customs was not enough. Neither did the treatise "Defense of the Legitimacy of the Rule of the King of Spain in the Indies" wholly satisfy the Viceroy or the conquistadores and their descendants. What the situation really required, they felt, was a history—a true history, which would supplant the false histories then current. . . .

The widespread and intense dissatisfaction among the Spanish rulers of Peru with the historical accounts of Spanish deeds in the New World and with the justification of Spanish rule in Peru is well-illustrated by the expressive memorial drawn up by the Town Council of Cuzco and forwarded to the Council of the Indies on October 24, 1572. These worthies wrote in an injured tone as follows:

Not only did the Greek and Roman historians have a high opinion of the importance of writing history, but even barbarians who have no knowledge of writing still have by a natural instinct sought means to record their past with paintings and marks, and in Peru by a system of threads and knots and registers. Certain persons were appointed whose sole duty was to teach the meaning of it all. Such care has been taken by these Indians that they have a record for the past three hundred years of their deeds, their achievements, their edifices, their wars, and the events of their history. Truly this is to be admired and it is difficult to believe unless one has seen it with his own eyes. All the greater, then, is the fault of the discoverers, the conquistadores, and the colonizers who, having performed great feats and having labored more greatly and with more determination than any other nation in the world, permit these deeds to be forgotten.

Many of those who conquered this realm still live, and we understand that chroniclers who never were here are writing the story of our deeds without ascertaining the truth. These writers do this only to get money by publishing, and sometimes to the detriment of the estates and the honor of those whose deeds they describe. Thus there has resulted a world of conflicting opinions which have left the people disturbed and depressed. When we read the histories written about us, we think they must be describing another kind of people.

We believe ours the most justified cause of all that we know because the basis was the concession which Our Lord and His Vicar-General of our Church made to the Kings of Castile, giving them sovereign dominion and making them patrons in spiritual matters charged with the conversion and evangelical preaching, with general authority to concern themselves in everything discovered and to be discovered without any limitation whatsoever.

This spiritual obligation has been fulfilled. In Cuzco alone there are five monasteries of ecclesiastics and one convent of sisters and a hospital. In this district alone are more than one hundred and twenty priests laboring for the conversion and indoctrination of the natives, not counting the priests Your Excellency has ordered to be added whose expenses are so heavy that they amount to more than one hundred thousand *castellanos*. Moreover, there are only Spanish inhabitants here and they are poor.

Therefore, considering the expense which Your Majesty bears with five tribunals of judges, and mayors, and so many *corregimientos* and the many other salaries which are paid, which consume almost all the revenue gained in Peru, we do not know if there exists in the world a dominion possessed by such just and such reasonable titles, and from which such usefulness and benefit have resulted for the service of God and the increase of His Holy Roman Church.

Moreover, those who are curious to know the origin and basis of other dominions that are in France, Germany, and many other places will discover that most of them have their rights to possession written in the bones of men. And though they have no other reason or basis for their rule than this, they have lived and continue to live so quietly and peacefully that all they have to do is maintain their defenses. They do not have to reply to scruples because nobody raises them. We, the inhabitants of this land, have been less fortunate.

Then the Spaniards resident in Cuzco in 1572 proceeded to describe the tyranny of the Incas, to deplore their bad customs—in much the same vein as the *Informaciones*—and to approve heartily Viceroy Toledo's inquiry. They concluded with the statement that of the one thousand *encomenderos* appointed by the King in Peru, eight hundred have been killed in putting down rebellions and in defense of the realm and those who remained required assistance and favors. It was to satisfy the demands for an honesty history, and to meet the threat to Spanish rule in America that Toledo . . . commissioned Pedro Sarmiento de Gamboa to write a history to set at rest forever the doubts concerning the justice of Spain's rule in Peru.

Sarmiento was one of that group of able officials with whom the Viceroy had surrounded himself, and upon whom he leaned heavily in the administration of his far-flung realm. As a soldier, astronomer, and later explorer of the Solomon Islands and the Straits of Magellan, Sarmiento was typical of the principal Spanish administrative officers who kept the large and complicated machinery of empire in motion. For two years he had been traversing Peru, drawing out from the oldest inhabitants their recollection of the events of the past. To a considerable extent Sarmiento depended upon the *Informaciones* brought forth by Toledo's inquiry, but he had also carried on other investigations in the Valley of the Jauja, in Guamanga, but principally in Cuzco where the Incas had made their capital and where the best informants still lived.

Sarmiento officially presented his history to the Viceroy on February 29, 1572, for examination and correction. Toledo thereupon ordered the "principal and most able descendants" of the Incas to be brought together to listen to a reading of the history. Each Indian swore by the Cross to tell the truth and to indicate, by means of an interpreter, whatever corrections he considered necessary. Day after day the history was read, chapter by chapter. Now and then some name was corrected, or other minor change made, as when Doña María Cusi Guarcai objected to the prominent place accorded to certain Inca not of her own family, but all the listeners declared that they found the history good and true and according to the tales handed down by their fathers. The four living conquistadores who had entered Peru with Pizarro almost half a century before also testified that the history coincided with what they had been told by other Indians.

The corrected version was then legally certified and despatched to the king, with a covering letter from the Viceroy, a genealogical tree, and four painted cloths illustrating certain events of Inca history. These paintings had also been examined by various competent Indians and pronounced good. The Viceroy suggested in his letter to the king that such an accurate history, which would serve as the best possible justification of Spain's title to America, should be published, "in order to refute the other false and lying books that have circulated in these parts, and to explain the truth, not only to our own people but to foreign nations as well."

The *Historia Indica* of Sarmiento described in detail the history of the Incas, their cruelty, their revolting customs, and their tyranny, in a tone and in a spirit reminiscent of that in which Las Casas had denounced the conquistadores in his *Very Brief Account of the Destruction of the Indies.* Sarmiento concluded that because of the sins of the Incas against the law of nature they should be forced to obey this law, "as had been taught by the Archbishop of Florence and confirmed by Friar Francisco de Vitoria in the discussion he made concerning the title of the Indies. Therefore, Your Majesty, by this title alone holds just as sufficient and legitimate title to the Indies as any prince in the world holds to any realm whatsoever, because in all the lands thus far discovered in the two seas to the North and to the South there has been found this general violation of the law of nature." But the king never published the history so laboriously compiled by Pedro Sarmiento de Gamboa. It was allowed to remain in obscurity and not permitted to be spread abroad through Europe in opposition to the writings of Bishop Bartolomé de las Casas; indeed, it has never been published in Spain and only saw the light of day in 1906, because of the interest of a German scholar.

Nor was Toledo able to convince all the Spaniards in Peru. The Jesuit José de Acosta, perhaps the outstanding ecclesiastic of the time, without mentioning Sarmiento by name, rejected the theory that Indians could be deprived of dominion if they persisted in error. Acosta affirmed: "We must reject those false titles of dominion which some persons are trying to propagate, unnecessary defenders of the royal authority in my opinion, not to say deceivers, who would prove their assertions by the tyranny of the Incas . . . which we do not understand and do not admit. For it is not lawful to rob a thief, nor does the crime committed by some one else add to our own justice."

Another prominent figure of the time, Juan de Matienzo, jurist and adviser of Toledo, was just as certain that the Viceroy was absolutely right. In the *Gobierno del Perú,* not published until three hundred years after it was written, Matienzo followed the same view set forth in Sarmiento's history. He first described the cruelty and tyranny of the Incas, how they killed five thousand persons at one time in one place and jerked out their hearts, how they sacrificed boys to their idols, how they burned alive the women and children of their chief men, and how the Incas governed in their own interest, and not for the welfare of their people. Then Matienzo made a rousing justification of Spanish rule, declaring:

> The Indies were justly won. By the concession of the pope, or because those kingdoms were found deserted by the Spaniards. Or because of their abominable sins against nature. Or because of their infidelity. Although this last reason alone would be sufficient, as would each of the others, the tyranny of the Indians is enough to establish the fact that the kingdom of Peru was justly gained and that His Majesty has a very just title to it. . . . Moreover, the Indians have learned to trade and thereby win profits, and to use mechanical and agricultural instruments, which is no less a just title than the others.

Curiously enough, just as certain historians today accuse the Spaniards of hypocritically seeking to justify their rule, so Polo de Ondegardo, another important adviser to Toledo, stated that the Incas, one they had determined upon a particular conquest. "looked for some title and pretext to accomplish what they wanted to do, which is only natural." . . .

Today there still exist two well-defined attitudes toward the history compiled by Sarmiento de Gamboa at the behest of Viceroy Toledo, similar to the divergence of opinion on the *Informaciones*. Markham attempted to discredit Sarmiento's work, and Means considers it "an abominably unjust and inaccurate account of a great but fallen dynasty" and the author a pliant tool who was willing to aid in the Viceroy's "nefarious literary attack." Levillier, on the other hand, stoutly defends the essential truthfulness of Sarmiento's history, lashes out at Markham for what appear to be his plain mendacity, and supports Viceroy Toledo at every point. Today, just as almost four hundred years ago, the differences of opinion on the justice of Spanish rule in Peru are deep, bitter, and apparently irreconcilable.

A MODERN INTERPRETATION

5. "The Incas Combined the Most Absolute Kind of Despotism with the Greatest Tolerance Toward the Social and Political Order of Its Subject Peoples"

ALFRED MÉTRAUX

The late Dr. Métraux was one of the most active anthropologists during the last quarter century in the study of South American Indians. He conducted field research as well as library investigations, which help to explain his balanced judgment on such a controversial issue as the true nature of Inca rule.

The true character of the Inca Empire is poorly set forth in works dealing with its economic and social structure. Too many historians or sociologists have attempted, in their enthusiasm, to make of it a state corresponding to a modern formula: a socialist, a totalitarian or a welfare state. From the sixteenth century on, how many arbitrary pictures have been drawn, propped up by quotations! In fact among the chronicles and reports and documents which Spain, that rummager of old papers, has handed down to us, and in the accounts of the Indians themselves, one finds enough mixed-up assertions and facts to bolster or justify the most diverse interpretations. Reality has frequently been confused with a schematic, abstract order which was the fruit of frequently gratuitous speculations.

Undoubtedly, the Indians who described their system of government to the Spaniards gave them a somewhat idealized image, exaggerating the geometrical order and the rigorous discipline which it implied. The perfection attributed to this administrative machine, in its functioning as much as in its intentions, cannot but fail to arouse suspicion in our minds. The Inca Empire, as it is usually evoked, escapes history. It is a Utopian republic and not a kingdom of this world which collapsed in a few months under the aggression of a band of adventurers. The terms

From "The Inca Empire: Despotism or Socialism?" by Alfred Métraux from *Diogenes* (A Journal of the International Council for Philosophy and Humanistic Studies, Paris; published by Mario Casalini, Montreal) 35 (Fall 1961): 78–98, passim. Reprinted by permission.

used to define its institutions constantly creating false associations, only add to the disease. Even contemporary authors often speak of the Empire of the Sun as did their colleagues of the sixteenth and seventeenth centuries who attributed the customs of its inhabitants to legislators as beneficent as they were wise and ingenious.

Professor Baudin, in a celebrated work, *The Socialist Empire of the Incas,* while admitting the traditional character of the rural communities, considers all the other institutions as a form of organization bearing the true trademark of socialism, for, as he explains, "it is an attempt at the rationalization of society." For this eminent economist, this organization would seem to respond to a preconceived plan tending "to realize a veritable absorption of the individual into the State, the well-being of the first being assured only in order to redound to the grandeur of the second. . . . " One of the aims of this article is to confront this concept of the Inca Empire with new interpretation of the facts. . . .

The myth of the great socialist State of the Incas is based upon a rather summary notion of its institutions. The property system, especially, as well as the duties of the subjects toward the emperor, have been interpreted according to a terminology and spirit only vaguely corresponding to a civilization which was still archaic despite its complexity and subtlety.

Based on Garcilaso, a picture has been drawn of an Inca economic and social system, thus briefly summed up: the monarchs of ancient Peru, seeking to establish a reign of justice and prosperity among their people, once a province was conquered, "divided it into three parts, the first for the Sun, the second for the king and the third for the natives of the country."

The fields of the Sun were cultivated for the needs of the cult and their products served to support a numerous clergy. The domain of the Inca, exploited for the government's profit, were drawn upon as from a safety vault, when disaster struck some province. Finally, the third group of arable lands were annually divided into equal lots, then redivided among the families of each community according to their members. Each individual's private property was reduced to possession of a hut, an enclosure, some domestic animals, and household goods such as clothes and utensils. All the rest belonged to the State. The inhabitants of the Empire worked for the emperor, who, in exchange, left the free disposition of the communal lands to them and equitably redistributed a part of the fruits of their labor. If the economic structure of the Inca Empire was carried on in this manner, one would more accurately entitle it State Socialism grafted upon agrarian collectivism. Did the reality correspond to the ideal image here evoked?

As a matter of fact, the Incas combined the most absolute kind of despotism with the greatest tolerance toward the social and political order of its subject peoples. The emperor's will was primary, but this will reached the common man via the intermediary of local chiefs whose authority and privileges were maintained and reinforced.

The centralizing tendencies of power harmonized with the practice of indirect government, a good and bad harmony—if such an anachronism may be permitted us.

The most original aspects of Inca civilization—the tripartite division of the land, the convents of the Virgins of the Sun, the State granaries, the system of statistics transcribed by means of knotted cords, the network of roads—reflect, in great detail, the conception of the subject's obligations toward his sovereign, and a most ingenious exploitation of resources—both in manpower and products—which a brutally imperialist political system had set up for itself in less than a century. . . .

The forced labor system which the Incas imposed within their Empire derives directly from the work-payments out of which they formerly profited when they were only chiefs of rural communities. The peasants for whom they had been, in bygone times, the *koraka* ("elders") followed them to war, cultivated their fields, and, in turn, took it upon themselves to serve them. Having become masters of a great empire the Incas organized it in such a way as to derive the same advantages from it, but on an incomparably vaster scale. . . .

The evidence of our sources is unanimous: the Incas avoided crushing their subjects under the weight of too-heavy tributes, and, as a rule, distributed personal services equitably. Despite its implacable discipline their government appears to us paternalistic by comparison with the truly ferocious régime which the Spaniards introduced into Peru. Perhaps we are baptising with the name of wisdom and political sense that which was only respect for norms of behavior and archaic traditions to which the Incas adapted themselves like the smallest community chief. Was not the structure of the imperial *ayllu* identical with that of other Andean *ayllu*, and did not their conceptions of the chief, as well as that of community rights, fit into the general ethic held by peoples of the same stock? What was at the beginning a simple confederation of agrarian communities in a Sierra valley was transformed into a hegemony over immense territories without fundamentally altering the primordial relationships between the ruling and ruled groups. In the mountainous region the relatively fertile earth derived its main value from the manpower available for its exploitation. Masters of an empire, the Incas imposed the obligations of work with much severity and made it a moral duty. Undoubtedly, the only condemnable idleness was that which harmed the state and which constituted for this reason an undisciplined act, almost a rebellion.

To read the numerous works treating of the Incas one would gather the impression that at the time of the Spanish conquest, their civilization had reached a dead point and that their empire had become inert in its rigidity and perfection. If one objectively examines the sources, devoting oneself to the exegesis of Spanish documentation without neglecting the teaching of modern ethnography, one would perceive that the Empire's institutions were in full evolution, and that in this apparently so harmonious system, the Incas had introduced innovations which would sooner or later have modified the structure of the State.

These as yet scarcely indicated tendencies, however, are sufficient to permit us to imagine an epoch in which, after repeated gifts, the nobles and high officials would have ended by carving out vast lordships for themselves. The Inca then would have been able to satisfy the ambition of his aides only by dispossessing a growing number of communities whose members would have changed status from freedom to servitude. Among these people uprooted from their *ayllu* were the specialized artisans, servants or tenants, Virgins of the Sun and the *mitima,* farmers transferred to conquered territories. They formed a new category of men whose status was not determined by blood ties, weakening, in proportion, the traditional communities.

Civic officials to whom land had been granted would have also been able to form a new class whose mentality and mode of life would no longer conform to the idea of old Andean society. If the Empire's evolution had not been brutally interrupted by the Spanish conquest, would it have transformed itself into a kingdom with a structure similar in many ways with that of the late Roman Empire or the decadent Carolingians? With the multiplication of large domains, would not the ruling class have constituted a powerful aristocracy and would it not have been opposed to the central power? The number of *yana,* domestic servants of the great and tenant farmers on their properties, would certainly have augmented at the expense of free peasants. These, of course, are only conjectures based on limited clues but these do reveal the possibilities of transformation which would have operated in a directly opposed sense to the idea of a "Socialist State of the Sun."

Let us consider the political and economic system described here in terms of the famous definition of Socialism by Bertrand Russell. For him, socialism essentially means common ownership of land and capital under a democratic form of government. It implies production for use and not for profit and distributed, if not equally to all, at any rate according to inequalities justified only in the public interest.

The Inca Empire hardly corresponds to these qualifications. Subjected to the despotism of a caste, its aristocratic tendencies were emphasized as a result of the consecration which the authority of the petty kings and local chiefs had received from the conquerors. Besides, in addition to the traditional privileges enjoyed by the *koraka,* were added those deriving from their status as Inca officials. An increasing distance separated them from their former subjects. Agrarian collectivism existed only on the level of the rural communities (*ayllu*) and represented an ancient system whose equivalent may be found in the Old as well as the New World. Therefore, it is certainly a peculiar anachronism to apply a term applicable only to industrial societies to the collective property of archaic societies.

Production was only partially influenced according to the needs of the subjects, the entire surplus reverting to a ruling caste and to its administration. Certainly a part of the excess was redistributed under the form of provisions and material allocated to work crews and soldiers or as presents made to noblemen, clergy, and officials. Assistance to the aged and to the sick which one would be tempted to compare with our social security was an obligation of the village and not of the State. This responsibility simply expressed the old group solidarity still present today among primitive farmers of the Amazon and the peasants of modern Peru.

Socialism, as its theoreticians have emphasized, is not limited to State ownership but implies that the latter be put to the service of the collectivity. In the Inca Empire the tribute paid in personal services and wrought objects profited a caste whose riches and power were growing.

The classical tradition, extolled by the Spanish chroniclers, was imposed on modern historians and sociologists, who, vying with each other, compared the Inca Empire to ancient Rome, to modern States, and to utopian Republics, but hardly ever dreamed of comparing it with States which existed or still exist among people characterized, for good or evil, as "primitive.". . .

The conquistadores accustomed to fight "naked and savage" Indians were dazzled by the manifestations of high civilization among peoples whom they were naturally inclined to treat as irrational barbarians. Nothing astonished them so much as the discipline ruling the Empire. Later, the old order seemed even more just and humane to the degree that the rule introduced by the Spaniards was marked by wretchedness and cruelty. By contrast with the horrors of the conquest and colonization, the Inca despotism was molded in memory into an age of gold. And so it, was, to the degree that the Cuzco emperors, respecting millennary customs, managed their subjects, and under the *pax Incaica,* guaranteed their well-being and happiness.

The arrival of the Spanish in Tenochtitlán. This Aztec illustration of the meeting between Cortés and Montezuma shows clearly the role of La Malinche as interpreter. The drawing was adapted by Alberto Beltran from a painting contained in a manuscript known as the Florentine Codex, an important source for information about the native view of the Spanish Conquest. In the late 1540s the Spanish missionary and ethnographer, Bernardino de Sahagún, began amassing data for a book on Aztec culture, devoting the following three decades of his life to the project. The information was gathered orally by interviewing the elders of the Indian towns or through paintings such as the one above. A team of associates put the collected data into Nahuatl and Latin. Sahagún then revised the information and translated it into Spanish. The result was his Historia general de las cosas de Nueva España *(General History of the Things of New Spain), profusely illustrated and better known as the Florentine Codex. Although completed in 1577, the work was largely unknown until the eighteenth century and was first printed in 1829–30. The illustration is one of many which Miguel León Portilla included in* The Broken Spears: The Aztec Account of the Conquest of Mexico *(Reading 3) and is reprinted by permission of Beacon Press.*

SECTION III

Patterns of Conquest

THE ERA OF THE CONQUISTADOR

Between 1492 and 1550 small groups of Spaniards, initially numbering a few hundred men, conquered the Aztec and Inca empires, which had populations in the millions, large armies, and militarist traditions of their own. The speed of this achievement, the courage and resourcefulness of Cortés and Pizarro, and the drama of their confrontations with Montezuma and Atahualpa were recorded by some of the participants. One of the best-known of these firsthand accounts was written by Bernal Díaz del Castillo, who was a foot soldier in the little band of warriors with which Cortés toppled the Aztec empire in Mexico. In the excerpt reprinted here, Díaz describes in awestruck tones their first battle with the Indians and their first view of the great city of Tenochtilán and of Montezuma and his court (Reading 2). Since the sixteenth century, Spanish historians have used this and similar accounts to recount what they regard as the one of the most glorious achievements of their nation. For the Anglo-Dutch enemies of Spain, however, it was the barbarity of the conquest that captured their attention. They quickly seized upon the polemical description of the wholesale slaughter of the peoples of the Caribbean and Meso-america written by the Dominican friar, Bartolomé de las Casas (Reading 1), to bolster their propaganda war against Spain that has come to be known as "The Black Legend."

CHANGING VIEWS OF THE CONQUEST

During the nineteenth and early twentieth centuries a great deal of effort was devoted to examining narrative accounts of the conquest and writing biographical studies of individual conquistadors. The first North American historian of Latin America, William Hinkling Prescott, made this era the subject of his classic works, *History of the Conquest of Mexico* (New York, 1843) and *History of the Conquest of Peru* (New York, 1847). Prescott's narratives are of epic proportions, and though written over a hundred years ago remain accurate and valuable.[1]

More recently scholars have focused on the social background of the conquistadors as a collective group,[2] and they have explored the role of women (Reading 6).[3] In addition, the growth of ethnohistorical research has made available native sources that have transformed our knowledge of American societies before and after the conquest and provided new perspectives on Indian responses to the European invasion. The Mexican anthropologist, Miguel León Portilla, has skillfully pieced together the fragments of Indian documentation recording their reaction to the Spaniards and the conquest, which is a moving statement with true poetic power (Reading 3). In a similar vein Nathan Wachtel has captured the reactions of the Incas in *The Vision of the Vanquished* (Sussex, 1977). In his careful study of pre-conquest Aztec society, Professor Ross Hassig has shown that the Spanish could not have won such a swift victory without the assistance of tens and even hundreds of thousands of Indian allies (Reading 4).

NOT ALL NATIVE SOCIETIES WERE DEFEATED

Other historians have pointed out that not all native American societies were defeated so quickly. If victory over the Aztecs was won in three years, the final surrender of the last Inca chief did not come until 1572, and only after the Spanish had fought a full-scale civil war that did not end until the arrival of the Spanish Viceroy Francisco de Toledo. In their survey of colonial Latin American history, Mark A. Burkholder and Lyman Johnson note that "throughout the Americas, indigenous peoples with decentralized political structures and little agriculture or urbanization resisted Spanish domination more effectively than did the rigid and disciplined Aztec and Incan states. Much of this success came from employing guerrilla tactics that dispersed Spanish resources and neutralized the advantages of superior arma-

---

1. Hugh Thomas, the author of the most recent study of the Mexican conquest, *Conquest: Montezuma, Cortés, and the Fall of Old Mexico* (New York: Touchstone, 1995), incorporates much new material that has come to light since Prescott's day but he pays tribute to Prescott's book describing it as "an astonishing achievement for any historian, even more so for one who was almost blind." (p. xiv)

2. A pioneering work in this vein is James Lockhart, *The Men of Cajamarca* (Austin: University of Texas Press, 1972). In *The Conquerors of the New Kingdom of Granada* (Albuquerque: University of New Mexico Press, 1995) José Ignacio Avellaneda has conducted a similar investigation of the six expeditions that conquered the indigenous people of Colombia between 1537 and 1543.

3. See, for example, Peter Boyd-Bowman, "Patterns of Spanish Emigration to the Indies until 1600," *Hispanic American Historical Review* 56:4 (Nov. 1976): 580–604, and Luis Martín, *Daughters of the Conquistadores: Women of the Viceroyalty of Peru* (Dallas: Southern Methodist University Press, 1989).

ments."[4] In the Yucatán Peninsula the Maya drove back the first Spanish army led by Francisco de Montejo in 1535 after eight years of fierce fighting, and it was only after the Spanish regrouped and returned in 1540 under the leadership of Montejo's son that they were defeated in 1545 (Reading 5). One of the most successful groups of all were the Araucanians on the southern frontier of Chile who found numerous ways to adopt and adapt to Spanish military techniques, and thereby maintained their independence until the end of the colonial era (Reading 7).

THE TRAUMA OF CONQUEST REMAINS

Even if some natives willingly joined the conquistadors and others survived by the good fortune of having time to convert to a new style of warfare, the conquest era was a traumatic period for both sides. As historian E. Bradford Burns has observed, "Two quite diverse peoples met. One conquered and imposed, forcing the Americas to conform to European trade demands. The other was conquered, yet resisted. Those realities shaped the attitudes and institutions of the hemisphere."[5] That this cultural tension remains plainly visible after five centuries is demonstrated by the fact that the hero of twentieth century Mexican nationalism is not Hernán Cortés but the last Aztec emperor, Cuauhtemoc, whose valor is celebrated in everything from post-Revolutionary murals to a statue gracing a traffic circle on Mexico City's Paseo de la Reforma.[6]

4. Mark A. Burkholder and Lyman L. Johnson, *Colonial Latin America*, 3rd ed. (New York: Oxford University Press, 1998), p. 61.

5. E. Bradford Burns, *Latin America: Conflict and Creation: A Historical Reader* (Englewood Cliffs: Prentice-Hall, 1993), p. 1.

6. Robert Haskett, "Cuahtemoc," in *Encyclopedia of Latin American History*, ed. Barbara Tenebaum, 5 vols. (New York: Charles Scribner's Sons, 1996), 2: 305.

HISPANIOLA

1. "They Slaughtered Anyone and Everyone in Their Path"

BARTOLOMÉ DE LAS CASAS

The Dominican friar Bartolomé de Las Casas (1474–1566) devoted the better part of his long life to defending the rights of the indigenous peoples of the New World. In 1552 in an attempt to persuade the Crown to abolish the encomienda, Las Casas wrote *A Short Account of the Destruction of the Indies* in which he declared that the Spanish had slaughtered millions of Indians in the conquest of the Caribbean, Mesoamerica, and Peru. Spanish apologists accused the Dominican of gross exaggeration, but Spain's enemies found his vivid documentation of genocide totally convincing. Translated into six languages and illustrated with vivid engravings by the Flemish publisher Theodor de Bry, the book enjoyed wide distribution in Western Europe and became the cornerstone of the Black Legend.

As we have said, the island of Hispaniola was the first to witness the arrival of Europeans and the first to suffer the wholesale slaughter of its people and the devastation and depopulation of the land. It all began with the Europeans taking native women and children both as servants and to satisfy their own base appetites; then, not content with what the local people offered them of their own free will (and all offered as much as they could spare), they started taking for themselves the food the natives contrived to produce by the sweat of their brows, which was in all honesty little enough. Since what a European will consume in a single day normally supports three native households of ten persons each for a whole month, and since the newcomers began to subject the locals to other vexations, assaults, and iniquities, the people began to realize that these men could not, in truth, have descended from the heavens. Some of them started to conceal what food they had, others decided to send their women and children into hiding, and yet others took to the hills to get away

From *A Short Account of the Destruction of the Indies* by Bartolomé de las Casas. Ed. and trans. Nigel Griffin (New York: Penguin Books, 1992), pp. 14–17. Translation copyright © Nigel Grifin, 1992. Reprinted by permission of Penguin Books Ltd.

from the brutal and ruthless cruelty that was being inflicted on them. The Christians punched them, boxed their ears and flogged them in order to track down the local leaders, and the whole shameful process came to a head when one of the European commanders raped the wife of the paramount chief of the entire island. It was then that the locals began to think up ways of driving the Europeans out of their lands and to take up arms against them. Their weapons, however, were flimsy and ineffective both in attack and in defence (and, indeed, war in the Americas is no more deadly than our jousting, or than many European children's games) and, with their horses and swords and lances, the Spaniards easily fended them off, killing them and committing all kind of atrocities against them.

They forced their way into native settlements, slaughtering everyone they found there, including small children, old men, pregnant women, and even women who had just given birth. They hacked them to pieces, slicing open their bellies with their swords as though they were so many sheep herded into a pen. They even laid wagers on whether they could manage to slice a man in two at a stroke, or cut an individual's head from his body, or disembowel him with a single blow of their axes. They grabbed suckling infants by the feet and, ripping them from their mothers' breasts, dashed them headlong against the rocks. Others, laughing and joking all the while, threw them over their shoulders into a river, shouting: 'Wriggle, you little perisher.' They slaughtered anyone and everyone in their path, on occasion running through a mother and her baby with a single thrust of their swords. They spared no one, erecting especially wide gibbets on which they could string their victims up with their feet just off the ground and then burn them alive thirteen at a time, in honour of our Saviour and the twelve Apostles, or tie dry straw to their bodies and set fire to it. Some they chose to keep alive and simply cut their wrists, leaving their hands dangling, saying to them: 'Take this letter'—meaning that their sorry condition would act as a warning to those hiding in the hills. The way they normally dealt with the native leaders and nobles was to tie them to a kind of griddle consisting of sticks resting on pitchforks driven into the ground and then grill them over a slow fire, with the result that they howled in agony and despair as they died a lingering death.

It once happened that I myself witnessed their grilling of four or five local leaders in this fashion (and I believe they had set up two or three other pairs of grills alongside so that they might process other victims at the same time) when the poor creatures' howls came between the Spanish commander and his sleep.

He gave orders that the prisoners were to be throttled, but the man in charge of the execution detail, who was more bloodthirsty than the average common hangman (I know his identity and even met some relatives of his in Seville), was loath to cut short his private entertainment by throttling them and so he personally went round ramming wooden bungs into their mouths to stop them making such a racket and deliberately stoked the fire so that they would take just as long to die as he himself chose. I saw all these things for myself and many others besides. And, since all those who could do so took to the hills and mountains in order to escape the clutches of these merciless and inhuman butchers, these mortal enemies of human kind trained hunting dogs to track them down—wild dogs who would savage a native to death as soon as look at him, tearing him to shreds and devouring his flesh as though he were a pig. These dogs wrought havoc among the natives and were responsible for much carnage. And when, as happened on the odd occasion, the locals did kill a European, as, given the enormity of the crimes committed against them, they were in all justice fully entitled to, the Spanish came to an unofficial agreement among themselves that for every European killed one hundred natives would be executed.

They spared no one, erecting especially wide gibbets on which they could string their victims up with their feet just off the ground and then burn them alive. (Illustrated by Theodor de Bry)

MESOAMERICA

2. The True History of the Conquest of Mexico

BERNAL DÍAZ DEL CASTILLO

One of the classics of the conquest is *The True History of the Conquest of New Spain*, written down long after the events by Bernal Díaz del Castillo, one of the small number of conquistadors who fought under Hernando Cortés in the conquest of Mexico. His honest and forthright account gives us a lifelike picture of how it all really happened. A more official account may be found in the letters Cortés sent back to Spain to impress the king and court of his great deeds in the New World.* The foot soldier's story is in a more familiar tone; Bernal Díaz was blunt, too, for he was responsible for that pithy explanation of why Spaniards went to America: "We came to serve God, and also to get rich."

Bernal Díaz throughout his detailed *True History* displayed a respect and admiration for many aspects of Indian culture, but like practically all Spaniards the human sacrifices practiced by the Indians revolted him from the first time he heard of them:

> Thirty of us soldiers, well armed, went in two boats to the Island [of San Juan de Ulúa] and we found there a temple where there was a very large and ugly idol which was called Tescatepuca and in charge of it were four Indians with very large black cloaks and hoods, such as the Dominicans or canons wear . . .
>
> They had this day sacrificed two boys and cut open their chests, and offered the blood and hearts to that cursed idol. The priests came towards us to fumigate us with the incense with which they had fumigated their Tescatepuca, for when we approached them they were burning something which had the scent of incense, but we would not allow them to fumigate us for we felt much pity at seeing those two boys who had just been killed and at beholding such great cruelty.†

The Indian prisons also brought stern condemnation by Bernal Díaz:

> In Tlaxcala we found wooden houses furnished with gratings, full of Indian men and women imprisoned in them, being fed up until they were fat enough to be

---

Hernando Cortés: Five Letters, 1519–1526 (New York: Norton, 1962). The most recent and best edition is *Hernán Cortés: Letters from Mexico*, trans. and ed. A. R. Pagden (New York: Grossman, 1971).

†*The True History of the Conquest of New Spain, by Bernal Díaz del Castillo*, trans. and ed. Alfred Percival Maudslay (London: The Hakluyt Society, 1908), vol. 1, pp. 55–56.

sacrificed and eaten. These prisons we broke open and destroyed, and set free the prisoners who were in them, and these poor Indians did not dare to go in any direction only to stay there with us and thus escaped with their lives. From now on in all the towns that we entered the first thing our Captain ordered us to do was to break open these prisons and set free the prisoners.‡

The True History deserves to be read in its entirely, and good paperback editions are available.** Here are a few selections in which Bernal Díaz records his early impressions of Mexico and the Mexican Indians.

1. HOW ALL THE CACIQUES OF TABASCO AND ITS DEPENDENCIES ATTACKED US, AND WHAT CAME OF IT

I have already said how we were marching along when we met all the forces of the enemy which were moving in search of us, and all of the men wore great feather crests and they carried drums and trumpets, and their faces were coloured black and white, and they were armed with large bows, and arrows, lances and shields and swords shaped like our two-handed swords, and many slings and stones and fire-hardened javelins, and all wore quilted cotton armour. As they approached us their squadrons were so numerous that they covered the whole plain, and they rushed on us like mad dogs completely surrounding us, and they let fly such a cloud of arrows, javelins and stones that on the first assault they wounded over seventy of us, and fighting hand to hand they did us great damage with their lances, and one soldier fell dead at once from an arrow wound in the ear, and they kept on shooting and wounding us. With our muskets and crossbows and with good sword play we did not fail as stout fighters, and when they came to feel the edge of our swords little by little they fell back, but it was only so as to shoot at us in greater safety. Mesa, our artilleryman, killed many of them with his cannon, for they were formed in great squadrons and they did not open out so that he could fire at them as he pleased, but with all the hurt and wounds which we gave them, we could not drive them off. I said to Diego de Ordás, "It seems to me that we ought to close up and charge them," for in truth they suffered greatly from the strokes and thrusts of our swords, and that was why they fell away from us, both from fear of these swords, and the better to shoot their arrows and hurl their javelins and the hail of stones. Ordás replied that it

‡ Ibid., pp. 288–89.
**Bernal Díaz, *The Conquest of New Spain*, trans. J. M. Cohen (Baltimore: Penguin Books, 1967), and *The Discovery and Conquest of Mexico by Bernal Díaz del Castillo*, trans. with notes by A. P. Maudslay, intro. by Irving A. Leonard (New York: Grove Press, 1958).

From *The True History of the Conquest of New Spain,* by Bernal Díaz del Castillo, trans. with notes by Alfred Percival Maudslay (London: The Hakluyt Society, 1908–1910), vol. 1, pp. 118–21; vol. 2, pp. 34–63, passim.

was not good advice, for there were three hundred Indians to every one of us, and that we could not hold out against such a multitude,—so there we stood enduring their attack. However, we did agree to get as near as we could to them, as I had advised Ordás, so as to give them a bad time with our swordsmanship, and they suffered so much from it that they retreated towards a swamp.

During all this time Cortés and his horsemen failed to appear, although we greatly longed for him, and we feared that by chance some disaster had befallen him.

I remember that when we fired shots the Indians gave great shouts and whistles and threw dust and rubbish into the air so that we should not see the damage done to them, and they sounded their trumpets and drums and shouted and whistled and cried "Alala! Alala!"

Just at this time we caught sight of our horsemen, and as the great Indian host was crazed with its attack on us, it did not at once perceive them coming up behind their backs, and as the plain was level ground and the horsemen were good riders, and many of the horses were very handy and fine gallopers, they came quickly on the enemy and speared them as they chose. As soon as we saw the horsemen we fell on the Indians with such energy that with us attacking on one side and the horsemen on the other, they soon turned tail. The Indians thought that the horse and its rider was all one animal, for they had never seen horses up to this time.

The savannas and fields were crowded the Indians running to take refuge in the thick woods near by.

After we had defeated the enemy Cortés told us that he had not been able to come to us sooner as there was a swamp in the way, and he had to fight his way through another force of warriors before he could reach us, and three horsemen and five horses had been wounded.

As soon as the horsemen had dismounted under some trees and houses, we returned thanks to God for giving us so complete a victory.

As it was Lady day we gave to the town which was afterwards founded here the name of Santa Maria de la Victoria, on account of this great victory being won on Our Lady's day This was the first battle that we fought under Cortés in the New Spain.

After this we bound up the hurts of the wounded with cloths, for we had nothing else, and we doctored the horses by searing their wounds with the fat from the body of a dead Indian which we cut up to get out the fat, and we went to look at the dead lying on the plain and there were more than eight hundred of them, the greater number killed by thrusts, the others by cannon, muskets and crossbows, and many were stretched on the ground half dead. Where the horsemen had passed, numbers of them lay dead or groaning from their wounds. The battle lasted over an hour, and the Indians fought all the time like brave warriors, until the horsemen came up.

We took five prisoners, two of them Captains. As it was late and we had had enough of fighting, and we had not eaten anything, we returned to our camp. Then we buried the two soldiers who had been killed, one by a wound in the ear, and the other by a wound in the throat, and we smeared the wounds of the others and of the horses with the fat of the Indian, and after posting sentinels and guards, we had supper and rested.

2. [THE GREAT CITY OF MEXICO]

As soon as the messengers had been despatched, we set out for Mexico, and as the people of Huexotzingo and Chalco had told us that Montezuma had held consultations with his idols and priests whether he should allow us to enter Mexico, or whether he should attack us, and all the priests had answered that his Huichilobos had said he was to allow us to enter and that then he could kill us, as I have already related in the chapter that deals with the subject, and as we are but human and feared death, we never ceased thinking about it. As that country is very thickly peopled we made short marches, and commended ourselves to God and to Our Lady his blessed Mother, and talked about how and by what means we could enter [the City], and it put courage into our hearts to think that as our Lord Jesus Christ had vouchsafed us protection through past dangers, he would likewise guard us from the power of the Mexicans.

We went to sleep in a town called Iztapalatengo where half the houses are in the water and the other half on dry land. where there is a small mountain (and now there is an Inn there) and there they gave us a good supper. . . .

The next day, in the morning, we arrived at a broad Causeway, and continued our march towards Iztapalapa, and when we saw so many cities and villages built in the water and other great towns on dry land and that straight and level causeway going towards Mexico, we were amazed and said that it was like the enchantments they tell of in the legend of Amadis, on account of the great towers and cues and buildings rising from the water, and all built of masonry. And some of our soldiers even asked whether the things that we saw were not a dream? It is not to be wondered at that I here write it down in this manner, for there is so much to think over that I do not know how to describe it, seeing things as we did that had never been heard of or seen before, not even dreamed about.

Thus, we arrived near Iztapalapa, to behold the splendour of the other Caciques who came out to meet us, who were the Lord of the town named Cuitlahuac, and the Lord of Culuacan, both of them near relations of Montezuma. And then when we entered that city of Iztapalapa, the appearance of the palaces in which they lodged us! How spacious and well built they were of beautiful stone work and cedar wood, and the wood of other sweet scented trees, with great rooms and courts, wonderful to behold, covered with awnings of cotton cloth.

When we had looked well at all of this, we went to the orchard and garden, which was such a wonderful thing to see and walk in, that I was never tired of looking at the diversity of the trees, and noting the scent which each one had and the paths full of roses and flowers, and the many fruit trees and native roses, and the pond of fresh water. There was another thing to observe, that great canoes were able to pass into the garden from the lake through an opening that had been made so that there was no need for their occupants to land. And all was cemented and very splendid with many kinds of stone [monuments] with pictures on them, which gave much to think about. Then the birds of many kinds and breeds which came into the pond. I say again that I stood looking at it and thought that never in the world would there be discovered other lands such as these, for at that time there was no Peru, nor any thought of it. [Of all these wonders that I then beheld] to-day all is overthrown and lost, nothing left standing. . . .

Early next day we left Iztapalapa with a large escort of those great Caciques whom I have already mentioned. We proceeded along the Causeway which is here eight paces in width and runs so straight to the City of Mexico that it does not seem to me to turn either much or little, but, broad as it is, it was so crowded with people that there was hardly room for them all, some of them going to and others returning from Mexico, besides those who had come out to see us, so that we were hardly able to pass by the crowds of them that came; and the towers and cues were full of people as well as the canoes from all parts of the lake. It was not to be wondered at, for they had never before seen horses or men such as we are.

Gazing on such wonderful sights, we did not know what to say, or whether what appeared before us was real, for on one side, on the land, there were great cities, and in the lake ever so many more, and the lake itself was crowded with canoes, and in the Causeway were many bridges at intervals, and in front of us stood the great City of Mexico, and we,—we did not even number four hundred soldiers! and we well remembered the words and warnings given us by the people of Huexotzingo and Tlaxcala and Tiamanalco, and the many other warnings that had been given that we should beware of entering Mexico, where they would kill us, as soon as they had us inside.

Let the curious readers consider whether there is not much to ponder over in this that I am writing. What men have there been in the world who have shown such daring? But let us get on, and march along the Causeway. When we arrived where another small causeway branches off (leading to Coyoacan, which is another city) where there were some buildings like towers, which are their oratories, many more chieftains and Caciques approached clad in very rich mantles, the brilliant liveries of one chieftain differing from those of another, and the causeways were crowded with them. The Great Montezuma had sent these great Caciques in advance to receive us, and when they came before Cortés they bade us welcome in their language, and as a sign of peace, they touched their hands against the ground, and kissed the ground with the hand. . . .

3. [MONTEZUMA AND HIS SPLENDID COURT]

The Great Montezuma was about forty years old, of good height and well proportioned, slender, and spare of flesh, not very swarthy, but of the natural colour and shade of an Indian. He did not wear his hair long, but so as just to cover his ears, his scanty black beard was well shaped and thin. His face was somewhat long, but cheerful, and he had good eyes and showed in his appearance and manner both tenderness and, when necessary, gravity. He was very neat and clean and bathed once every day in the afternoon. He had many women as mistresses, daughters of Chieftains, and he had two great Cacicas as his legitimate wives, and when he had intercourse with them it was so secretly that no one knew anything about it, except some of his servants. He was free from unnatural offences. The clothes that he wore one day, he did not put on again until four days later. He had over two hundred chieftains in his guard, in other rooms close to his own, not that all were meant to converse with him, but only one or another, and when they went to speak to him they were obliged to take off their rich mantles and put on others of little worth, but they had to be clean, and they had to enter barefoot and their eyes lowered to the ground, and not to look up in his face. And they made him three obeisances, and said ; "Lord, my Lord, my Great Lord," before them came up to him, and then they made their report and with a few words he dismissed them, and on taking leave they did not turn their backs, but kept their faces toward him with their eyes to the ground, and they did not turn their backs until they left the room. I noticed another thing, that when other great chiefs came from distant lands about disputes or business, when they reached the apartments of the Great Montezuma, they had to come barefoot and with poor mantles, and they might not enter directly into the palace, but had to loiter about a little on one side of the Palace door, for to enter hurriedly was considered to be disrespectful.

For each meal over thirty different dishes were prepared by his cooks according to their ways and usage, and they placed small pottery brasiers beneath the dishes so that they should not get cold. They prepared more than three hundred plates of the food that Montezuma was going to eat, and more than a thousand for the guard. When he was going to eat, Montezuma would sometimes go out with his chiefs and stewards, and they would point out to him which dish was best, and of what birds and other things it was composed, and as they advised him, so he would eat, but it was not often that he would go out to see the food, and then merely as a pastime.

I have heard it said that they were wont to cook for him the flesh of young boys, but as he had such a variety of dishes, made of so many things, we could not succeed in seeing if they were of human flesh or of other things, but they daily cooked fowls, turkeys, pheasants, native partridges, quail, tame and wild ducks, venison, wild boar, reed birds, pigeons, hares and rabbits, and many sorts of birds and other things which are bred in this country, and they are so numerous that I cannot finish naming them in a hurry; so we had no insight into it, but I know for certain that after our Captain censured the sacrifice of human beings, and the eating of their flesh, he ordered that such food should not be prepared for him thenceforth.

Let us cease speaking of this and return to the ways things were served to him at meal times. It was in this way: if it was cold they made up a large fire of live coals of a firewood made from the bark of trees which did not give off any smoke, and the scent of the bark from which the fire was made was very fragrant, and so that it should not give off more heat than he required, they placed in front of it a sort of screen adorned with figures of idols worked in gold. He was seated on a low stool, soft and richly worked, and the table, which was also low, was made in the same style as the seats, and on it they placed the table cloths of white cloth and some rather long napkins of the same material. Four very beautiful cleanly women brought water for his hands in a sort of deep basin which they call "xicales," and they held others like plates below to catch the water, and they brought him towels. And two other women brought him tortilla bread, and as soon as he began to eat they placed before him a sort of wooden screen painted over with gold, so that no one should watch him eating. Then the four women stood aside, and four great chieftains who were old men came and stood beside them, and with these Montezuma now and then conversed, and asked them questions, and as a great favour he would give to each of these elders a dish of what to him tasted best. they say that these elders were his near relations, and were his counsellors and judges of law suits, and the dishes and food which Montezuma gave them they ate standing up with much reverence and without looking at his face. He was served on Cholula earthenware either red or black. While he was at his meal the men of his guard who were in the rooms near to that of Montezuma, never dreamed of making any noise or speaking aloud. They brought him fruit of all the different kinds that the land produced, but he ate very little of it. From time to time they brought him, in cup-shaped vessels of pure gold, a certain drink made from cacao which they said he took when he was going to visit his wives, and at the time he took no heed of it, but what I did see was that they brought over fifty great jugs of good cacao frothed up, and he drank of that, and the women served this drink to him with great reverence.

Sometimes at meal-times there were present some very ugly humpbacks, very small of stature and their bodies almost broken in half, who are their jesters, and other Indians, who must have been buffoons, who told him witty sayings, and others who sang and danced, for Montezuma was fond of pleasure and song, and to these he ordered to be given what was left of the food and jugs of cacao. Then the same four women removed the table cloths, and with much ceremony they brought water for his hands. And Montezuma talked with those four old chieftains about things that interested him, and they took leave of him with the great reverence in which they held him, and he remained to repose. . . .

3. The Grief of the Conquered:
"Broken Spears Lie in the Roads"

MIGUEL LEÓN PORTILLA

Spanish chronicles present only one side of the story, that of the conquerors. The Mexican anthropologist Miguel León Portilla was the first to bring together a selection of the accounts by the Indians, some written as early as 1528, only seven years after the fall of Mexico City. These writings give a brief history of the dramatic confrontation of Indians and Spaniards as told by the victims, and include reports by native priests and wise men who managed to survive the persecution and death that took place during the final struggle.

The selection begins with the story of how frightened Montezuma was by the reports of the messengers he had sent to see Cortés and his soldiers.

MOTECUHZOMA GOES OUT TO MEET CORTES

The Spaniards arrived in Xoloco, near the entrance to Tenochtitlan. That was the end of the march, for they had reached their goal.

Motecuhzoma now arrayed himself in his finery, preparing to go out to meet them. The other great princes also adorned their persons, as did the nobles and their chieftains and knights. They all went out together to meet the strangers.

They brought trays heaped with the finest flowers—the flower that resembles a shield, the flower shaped like a heart; in the center, the flower with the sweetest aroma; and the fragrant yellow flower, the most precious of all. They also brought garlands of flowers, and ornaments for the breast, and necklaces of gold, necklaces hung with rich stones, necklaces fashioned in the petatillo style.

Thus Motecuhzoma went out to meet them, there in Huitzillan. He presented many gifts to the Captain and his commanders, those who had come to make war. He showered gifts upon them and hung flowers around their necks; he gave them

From *The Broken Spears: The Aztec Account of the Conquest of Mexico*, ed. Miguel León Portilla (Boston: Beacon Press, 1962), pp. 29–149, passim. Copyright © 1962 and 1990 by Beacon Press; originally published in Spanish under the title of *Vision de los vencidos*: copyright © 1959 by Universidad Nacional Autónoma de México. Reprinted by permission of Beacon Press.

necklaces of flowers and bands of flowers to adorn their breasts; he set garlands of flowers upon their heads. Then he hung the gold necklaces around their necks and gave them presents of every sort as gifts of welcome. . . .

MOTECUHZOMA AWAITS WORD FROM THE MESSENGERS

While the messengers were away, Motecuhzoma could neither sleep nor eat, and no one could speak with him. He thought that everything he did was in vain, and he sighed almost every moment. He was lost in despair, in the deepest gloom and sorrow. Nothing could comfort him, nothing could calm him, nothing could give him any pleasure.

He said: "What will happen to us? Who will outlive it? Ah, in other times I was contented, but now I have death in my heart! My heart burns and suffers, as if it were drowned in spices . . .! But will our lord come here?"

Then he gave orders to the watchmen, to the men who guarded the palace:

"Tell me, even if I am sleeping. The messengers have come back from the sea." But when they went to tell him, he immediately said: "They are not to report to me here. I will receive them in the House of the Serpent. Tell them to go there." And he gave this order: "Two captives are to be painted with chalk."

The messengers went to the House of the Serpent, and Motecuhzoma arrived. The two captives were then sacrificed before his eyes: their breasts were torn open, and the messengers were sprinkled with their blood. This was done because the messengers had completed a difficult mission: they had seen the gods, their eyes had looked on their faces. They had even conversed with the gods!

THE MESSENGERS' REPORT

When the sacrifice was finished, the messengers reported to the king. They told him how they had made the journey, and what they had seen, and what food the strangers ate. Motecuhzoma was astonished and terrified by their report, and the description of the strangers' food astonished him above all else.

He was also terrified to learn how the cannon roared, how its noise resounded, how it caused one to faint and grow deaf. The messengers told him: "A thing like a ball of stone comes out of its entrails: it comes out shooting sparks and raining fire. The smoke that comes out with it has a pestilent odor, like that of rotten mud. This odor penetrates even to the brain and causes the greatest discomfort. If the cannon is aimed against a mountain, the mountain splits and cracks open. If it is aimed against a tree, it shatters the tree into splinters. This is a most unnatural sight as if the tree had exploded from within."

The messengers also said: "Their trappings and arms are all made of iron. They dress in iron and wear iron casques on their heads. Their swords are iron: their bows are iron, their shields are iron; their spears are iron. Their deer carry them on their backs wherever they wish to go. These deer, our lord, are as tall as the roof of a house.

"The strangers' bodies are completely covered, so that only their faces can be seen. Their skin is white, as if it were made of lime. They have yellow hair, though some of them have black. Their beards are long and yellow, and their moustaches are also yellow. Their hair is curly, with very fine strands.

"As for their food, it is like human food. It is large and white, and not heavy. It is something like straw, but with the taste of a corn stalk, of the pith of a corn stalk. It is a little sweet, as if it were flavored with honey; it tastes of honey, it is sweet-tasting food.

"Their dogs are enormous, with flat ears and long, dangling tongues. The color of their eyes is a burning yellow; their eyes flash fire and shoot off sparks. Their bellies are hollow, their flanks long and narrow. They are tireless and very powerful. They bound here and there, panting, with their tongues hanging out. And they are spotted like an ocelot."

When Motecuhzoma heard this report, he was filled with terror. It was as if his heart had fainted, as if it had shriveled. It was as if he were conquered by despair. . . .

THE SPANIARDS TAKE POSSESSION OF THE CITY

When the Spaniards entered the Royal House, they placed Motecuhzoma under guard and kept him under their vigilance. They also placed a guard over Itzcuauhtzin, but the other lords were permitted to depart.

Then the Spaniards fired one of their cannons, and this caused great confusion in the city The people scattered in every direction; they fled without rhyme or reason; they ran off as if they were being pursued. It was as if they had eaten the mushrooms that confuse the mind, or had seen some dreadful apparition. They were all overcome by terror, as if their hearts had fainted. And when night fell, the panic spread through the city and their fears would not let them sleep.

In the morning the Spaniards told Motecuhzoma what they needed in the way of supplies: tortillas, fried chickens, hens' eggs, pure water, firewood and charcoal. Also: large clean cooking pots, water jars, pitchers, dishes and other pottery. Motecuhzoma ordered that it be sent to them. The chiefs who received this order were angry with the king and no longer revered or respected him. But they furnished the Spaniards with all the provisions they needed—food, beverages and water, and fodder for the horses.

THE SPANIARDS REVEAL THEIR GREED

When the Spaniards were installed in the palace, they asked Motecuhzoma about the city's resources and reserves and about the warriors' ensigns and shields. They questioned him closely and then demanded gold.

Motecuhzoma guided them to it. They surrounded him and crowded close with their weapons. He walked in the center, while they formed a circle around him.

When they arrived at the treasure house called Teucalco, the riches of gold and feathers were brought out to them: ornaments made of quetzal feathers, richly worked shields, disks of gold, the necklaces of the idols, gold nose plugs, gold greaves and bracelets and crowns.

The Spaniards immediately stripped the feathers from the gold shields and ensigns. They gathered all the gold into a great mound and set fire to everything else, regardless of its value. Then they melted down the gold into ingots. As for the precious green stones, they took only the best of them; the rest were snatched up by the Tlaxcaltecas. The Spaniards searched through the whole treasure house, questioning and quarreling, and seized every object they thought was beautiful.

THE SEIZURE OF MOTECUHZOMA'S TREASURES

Next they went to Motecuhzoma's storehouse, in the place called Totocalco [Place of the palace of the Birds], where his personal treasures were kept. The Spaniards grinned like little beasts and patted each other with delight.

When they entered the hall of treasures, it was as if they had arrived in Paradise. They searched everywhere and coveted everything; they were slaves to their own greed. All of Motecuhzoma's possessions were brought out: fine bracelets, necklaces with large stones, ankle rings with little gold bells, the royal crowns and all the royal finery—everything that belonged to the king and was reserved to him only. They seized these treasures as if they were their own, as if this plunder were merely a stroke of good luck. And when they had taken all the gold, they heaped up everything else in the middle of the patio.

La Malinche called the nobles together. She climbed up to the palace roof and cried: "Mexicanos, come forward! The Spaniards need your help! Bring them food and pure water. They are tired and hungry; they are almost fainting from exhaustion! Why do you not come forward? Are you angry with them?"

The Mexicans were too frightened to approach. They were crushed by terror and would not risk coming forward. They shied away as if the Spaniards were wild beasts, as if the hour were midnight on the blackest night of the year yet they did not abandon the Spaniards to hunger and thirst. They brought them whatever they needed, but shook with fear as they did so. They delivered the supplies to the Spaniards with trembling hands, then turned and hurried away. . . .

THE MASSACRE IN THE MAIN TEMPLE DURING THE FIESTA OF TOXCATL

At this moment in the fiesta, when the dance was loveliest and when song was linked to song, the Spaniards were seized with an urge to kill the celebrants. They all ran forward, armed as if for battle. They closed the entrances and passageways, all the gates of the patio: the Eagle Gate in the lesser palace, the Gate of the Canestalk and the Gate of the Serpent of Mirrors. They posted guards so that no one could escape, and then rushed into the Sacred Patio to slaughter the celebrants. They came on foot, carrying their swords and their wooden or metal shields.

They ran in among the dancers, forcing their way to the place where the drums were played. They attacked the man who was drumming and cut off his arms. Then they cut off his head, and it rolled across the floor.

They attacked all the celebrants, stabbing them, spearing them, striking them with their swords. They attacked some of them from behind, and these fell instantly to the ground with their entrails hanging out. Others they beheaded: they cut off their heads, or split their heads to pieces.

They struck others in the shoulders, and their arms were torn from their bodies. They wounded some in the thigh and some in the calf. They slashed others in the abdomen, and their entrails all spilled to the ground. Some attempted to run away, but their intestines dragged as they ran; they seemed to tangle their feet in their own entrails. No matter how they tried to save themselves, they could find no escape.

Some attempted to force their way out, but the Spaniards murdered them at the gates. Others climbed the walls, but they could not save themselves. Those who ran into the communal houses were safe there for a while; so were those who lay down among the victims and pretended to be dead. But if they stood up again, the Spaniards saw them and killed them.

The blood of the warriors flowed like water and gathered into pools. The pools widened, and the stench of blood and entrails filled the air. The Spaniards ran into the communal houses to kill those who were hiding. They ran everywhere and searched everywhere, they invaded every room, hunting and killing.

THE SIEGE OF TENOCHTITLAN

Now the Spaniards began to wage war against us. They attacked us by land for ten days, and then their ships appeared. Twenty days later, they gathered all their ships together near Nonohualco, off the place called Mazatzintamalco. The allies from Tlaxcala and Huexotzinco set up camp on either side of the road.

Our warriors from Tlatelolco immediately leaped into their canoes and set out for Mazatzintamalco and the Nonohualco road. But no one set out from Tenochtitlan to assist us: only the Tlatelolcas were ready when the Spaniards arrived in their ships.

On the following day, the ships sailed to Xoloxo.

The fighting at Xoloco and Huitzillan lasted for two days. While the battle was under way, the warriors from Tenochtitlan began to mutiny. They said: "Where are our chiefs? They have fired scarcely a single arrow! Do they think they have fought like men?" Then they seized four of their own leaders and put them to death. The victims were two captains, Cuauhnochtli and Cuapan, and the priests of Amantlan and Tlalocan. This was the second time that the people of Tenochtitlan killed their own leaders. . . .

THE FIGHTING IS RENEWED

The Spaniards made ready to attack us, and the war broke out again. They assembled their forces in Cuepopan and Cozcacuahco. A vast number of our warriors were killed by their metal darts. Their ships sailed to Texopan, and the battle there lasted three days. When they had forced us to retreat, they entered the Sacred Patio, where here was a four-day battle. Then they reached Yacacolco.

The Tlatelolcas set up three racks of heads in three different places. The first rack was in the Sacred Patio of Tlilancalco [Black House.], where we strung up the heads of our lords the Spaniards. The second was in Acacolco, where we strung up Spanish heads and the heads of two of their horses. The third was in Zacatla, in front of the temple of the earth-goddess Cihuacoatl, where we strung up the heads of Tlaxcaltecas.

The women of Tlatelolco joined in the fighting. They struck at the enemy and shot arrows at them; they tucked up their skirts and dressed in the regalia of war.

The Spaniards forced us to retreat. Then they occupied the market place. The Tlatelolcas—the Jaguar Knights, the Eagle Knights, the great warriors—were defeated, and this was the end of the battle. It had lasted five days, and two thousand Tlatelolcas were killed in action. During the battle, the Spaniards set up a canopy for the Captain in the market place. They also mounted a catapult on the temple platform.

EPIC DESCRIPTION OF THE BESIEGED CITY

And all these misfortunes befell us. We saw them and wondered at them; we suffered this unhappy fate.

> Broken spears lie in the roads;
> we have torn our hair in our grief.
> The houses are roofless now, and their walls
> are red with blood.

Worms are swarming in the streets and plazas,
and the walls are splattered with gore.
The water has turned red, as if it were dyed,
and when we drink it,
it has the taste of brine.

We have pounded our hands in despair
against the adobe walls,
for our inheritance, our city, is lost and dead.
The shields of our warriors were its defense,
but they could not save it.

We have chewed dry twigs and salt grasses;
we have filled our mouths with dust and bits of adobe;
we have eaten lizards, rats and worms . . . .

When we had meat, we ate it almost raw. It was scarcely on the fire before we snatched it and gobbled it down.

They set a price on all of us: on the young men, the priests, the boys and girls. The price of a poor man was only two handfuls of corn, or ten cakes made from mosses or twenty cakes of salty couch-grass. Gold, jade, rich cloths, quetzal feathers—everything that once was precious was now considered worthless.

The captains delivered several prisoners of war to Cuauhtemoc to be sacrificed. He performed the sacrifices in person, cutting them open with a stone knife . . . .

ELEGIES ON THE FALL OF THE CITY

INTRODUCTION. By way of conclusion, we present three "songs of sorrow," true elegies written by the post-Conquest Aztec poets. The first song, from the collection of *Cantares Mexicanos* in the National Library of Mexico, was probably composed in 1523. The second is part of a whole series of poems recounting the Conquest from the arrival of the Spaniards in Tenochtitlan to the ultimate defeat of the Aztecs. We have selected only the most dramatic moments from the last section of this series. The third song, also from the *Cantares Mexicanos,* recalls the traditional symbolism of "flowers and songs." It laments that only grief and suffering remain in the once proud capital.

These elegies are among the first and most poignant expressions of what Dr. Garibay has called "the trauma of the Conquest." They reveal, with greater eloquence than the other texts, the deep emotional wound inflicted on the Indians by the defeat. (Introductory note by Miguel León Portilla.)

The Fall of Tenochtitlan

Our cries of grief rise up
And our tears rain down,
For Tlatelolco is lost.
The Aztecs are fleeing across the lake,
They are running away like women.

How can we save our homes, my people?
The Aztecs are deserting the city:
the city is in flames, and all
is darkness and destruction.

Motelchiuhtzin the Huiznahuacatl,
Tlacotzin, the Tlailotlacatl,
Oquitzin the Tlacatecuhtli
are greeted with tears.

Weep, my people:
know that with these disasters
we have lost the Mexican nation.
The water has turned bitter,
our food is bitter!
These are the acts of the Giver of Life. . . .

The Imprisonment of Cuauhtemoc

The Aztecs are besieged in the city;
the Tlatelolcas are besieged in the city!

'The walls are black,
the air is black with smoke,
the guns flash in the darkness.
They have captured Cuauhtemoc;
they have captured the princes of Mexico.

The Aztecs are besieged in the city;
the Tlatelolcas are besieged in the city!
After nine days, they were taken to Coyoacan:

Cuauhtemoc, Coanacoch, Tetlepanquetzaltzin.
The kings are prisoners now.

Tlacotzin consoled them:
"Oh my nephews, take heart!
The kings are prisoners now;
they are bound with chains."

The king Cuauhtemoc replied:
"Oh my nephew, you are a prisoner;
they have bound you in irons.

"But who is that at the side of the Captain-General?
Ah, it is Dona Isabel, my little niece!
Ah, it is true: the kings are prisoners now!

"You will be a slave and belong to another:
the collar will be fashioned in Coyoacan,
where the quetzal feathers will be woven.

"Who is that at the side of the Captain-General?
Ah, it is Dona Isabel, my little niece!
Ah, it is true: the kings are prisoners now!"

Flowers and Songs of Sorrow

Nothing but flowers and songs of sorrow
are left in Mexico and Tlatelolco,
where once we saw warriors and wise men.

We know it is true
that we must perish,
for we are mortal men.
You, the Giver of Life,
You have ordained it.

We wander here and there
in our desolate poverty.
We are mortal men.
We have seen bloodshed and pain

where once we saw beauty and valor.

We are crushed to the ground;
we lie in ruins.
There is nothing but grief and suffering
in Mexico and Tlatelolco,
where once we saw beauty and valor.

Have you grown weary of your servants?
Are you angry with your servants,
O Giver of Life?

4. "The Conquest of Mexico was Not the Victory of a Spanish Juggernaut"

ROSS HASSIG

To tell the story of the conquest from the native point of view, Ross Hassig, a Professor of Anthropology at the University of Oklahoma, has surveyed in a series of volumes the long pre-conquest historical development of Mexico, paying particular attention to the emergence of the Aztecs and their tense and inherently unstable relations with the other Indian cultures of the region. He assessed their political organization, highlighting the formidable nature of Aztec warfare, and showing why hostility to the Aztecs led so many Indians to ally themselves with the invaders. As this excerpt shows, Hassig argues that it was the fragmented organization and divided aims of the Indians rather than Spanish military might that brought about their defeat.

The conquest of Mexico was not the victory of a Spanish juggernaut. It was a campaign fought in fits and starts and was very much a learning experience for both sides. All participants regarded the others as something different from what they really were: the Spaniards saw the Indians as inferior and easily defeated, while the Indians viewed the Spaniards as perhaps supernatural and powerful, if not invincible. Although these perceptions changed with harsh experience, they patterned the behaviour of both sides, leading to miscalculations that profoundly affected the meeting of Old and New Worlds.

The Spanish arrival presented groups such as the Cempohualtecs and Tlaxcaltecs with new political opportunities that they ultimately seized. Both Indians and Spaniards sought alliances in their own fashion. The Indians frequently gave the Spaniards the daughters of kings and nobles in effort to link the two sides through elite marriages. But the Spaniards failed to recognize the significance of these acts and accepted the women largely as concubines. For their part, the Spaniards claimed to seek alliances through religious conversion, but both these claims and their actions were primarily motivated by political purposes, to justify the war.

The Spaniards did not vigorously pursue religious conversions. Combatants on both sides prayed to their gods, but meaningful conversion in the sense that Roman

From *Mexico and the Spanish Conquest* by Ross Hassig (New York: Longman Publishing, 1994), pp. 144–49, passim. Reprinted by permission of Addison Wesley Longman Ltd.

Catholic religious doctrine was transmitted, understood and believed, almost surely did not occur during the Conquest period. Whatever conversion effects did occur would have satisfied both the Spaniards' legal and religious obligations, but Christianity was still culturally impenetrable to the Indians and true comprehension was not what the conquistadors sought. Rather, public conversions were political statements and occurred only after an alliance had been established and the Indians could no longer back out. This happened at Cempohuallan after the attack on the Aztecs for which the Indians would be blamed, and at Tlaxcallan after the Spaniards had fled Tenochtitlan, renegotiated their alliance, and promised the Tlaxcaltecs vassalage over adjacent city-states.

Despite its superficiality, the Christianization of Indian rulers was the price of Spanish assistance and meant a breach in traditional patterns of authority. Conversion prized rulers away from the local priesthood and made them dependent on Spanish support because, unaided, the rulers could not withstand the internal opposition that their conversions generated. Public conversion did not signal an actual change in belief, but rather a political alliance from which there was no escape. Thus, there was a pattern of apparent conversion of allied rulers to Christianity. Conversion would alienate the native priesthood and at least some of the populace, but it nevertheless occurred when the loss of internal support was offset by the power and political support gained from the Spaniards. By contract, religious conversions did not take place in Tenochtitlan, not because the Aztecs were more devout, but because they were at the political apex in Mesoamerica. They did not need Spanish support to maintain their position and were thus not compelled to undergo public conversion. Only the Aztecs did not need Spanish power to advance their political position in the existing power structure of Mesoamerica, which is why only they rejected even the superficial trappings of Christianity.

Thus, neither a Spanish religious imperative nor an Aztec loss of faith explains the success of the Conquest. The fate of both Aztecs and Spaniards was tied to their political situations and both had little choice but to follow the courses they selected. The Aztecs could resist or lose their empire: the Spaniards could conquer Mesoamerica, be killed by the Aztecs or be tried for treason in Cuba. The main protagonists were on a collision course: while both sides chose that course, neither saw the consequences clearly. Circumstances and events forced decisions on them, but the costs and consequences were beyond their anticipation.

Cortés unquestionably brought new and effective military technologies to the confrontation. Steel swords, metal armour, harquebuses, crossbows, cannons, horses and ships all gave the Spaniards a great technological advantage The Aztecs successfully altered their tactics and countered some of these innovations but they could not counter them all. Instead, the Aztecs' main advantage lay in the size, skill and organization of their military. Although the casualties would have been high, early in the Conquest the massive Aztec armies could have crushed the Spaniards though numbers alone, despite the technological unbalance.

What made the conquest of Mexico possible was not the Spaniards' military might, which was always modest, but the assistance of tens and even hundreds of thousands of Indian allies—labourers, porters, cooks and especially soldiers. The Spaniards were so few that it was not their technology alone that was important, but the way it was coupled with Indian forces. Spanish arms could disrupt opposing formations in a way that native arms could not, but victories were typically won by large numbers of allied troops who could exploit these breaches. The Spaniards' most serious threat was the way they could convert relatively unimportant groups into a significant offensive force. This was a world-shattering alteration of the political landscape, but the Aztecs did nothing about it, either because they failed to recognize it in time or, perhaps, because of ineffective political leadership and tributary control problems. The self-serving conquistador accounts notwithstanding, the Conquest was not simply a matter of Spanish brains versus Indian brawn.

Spanish technology was important, but the key to the success of the Conquest was acquiring native allies who magnified the impact of those arms. Doing this required a thorough understanding of the political organization of Mesoamerican states and empires, the nature of rule and patterns of royal succession, and the individuals and factions involved. Cortés had some grasp of the situation, but not the detailed knowledge or understanding necessary to determine which faction to attack and which to support: only the Indians had this knowledge. The political manipulations that funnelled men and materiel to the Spaniards were engineered by the Indians in the furtherance of their own factional interests. The Tlaxcaltecs could have destroyed the Spaniards, either in their initial clashes or after their flight from Tenochtitlan, and some factions wanted to do so. But the Tlaxcaltec leaders saw the advantages of an alliance, given their own imperilled position *vis-à-vis* the Aztecs and *chose* to ally with Cortés. The Conquest was not primarily a conflict between Mexico and Spain, but between the Aztecs and the various Mesoamerican groups supporting Cortés. The clash was centred on issues internal to Mesoamerica; Cortés neither represented the forces of Spain nor had formal Spanish backing. Instead, he fought on his own behalf in hope of eventual Spanish royal support and legitimation.

The Aztecs fought a Mesoamerican war and lost. They chose to defend their capital on the assumption that they would gain a defensive military advantage and the stringent logistical constraints on Mesoamerican warfare would work in their favour. However, technological innovations and, more importantly, political shifts stripped the Aztecs of these advantages. But if the conquest of Mexico was an Indian victory over Indians rather than a Spanish victory over Indians, why did all of the Indians fare so poorly thereafter? The answer can be largely found in the different goals pursued by the Indians and the Spaniards. . .

The Conquest meant very different things to the Spaniards from what it did to the Indians. To the Indians who allied with Cortés, it meant the removal of an enemy and/or tributary lord, which benefited them. The Indian allies used the situation to improve their immediate circumstances by removing the Aztec threat. They foresaw only what they could: an overthrow similar to others in Mesoamerica that shifted the existing situation in ways more favourable to themselves.

The Spaniards, by contrast, saw the Conquest as a means of bringing all of the Indians under their rule. The Spaniards had a longer-term view based on their experiences in Europe; to them, the Conquest meant the removal of the only significant competing Mesoamerican power, which left the Indians fully exposed to the expansion of Spanish control. The Indians could only have assumed the continuation of a hegemonic imperial system, which is what they had known, and could not have anticipated the territorial one that the Spaniards were to impose. The Spaniards focused on what was to become the national level—the control of all groups in Mesoamerica, the imposition of centralized rule, and the collection of tribute on a massive scale. For the Spaniards, this was one more step in their imperial success, but for the Indians, it was a world-shattering event, although this was not immediately clear to all of them.

The Tlaxcaltecs aided the Spaniards in the continued conquest of other areas in Mesoamerica, presumably because they thought it was to their advantage. But these conquered areas felt no particular allegiance to Tlaxcallan, so the Tlaxcaltecs conquered areas that the Spaniards then controlled and used against them. Tlaxcallan emerged from the Conquest as a power, but did not parlay that into a ruling position in Mesoamerica. One reason that they failed to do so was that they were poorly positioned both geographically and socially. The Tlaxcaltecs lacked the overarching power that enabled the Aztecs to dominate large areas and the Spaniards were unchallengeable after they established reliable allies elsewhere, as with Tetzcoco. The Spaniards supported groups favourable to themselves and played them off against each another. Moreover, the Spaniards had no interest in increasing the Tlaxcaltecs' power after the Conquest, as they were doubtlessly seen as the main potential competitors. . . .

Mexico was not conquered from abroad but from within. The Spaniards were important and quickly took full credit even when they served only as the most visible, if not the most crucial, element. The Aztecs did not lose their faith, they lost a war. And it was a war fought overwhelmingly by other Indians, taking full advantage of the Spanish presence, but exploiting their own unique inside understanding of Mesoamerican political dynamics that Cortés could never master. The war was more of a coup or, at most, a rebellion, than a conquest. Conquest came later, after the battles, as the Spaniards usurped the victory for which their Indian allies had fought and died.

5. The Conquest of Yucatán

INGA CLENDINNEN

The Spanish conquest of the Yucatán peninsula was a long and bloody affair because the Maya put up a formidable resistance. In her prize-winning book, *Ambivalent Conquests: Maya and Spaniard in Yucatan, 1517–1570*, Professor Clendinnen uses fragmentary native sources to analyze Mayan actions from their own point of view. In this section she explains various environmental and cultural factors that ultimately brought about their defeat.

By 1535 there were no Spaniards in the peninsula. While later a tiny group under orders from Montejo clung on at Campeche, it was not until 1540 that the Maya were once again under foreign attack. Those Spaniards who regrouped under his son in 1540 to renew the assault on the peninsula were determined but disillusioned men. They knew the country held no promise of treasure; they knew its resistant people and it resistant terrain. They returned because they no longer hoped for riches. They knew they had missed the big prizes. Many of them middle-aged, many of them with family responsibilities, they sought some modest but secure recompense for their years of marching and fighting and going on short rations in the New World. And Yucatan, poor as it was, had some potential. The intricately embroidered cotton garments now spoke to more chastened men of a raw material, local technical skill, and the chance of a commercial product tuned to European needs. Honey, wax, indigo, cacao, all suggested the possibility of a modest but useful trade. Above all, there were the Maya themselves, sturdy, vigorous, accustomed to regular labour, and conveniently close to the chronically labour-hungry mines of the islands, which had only sick and dying Indians to work them. The enslavement and export of the native population was the most promising road to profit.

The Maya had not used their five years' grace well. They probably believed the foreigners had quit their territory for good; after all, they had driven them away before: at Campeche, at Champoton, they had beaten the invaders back to their boats, so they had not dared to venture inshore again for many years. Then they had

From *Ambivalent Conquests: Maya and Spaniard in Yucatán, 1517–1570* (New York: Cambridge University Press, 1988), pp. 29–37, passim. Reprinted by permission of Cambridge University Press.

come back, blundering from province to province, but they had finally given up, and gone away. Guerrero's advice, and their own observations, must also have informed the Maya of the centrality of gold as a fuel of Spanish energy. Yet their behaviour over that half decade seems to go beyond misplaced insouciance. It suggests that Spanish intrusions both direct and indirect, into the rhythm of Maya life had been more socially disruptive and psychologically disturbing than the flawed mirror of Spanish accounts implies. A missionary friar was later to record what he was told had happened in those years. First, after the Spaniards had left, there came a great drought. Few communities had been left with reserves. The bearded foreigners had neither planted nor harvested, and fought and looted when they chose, even through the time for planting, when no Maya thought of war. So famine followed on the heels of drought, and the people had to abandon their villages to live as best they could. It was in these desperate circumstances, with the ritual life of the villages tattered, that the Xiu of Mani decided to make pilgrimage to the Sacred Cenote at Chichen Itza, to make offerings to the gods of rain. To reach the Sacred Cenote they had to cross the territory of their traditional enemies the Cocom of Sotuta. They therefore explained their mission which was clearly requested, and were granted, safe conduct. Then, at the Cocom town of Otzmal, where the Xiu lords had been lodged together in one large house, the Cocom set the structure on fire, and killed all those who managed to escape the flames. . . .

Whatever their mutterings about the miserable poverty of the country and the suicidal obstinacy of its intractable inhabitants, the Spaniards would never again withdraw. Nor would they repeat the errors of the first phase. There were no more ambitious wanderings by small, isolated bands: now each group operated from a secure base, and ventured out only in effective force. Methods changed. As the Maya fouled their precious wells, destroyed their food supplies, and even performed the sacrilege of smashing down the growing corn to deny the invaders any prize beyond the blackened shell of what had once been a village, so the Spaniards destroyed those villages they could take by surprise, and massacred or enslaved their inhabitants. In the southernmost province of Uaymil-Chetumal, where the renegade Spaniard Gonzalo Guerrero had once exhorted and explained and organised, the Spaniards pursued deliberate policies of terror which must have vindicated his worst warnings. It was in the south that Montejo at last got his permanent 'Salamanca', with the founding of Salamanca de Bacalar on the south-western shore of Lake Bacalar late in 1544. It was an ironic monument to his earlier dreams. Eight Spanish citizens formed its corporation. They ruled what had once been one of the most populous and prosperous of the provinces, now effectively depopulated, haunted only by a few ghostly survivors of the years of war.

The Maya had defended their villages for as long as they could, and then destroyed them. Scattered through the forest, they had watched and killed when they were able. After five years of fighting it seemed their resistance was at last at an end. An unknown number withdrew, as the Maya had done and would do again in other times of foreign intrusion, first to provinces not yet subjugated, and then, as Spanish pressure increased, to the swamps and lagoons of the southern rainforests, the independent Itza kingdom at Lake Peten, or the remote zones of refuge which were to offer sanctuary to those other irreconcilables, the Maya rebels of the Caste War of the mid nineteenth century, when once again the Maya demonstrated their hatred of foreign masters. But most drifted back to their villages, and so became vulnerable to Spanish control and exploitation.

A question remains. Why was a people so resolute and so resourceful defeated by a band of adventurers? On that issue the few Maya writings are laconic to the point of muteness, but Spanish accounts, angled though they were to maximise Spanish gallantry and Spanish tenacity, yield enough to puzzle. The Maya had enjoyed the substantial advantage of local knowledge of a terrain hostile to outsiders. Despite progressive and accelerating depletion, they had at all times overwhelming numerical superiority: Montejo rarely had more than 400 men under his command, and those men were distributed between three or four separate camps. Historians' acknowledgment of that great imbalance in numbers (true for Mexico and for Peru, as well as for Yucatan), is usually accompanied by an obeisance (slightly baffled) to 'European technical and cultural superiority' or a reference (slightly embarrassed) to the unfortunate rigidity of 'traditional native thought' when confronted by novel challenges. It is worth bringing these abstractions down to the ground of actual episodes and encounters, to see what sense there is in them.

'European cultural superiority' is usually seen as manifesting itself in a greater capacity for flexible and rational thought, and a pragmatic allocation of energy and material resources. It is difficult to see much of either in the Spanish campaigns, especially those led by the senior Montejo, where bad decisions were taken, and obstinately adhered to. The early stages of the campaign resemble nothing so much as a disorderly game of Blind Man's Buff, with the Spaniards, blundering about with very little sense of direction or purpose, in the role of victims; being spun and shoved from town to town, province to province, and finally out of the peninsula altogether. The conduct of the campaigns improved under Montejo the Younger, but it remains difficult to regard it as a distinguished by rationality.

Possibly more important, at least for Spanish survival if not for final victory, was the Spaniards' superb discipline under pressure (and only under pressure; solidarity evaporated like morning dew as soon as necessity was removed). The last stages of the conquest were fought by seasoned men, who learnt to move almost instinctively into the tight formation fighting which had made the steadiness of Spanish swordsmen and pikemen a legend in Europe. Awareness of the military value of every Spanish life, intensified by the deeper loyalty to one's own kind in a world both alien and hostile, meant that no man in jeopardy would be abandoned if his comrades could prevent it. In warfare at least, Spanish lives were neither lightly wasted nor easily yielded. Above all, while the Indians were fighting on their home ground, with all that implies of inhibition, vulnerability, and anxiety for the morrow, the Spaniards could move through the land with no scruple as to the destructiveness and the human cost of their actions: those considerations could wait on victory. The 'technical superiority' argument usually pays particular attention to Spanish military equipment. Yucatan did not provide a favourable venue for the Spanish cavalryman, the tank of the New World. The man on horseback enjoys enormous advantages in height and reach and less measurable, but perhaps even more potent, in psychological superiority over the man on foot, as anyone unlucky enough to have confronted a mounted policeman knows. Those advantages evaporate where the horse is not sure of its footing, as on the nightmare causeways of Tenochtitlan, where the incomparable Cortés suffered a smashing defeat—or along the narrow stony paths of Yucatan. In those few places in the peninsula where the terrain happened to suit them, Montejo's horsemen enjoyed their usual success. But it was the crossbows and muskets, together with Spanish mastiffs, the great dogs trained for war, which the Spaniards most valued and the Indians most feared.

But the puzzle remains. Most of the encounters were fought at close quarters, and in hand-to-hand combat the Maya were skilled and tough. Each community sustained a body of at least semi-professional fighting men, and prowess was valued and measured in the endemic slave-raids and more formal battles between towns and provinces. The Spaniards had no doubt as to the Mayas' toughness: the Mérida *cabildo* judged them 'bellicose, valiant and experienced in war', and Spaniards did not distribute such reputations lightly, especially to Indians. Is the crucial factor then some real difference in 'how natives think', some stultifying rigidity which rendered them helpless before European invention?

We have examples of Maya 'creative innovation' in response to European threats. Pits with stakes devised to cripple the horses were effective, and on the organisational level we can trace throughout the course of the conquest a development in the range and reliability of Maya alliances. The coalitions of forces resulting from those alliances could win major victories, as when Montejo the Younger, desperately holding out at Chichen Itza against a great Maya army drawn from four or five provinces lost 150 men, with all of the surviving one hundred men badly wounded, in the course of a single day. Yet there are oddities in Maya behaviour, at least as we can reconstruct it from the sketchy and partial Spanish account. The aftermath of that spectacular Maya victory at Chichen Itza provides an instructive example. The little Spanish encampment was meant to be held under close seige, but the bloodied, fatigued Spaniards managed to escape by a stratagem. Their trail was quickly picked up by the Indians. The Spaniards laid an ambush; there was a brief, sharp encounter, and the Indians pulled back. Then they followed the fleeing Spaniards at a wary distance, escorting rather than molesting them, until Montejo the Younger was able to join forces with his father at Tiho, with consequences ultimately disastrous for the Maya. There was, on that occasion as on others, a curious lethargy in Maya response, a tentativeness in following through the victory—at least according to our expectations. Are we then looking at an example of 'native thought', capable only of reaction and not effective prosecution? Was each group of Maya still obstinately parochial, despite their coalitions, and concerned only to see the intruders leave their own territory? Or were they persuaded, on sufficiently 'rational' grounds, given past experience, that the Spaniards were essentially birds of passage who would, if sufficiently discouraged, remove themselves from the peninsula once more and for good?

Probably—as far as the relatively opaque sources permit us to see—something of each of the last two elements shaped Maya response. Throughout the conquest, whenever the Spaniards made unequivocal their intention to settle, by establishing permanent towns and demanding regular tribute, even 'pacified' and previously docile Indians rose in revolt. At other times, when they appeared as transients, the Spaniards were permitted to wander blindly through the forests, meeting opposition only when they attempted to retrace their steps. We also have hints of discord between different provinces, and of some unreadiness to pursue the Spaniards across local boundaries: intent on the familiar game of peninsular politics, the Maya were too little aware of the threat the new players posed to the game itself.

It is also true that some Maya 'strategies' appear at first sight to be self-defeating. In the early as well as in the later stages of the campaign it was a standard Maya response to withdraw from a threatened town. After the Spaniards had entered unopposed and taken possession of the town, attack sometimes followed, with the attackers being, of course, at a significant disadvantage. These Maya actions, superficially irrational, make more sense when we recall that in traditional Maya warfare the taking of loot and captives, not the possession of places, was the prime aim. The Maya were capable of drawing radical lessons from their experience, as when they signalled their recognition of the Spaniards as a new kind of enemy by their own unprecedented destruction of their precious wells, and the sacred maize.

The meaning of other strategies, or at least frequently reported actions, is harder to penetrate. As the campaigns dragged on, the Spaniards often encountered defensive earthworks and barricades on the approaches to a town or village—earthworks which must have taken many man-hours to construct. Yet they were frequently left unmanned, or so lightly defended as to be easily brushed aside. We could perhaps be looking here at some magical exercise, or only partially realised innovation, but my own guess is that we are glimpsing desperate attempts, effective and inadequate in their own terms, by communities exhausted and depleted but still determined to resist.

There is, unhappily, no direct way of demonstrating the truth of that guess. I have already commented on the acute selectivity, the characteristically blinkered vision, of the Spanish reports, and in these early encounters the Spaniards were not, nor could we expect them to be, sensitive to indications of flux and disorder. Yet the Maya must have been constantly responding to novel experiences: to the intrusion of new diseases, and of enemies who thought and who fought in new ways. We cannot know how those experiences were accommodated in social relations, but major adjustments must have been necessary, if only because of a massive reduction in population. Chauaca, the town so large that it took the best part of an afternoon to march from its outskirts to the town centre, could muster only 200 tribute payers in 1549, and Champoton, with its estimated 8,000 horses in 1517, had a population of not more than 2,000 thirty years later. From a native population of perhaps 800,000 at the time of the first smallpox epidemic, before the beginning of the military campaign, Yucatan was reduced to about 250,000 people when the fighting stopped.

It is difficult to begin to grasp the human experience distilled in those figures. We do not even know what age groups were most vulnerable, or in what form death most often came. Introduced diseases probably killed indiscriminately, and perhaps the men killed in battle did not outnumber the women and children and the old people who died of exposure, hunger or at the hands of the Spaniards during the prolonged anguish of the conquest. Certainly the depleted populations and the forced migrations must have fractured social life, and frighteningly disrupted the reassuring pulse of collective ritual activity. The survivors were reduced to being refugees in their own land, striving to pull together some of the old strands of life as they regrouped in the desolate villages, among the empty houses and the silent places. If we remember the psychological tension which must attend the attempt to deal with strangers who appeared ignorant of the most taken-for-granted rules of conduct, who fought even when with the coming of the rains the planting had to begin, or during the inauspicious and deeply dangerous days which fell between the old and the new year; who had no understanding of the warrior codes Maya behaviour ceases to puzzle. Roles must have been elided, transformed, even excised, as men strove to sustain the activities and routines they identified as most essential, while organising to meet as best they could, with what time and energy they could muster, the unpredictable threat from outside. When that threat was removed, or rather institutionalised, by the fact of defeat, and the villages were left by their Spanish masters to reconstitute themselves, those little societies had already been profoundly transformed.

THE SOUTH AMERICAN FRONTIER

6. "The Men Became So Weak that All the Tasks Fell on the Poor Women"

DOÑA ISABEL DE GUEVARA

It has been argued that the Spanish conquest was a "conquest of women," for in the process of defeating their enemies, the Spanish obtained native girls both by force and by peaceful means. This seizure of women was simply one element in the general enslavement of Indians that took place in the New World during the first decades of the sixteenth century.* European women, on the other hand, were not central figures in the conquest era. Most of the expeditions organized to conquer the more remote parts of South America set out with no Spanish women at all or at most with one or two camp followers or mistresses of leaders, like the well-known Inés Suárez in Chile. But in the relay system of conquest, there would always be wives and female relatives of the conquerors at the more established base from which the expedition left, who would begin to appear in the new country almost before the fighting was over.

Paraguay was one of the most remote regions that the Spanish would enter, but this fact was not known in Spain in 1535 when don Pedro de Mendoza, expecting another Peru, brought a great expedition directly from Seville to the Río de la Plata that included no small number of women who were not camp followers but women of noble birth. One of them was Doña Isabel de Guevara who wrote the following letter in 1556 to Princess doña Juana, then regent in Spain, requesting that the crown grant her an encomienda of Indians as compensation for her contributions in the founding of the colony at Asunción.

Very high and powerful lady:

Several women came to this province of the Rio de la Plata along with its first governor don Pedro de Mendoza, and it was my fortune to be one of them. On reaching the port of Buenos Aires, our expedition contained 1,500 men, but food was scarce, and the hunger was such that within three months 1,000 of them died;

---

*Magnus Mörner, *Race Mixture in the History of Latin America* (Boston: Little, Brown and Company, 1967), 23.

From *Letters and People of the Spanish Indies: The Sixteenth Century,* ed. James Lockhart and Enrique Otte (Cambridge: Cambridge University Press, 1976), pp. 14–17. Reprinted with the permission of Cambridge University Press.

it was such a famine that the one of Jerusalem cannot equal it, nor any other be compared to it. The men became so weak that all the tasks fell on the poor women, washing the clothes as well as nursing the men, preparing them the little food there was, keeping them clean, standing guard, patrolling the fires, loading the crossbows when the Indians came sometimes to do battle, even firing the cannon, and arousing the soldiers who were capable of fighting, shouting the alarm through the camp, acting as sergeants and putting the soldiers in order, because at that time, as we women can make do with little nourishment, we had not fallen into such weakness as the men. Your highness will readily believe that our contributions were such that if it had not been for us, all would have perished; and were it not for the men's reputation, I could truthfully write you much more and give them as the witnesses. I believe others will write this story to your highness at greater length, so I will cease.

When this so perilous turbulence was over, the few who were still alive decided to ascend the river, weak as they were and with winter coming on, in two brigantines, and the weary women nursed them and looked after them and cooked their meals, carrying firewood on their backs from off the ship, and encouraging them with manly words not to let themselves die, that soon they would reach fertile land, and carrying them on our shoulders to the brigantines with as much tenderness as if they were our own sons. And when we came upon a kind of Indians called Timbues who are great fishmen, again we served the men in finding different sorts of dishes so that they wouldn't get sick from eating fish without bread when they were so weak.

Afterwards they decided to ascend the Paraná in search of provisions, in which voyage the unfortunate women underwent such hardships that God gave them life miraculously because he saw the men's lives depended on them, for they took all the tasks of the ship so to heart that a woman who did less than another felt affronted; they worked the sail, steered the ship, sounded the depth, bailed out the water, took the oar when a soldier was unable to row, and exhorted the soldiers not to be discouraged, that men were meant for hardships. And the truth is, no one forced the women to do those things, nor did they do them out of obligation; only charity obliged them. Thus they arrived at this city of Asunción, which though today it is very rich in provisions, was then greatly in need of them, and the women had to turn to their tasks anew, making clearings with their own hands, clearing and hoeing and sowing and harvesting the crop with no one's aid until such time as the soldiers recovered from their weakness and began to rule the land, acquiring the service of Indian men and women, until the country at last attained its present state.

I wanted to write this and bring it to your highness' attention to let you know how ungratefully I have been treated in this land, because recently most of it was distributed among the Spaniards here, both the first-comers and the new arrivals, without any consideration of me and my hardships, and I was left out without being given the service of a single Indian. I greatly wish, I were free to present myself before your highness and tell you the services I have done his majesty and the injustices they are now doing me, but that is not in my power, since I am married to a gentleman of Seville named Pedro de Esquivel, who, through serving his majesty, was the reason my hardships were forgotten and now are renewed, because three times I have taken the executioner's knife away from his throat, as your highness may know. So I beg you to order that my encomienda be granted to me in perpetuity, and that in gratification of my services my husband be appointed to some office suiting the quality of his person, since for his own part, his services merit it. Our Lord prolong your royal life and estate for many years. From this city of Asunción, 2nd of July, 1556.

Your highness' servant who kisses your royal hands,

Doña Isabel de Guevara

7. In Fighting Ability, the Araucanians Soon Surpassed the Spaniards

LOUIS DE ARMOND

The Araucanians once inhabited the whole of Chile. Isolated from Peru by the Atacama desert they were influenced only peripherally by the Inca empire, and they never abandoned their independent village-farming culture to create chiefdoms. After a Spanish force led by Pedro de Valdivia founded a settlement at Santiago in 1541, the Araucanians found numerous ways to adopt and adapt to Spanish military techniques and thereby maintain their independence until the end of the colonial era. In writing this essay in 1954 from the point of view of the Araucanians, Professor de Armond, who served as a Foreign Service office in Chile from 1942 to 1944 and received a Ph.D. in history from the University of California at Berkeley in 1950, was well ahead of his time.

Warfare between Indians and Spaniards in sixteenth-century Chile saw a very nearly regular rise in the warrior capacity of the Araucanians and a steadily declining military potential on the part of the Spaniards. Factors quite apart from numbers account for the changing fortunes of the contenders. The 150 troops who accompanied Pedro de Valdivia on his first trip to Chile were but a handful compared with the Spanish army of the early seventeenth century, which numbered well over a thousand. Conversely, the Araucanian population had diminished notably by the end of the sixteenth century. Nonetheless, a competent observer estimated that the area south of the Bío Bío River still held something more than twenty thousand Indian warriors.

Whatever the accuracy of the population estimates extant, they clearly indicate that the Araucanians, despite the recurrent ravages of smallpox and other diseases, still enjoyed an overwhelming numerical advantage over the Spaniards. Given this preponderance, one wonders why they did not expel the small and miserably poor Spanish population.

Paradoxically, the very circumstance which made it virtually impossible for the Spaniards to end the war with the Indians seems also to have rendered the Indians incapable of ousting their European enemy. This factor was the basic nature of the

From "Frontier Warfare in Colonial Chile" by Louis de Armond. Reprinted by permission from *Pacific Historical Review,* Vol. 23, No. 2, May 1954, pp. 125–32 passim. © 1954 by the American Historical Association, Pacific Coast Branch.

Indian social order, which was characterized by an extraordinary degree of individualism and, in a manner, rude democracy. The Spaniards were quite unable to find any single individual or group against whom they could direct their energies in an effort to conclude the war. The correspondence of governors, judges of the audiencia, and army officers is replete with annoyed references to the fact that there was no Indian chieftain responsible for the conduct of all the natives of Chile. Conversely, the Araucanians were never able, if ever they sought, to mass their entire potential against the Spaniards. Thus the early seventeenth century found the war in Chile in a state of uneasy equilibrium. The Spaniards were unable to push deeper into Indian territory, while the natives engaged mostly in limited raids across the frontier of the Spanish area.

A major cause bringing about this balance was that the Araucanians soon surpassed the Chilean Spaniard in equestrian ability and acquired the talents that make today's Chilean *huaso* in every respect the equal of Argentina's now- disappearing Gaucho. From the time they stole their first horses from Pedro de Valdivia, the Araucanians steadily augmented their mounted troops and came to place growing reliance on cavalry in encounters with the Spaniard. Clear proof of the fact would seem to lie in their penchant for stealing horses from the Spaniards.

Not alone through their adoption of the horse did the Indians enhance their fighting potential. Other facets of acculturation had raised their individual capacity to meet the second-rate Spanish troops in Chile. Most of the changes, however, occurred in strategy rather than in the weapons used. The weapons of Araucanian infantry in the seventeenth century remained largely those of the pre-Spanish period and comprised pikes, arrows, and clubs. The pikes, though not as durable as their Spanish counterpart, were formidable weapons from twenty to twenty-two feet long. The bows were smaller and heavier than those used in many other parts of America, for they were only about three and a half feet long; the arrows were comparably short, and were customarily tipped with a variety of materials that often remained in the wound. Used less frequently were the clubs, shaped roughly like a hockey stick, in cross section as large as a man's wrist, and perhaps seven feet long.

In their attacks on Pedro de Valdivia and his men, the Indians had displayed heroic valor but their superior numbers were neutralized by the Spanish soldier's lance, sword, and, above all, discipline. Within a very few years, however, the Araucanians had learned their first lesson. In the attack that led to the capture and death of Pedro de Valdivia, instead of attacking *en masse*, the Indians formed in several squadrons. The first descended on Valdivia and his men and fought until forced to break and run. It was at once replaced by another, which was then replaced by a third. While successive squadrons were engaging the Spanish troops, the first groups reformed and, in turn, attacked. Thus through sheer force of numbers and despite heavy losses, the Indians fought without cease until the Spaniards were literally so tired they could not lift their sword arms and fell under the weight of Indian numbers.

Soon thereafter the Araucanians used lassos of *liana*, with considerable effect, to pull Spanish troops from their horses and bring them within reach of Indian hand weapons. A change in tactics as well quickly became apparent. In 1555 occurred the first instance in which the Araucanians took a leaf from the Spaniards' book and used fortifications. In December of that year they overnight silently occupied an excellent defensive position overlooking Concepción, prepared a rude stockade of poles they had carried with them, and then waited for the Spaniards to attack. The Spaniards did attack, but despite their horses and arquebuses they failed completely to dislodge the enemy. Returning to their own stockade, the Spaniards found themselves besieged and finally were forced to retire over trails made difficult by trees the Indians had felled.

As early as 1558 the natives had lost their fear of firearms. Thereafter, though grossly inaccurate in their aim and usually short of powder, they used firearms whenever circumstances permitted. Soldiers of the Spanish army, usually mestizos from the ranks, from time to time fled to join the Indians. According to one Spanish officer, these renegades afforded the Araucanians a limited force of arquebusiers who were effective only to the extent that powder could be taken from the Spaniards.

Refinements in Indian methods of fortification soon included the practice of digging trenches and camouflaged holes to trap the Spanish horses. The effectiveness of the practice became evident in a pitched battle of 1563, which also gave clear evidence of the deterioration of the Spanish military. In that year a group of ninety Spaniards attacked such an Indian fort with disastrous results. As they approached the palisade, many of the horses and their riders fell into the holes prepared for them. Thrown from their mounts, the Spaniards were easy targets for Araucanian arrows. Thus the Spanish attack was promptly converted into a rout from which the attackers fled in complete disorder and with heavy toll of lives.

The same year witnessed other instances of the inventiveness of Indian resistance. An excellent illustration of this adaptability is in their laying siege to Arauco fort. They took up position just beyond the range of the few artillery pieces in the Spanish fort and there waited for the Spaniards to exhaust their scant food supplies. Finding that the enemy was getting water from a ravine within the cover of his artillery, the Indians under cover of darkness threw bodies and other decaying matter into the pool. The extremity of the Spaniards was such, however, that they continued to use the water despite its contamination The Araucanians thereupon dug a ditch and drained the pool.

Finally, the natives attacked the besieged soldiers with a grisly form of psychological warfare. Another body of Indians had felled part of a group of Spanish troops who sought to lift the siege of Arauco. The heads of the hapless Spaniards were proptly brought to Arauco and lifted high on pikes. Seeing them, the trapped Spaniards were assured that Concepción had fallen and than they were the only Christians remaining in all of southern Chile. Whatever the effectiveness of this unusual bit of strategy, the Araucanians maintained such a tight siege that Arauco fort was abandoned after two months of isolation.

In all these engagements the Indians were gaining increasing quantities of Spanish matériel, including swords, pikes, and guns, as well as protective helmets and leather jackets that rendered the Spanish soldiers' swords less dangerous. Most important, however, were the horses which the Indians were taking in steadily increasing numbers. As a single instance, when the Spaniards evacuated Arauco (re-established after its loss in 1563) and Cañete forts in 1566, they left behind 360 horses and a quantity of saddles. Within a relatively brief span these and other horses gained by the Indians enabled them to mount cavalry forces far superior to those of the Spaniards. The first governor of Chile in the seventeenth century lamented that "all the enemy who can, move on horseback and therefore enter and leave our territory with increasing ease and speed. . . ." The maximum body of cavalry the natives could mass, according to an authoritative estimate of 1614, was an impressive six thousand. By this time the native cavalry could boast of defensive armor for both horse and rider that was fully the equal of the Spaniards'. The only weapon carried by the Indian cavalryman was a lance.

The Indian military position in Chile was further enhanced by the nature of Spanish soldiery. Letters and reports of the early seventeenth century unvaryingly speak of the exceptionally low moral and military level of troop reinforcements that reached Chile, whether they came from Peru or, much less often, from Spain. One of the most serious penalties assessed for wrongdoing in Peru was exile to Chile and service in the army there. Thus many of the soldiers sent from Lima were habitual criminals. Whether criminals or not, they were of little or no value in the struggle with the Araucanians.

The practice of allowing these soldiers to winter in Santiago was a major reason for the regular diminution of the army's numbers and the seed for its aperiodic reinforcement. Indeed, more soldiers were lost to the army in peaceful Santiago than were lost in the war. Statistical details are not available for the rate of attrition of the army in the period as a whole. But there is record that from November, 1591, to late 1593 thirty-two soldiers died from causes growing out of action against the Indians, while at least three times that number were lost in Santiago through death from disease, flight from the country, or escape into a religious order.

The fact that fewer soldiers were lost to the army in the war than in Santiago was a direct result of the deplorable conditions under which the soldiers lived. One army officer, writing in 1594, asserted that "the name Chile grows daily more hateful" and "today not one man of those who serve there and are not settled would remain if he were given permission to leave. . . ." The men were ill-clothed, ill-fed, and ill-equipped. They were the victims of exploitation by merchants, *encomenderos*, and their own officers. Competition among these persons for a share of the soldiers' wage was keen, but competitive price-cutting was not a feature of this contest.

The supply situation of the garrison troops in the more remote fontier forts was particularly difficult. Sometimes rations were completely exhausted and they were forced to forage for food in the areas surrounding the forts. They were usually forced to remain near the forts for fear of Indian ambush if they ranged too far afield. The hardships that resulted were sometimes extreme, as is illustrated by the account given by one officer of the plight of the garrison of a small fort near the junction of the Laja and Bío Bío rivers:

> When the reduced rations of wheat and barley were exhausted I first ordered that, of the two companies I had with me, one should go out each day into the unproductive and barren countryside to bring back thistles. . . , which were the most substantial thing to be found. . . . When these were gone we collected other unfamiliar plants, from which some became ill. . . . I went out daily in a little boat we had there and went upstream (collecting) the leaves, larger than a shield, of a plant called *pangue*. . . . it was necessary to distribute these leaves with sword in hand. . . . Finally the state of hunger reached such extremes that no shield or other thing made of leather remained. . . . Even the palisade of the fort was torn apart for the leather thongs, rotted by sun and water, with which the timbers were lashed together. . . . Despite the precaution of seeing that no soldier who guarded the wall at night should carry a knife or sword . . . we woke one morning to find the fort torn apart and open in a score of places . . . and (soldiers) roasting the thongs over the coals of a fire.

In the light of these multiple problems, army leaders in the late sixteenth century initiated a battle strategy which became the norm. An unstable frontier roughly paralleling the Bío Bío River had come into being. Now the *maloca*, or summer campaign, was initiated. It was essentially defensive, for it sought to prevent the Araucanians, through destruction of their crops and their homes, from mounting any major attack. In the main, the strategy was effective, for only once in the next twenty years did the Indians coalesce their forces into a general movement that for a brief time threatened the entire Spanish position south of the Maule River. During the rest of this period the Araucanians for the most part confined themselves to guerrilla raids by small groups of mounted troops.

Perhaps a more important reason for the success of the maloca in maintaining relative peace north of the Bío Bío was that the Indian rebels soon came to look upon it with what amounted to approval. They noted that the campaign began at approximately the same time from year to year and usually followed a rather closely prescribed route through the central valley. They continued to plant some corn within reach of the campaigning Spanish army, but they also planted larger crops far back in mountain valleys where the Spaniards feared to go. Most of the Indians retired to these same mountain retreats.

The circumstances suggest that the Indians continued plantings in the central valley only as bait designed to persuade the Spaniards to continue their annual campaign. The truth is that the Indians promptly made of the *maloca* a positive benefit to themselves. Wrote one Spanish soldier:

Each year [they] look forward to our *campeada* as an excellent and abundant fair where they know they can abundantly replace whatever time has consumed. . . . From our campaigns they provide themselves with many horses . . . , as well as so many bridles, spurs, and stirrups that they have stopped using those . . . made of whale bone and wood. . . . The offensive arms the Indians gain in greatest numbers . . . are swords which provide them with iron for their pike and lance [tips]. But now they have so many that . . . their infantry attach [compete swords] to the long and pliable poles of their pikes. . . . Besides the swords, they get knives, machetes, mattocks, and axes in great quantity. Among all the tools they esteem the axes most, for they are very useful to them. [With them] they speedily fell trees that fall across . . . the trails and hinder the passage of our cavalry. . . .

Not along by dint of seizure did the Araucanians gather Spanish artifacts. At once suggesting the advantage enjoyed by the Indians as a result of these campaigns and indicative of the extraordinarily low position of the Spanish army was the willing part played by Spanish soldiery itself. Many of the Spanish troops participated in an unusual trade with the enemy wherein they bartered their swords and even the matchlocks and supporting hooks of their arquebuses in exchange for a little fruit or grain meal. Sometimes their hunger reached such extremes that they even handed gunpowder to the enemy in return for food. It might be added parenthetically that the clandestine trade gave clear evidence that the Araucanians were completely familiar with the functioning of the arquebus. They readily took matchlocks in this commerce, not because of any intrinsic value, but because the Spanish firing pieces were thus very effectively immobilized.

Such were some of the aspects of warfare in colonial Chile. It was a war that by the seventeenth century found the Spaniards on the horns of a dilemma. On the one hand, they did not have the strength to deal the Indians a definitive blow. On the other, much as they might suffer directly or indirectly, they felt they had to continue the war in an effort to prevent the Indians from becoming predominantly stronger, to keep in force the royal subsidy of the army in chile, and to provide some replenishment of encomienda labor. As the seventeenth century wore into the eighteenth and as the European population of Chile mounted—albeit very slowly—they emerged what was essentially a stalemate broken by brief flurries of warfare. This unhappy situation was not to end until the diplomacy of an independent Chile finally brought solution in the late nineteenth century.

Bartolomé de Las Casas. Spanish Dominican and Bishop of Chiapas, Mexico. Las Casas became the best-known champion of the Indians in the New World by challenging the racist and imperialist assumptions of the conquistadors. He emphasized Christian teaching about human dignity as developed by St. Thomas Aquinas, and throughout his long career, he defended Indian culture as the equal of the European. In his celebrated debate at Valladolid in 1550 with the Aristotelian scholar, Juan Ginés de Sepúlveda, Las Casas denounced Spain's war against the Indians and with ringing words proclaimed, "All the peoples of the world are men." (Reading 7)

Bartolomé de las Casas and the Spanish Struggle for Justice

THE STRUGGLE FOR JUSTICE

In building an empire in the New World, Spain exercised its conscience as well as its sword. After the return of Columbus to Spain in 1492, the Catholic Sovereigns applied to Pope Alexander VI for ratification of their claim to the new lands that Columbus had discovered. The Papal bulls issued by Alexander VI and his successor Julius II conferred upon the crown great power to direct the administration of church affairs in America and the obligation to provide for the Christianization of the indigenous peoples (Reading 2). As the conquest proceeded throughout the sixteenth century, Spanish theologians and scholars attempted to define what means ought to be employed to secure the new empire and what ultimate purposes it ought to serve. A fundamental question concerned the nature of the indigenous peoples. Were the Indians rational beings, and, if so, what were their rights? How should the faith be preached to them; under what circumstances could they be made to work for Spaniards and when could war be justly waged against them? All these and other questions were asked and heatedly debated throughout the sixteenth century in both Spain and America. The materials in this section have been selected to provided an outline of what has been called the "Spanish Struggle of Justice."

THE FIRST CRY FOR JUSTICE

The struggle for justice for the Indians began in Santo Domingo, Hispaniola, when a Dominican friar named Antonio de Montesinos delivered a sermon in 1511 accusing the colonists of gross mistreatment of the native people (Reading 1). The consternation caused by this event on the island and in Spain prompted King Ferdinand in 1512 to issue the Laws of Burgos which recognized the freedom of the Indians but concluded that they must be governed closely by the Spaniards in order that their conversion be effected. At about the same time, in order to ensure that the war waged on non-subjugated Indians was just, the King's jurists and theologians drew up a document known as the Requirement of 1513 which was to be read to all natives before the Spanish could make war on them (Reading 3).

BARTOLOMÉ DE LAS CASAS

At this point a new voice on behalf of the indigenous people made itself heard. Bartolomé de Las Casas had come to Hispaniola in 1502 as a *doctrinero* (teacher of Christian doctrine), but his daily life was that of an encomendero (holder of Indians) even after he became the first priest ordained in the New World in 1512. He was increasingly troubled by Spanish exploitation of the Indians, and in 1514 after reading a text from Ecclesiastes 34, "Tainted his gifts who offers in sacrifice ill-gotten goods," he experienced a profound conversion. He gave up his encomienda and journeyed to Spain to fight for Indian rights at court. Between 1516 and 1522 he proposed several substitutes for the encomienda, but when all of these alternatives failed, he entered the Dominican order in 1524 and spent several years in meditation and self-education through extensive reading.

Las Casas returned to an activist role in the 1530s, preaching against a proposed conquest of Indians in Nicaragua and organizing a Dominican mission to Verapaz, Guatemala in 1537–39. He argued at the Spanish court for the abolition of the encomienda, and for this purpose he wrote *A Short Account of the Destruction of the Indies* (see Section III, Reading 1). Las Casas was gratified when King Charles V issued the New Laws of 1542 (Reading 4), and in 1545–46 he returned to the New World as Bishop of Chiapas, a region adjoining Verapaz. Failing to persuade his hostile congregation to restore wealth taken from the Indians and angry that rebellious colonies forced Charles to modify the New Laws, Las Casas resigned his bishopric in 1550 to take up the fight again in Spain.

THE VALLADOLID DEBATE

Las Casas and the other religious who defended the indigenous people had raised enough questions about the nature of Spanish rule in the New World that on April 16, 1550 King Charles V ordered that all conquests be suspended until a special group of theologians and counselors should decide upon a just method of conducting them. In August of that year, a debate was held in Valladolid on the question, "Is the current method of carrying on conquests in America just or unjust?" Arguing on behalf of the conquistadors was Juan Ginés de Sepúlveda, a renowned humanist scholar specializing in Aristotle and author of a book, *Democrates alter,* in which he maintained that the Indians were, in Aristotle's phrase, "slaves by nature," who must be subjected before they could be converted (Reading 6). Las Casas argued on behalf of the Indians drawing on his 550-page Latin treatise, the *Argumentum apologiae*, which he had written to refute the doctrine Sepúlveda had set forth in *Democrates alter* (Reading 7).

The two men made their case before a council of fourteen advisors to the king. As Lewis Hanke recounts:

> On the first day of the session Sepúlveda spoke for three hours, giving a résumé of his book, *Democrates alter*. On the second day Las Casas appeared, armed with his monumental treatise which he proceeded to read word for word seriatim, as he himself states. This scholastic onslaught continued for five days, until the reading was completed, or until the members of the junta could bear no more, as Sepúlveda suggested. The two opponents did not appear together before the council, but the judges seem to have discussed the issues with them separately as they stated their positions. The judges also carried on discussions among themselves.[1]

When the oral arguments were completed, the judges departed to their homes taking with them copies of a summary of the arguments and agreeing to reconvene on January 20, 1551 for a final vote. Unfortunately there is no evidence that this meeting ever took place or that the judges ever came to a definite decision. Both Sepúlveda and Las Casas claimed victory, but the facts now available do not support either contestant. On the one hand, the king permitted the conquests to begin again, which would have been a point in Sepúlveda's favor. On the other hand, the new Royal Ordinances on "Pacification" of July 13, 1573, which replaced the Requirement, were probably drawn up in such generous terms because of the battle Las Casas fought at Valladolid (Reading 5). During the last sixteen years of his life Las Casas blocked an attempt by the conquistadors of Peru to have their encomiendas made perpetual, organized new missions to the New World, and completed his major writings. He died in Madrid on July 18, 1566.

INTERPRETATIONS

Historians have offered different views of the importance of the Spanish struggle for justice. In Reading 9 Lewis Hanke points out that of all the European countries that colonized the New World, only Spain seriously debated the legality of its rule and the justice of its control over the indigenous people, and that in waging a battle

---

1. Lewis Hanke, *The Spanish Struggle for Justice* (Boston: Little, Brown and Company, 1965), p. 118.

to win recognition of the humanity of the Indians and to understand their culture, Las Casas was a man far ahead of his time. For Charles Gibson, on the other hand, the efforts of one man or a group of men cannot outweigh the Spanish exploitation of the indigenous people which brought about the near-total collapse of the pre-Columbian cultures (Reading 8).

THE FIRST CRY FOR JUSTICE IN AMERICA

1. The Sermons of Friar Antonio de Montesinos, 1511

LEWIS HANKE

It is symbolic that the struggle for justice was touched off by an almost unknown friar. No writings of Montesinos have come down to us, nor any picture of him, and of his life after his famous sermons on the Caribbean island of Hispaniola we know little, except that he spoke once at court in Spain on behalf of the Indians and met his death whlie protecting them in Venezuela. Millions of Americans have never heard his name or been aware of his first cry on behalf of human liberty in the New World, which Pedro Henríquez Ureña termed one of the great events in the spiritual history of mankind. Our own records of his great moment in history appear in the royal instruction ordering him to be silent and in the *History of the Indies* by Bartolomé de Las Casas, whose description, written over four hundred years ago, vividly conveys to us the passion and the force of this first dramatic blow struck for freedom in the New World.

On the Sunday before Christmas in 1511 a Dominican friar named Antonio de Montesinos preached a revolutionary sermon in a straw-thatched church on the island of Hispaniola. Speaking on the text "I am a voice crying in the wilderness," Montesinos delivered the first important and deliberate public protest against the kind of treatment being accorded the Indians by his Spanish countrymen. This first cry on behalf of human liberty in the New World was a turning point in the history of America and, as Pedro Henríquez Ureña termed it, one of the great events in the spiritual history of mankind.

The sermon, preached before the "best people" of the first Spanish town established in the New World, was designed to shock and terrify its hearers. Montesinos thundered, according to Las Casas:

In order to make your sins against the Indians known to you I have come up on this pulpit, I who am a voice of Christ crying in the wilderness of this

From *The Spanish Struggle for Justice in the Conquest of America* by Lewis Hanke (Boston: Little, Brown and Company 1965), pp. 17–18. Reprinted by permission.

island, and therefore it behooves you to listen, not with careless attention, but with all your heart and senses, so that you may hear it; for this is going to be the strangest voice that ever you heard, the harshest and hardest and most awful and most dangerous that ever you expected to hear. . . . This voice says that you are in mortal sin, that you live and die in it, for the cruelty and tyranny you use in dealing with these innocent people. Tell me, by what right or justice do you keep these Indians in such a cruel and horrible servitude? On what authority have you waged a detestable war against these people, who dwelt quietly and peacefully on their own land?

. . . Why do you keep them so oppressed and weary, not giving them enough to eat nor taking care of them in their illness? For with the excessive work you demand of them they fall ill and die, or rather you kill them with your desire to extract and acquire gold every day. And what care do you take that they should be instructed in religion? . . . Are these not men? Have they not rational souls? Are you not bound to love them as you love yourselves? . . . Be certain that, in such a state as this, you can no more be saved than the Moors or Turks.

Montesinos thereupon strode out of the church with head high, leaving a muttering crowd of colonists and officials behind him, who were astounded, but not one was converted. He had come as near to convincing his hearers of their wrongdoing as would a theological student in our day who delivered a soapbox philippic in Wall Street on the biblical text "Sell that which thou hast and give to the poor, and thou shalt have treasure in heaven."

The colonists gathered at the house of the governor, Diego Columbus, protested against the sermon as a scandalous denial of the lordship of the king in the Indies, and delegated a group which went indignantly to the monastery to exact an apology and disavowal. The vicar, Pedro de Córdoba, unimpressed by the delegation's threat to expel the offensive friar, assured them that Montesinos had spoken for the Dominican group. He promised, however, that Montesinos would preach the next Sunday on the same topic. The colonists thereupon retired, believing they had won their point.

Word of the expected retreat spread quickly, and the following Sunday most of the leading Spaniards crowded into the church. Montesinos mounted the pulpit and announced the disquieting text "Suffer me a little, and I will show thee that I have yet to speak on God's behalf." Rather than explaining away his previous sermon with dialectic subtleties, he proceeded to belabor the colonists anew, and with even more passion than before, warning them that the friars would no more receive them for confession and absolution than if they were so many highway robbers. And they might write home what they pleased, to whom they pleased.

These words were soon heard in Spain, even by the King. On March 20, 1512, Ferdinand ordered Governor Diego Columbus to reason with Montesinos. If the Dominican and his brothers persisted in their error, previously condemned by the canonists, theologians, and learned men gathered to deliberate on the problem ten years before, the Governor was instructed to send them to Spain by the first ship so that their Superior might punish them "because every hour that they remain in the islands holding such wrong ideas they will do much harm."

Three days later on March 23, 1512, the Dominican Superior in Spain, Alonso de Loaysa, reproved Montesinos in an official communication to the Dominican Provincial in Hispaniola and ordered him to prevail upon the friars to stop preaching such scandalous doctrine. The Provincial was warned that no more friars would be sent if such preaching were permitted to continue.

Thus began the first great struggle for justice in the New World.

FUNDAMENTAL LAWS

2. Inter Caetera, the Papal Bull of 1493

Columbus's account in 1493 of his first voyage brought immediate protest from the Portuguese that he had encroached on an area in the Atlantic reserved to Portugal by the Treaty of Alcaçovas-Toledo signed with Spain in 1479–80. To resolve the conflict, Ferdinand and Isabel appealed to Pope Alexander VI, who being a Spaniard himself, was inclined to look with favor on their claims. The pontiff complied by issuing a series of four papal decrees (known as bulls because they bear the pope's official seal or *bullarum*) advancing Castilian interests in the Atlantic. In the bull reprinted below known as *Inter caetera* (the first words of its text) the pope divided the world between the Spanish and the Portuguese by drawing an imaginary north-south line 100 leagues (375–400 miles) west of the Azores and the Cape Verdes. For the purposes of evangelization the Portuguese were to hold sway east of the line, while the Spanish would be responsible for all the islands and mainlands discovered or to be discovered toward the west and south. In the years to come *Inter Caetera* served as the fundamental legal document on which Spain would justify its conquest of America.

Alexander, bishop, servant of the servants of God, to the illustrious sovereigns, our very dear son in Christ, Ferdinand, king, and our very dear daughter in Christ, Isabella, queen of Castile, León, Aragón, Sicily, and Granada, health and apostolic benediction.

Among other works well pleasing to the Divine Majesty and cherished of our heart, this assuredly ranks highest, that in our times especially the Catholic faith and the Christian religion be exalted and be everywhere increased and spread, that the health of souls be cared for and that barbarous nations be overthrown and brought to the faith itself.

Wherefore inasmuch as by the favor of divine clemency, we, though of insufficient merits, have been called to this Holy See of Peter, recognizing that as true Catholic kings and princes, such as we have known you always to be, and as your illustrious deeds already known to almost the whole world declare, you not only eagerly desire but with every effort, zeal, and diligence, without regard to hardships, expenses, dangers, with the shedding even of your blood, are laboring to that end;

From *European Treaties Bearing on the History of the United States and Its Dependencies to 1648* edited by F. G. Davenport, 4 vols. (Washington, D.C., 1917–37), 1: 75–78.

recognizing also that you have long since dedicated to this purpose your whole soul and all your endeavors—as witnessed in these times with so much glory to the Divine Name in your recovery of the kingdom of Granada from the yoke of the Saracens [Muslims]—we therefore are rightly led, and hold it as our duty, to grant you even of our own accord and in your favor those things whereby with effort each day more hearty you may be enabled for the honor of God himself and the spread of the Christian rule to carry forward your holy and praiseworthy purpose so pleasing to immortal God.

We have indeed learned that you, who for a long time had intended to seek out and discover certain islands and mainlands remote and unknown and not hitherto discovered by others, to the end that you might bring to the worship of our Redeemer and profession of the Catholic faith their residents, and inhabitants, having been up to the present time greatly engaged in the siege and recovery of the kingdom itself of Granada were unable to accomplish this holy and praiseworthy purpose; but the said kingdom having at length been regained, as was pleasing to the Lord, you, with the wish to fulfill your desire, chose our beloved son, Christopher Columbus, a man assuredly worthy and of the highest recommendations and fitted for so great an undertaking, whom you furnished with ships and men equipped for like designs, not without the greatest hardships, dangers, and expenses, to make diligent quest for these remote and unknown mainlands and islands through the sea, where hitherto no one had sailed; and they at length, with divine aid and with the utmost diligence sailing in the ocean sea, discovered certain very remote islands and even mainlands that hitherto had not been discovered by others; wherein dwell very many peoples living in peace, and, as reported, going unclothed, and not eating flesh.

Moreover, as your aforesaid envoys are of opinion, these very peoples living in the said islands and countries believe in one God, the Creator in heaven, and seem sufficiently disposed to embrace the Catholic faith and be trained in good morals. And it is hoped that, were they instructed, the name of the Savior, our Lord Jesus Christ, would easily be introduced into the said countries and islands. Also, on one of the chief of these aforesaid islands the said Christopher has already caused to be put together and built a fortress fairly equipped, wherein he has stationed as garrison certain Christians, companions of his, who are to make search for other remote and unknown islands and mainlands. In the islands and countries already discovered are found gold, spices, and very many other precious things of divers kinds and qualities.

Wherefore, as becomes Catholic kings and princes, after earnest consideration of all matters, especially of the rise and spread of the Catholic faith, as was the fashion of your ancestors, kings of renowned memory, you have purposed with the favor of divine clemency to bring under your sway the said mainlands and islands with their residents and inhabitants and to bring them to the Catholic faith.

Hence, heartily commending in the Lord this your holy and praiseworthy purpose, and desirous that it be duly accomplished, and that the name of our Savior be carried into those regions, we exhort you very earnestly in the Lord and by your reception of holy baptism, whereby you are bound to our apostolic commands, and by the bowels of the mercy of our Lord Jesus Christ, enjoin strictly, that inasmuch as with eager zeal for the true faith you design to equip and dispatch this expedition, your purpose also, as is your duty, to lead the peoples dwelling in those islands and countries to embrace the Christian religion, nor at any time let dangers or hardships deter you therefrom, with the stout hope and trust in your hearts that Almighty God will further your undertakings.

And, in order that you may enter upon so great an undertaking with greater readiness and heartiness endowed with the benefit of our apostolic favor, we, of our own accord, not at your insistence nor the request of anyone else in your regard, but of our own sole largess and certain knowledge and out of the fullness of our apostolic power, by the authority of Almighty God conferred upon us in blessed Peter and of the vicarship of Jesus Christ, which we hold on earth, do by tenor of these presents, should any of said islands have been found by your envoys and captains, give, grant, and assign to you and your heirs and successors, kings of Castile and León, forever, together with all their dominions, cities, camps, places, and villages, and all rights, jurisdictions, and appurtenances, all islands and mainlands found and to be found, discovered and to be discovered towards the west and south, by drawing and establishing a line from the Arctic pole, namely the north, to the Antarctic pole, namely the south, no matter whether the said mainlands, and islands are found and to be found in the direction of India or towards any other quarter, the said line to be distant one hundred leagues towards the west and south from any of the islands commonly known as the Azores and Cape Verde.

With this proviso however, that none of the islands and mainlands, found and to be found, discovered and to be discovered, beyond that said line towards the west and south, be in the actual possession of any Christian king or prince up to the birthday of our Lord Jesus Christ just past from which the present year one thousand four hundred and ninety-three begins.

3. The Requirement, 1513, a Most Remarkable Document

By 1513 the agitation caused by Montesinos's sermons and the dwindling native population on Hispaniola brought to the fore the larger question of the legality of Spain's claim to the Indies. To satisfy the royal conscience a committee of jurists and theologians met in Valladolid, Spain to draw up a manifesto that would base the conquest on what they considered to be the unassailable truths of the Bible, the medieval theory of Just War, and European ideas concerning national sovereignty. This document, known as the Requirement, was designed to be read to Indians before hostilities could be legally launched, and was first employed in 1514 by the aged and vitriolic conquistador Pedrarias Dávila near Santa Marta. Later it was made part of the baggage that every conquistador carried to America, and it was used in a number of curious circumstances. As Lewis Hanke writes:

> The Requirement was read to trees and empty huts when no Indians were to be found. Captains muttered its theological phrases into their beards on the edge of sleeping Indian settlements, or even a league away before starting the formal attack, and at times some leather-lunged Spanish notary hurled its sonorous phrases after the Indians as they fled into the mountains. Once it was read in camp before the soldiers to the beat of the drum. Ship captains would sometimes have the document read from the deck as they approached an island, and at night would send out enslaving expeditions, whose leaders would shout the traditional Castilian war cry "Santiago!" rather than read the Requirement before they attacked the near-by villages.*

Modern historians have usually treated the Requirement in a derisive or ironical spirit. Spaniards themselves, when describing this document, have often shared the dilemma of Las Casas, who confessed on reading it that he could not decide whether to laugh or to weep. He roundly denounced it on practical as well as theoretical grounds. Even its principal author, the jurist Juan López Palacio Rubios, "laughed often" when he was told of how it was applied in the New World, though the learned doctor still believed that it satisfied the demands of Christian conscience when executed in the manner originally intended.

On the part of the King, don Fernando, and of doña Juana, his daughter, Queen of Castille and Leon, subduers of the barbarous nations, we their servants notify and

---

*Lewis Hanke, *The Spanish Struggle for Justice*, p. 34.

Based upon the translation given in Arthur Helps, *The Spanish Conquest in America and its Relation to the History of Slavery and to the Government of the Colonies*, vol. 1 (London, 1900), pp. 264–67.

make known to you, as best we can, that the Lord our God, Living and Eternal, created the Heaven and the Earth, and one man and one woman, of whom you and I, and all the men of the world, were and are descendants, and all those who come after us. But, on account of the multitude which has sprung from this man and woman in the five thousand years since the world was created, it was necessary that some men should go one way and some another, and that they should be divided into many kingdoms and provinces, for in one alone they could not be sustained.

Of all these nations God our Lord gave charge to one man, called St. Peter, that he should be Lord and Superior of all the men in the world, that all should obey him, and that he should be head of the whole human race, wherever men should live, and under whatever law, sect, or belief they should be; and he gave him the world for his kingdom and jurisdiction.

And he commanded him to place his seat in Rome, as the spot most fitting to rule the world from; but also he permitted him to have his seat in any other part of the world, and to judge and govern all Christians, Moors, Jews, Gentiles, and all other sects. This man was called Pope, as if to say, Admirable Great Father and Governor of men. The men who lived in that time obeyed that St. Peter, and took him for Lord, King, and Superior of the universe; so also have they regarded the others who after him have been elected to the Pontificate, and so it has been continued even until now, and will continue until the end of the world.

One of these Pontiffs, who succeeded that St. Peter as Lord of the world, in the dignity and seat which I have before mentioned, made donation of these isles and Terra-firme to the aforesaid King and Queen and to their successors, our lords, with all that there are in these territories, as is contained in certain writings which passed upon the subject as aforesaid, which you can see if you wish.

So their Highnesses are kings and lords of these islands and land of Terra-firme by virtue of this donation; and some islands, and indeed almost all those to whom this has been notified, have received and served their Highnesses, as lords and kings, in the way that subjects ought to do, with good will, without any resistance, immediately, without delay, when they were informed of the aforesaid facts. And also they received and obeyed the priests whom their Highnesses sent to preach to them and to teach them our Holy Faith; and all these, of their own free will, without any reward or condition, have become Christians, and are so, and their Highnesses have joyfully and benignantly received them, and also have commanded them to be treated as their subjects and vassals; and you too are held and obliged to do the same. Wherefore as best we can, we ask and require you that you consider that we have said to you, and that you take the time that shall be necessary to understand and deliberate upon it, and that you acknowledge the Church as the Ruler and Superior of the whole world and the high priest called Pope, and in his name the King and Queen doña Juana our lords, in his place, as superiors and lords and kings of these islands and this Terra-firme by virtue of the said donation, and that you consent and give place that these religious fathers should declare and preach to you the aforesaid.

If you do so, you will do well, and that which you are obliged to do to their Highnesses, and we in their name shall receive you in all love and charity, and shall leave you your wives, and your children, and your lands, free without servitude, that you may do with them and with yourselves freely that which you like and think best, and they shall not compel you to turn Christians, unless you yourselves, when informed of the truth, should wish to be converted to our Holy Catholic Faith, as almost all the inhabitants of the rest of the islands have done. And besides this, their Highnesses award you many privileges and exceptions and will grant you many benefits.

But if you do not do this, and wickedly and intentionally delay to do so, I certify to you that, with the help of God, we shall forcibly enter into your country and shall make war against you in all ways and manners that we can, and shall subject you to the yoke and obedience of the Church and of their Highnesses; we shall take you and your wives and your children, and shall make slaves of them, and as such shall sell and dispose of them, as their Highnesses may command; and we shall take away your goods, and shall do all the harm and damage that we can, as to vassals who do not obey, and refuse to receive their lord, and resist and contradict him; and we protest that the deaths and losses which shall accrue from this are your fault, and not that of their Highnesses, or ours, nor of these cavaliers who come with us. And that we have said this to you and made this Requirement, we request the notary here present to give us his testimony in writing, and we ask the rest who are present that they should be witnesses of this Requirement.

4. The New Laws, 1542

The "Laws and ordinances newly made by His Majesty for the government of the Indies and good treatment and preservation of the Indians" contain detailed regulations so sweeping and so strongly in favor of the Indians that Las Casas himself might well have drafted them. Some of the most stringent laws were subsequently revoked because of the fierce opposition in Mexico and in Peru where the viceroy was killed when he attempted to enforce them.

The battles over the New Laws revealed the power of the feudalists who favored the encomienda system because it maintained society as in the Old World, while the regalists feared that the granting of encomiendas in perpetuity would seriously diminish the king's power in the New World. Ecclesiastics were just as keen as most conquistadors to use Indian labor. The crown finally decided to allow encomiendas to continue, under certain limitations, and their reasons were both political and humanitarian.

In attempting to assess the importance of laws in the Spanish Conquest one must always remember that laws are frequently broken, especially in times of war and stress. Yet Spanish preoccupation with law and juridical procedures had a firm basis in Spanish history and Spanish character. Spaniards in the sixteenth century well exemplified the truth of the observation by the philosopher Wilhelm Dilthey that "the energy which determined the fundamental direction of an age can be found in its legislation."*

Charles by the divine clemency Emperor ever August, King of Germany. . . . To the Most Illustrious Prince Don Philip our very dear and very beloved grandson and son, and to the Infantes our grandsons and sons, and to the President, and those of our Council of the Indies, and to our Viceroys, Presidents and Auditors of our Audiencias and royal Chanceries of our said Indies, Islands and Continent of the Ocean Sea; to our governors, Alcaldes mayores and our other Authorities thereof, and to all the Councils, magistrates, regidores, knights, esquires, officers, and commoners of all the cities, towns, and villages of our said Indies, Islands, and Tierrafirme of the Ocean Sea, discovered and to be discovered; and to any other persons, captains, discoverers, settlers, and inhabitants dwelling in and being natives thereof, of whatever state, quality, condition and pre-eminence they may be. . . .

Know ye, That having for many years had will and intention as leisure to occu-

*As quoted by José Honório Rodrigues, in *Perspectives on Brazilian History*, ed. E. Bradford Burns (New York: Columbia University Press, 1967), pp. 133–34.

From *The New Laws of the Indies*, ed. Henry Stevens (London: Chiswick Press, 1893), pp. iii–xvii, passim.

py ourselves with the affairs of the Indies, on account of their great importance, as well in that touching the service of God our Lord and increase of his holy Catholic faith, as in the preservation of the natives of those parts and the good government and preservation of their persons; and although we have endeavoured to disengage ourselves to this effect, it has not been possible through the many and continual affairs that have occurred from which we were not able to excuse ourselves, and through the absences from these kingdoms which I the King have made for most necessary causes, as is known to all: and although this incessant occupation has not ceased this present year, nevertheless we commanded persons to assemble of all ranks, both prelates and knights and the clergy with some of our Council to discuss and treat of the things of most importance, of which we had information that they ought to be provided for: the which having been maturely debated and consulted upon, and in present of me the King divers times argued and discussed: and finally having taken the opinion of all, we resolved on commanding to enact and ordain the things contained below: which besides the other Ordinances and Provisions that at different times we have commanded to be made, as by them shall appear, we command to be from henceforwards kept inviolably as laws. . . .

Whereas one of the most important things in which the Audiencias are able to serve us is in taking very especial care of the good treatment of the Indians and preservation of them. We command that the said Audiencias enquire continually into the excesses or ill treatment which are or shall be done to them by governors or private persons; and how the ordinances and instructions which have been given to them, and are made for the good treatment of the said Indians have been observed. And if there had been any excesses, on the part of the said Governors, or should any be committed hereafter, to take care that such excesses are properly corrected, chastizing the guilty parties with all rigour conformably to justice. The Audiencias must not allow that in the suits between Indians, or with them, there be ordinary proceedings at law, nor dilatory expedients, as is wont to happen through the malice of some advocates and solicitors, but that they be determined summarily, observing their usages and customs, unless they be manifestly unjust; and that the said Audiencias take care that this be so observed by the other, inferior judges.

Item, We ordain and command that from henceforward for no cause of war nor any other whatsoever, though it be under title of rebellion, nor by ransom nor in other manner can an Indian be made a slave, and we will that they be treated as our vassals of the Crown or Castile since such they are.

No person can make use of the Indians by way of Naboria or Tapia or in any other manner against their will.

As We have ordered provision to be made that from henceforward the Indians in no way be made slaves, including those who until now have been enslaved against all reason and right and contrary to the provisions and instructions thereupon, We ordain and command that the Audiencias having first summoned the parties to their presence, without any further judicial form, but in a summary way, so that the truth may be ascertained, speedily set the said Indians at liberty unless the persons who hold them for slaves, show title why they should hold and possess them legitimately. And in order that in default of persons to solicit the aforesaid, the Indians may not remain in slavery unjustly, We command that the Audiencias appoint persons who may pursue this cause for the Indians and be paid out of the Exchequer fines, provided they be men of trust and diligence.

Also, We command that with regard to the lading of the said Indians the Audiencias take especial care that they be not laden, or in case that in some parts this cannot be avoided that it be in such a manner that no risk of life, health and preservation of the said Indians may ensue from an immoderate burthen; and that against their own will and without their being paid, in no case be it permitted that they be laden, punishing very severely him who shall act contrary to this. In this there is to be no remission out of respect to any person.

Because report has been made to us that owing to the pearl fisheries not having been conducted in a proper manner deaths of many Indians and Negroes have ensued. We command that no free Indian be taken to the said fishery under pain of death, and that the bishop and the judge who shall be at Veneçuela direct what shall seem to them most fit for the preservation of the slaves working in the said fishery, both Indians and Negroes, and that the deaths may cease. If, however, it should appear to them that the risk of death cannot be avoided by the said Indians and Negroes, let the fishery of the said pearls cease, since we value much more highly (as is right) the preservation of their lives than the gain which may come to us from the pearls.

Whereas in consequence of the allotments of Indians made to the Viceroys, Governors, and their lieutenants, to our officials, and prelates, monasteries, hospitals, houses of religion and mints, offices of our Hazienda and treasury thereof, and other persons favoured by reason of their offices, disorders have occurred in the treatment of the said Indians, it is our will, and we command that forthwith there be placed under our Royal Crown all the Indians whom they hold and possess by any title and cause whatever, whoever the said parties are, or may be, whether Viceroys, Governors, or their lieutenants, of any of our officers, as well of Justice as of our Hazienda, prelates, houses of religion, or of our Hazienda, hospitals confraternities, or other similar institutions, although the Indians may not have been allotted to them by reason of the said offices; and although such functionaries or governors may say that they wish to resign the offices or governments and keep the Indians, let this not avail them nor be an excuse for them not to fulfill what we command.

Moreover, We command that from all those persons who hold Indians without proper title, having entered into possession of them by their own authority, such

Indians be taken away and be placed under our Royal Crown.

And because we are informed that other persons, although possessing a sufficient title, have had an excessive number of Indians allotted to them, We order that the Audiencias, each in its jurisdiction diligently inform themselves of this, and with all speed, and reduce the allotments made to the said persons to a fair and moderate quantity, and then place the rest under our Royal Crown notwithstanding any appeal or application which may be interposed by such persons: and send us a report with all speed of what the said Audiencias have thus done, that we may know how our command is fulfilled. And in New Spain let it be especially provided as to the Indians held by Joan Infante, Diego de Ordas, the Maestro Roa, Francisco Vasquez de Coronado, Francisco Maldonado, Bernardino Vazquez de Tapia, Joan Xaramillo, Martin Vazquez, Gil Gonçales de Venavides, and many other persons who are said to hold Indians in very excessive quantity, according to the report made to us. And, whereas we are informed that there are some persons in the said New Spain who are of the original Conquistadores and have no repartimiento of Indians, We ordain that the President and Auditors of the said New Spain do inform themselves if there be any persons of this kind, and if any, to give them out of tribute which the Indians thus taken away have to pay, what to them may seem fit for the moderate support and honourable maintenance of the said original Conquistadores who had no Indians allotted to them.

So also, the said Audiencias are to inform themselves how the Indians have been treated by the persons who have held them in encomienda, and if it be clear that in justice they ought to be deprived of the said Indians for their excesses and the ill-usage to which they have subjected them, We ordain that they take away and place such Indians under our Royal Crown. And in Peru, besides the aforesaid, let the Viceroy and Audiencia inform themselves of the excesses committed during the occurrences between Governors Pizarro and Almagro in order to report to us thereon, and from the principal persons whom they find notoriously blameable in those feuds they then take away the Indians they have, and place them under our Royal Crown.

Moreover, We ordain and command that from henceforward no Viceroy, Governor, Audiencia, discoverer, or any other person have power to allot Indians in encomienda by new provision, or by means of resignation, donation, sale, or any other form or manner, neither by vacancy nor inheritance, but that the person dying who held the said Indians, they revert to our Royal Crown. And let the Audiencias take care to inform themselves then particularly of the person who died, of his quality, his merits and services, of how he treated the said Indians whom he held, if he left wife and children or what other heirs, and send us a report thereof with the condition of the Indians and of the land, in order that we may give directions to provide what may be best for our service, and may do such favour as may seem suitable to the wife and children of the defunct. If in the meantime it should appear to the Audiencia that there is a necessity to provide some support for such wife and children, they can do it out of the tribute which the said Indians will have to pay, or allowing them a moderate pension, if the said Indians are under our Crown, as aforesaid.

Item, We ordain and command that our said Presidents and Auditors take great care that the Indians who in any of the ways above mentioned are taken away, and those who may become vacant be very well treated and instructed in the matters of our holy Catholic faith, and as our free vassals. This is to be their chief care, that on which we principally desire them to report, and in which they can best serve us. They are also to provide that they be governed with justice in the way and manner that the Indians who are under our Royal Crown are at present governed in New Spain. . . .

5. Royal Ordinances on "Pacification," 1573

The most important doctrinal discussion occurred in 1550–51 in Valladolid, where Bartolomé de Las Casas bitterly opposed the proposal of Juan Ginés de Sepúlveda before a royal commission that Indians be considered "natural slaves" of Spaniards in accordance with the theory elaborated centuries before by Aristotle. Apparently no formal decision was handed down by the commission, but probably the standard law of 1573 on new discoveries was drawn up in such generous terms because of the battle Las Casas fought at Valladolid.

All regulations made for conquistadors since the Requirement was approved in 1513 were superseded by a general ordinance promulgated by Philip II on July 13, 1573, which was designed to regulate all future discoveries and pacifications by land or by sea. A detailed study of its provisions will show how far the king had departed from the Requirement policy. This general order governed conquests as long as Spain ruled her American colonies, even though some Spaniards could always be found who thought that the Indians could be subjugated by force of arms because of their infidelity.

. . . Discoveries are not to be called conquests. Since we wish them to be carried out peacefully and charitably, we do not want the use of the term "conquest" to offer any excuse for the employment of force or the causing of injury to the Indians. . . .

After a town has been laid out and its buildings constructed, but not before, the government and settlers are to attempt peacefully to win all the natives of the region over to the Holy Church and obedience to our rule. In this they are to show great diligence and holy zeal and to use the best means at their disposal, including the following:

They are to gather information about the various tribes, languages, and divisions of the Indians in the province and about the lords whom they obey. They are to seek friendship with them through trade and barter, showing them great love and tenderness and giving them objects to which they will take a liking. Without displaying any greed for the possessions of the Indians, they are to establish friendship and cooperation with the lords and nobles who seem most likely to be of assistance in

From "Ordenanzas de Su Magestad para los nuevos descubrimientos, conquistas y pacificaciones.—Julio de 1573," *Colección de documentos inéditos relativos al descubrimiento, conquista y organización de las antiguas posesiones españolas de América y Oceanía, sacados de los archivos del reino y muy especialmente del de Indias* (Madrid, 1864–1884), vol. 16, pp. 142–87, passim.

the pacification of the land.

Once peace and amity with the Indians have been assured, the Spaniards will try to bring them together in one spot. Then the preachers, with as much solemnity as possible, will start to teach our Holy Faith to those who wish to be instructed in it, using prudence and discretion and the gentlest methods possible. Accordingly, they are not to begin by rebuking the Indians for their vices and idolatry, nor by taking away their women and idols, so that they will not be shocked and form an aversion to Christian doctrine. Instead, it should be taught to them first, and after they have been instructed in it, they should be persuaded to give up of their own free will those things that are contrary to our Holy Catholic Faith and evangelical doctrine.

The Indians should be brought to an understanding of the position and authority which God has given us and of our zeal in serving Him by bringing to His Holy Catholic Faith all the natives of the Western Indies. They should also learn of the fleets and armies that we have sent and still send for this purpose, as well as of the many provinces and nations that have rendered us obedience and of the many benefits which they have received and are receiving as a result, especially that we have sent ecclesiastics who have taught them the Christian doctrine and faith by which they could be saved. Moreover, we have established justice in such a way that no one may aggravate another. We have maintained the peace so that there are no killings, or sacrifices, as was the custom in some parts. We have made it possible for the Indians to go safely by all roads and to peacefully carry on their civil pursuits. We have taught them good habits and the custom of wearing clothes and shoes. We have freed them from burdens and servitude; we have made known to them the use of bread, wine, oil, and many other foods, woollen cloth, silk, linen, horses, cows, tools, arms, and many other things from Spain; we have instructed them in crafts by which they live excellently. All these advantages will those Indians enjoy who embrace our Holy Faith and render obedience to us.

Even if the Indians are willing to receive the faith and the preachers in peace, the latter are to approach their villages with prudence and with precautions for their own safety. In this manner if the Indians should prove unruly, they will not be inclined to show disrespect to the preachers; otherwise, the guilty persons would have to be punished, causing great damage to the work of pacification and conversion. Although the preachers should keep this in mind when they visit the Indian settlements, it should be concealed form the natives so that they will not feel any anxiety. Difficulties may be avoided if the children of the caciques and nobles are brought to the Spanish settlements and are kept there as hostages under the pretext of entertaining them and teaching them to wear cloths. By means such as these is conversion to be undertaken in all the Indian communities which wish to receive the preachers in peace.

In areas where the Indians refuse to accept Christian doctrine peacefully, the following procedure may be used. An arrangement should be made with the principal lord who is a proponent of peace so that he will invite the belligerent Indians to his territory on one pretext or another. On this occasion the preachers, together with some Spaniards and friendly Indians should be hidden nearby. At the opportune moment they should disclose themselves and begin teaching the faith with the aid of interpreters. In order that the Indians may hear the faith with greater awe and reverence, the preachers should carry the Cross in their hands and should be wearing at least albs or stoles; the Christians are also to be told to listen to the preaching with great respect and veneration, so that by their example the non-believers will be induced to accept instruction. If it seems advisable, the preachers may attract the attention of the non-believers by using music and singers, thereby encouraging them to join in. If the Indians seem inclined to be peaceful and request the preachers to go to their territory, the latter should do so, taking the precautions previously described. They should ask for their children under the pretext of teaching them and keep them as hostages; they should also persuade them to build churches where they can teach so that they may be safer. By these and other means are the Indians to be pacified and indoctrinated, but in no way are they to be harmed, for all we seek is their welfare and their conversion.

Once the region has been pacified and the Indian lords and subjects have tendered us their fealty, the Governor, with their consent, is to distribute the land among the settlers who are to take charge of the natives in their parcels, defending and protecting them and providing them with clerics to teach them Christian doctrine and administer the sacraments. They should also teach them to live in an orderly fashion and fulfill all the obligations of encomenderos as set forth in the clauses dealing with this subject.

The Indians who offer us obedience and are distributed among Spaniards are to be persuaded to acknowledge our sovereignty over the Indies. They are to give us tributes of local produce in moderate amounts, which are to be turned over to their Spanish encomenderos so that the latter may fulfill their obligations, reserving to us the tributes of the principal villages and the seaports, as well as an amount adequate to pay the salaries of our officials. If it appears that the pacification of the natives will be accomplished more easily by temporarily exempting them from tribute payments or by granting them other privileges, this should be done; and whatever is promised should be carried out. . . .

THE VALLADOLID DEBATE

6. *"War Against These Barbarians Can Be Justified"*

JUAN GINÉS DE SEPÚLVEDA

Juan Ginés de Sepúlveda (1490–1573) was a distinguished scholar of the works of the ancient Greek philosopher Aristotle and a master of Latin style. He was also an ardent nationalist who was much impressed by the achievements of his compatriots. In 1547, when the activities of Las Casas were beginning to force the crown to reconsider the methods by which the conquest of America was being carried out, Sepúlveda wrote *Demócrates Alter*, a spirited defense of the settlers in the form of a dialogue in which a man named Demócrates argues with a German Lutheran who initially believes the conquest to be unjust, but is finally convinced that the king of Spain is obliged to wage war against the natives. In this dialogue, Demócrates maintains that war against the Indians was just for four reasons: First, the Indians had committed grave sins by their idolatry and sins against nature. Second, their "natural rudeness and inferiority" corresponded with Aristotle's view that some people were born natural slaves. Third, military conquest was the most efficacious method of converting Indians to Christianity, and finally, conquering Indians made it possible to protect the weak amongst them.

Sepúlveda seems ethnocentric today, but he was a passionate and sincere nationalist, and his position was popular with the colonists. He was also one of the first defenders of modern imperialism. As translator John L. Phelan observes, he "invented a central justification for imperialism (reformulated by Rudyard Kipling as 'taking up the white man's burden') that was to be invoked from the sixteenth to the twentieth centuries." In the passages reprinted below, Sepúlveda applies Aristotle's doctrine of natural slavery to the Indians and strikes a note of ardent Spanish nationalism, at the same time downgrading Indian civilization. He concludes with an explanation of his concept of the "just war."

You should remember that authority and power are not only of one kind but of several varieties, since in one way and with one kind of law the father commands his children, in another the husband commands his wife, in another the master commands his servants, in another the judge commands the citizens, in another the king

From Juan Ginés de Sepúlveda. "Demócrates alter de justis belli causis apud Indios." In *Latin American History: Select Problems,* ed. Frederick B. Pike, trans. John L. Phelan (New York, Harcourt, Brace & Company, 1969), 47–52. Reprinted by permission of the publisher.

commands the peoples and human beings confined to his authority. . . .

And thus we see that among inanimate objects, the more perfect directs and dominates, and the less perfect obeys its command. This principle is even clearer and more obvious among animals, where the mind rules like a mistress and the body submits like a servant. In the same way the rational part of the soul rules and directs the irrational part, which submits and obeys. All of this derives from divine and natural law, both of which demand that the perfect and most powerful rule over the imperfect and the weaker. . . .

The man rules over the woman, the adult over the child, the father over his children. That is to say, the most powerful and most perfect rule over the weakest and most imperfect. This same relationship exists among men, there being some who by nature are masters and others who by nature are slaves. Those who surpass the rest in prudence and intelligence, although not in physical strength, are by nature the masters. On the other hand, those who are dim-witted and mentally lazy, although they may be physically strong enough to fulfill all the necessary tasks, are by nature slaves. It is just and useful that it be this way. We even see it sanctioned in divine law itself, for it is written in the Book of Proverbs: "He who is stupid will serve the wise man." And so it is with the barbarous and inhumane peoples [the Indians] who have no civil life and peaceful customs. It will always be just and in conformity with natural law that such people submit to the rule of more cultured and humane princes and nations. Thanks to their virtues and the practical wisdom of their laws, the latter can destroy barbarism and educate these [inferior] people to a more humane and virtuous life. And if the latter reject such rule, it can be imposed upon them by force of arms. Such a war will be just according to natural law.

One may believe as certain and undeniable, since it is affirmed by the wisest authors, that it is just and natural that prudent, upright, and humane men should rule over those who are not. On this basis the Romans established their legitimate and just rule over many nations, according to St. Augustine in several passages of his work, *The City of God*, which St. Thomas [Aquinas] colleted and cited in his work, *De regimine principum*. Such being the case, you can well understand . . . if you know the customs and nature of the two peoples, that with perfect right the Spaniards rule over these barbarians of the New World and the adjacent islands, who in wisdom, intelligence, virtue, and humanitas are as inferior to the Spaniards as infants to adults and women to men. There is as much difference between them as there is between cruel, wild peoples and the most monstrously intemperate peoples and those who are temperate and moderate in their pleasures, that is to say, between apes and men.

You do not expect me to make a lengthy commemoration of the judgment and talent of the Spaniards. . . . And who can ignore the other virtues of our people, their fortitude, their humanity, their love of justice and religion? I speak only of our princes and those who by their energy and industriousness have shown that they are worthy of administering the commonwealth. I refer in general terms only to those Spaniards who have received a liberal education. If some of them are wicked and unjust, that is no reason to denigrate the glory of their race, which should be judged by the actions of its cultivated and noble men and by its customs and public institutions, rather than by the actions of depraved persons who are similar to slaves. More than any other country, this country [Spain] hates and detests depraved individuals, even those who have certain of the virtues that are common to nearly all classes of our people, like courage and the martial spirit for which the Spanish legions have always provided examples that exceed all human credibility . . . And I would like to emphasize the absence of gluttony and lasciviousness among the Spaniards. Is there any nation in Europe that can compare with Spain in frugality and sobriety? Although recently I have seen the intrusion of luxury at the tables of the great as a result of commerce with foreigners, men of good will condemn this innovation, [and] it is to be hoped that in a short time the pristine and natural frugality of national customs may be restored. . . . How deeply rooted is the Christian religion in the souls of the Spaniards, even among those who live amidst the tumult of battle! I have observed many outstanding examples. The most notable among them, it appears to me, occurred after the sacking of Rome during the papacy of Clement VII [1527]. There was scarcely a single Spaniard among those who died from the plague who did not order all the goods he had stolen from the Roman citizens returned in his last will and testament. Not a single other nation that I know of fulfilled this Christian duty, and there were many more Italians and Germans than Spaniards there. I followed the army and noted everything down scrupulously. . . . And what will I say of the gentleness and humanity of our soldiers, who even in battle, after the attainment of victory, expressed great concern and care in saving the greatest possible number of the conquered, protecting them against the cruelty of their allies [the Germans and Italians]?

Now compare these natural qualities of judgment, talent, magnanimity, temperance, humanity, and religion with those of these pitiful men [the Indians], in whom you will scarcely find any vestiges of humanness. These people possess neither science nor even an alphabet, nor do they preserve any monuments of their history except for some obscure and vague reminiscences depicted in certain paintings, nor do they have written laws, but barbarous institutions and customs. In regard to their virtues, how much restraint or gentleness are you to expect of men who are devoted to all kinds of intemperate acts and abominable lewdness, including the eating of human flesh? And you must realize that prior to the arrival of the Christians, they did not live in that peaceful kingdom of Saturn that the poets imagine, but on the contrary they made war against one another continually and fiercely, with such fury that victory was of no meaning if they did not satiate their monstrous hunger with the flesh of their enemies. . . . These Indians are so cowardly and timid that they could scarcely resist the mere presence of our soldiers. Many times thousands upon thousands of them scattered, fleeing like women before a very few Spaniards, who amounted to fewer than a hundred.

In regard to those [of the Aztec and other Indian civilizations] who inhabit New Spain and the province of Mexico, I have already said that they consider themselves the most civilized people [in the New World]. They boast of their political and social institutions, because they have rationally planned cities and nonhereditary kings who are elected by popular suffrage, and they carry on commerce among themselves in the manner of civilized people. But . . . I dissent from such an opinion. On the contrary, in those same institutions there is proof of the coarseness, barbarism, and innate servility of these men. Natural necessity encourages the building of houses, some rational manner of life, and some sort of commerce. Such an argument merely proves that they are neither bears nor monkeys and that they are not totally irrational. But on the other hand, they have established their commonwealth in such a manner that no one individually owns anything, neither a house nor a field that one may dispose of or leave to his heirs in his will, because everything is controlled by their lords, who are incorrectly called kings. They live more at the mercy of their king's will than of their own. They are the slaves of his will and caprice, and they are not the masters of heir fate. The fact that this condition is not the result of coercion but is voluntary and spontaneous is a certain sign of the servile and base spirit of these barbarians. They had distributed their fields and farms in such a way that one third belonged to the king, another third belonged to the religious cult, and only a third part was reserved for the benefit of everyone; but all of this they did in such a way that they themselves cultivated the royal and religious lands. They lived as servants of the king and at his mercy, paying extremely large tributes. When a father died, all his inheritance, if the king did not decide otherwise, passed in its entirety to the oldest son, with the result that many of the younger sons would either die of starvation or subject themselves to an even more rigorous servitude. They would turn to the petty kings for help and would ask them for a field on the condition that they not only pay feudal tribute but also promise themselves as slave labor when it was necessary And if this kind of servitude and barbaric commonwealth had not been suitable to their temperament and nature, it would have been easy for them to take advantage of the death of a king, since the monarchy was not hereditary, in order to establish a state that was freer and more favorable to their interests. Their failure to do so confirms that they were born for servitude and not for the civil and liberal life. . . . Such are, in short, the character and customs of these barbarous uncultivated, and inhumane little men. We know that they were thus before the coming of the Spaniards. Until now we have not mentioned their impious religion and their abominable sacrifices, in which they worship the Devil as God, to whom they thought of offering no better tribute than human hearts. . . . Interpreting their religion in an ignorant and barbarous manner, they sacrificed human victims by removing the hearts form the chests. They placed these hearts on their abominable altars. With this ritual they believed that they had appeased their gods. They also ate the flesh of the sacrificed men. . . .

How are we to doubt that these people, so uncultivated, so barbarous, and so contaminated with such impiety and lewdness, have not been justly conquered by so excellent, pious, and supremely just a king as Ferdinand the Catholic was and the Emperor Charles now is, the kings of a most humane and excellent nation rich in all varieties of virtue?

War against these barbarians can be justified not only on the basis of their paganism but even more so because of their abominable licentiousness, their prodigious sacrifice of human victims, the extreme harm that they inflicted on innocent persons, their horrible banquets of human flesh, and the impious cult of their idols. Since the evangelical law of the New Testament is more perfect and more gentle than the Mosaic law of the Old Testament (for the latter was a law of fear and the former is a law of grace, gentleness, and clemency), so also [since the birth of Christ] wars are now waged with more mercy and clemency. Their purpose is not so much to punish as to correct evils. What is more appropriate and beneficial for these barbarians than to become subject to the rule of those whose wisdom, virtue, and religion have converted them from barbarians into civilized men (insofar as they are capable of becoming so), from being torpid and licentious to becoming upright and moral, from being impious servants of the Devil to becoming believers in the true God? They have already begun to receive the Christian religion, thanks to the prudent diligence of the Emperor Charles, an excellent and religious prince. They have already been provided with teachers learned in both the sciences and letters and, what is more important, with teachers of religion and good customs.

For numerous and grave reasons these barbarians are obligated to accept the rule of the Spaniards according to natural law. For them it ought to be even more advantageous than for the Spaniards, since virtue humanity, and the true religion are more valuable than gold or silver. And if they refuse our rule, they may be compelled by force of arms to accept it. Such a war will be just according to natural law. . . . Such a war would be far more just than even the war that the Romans waged against all the nations of the world in order to force them to submit to their rule [for the following reasons]. The Christian religion is better and truer than the religion of the Romans. In addition, the genius, wisdom, humanity, fortitude, courage, and virtue of the Spaniards are as superior to those same qualities among those pitiful little men [the Indians] as were those of the Romans vis-à-vis the peoples whom they conquered. And the justice of this war becomes even more evident when you consider that the Sovereign Pontiff, who represents Christ, has authorized it.

7. In Defense of the Indians

BARTOLOMÉ DE LAS CASAS

Like Sepúlveda, Las Casas drew upon an immense store of arguments from the Bible, the writings of the Church fathers, the pagan philosophers, and records of the conquest to prove that Spanish treatment of the Indians was a crime not only against humanity, but also contrary to the Christian faith. At Valladolid he had one great advantage over his opponent, for Sepúlveda had never been to America, while he could draw upon his firsthand experiences and observations of the Indian civilizations. The selections reprinted below are from a treatise Las Casas published in Seville in 1552. They reveal that he did not question the right of the Pope to give Spain authority to preach the gospel to the New World peoples, but he believed that the current method of carrying on the conquest was counter-productive to this goal and that the encomienda "was the most cruel sort of tyranny that can be imagined, and it is most worthy of infernal damnation."

PROPOSITION 1

The Roman Pontiff, canonically chosen vicar of Jesus Christ and successor of St. Peter, has the authority and the power of Christ himself, the Son of God, over all men in the world, believers or infidels, insofar as it is necessary to guide and direct men to the end of the eternal life and to remove any impediments to this goal. Although the Pontiff uses and ought to use such power in a special fashion with the infidels, who have never entered into holy baptism of the holy Church, especially those who never heard tidings of Christ nor of His faith, he uses another kind of authority with Christians and those who at one time were Christian.

PROPOSITION II

St. Peter and his successors had and have a necessary duty by the injunctions of God to adopt measures with the greatest care that the gospel and faith of Jesus Christ may be preached to all men throughout the whole world, and in my opinion it is

From Bartolomé de Las Casas, *Aquí se contienen treinta proposiciones muy jurídicas* (Seville, 1552). In *Latin American History: Select Problems,* ed. Frederick B. Pike, trans. John L. Phelan (New York: Harcourt, Brace & Company, Inc.), pp. 52–57. Reprinted by permission of the publisher.

unlikely that anyone will resist the preaching of the gospel and the Christian doctrine.

PROPOSITION IV

For the conversion of the infidels the Christian kings are very necessary for the Church, with their secular power, armed forces, and temporal wealth, they may help, protect, preserve, and defend the ecclesiastical and spiritual ministers. . . .

PROPOSITION VII

In order to avoid confusion, the vicar of Christ with his divine authority can and has wisely and justly divided the kingdoms and provinces of all the infidels, of whatever infidelity or sect they may be, among the Christian princes, charging and entrusting those princes with the task of spreading the holy faith, the expansion of the universal Church and the Christian religion, and the conversion and health of their souls as the ultimate end.

PROPOSITION VIII

This division, commission, or concession was not made (nor is it made, nor should the Sovereign Pontiff in the future make it) primarily or ultimately to concede grace or to increase the power of the Christian states and to bestow on these princes honor, titles, and riches, but primarily and ultimately for the spread of the divine worship, the glory of God, and the conversion and salvation of the infidels, which is the purpose and final intention of the King of kings and the Master of masters, Jesus Christ. He imposed a most dangerous duty and office upon the Christian princes, about which they will have to give the most meticulous account before divine judgment at the end of their lives. Thus, the said division and grant is more for the well-being and profit of the infidels than of the Christian princes.

PROPOSITION IX

It is a just and worthy thing that the primary reward of Christian kings for the services they render to God and the welfare of the universal Mother Church in their royal persons does not consist in worldly and earthly things—to which kings should not aspire, for they are transitory and of little value—but in co-reigning with Christ in heaven. . . . The Supreme Pontiff may concede and donate to Christian princes compensation in the kingdoms of the infidels in order to fulfill the purpose for which he originally entrusted those kingdoms to them. This is a just thing, which does not notably harm or damage the rights of those kings, princes, and notable individuals among the infidels.

PROPOSITION X

Among the infidels who have distant kingdoms that have never heard the tidings of Christ or received the faith, these are true kings and princes. Their sovereignty, dignity, and royal preeminence derive from natural law and the law of nations. . . . Therefore, with the coming of Jesus Christ to such domains, their honors, royal preeminence, and so on, do not disappear either in fact or in right.

PROPOSITION XI

The opinion contrary to that of the preceding proposition is erroneous and most pernicious. He who persistently defends it will fall into formal heresy. It is likewise most impious and iniquitous and has been the cause of innumerable thefts, violent disturbances, tyrannies, massacres, larcenies, irreparable damage, the gravest sins, infamy, stench, and hatred against the name of Christ and the Christian religion. . . .

PROPOSITION XII

The said infidels, monarchs or subjects, are not deprived of their domains, dignities, or other property by any sin of idolatry or any other sin, regardless of how grave or abominable it may be. . . .

PROPOSITION XIII

Infidels, especially those whose paganism is a simple denial, cannot be punished by any judge in the world for the sin of idolatry or for any other sin they committed during their infidelity, regardless of how enormous, extensive, or abominable such sins may have been, until they voluntarily receive the sacrament of holy Baptism. The only exceptions are those infidels who maliciously obstruct the preaching of the gospel and who refuse to desist after they have been sufficiently warned.

PROPOSITION XIV

The Sovereign Pontiff, Alexander VI, during whose reign the vast new world that we call the West Indies was discovered, had the duty by divine injunction to select a Christian king to whom he could entrust the task of preaching the gospel in those lands. That Christian king was also to have the responsibility of establishing and spreading the divine cult and the universal Church in all the kingdoms of the Indies. . . In compensation for this undertaking the Pope granted him the dignity and the imperial crown of [universal] sovereignty over all the kingdoms of the New World.

PROPOSITION XV

The kings of Castile and León, Ferdinand and Isabella, the Catholic kings, possessed more outstanding virtues than all the other Christian princes. For this reason, the Pope entrusted this task to them rather than to any other Christian prince. . . . among their notable virtues there are two in particular. First, inheriting from their royal ancestors the obligation to reconquer all of the Spanish kingdoms from the grip of tyrannical Muslim enemies of our holy Catholic faith, with their own royal persons and at a heavy expense they reconquered the great kingdom of Granada and at long last restored it to Christ and the universal Church. Secondly, at their own expense and upon their own initiative they sponsored an expedition commanded by the eminent Christopher Columbus, whom they honored and exalted with the title of first Admiral of the Indies, and he discovered the vast and extensive Indies.

PROPOSITION XVI

The Roman Pontiff, vicar of Jesus Christ, whose divine authority extends over all the kingdoms of heaven and earth, could justly invest the kings of Castile and León with the supreme and sovereign empire and dominion over the entire realm of the Indies, making them emperors over many kings. . . . If the vicar of Christ were to see that this was not advantageous for the spiritual well being of Christianity, he could without doubt, by the same divine authority, annul or abolish the office of emperor of the Indies, or he could transfer it to another prince, as one Pope did when he transferred the imperial crown from the Greeks to the Germans [at the coronation of Charlemagne in 800]. With the same authority, the Apostolic See could prohibit, under penalty of excommunication, all other Christian kings from going to the Indies without the permission and authorization of the kings of Castile. If they do the contrary, they sin mortally and incur excommunication.

PROPOSITION XVII

The kings of Castile and León are true princes, sovereign and universal lords and emperors over many kings. The rights over all that great empire and the universal jurisdiction over all the Indies belong to them by the authority, concession, and donation of the said Holy Apostolic See and thus by divine authority. This and no other is the juridical basis upon which all their title is founded and established.

PROPOSITION XIX

All the kings and princes, cities, communities, and towns of those Indies are obliged to recognize the kings of Castile as universal and sovereign lords and emperors in the said manner, after having received by their own free will our holy faith and the sacred baptism. If before baptism they do not wish to accept [the imperial sovereignty of Castile], they cannot be punished by any judge or justice.

PROPOSITION XX

The kings of Castile are obligated by the Apostolic See and also by divine law to procure, to provide, and to send with all diligence qualified ministers to preach the faith everywhere, calling and inviting the people in the Indies to come to the wedding and banquet of Christ. . . .

PROPOSITION XXI

The kings of Castile are obliged by divine law to ensure that the faith of Jesus Christ be preached in the same manner that He, the Son of God, established for His Church. [This method and this method only] was literally and without any change or diminution followed by His apostles, and the universal Church has made it customary law, enshrining it in its decrees and canons. The holy doctors expostulated and glorified it in their books. The gospel should be preached peacefully, with love, charity, sweetness, and affection, with meekness and good example. The infidels, especially the Indians (who by nature are very gentle, humble, and peaceful), should be persuaded by gifts and presents, and nothing should be taken away from them. And thus they will regard the God of the Christians as a good, gentle, and just God. Hence they will want to be His subjects and to receive His Catholic faith and holy doctrine.

PROPOSITION XXII

To conquer them first by war is contrary to the law, gentle yoke, light load, and sweetness of Jesus Christ. It is the same approach that Mohammed and the Romans followed when they disturbed and plundered the world. It is the same manner that the Turks and Moors have adopted today. . . .Therefore it is iniquitous, tyrannical, and infamous to the sweet name of Christ, causing infinite new blasphemies against the true God and against the Christian religion. And we have abundant evidence of the damage that this warlike approach has done and is still doing in the Indies. Since the Indians regard our God as the most cruel, unjust, and pitiless god of all, the conversion of the Indians has been hindered, and it has become impossible to convert infinite numbers of infidels. . . .

PROPOSITION XXV

The kings of Castile has prohibited wars against the Indians of the Indies from the time that the First Admiral [Columbus] discovered them, but the Spaniards never honored, observed, or fulfilled these orders and instructions that the kings issued. . . .

PROPOSITION XXVI

Since our kings never sanctioned just wars against the innocent Indians . . . we affirm that all such wars that have taken place in the Indies since their discovery have been, are, and will be unjust, iniquitous, and tyrannical. . . .

PROPOSITION XXVII

The kings of Castile are obliged by divine law to establish a government and administration over the native peoples of the Indies that will preserve their just laws and good customs and abolish the evil ones, which are very few. . . . Whatever defects their society may have had can be removed and corrected with the preaching and the spread of the gospel. . . .

PROPOSITION XXVIII

The Devil could invent no worse pestilence to destroy all that world and to kill all the people there . . . than the *repartimiento* and *encomienda*, the institution used to distribute and entrust Indians to the Spaniards.[1] This was like entrusting the Indians to a gang of devils or delivering herds of cattle to hungry wolves. The encomienda or repartimiento was the most cruel sort of tyranny that can be imagined, and it is most worthy of infernal damnation. The Indians were prevented from receiving the Christian faith and religion. The wretched and tyrannical Spanish encomenderos worked the Indians night and day in the mines and in other personal services. They colleted unbelievable tributes. The encomenderos forced the Indians to carry burdens on their backs for one hundred and two hundred leagues, as if they were less than beasts. They persecuted and expelled from the Indian villages the preachers of the faith. . . . And I solemnly affirm as God is my witness, that so long as these encomiendas remain, all the authority of the kings, even if they were resident in the Indies, will not be enough to prevent all the Indians from perishing.

1. [The encomienda was an institution in which the Crown distributed the Indian population among the Spanish colonists, who in turn collected a yearly tribute from the Indians assigned to them. Although the individual *encomienderos* were obligated to provide protection to their Indian wards, the system was subject to many abuses. Repartimiento refers to the actual distribution of the Indians among the encomenderos.]

INTERPRETATIONS

8. Spanish Exploitation of Indians in Central Mexico

CHARLES GIBSON

Every student of Latin American history must at some time tackle the problem of how to handle the Black Legend of Spanish cruelty and oppression in America. The literature on the subject is enormous, and the emotions involved are sometimes considerable. Here we see how one of the veteran scholars in the field judged Spain's work in Mexico. Professor Gibson's meticulous research, published in *The Aztecs under Spanish Rule*, gave him an excellent background for the task.

The Black Legend provides a gross but essentially accurate interpretation of relations between Spaniards and Indians. The Legend builds upon the record of deliberate sadism. It flourishes in an atmosphere of indignation, which removes the issue from the category of objective understanding. It is insufficient in its awareness of the institutions of colonial history. But the substantive content of the Black Legend asserts that Indians were exploited by Spaniards, and in empirical fact they were.

We have not commented in detail on the conquest itself, a separate subject, already much studied. The conquest has a bearing here not for its military events but for its consequences, and the over-all consequence of conquest was the condition of Spanish domination and Indian subjugation. Aztec peoples could not confront Spaniards as a unified nation, with diplomacy and negotiation. Conquest destroyed Aztec nationalism and fixed adjustments at a local level. Nearly everything that could be called imperial in Aztec affairs came to an end. If Aztec society be thought of as a graduated complex of progressively more inclusive units, from the family and calpulli at one end to the total empire at the other, it becomes evident that con-

Reprinted from *The Aztecs under Spanish Rule: A History of the Indians of the Valley of Mexico, 1519–1810* by Charles Gibson pp. 403–09 with the permission of the publishers, Stanford University Press. © 1964 by the Board of Trustees of the Leland Stanford Junior University.

quest eliminated all the more comprehensive structures while it permitted the local and less comprehensive ones to survive.

The demarcation or cut-off point was the jurisdiction of the tlatoani. This became the cabecera, the essential unit of the early colonial period, on which encomienda, the missionary church, cacicazgo, and tribute and labor exactions directly depended. The cabecera won out over alternative organizing principles of greater or lesser range. One may suppose that this followed in part from the role of the tlatoani in Indian society, a role than was repeatedly affirmed in the events of pre-conquest history. But it was the consequence also of relations between Spaniards and Indians. Conceivably a differently ordered Spanish rule might have made the tribe rather than the cabecera the essential colonial unit. An opposite type of Spanish power might have settled on the calpulli. We can glimpse some such alternative forces at work in the various readjustments and modifications made upon the standard cabecera, as when repartimiento reinvoked the tribal groups or when nontlatoani towns were granted in encomienda and allowed to become cabeceras.

The most evident changes in Indian society occurred during the first forty or fifty years. This was the time when Indian peoples, or some of them, met the Spanish influence part way and reached positive degrees of cultural accord. The mid-sixteenth century has a special interest in the history of humanistic tutelage, with the community of Santa Fe, the Gante school, and above all the Colegio of Santa Cruz in Tlatelolco. One can speak here of a cultural florescence for upper-class Indians, and we may cite again the remarkable Badianus Herbal, a systematic catalogue of plants, classified in a European tradition, painted in an Indian style, its glosses written in Nahuatl by one learned native commentator and translated into Latin by another. The herbal was composed in 1552, and it seemed to give promise, thirty years after the conquest, of a combined culture, with enduring Indian values enriched by a European admixture.

The total possible range of Indian reaction at this time was relatively extensive. Because two complicated societies were intermeshing, opportunities for new combinations continually arose. It is in the sixteenth century that we find the most diverse individual incidents and the most unsettled conditions in both societies. But the long-term tendencies were toward the solutions of the seventeenth and eighteenth centuries, and the scope of Indian response became more limited. As the Indian population was reduced in size, Spanish controls became fixed and the traditional leaders lost power. Colonial law only partially reacted to what occurred, and local customs acquired a greater force than law. After the sixteenth century few individuals stand out in either society, and the history becomes one of localized groups. The seventeenth and eighteenth centuries have a peculiarly leaderless quality, as if all alternative solutions had been discarded.

Neither society was at first unified in its response to the conditions proffered by the other. Indians were at first divided between the upper class and the maceguales. Both lines of division tended to disappear. But the geographical divisions in Indian society remained. The patterns of subordination, however, uniform in their abstract characteristics, were locally bounded. Cabecera jurisdictions, encomiendas, and haciendas were discrete manifestations of localism effectively preventing a consolidation of Indian interests. All native conduct was so confined. No two towns were ever capable of uniting in organized resistance. The common qualities of Indian towns were insufficient bases for concerted action.

In Spanish society friars and encomenderos were the main conflicting parties of the early period. The friars, almost alone among Spaniards, were guided by principles of Christian humanitarianism. It could be argued that even they exploited native peoples in their coercive indoctrination and their extirpation of pagan practices. Yet their effort as a whole may be distinguished from that of other Spaniards. What happened was that the spiritual component of Hispanic imperialism disappeared or concentrated its energies elsewhere. Its effect for Indians was confined to the early period. The church ceased to be active in Indian defense as ecclesiastics adopted the methods and attitudes of civilian colonists. Churchmen could oppose encomienda in part because they were prohibited from becoming encomenderos, but ecclesiastical condemnation of latfundium would have meant condemnation of an institution that was essential to ecclesiastical wealth and power. There were many other divisions, of course, within Spanish society, but none of them bore directly upon Indian life or livelihood. Thus the creoles despised the peninsulares, but the issue between them was not native welfare, and in some degree what they were disputing over was Indian spoils.

Tribute, labor, and land were the most clearly defined categories of Spanish demand. The three were differentiated in the colonial period, and the legal instruments were different in each case. Tribute and labor were state-controlled after the mid-sixteenth century, and their consequences for Indian society, however, serious, were less severe than in the case of land. Tribute and labor were periodically adjusted to population changes, and the extreme Spanish requirements were confined to the earliest times. Moreover, tribute and labor were already familiar types of pre-conquest exaction, and the degree of change between the one period and the other has often been overstated by critics of the Spanish regime.

Spanish usurpation of land has received less attention, probably because it followed the conquest by some years and did not occupy a major position among the Las Casas accusations. It occurred gradually, through many individual events over a long period, and phenomena that take place in this way lack the dramatic appeal of cataclysms like conquest. So deficient is the Black Legend with regard to land that until recently historians were interpreting hacienda as a direct outgrowth of encomienda. Only in our own time has this fundamental error been corrected, most effectively through the work of Silvio Zavala.

It is often said, with an implication of significance, that the lands of America were the property of the crown of Castile. But the point is at best legalistic, and for Indian history it is immaterial. The crown played an insignificant role either in fostering or in inhibiting latifundia. Legal possession of land by the crown did not mean that land usurpation, too, was a state-controlled enterprise. It was private and frequently illegal, though the state came to tolerate it and to profit from it through the devices of denuncia and composición. That it did not occur immediately is probably less the result of legal restriction than of sheer numbers of Indian people and the universality of Indian occupation of land. A prerequisite was available land, and this was not present when the Spaniards first came. Encomienda was therefore an appropriate institution for the early years But with Indian depopulation, land became accessible, and when it became accessible, it was usurped.

One consequence of the historical concern with selected Black Legend themes is a weakness in our knowledge of hacienda history. The sections of this book that deal with hacienda make some contribution to the subject, but they suffer from inadequate information and lack a secure conceptual frame. Hacienda, perhaps more than any other single colonial topic, still needs systematic investigation, not alone in the Valley of Mexico but in all areas. We cannot now confidently compare our documented examples of Valley of Mexico hacienda with the institution in other regions, and until we can the Valley conditions will remain imperfectly defined. . . . My own feeling is that the hacienda is a crucial institution, that for various reasons its study has been slighted, and that we would be well advised to make a concerted effort toward solving the historical problems that it raises.

With respect to land there can be no doubt that the hacienda came to be the dominant mode of control. In the tempo of its history it contrasts with tribute and labor. The extreme Spanish demands for tribute and labor occurred early, before much land was transferred to Spanish possession. This transfer, on the other hand, took place on a large scale only in the late sixteenth century and after, when private exploitation of tribute and labor had already been brought under state control. In a sense, land represented a new avenue of exploitation for Spaniards, after other avenues were blocked. But the hacienda combined its essential control of land with secondary controls over labor and tribute, and the result was the most comprehensive institution yet devised for Spanish mastery and Indian subordination. If there appeared, as we have thought, some benign features of hacienda, these are explicable in terms of the total matrix within which hacienda developed. Human character tends toward benevolence as well as toward cruelty, and the hacienda could afford certain kinds of benevolence that would have been incongruous with the harsher, more superficial, less subtle coercions of encomienda. Thus the hacendado could appear as the protector and advocate of his Indians against outside pressures. The encomendero was intended by law to play this same role, but he never did.

That land was important to Indians is obvious. Some of the most intimate and revealing documents of all Indian history are the native títulos for community land possession, The títulos were an Indian response to Spanish usurpation and Spanish legalism. Their purpose was to integrate community opposition against alienation. They speak only sparingly, or not at all, of conquest, tribute, and labor. They see the essential threat to community existence where in fact it lay, in Spanish seizures of land.

There had been seizures of land before the conquest, as in the "lands of Montezuma," but these had been accommodated within Indian practices of land disposition. The difference is one of degree. Moreover, the pre-conquest period, so far as we know, offers no comparable situation of population change. When Indian society seemed headed for extinction, in the late sixteenth and early seventeenth centuries, its practical need for land likewise diminished, and Indian gobernadores and others became the accomplices of Spaniards in the transfer of titles. When the population began to increase in the late seventeenth and eighteenth centuries the need for land correspondingly increased. But by then it was too late. Land transfer was cumulative in a way that tribute and labor exactions were not. Every increase in Indian population in the late colonial period meant an additional number that could not be incorporated in the traditional calpulli tenure, or could be incorporated only with a corresponding strain on other community institutions. The available land was hacienda land, and the new population could not be incorporated within colonial society only through the mediation of hacienda. When the hacendado authorized the towns to rent some of his lands or gave permission to individuals to occupy huts on the hacienda properties, both the hacendado and the Indian beneficiaries could regard the act as one of benevolence. All surrounding conditions were accepted as normal. An aristocracy had been created through innumerable acts over generations of time. Even if there had been an inclination to assign blame, there was no one to accuse, for no one was responsible. The institution and the ethos of the institution dominated all its members. A conquistador who killed or an encomendero who overcharged could be convincingly criticized on moral grounds, but similar criticism appeared excessive when turned against the hacendado, who had inherited most of his lands and played a paternalistic role in a society he had not created. . . .

The Indian community was further beset by a series of demands not comprehended in the three classifications of tribute, labor, and land. Most of these were designed to extract from its economy the increment remaining beyond minimum subsistence. Ecclesiastical fees fall in this category, as do the forced sales in corregimiento and the usurpations of produce. The political officials' handbook of 1777 openly declared the corregimiento of Chalco to be worth thirty times the corregidor's salary, a statement that suggests the extent of precedented extra-legal exploitation by officials appointed to uphold the law.

Variations occurred from area to area in the timing and intensity of these processes. Tacuba was an early victim. Xaltocan prospered for a time and yielded in the seventeenth century. Tepetlaoztoc made a late recovery based not on land but on a pack-train commerce. Chalco province attracted powerful hacendados and became an area of extreme land pressures. By contrast, Xochimilco lacked the kind of land that attracted haciendados and by a coincidence of circumstances maintained its craft economy and chinampa agriculture throughout the colonial period. Tenochtitlan and Tlatelolco, which lacked land from the start, remained virtually immune from the struggle against the hacienda. But Tenochtitlan made a more viable economic adjustment than Tlatelolco, which suffered progressively from drought, emigration, and neglect.

What we have studied is the deterioration of a native empire and civilization. The empire collapsed first, and the civilization was fragmented in individual communities. Some creativity appeared in the early stages of change, but the process as a whole could not be called a creative one for Indians. The community proved to be the largest Indian social unit capable of survival, and it survived in spite of manifold and severe stresses. The cofradía and the fiesta were enlisted to support it. Indians in general yielded to Spanish demands, protesting only in rare instances of community resistance. The civilization became infused with Hispanic traits at many points, but it retained an essential Indian character, partly through the conviction of its members, partly because it was depressed to a social status so low that it was given no opportunities for change. One of the earliest and most persistent individual responses was drink. If our sources may be believed, few people in the whole of history were more prone to drunkenness than the Indians of the Spanish colony.

9. The Dawn of Conscience in America

LEWIS HANKE

Generalizations are often dangerous because it is almost always difficult or even impossible to summarize in a few words a complicated historical event. Yet most of us concerned with the history of Spain in America sometimes indulge in generalizations, as they stimulate us to think about our work in large terms. Lewis Hanke's research on the career and writings of Las Casas helped to show that the Dominican friar was "not the lonely apostle waging a solitary struggle in defense of the Indian" portrayed by the traditional accounts, but the principal spokesman and ideologist of a reformist Spanish movement that sought to prevent "the destruction of the Indies."* Here are some of his "generalizations" that contributed to the twentieth-century revisionist school of U.S. writing on colonial Latin America.

The image many English-speaking people have of Spanish action in America is one of almost unrelieved cruelty to the Indians, and many unfavorable judgments have been made on Spanish action in the New World in comparison with English colonization. Spaniards naturally resented these judgments, and a "war of the myths" has resulted. One myth makes the Spaniards the heroes, the English the villains, and the Indians the victims and the opposing myth makes the Spaniards into villains, the English into heroes, but still casts the Indians in the role of victims. My aim is to present some relatively little known aspects of Spanish-Indian relations, not to present a well-rounded comparison of European colonial practices, and certainly not to engage into the war of the myths.

All European explorers and colonists who came to the New World encountered native peoples. But only the Spaniards met so many millions of natives, whom they called Indians, in the vast stretches of their empire which eventually reached from California to Patagonia. The very fact of large numbers of natives settled under the

---

*Benjamin Keen, "Obituary, Lewis Hanke (1905–1993)," *Hispanic American Historical Review* 73:4 (Nov. 1993): 663.

From "The Dawn of Conscience in America: Spanish Experiments and Experiences with Indians in the New World" by Lewis Hanke, *Proceedings of the American Philosophical Society* 107, no. 2 (April 1963): 83–92, passim. Reprinted by permission of the American Philosophical Society.

control of the Aztec, Inca, and Maya empires required the Spaniards to devise a different method of treating them from that worked out by the English, French, and Portuguese for the largely nomadic and much smaller number of natives they found sparsely scattered in their territories. . .

In the effort to govern the mass of Indians in their great empire the Spaniards adapted some institutions form their own medieval experience of long fighting against the Moslems and created others to meet the needs of New World conditions. The determination of the Crown and the Church to Christianize the Indians, the imperious demand of Spaniards for labor forces to exploit the new lands for revenues for the Crown and for themselves, and the attempts of some Spaniards to protect the Indians resulted in a very remarkable complex of relations, laws, and institutions which even today leads historians to contradictory conclusions on the reality of Spanish rule in America. The encomienda system, by which groups of Indians were assigned to Spaniards, a device to provide both labor and goods to the Spaniard and protection and religious instruction for the Indians, was both stoutly defended as necessary and bitterly attacked as un-Christian throughout the sixteenth century by Spaniards themselves. The Spanish imperial policy of attempting to civilize the Indians by organizing them led to many curious experiments and experiences, and in the end was fatal for large numbers of natives. George Kubler has pointed out in his substantial work on Mexican architecture:

> No building could be achieved without the prior urbanization of the participants. To urbanize the Indian populations was to dislocate and destroy the patterns of indigenous culture. Such cultural extirpation brought about, in turn, the biological decrease of the Indian race. . . . Each building, and each colonial artifact, was nourished by the destruction of a culture and the decline of a race.

Spain made many efforts to mitigate the lot of the Indians by appointing official "Protectors," setting up special courts to try cases involving them, and sending out numerous investigating groups to discover what might be done to help them. She tried many stratagems in the sixteenth century particularly to ensure that Indians would be brought under Spanish rule by peaceful means alone, and be persuaded to accept Christianity by reason instead of by force. To achieve this end the Dominican Bartolomé de Las Casas and his brother Dominicans attempted to preach the faith without the backing of the sword in Chiapas, and Vasco de Quiroga established his Utopian communities in Michoacan. In many places a system of Indian segregation was worked out by friars and royal officials to protect them from other Spaniards who would exploit them, and this practice was followed throughout the colonial period, culminating in the famous Jesuit missions in eighteenth-century Paraguay.

The difficult, indeed impossible, double purpose of the Crown to secure revenue and also to Christianize the Indians inevitably led in fact to a series of angry disputes, evil compromises, and some glorious episodes throughout the more than three centuries of Spanish rule in America.

Today, in looking back on the total encounter of Spaniards and Indians, two developments hold special interest for us, living as we do in a world society whose multiplicity and variety of cultures become daily more evident and more significant. For the first time in history one people—Spaniards—paid serious attention to the nature of the culture of the peoples they met; and, perhaps most striking of all, the controversies which developed in sixteenth-century Spain and America over the just method of treating the Indians led to a fundamental consideration of the nature of man himself. This "dawn of conscience in America" was only a faint daybreak; indeed, who can say that in the twentieth century we have reached high noon? The fact that we are still struggling ourselves to discover how to live justly in a world of many races and many cultures give the Spanish struggles of the sixteenth century a poignant and familiar ring. . . .

It was the friars, looking for souls to win, rather than the conquistadores, who first began to study Indian customs, history, and religion. The missionaries needed to know the names and attributes of Indian gods, the sacrifices made to them, and as accurately as possible the mentality of the Indians in order to lead them away from their pagan rites toward Christianity. The founder of American anthropology was Friar Ramón Pané, who accompanied Columbus on his second voyage for the express purpose of observing the natives and reporting on their ways and who was the first European to learn an Indian language.

The Crown encouraged ecclesiastics throughout the sixteenth century to study the Indians, and numerous volumes on their cultures were in fact prepared. Administration officials such as Alonso de Zurita also compiled reports, and the questionnaires sent out regularly to all Spanish governors in the New World by the Council of the Indies included a number of items on Indians. The result of all this enquiry is a magnificent body of linguistic, archaeological, and ethnographical material which is both contradictory are times and difficult to assess because so much remains in manuscript and even the printed editions available are often poor, lacking indexes and proper notes. . . .

Closely linked with these anthropological studies and with Spain's struggle to work out a just Indian policy was the much disputed question of the nature of the Indians. The first twinge of official conscience was expressed by Ferdinand and Isabella in 1495 when they learned that a shipload of Indians Columbus had sent back from Hispaniola had been sold as slaves because they had been taken in rebellion. The monarchs thereupon instructed Bishop Fonseca, who managed Indian affairs, that the money from this sale should not be accepted until their Highnesses could inform themselves from men learned in law whether these Indians could be sold with good conscience. No document that I know of has recorded the answer the sovereigns requested. A dramatic public protest in America against Indian slavery was made by a Dominican friar named Antonio de Montesinos, who in a revolutionary sermon preached in 1511 on the island of Hispaniola thundered:

> Tell me, by what right or justice do you keep these Indians in cruel servitude? On what authority have you waged a detestable war against these people, who dwelt quietly and peacefully on their own land? . . . Are these not men? Have they not rational souls?

This sermon led to serious disputes and discussions in Spain, out of which came the 1512 Laws of Burgos to govern relations between Spaniards and Indians as well as juridical treatises on the basis for Spanish dominion in the New World.

The legalistic and religious nature of the Spaniards led both to their intense preoccupation with the just basis for their newly discovered overseas territory and with the nature of the Indians whom they were attempting to draw into the Christian world. Francisco de Vitoria, a Dominican professor at the University of Salamanca, discussed these matters with great vision and clarity in his lectures and many of his students later went to America with their attitudes determined by his teachings. Vitoria remarked in one treatise, *De Indis:* "The Indians are stupid only because they are uneducated and, if they live like beasts, so for the same reason do many Spanish peasants." He also asserted that discovery alone gave Spaniards no more right to American territory than the Indians would have acquired had they "discovered" Spain. Vitoria and other Spanish political theorists of the time addressed themselves to the fundamental legal questions raised when Europe invaded America and, long before Grotius, laid down an enduring basis for international law.

Most significant of all, the Spanish inquiry into the nature of the Indians and their capacity for entering into the Christian commonwealth led Spaniards to grapple with that ultimate problem—the nature of man himself. Of all the ideas churned up during the early tumultuous years of American history, none had more dramatic implications than the attempts made to apply to the natives there the Aristotelian doctrine of natural slavery: that one part of mankind is set aside by nature to be slaves in the service of masters born for a life of virtue free of manual labor. Learned authorities such as the Spanish scholar Sepúlveda not only sustained this view with great tenacity and erudition but also concluded, without having visited America, that the Indians were in fact such rude and brutal beings that war against them to make possible their forcible Christianization was not only expedient but lawful. Many ecclesiastics, especially Las Casas, opposed this idea scornfully, with appeals to divine and natural laws as well as to their own experience in America. The controversy became so heated and the emperor's conscience so troubled over the question of how to carry on the conquest of the Indies in a Christian way that Charles V actually ordered the suspension of all expeditions to America while a junta of foremost theologians, jurists, and officials was convoked in the royal capital of Valladolid to listen to the arguments of Las Casas and Sepúlveda. All this occurred in 1550, after Cortez had conquered Mexico, Francisco Pizarro had shattered the Inca empire, and many other lesser-known captains had carried the Spanish banners to far corners of the New World.

Las Casas and Sepúlveda duly fought their great battle of ideas before the junta in Valladolid. The details of their arguments cannot be indicated here. The foundation on which Las Casas based his argument was that the Indians were truly men capable of becoming Christians. Drawing upon the information he had brought together in his massive anthropological work the *Apologetic History,* he documented his contention that the Indians had many skills and accomplishments and in fact possessed a culture worthy of respect. He cited their agricultural methods as well as their irrigation systems; illustrated their ingenuity by the way they derived twenty-two products from the maguey tree, contrived delicate ornamental collars of fish bones, and created remarkable gold jewelry. He drew special attention to their extraordinary capacity to learn Old World crafts which the Spaniards had brought with them, giving a careful account of the way the Indians made knives and rubber balls. He also described the cleverness of their painters, their feather work, their silver making with few tools, and, after little training, their competence in fashioning musical instruments, their work as carpenters, and their hand lettering so fine that it could sometimes not be distinguished from printing. The only thing he found an Indian could not do as well as a Spaniard was to shoe a horse. He described the Indian mining methods and included an account of their ball games. Above all, however, he claimed, the Indians excelled in the dramatic arts and demonstrated this with various illustrations. He described the military organization of both the Mexican Indians and the Incas of Peru, a topic on which relatively few data are provided by other works, and gave much information on their coca chewing and tobacco smoking, together with an excellent description of the great teeming market in Mexico City.

He devoted many pages to the religion of the Indians, and the most striking aspect of this section is his attitude toward Indian sacrifices. He considered that the most religious peoples were those which offered to God the most magnificent sacrifice, and those who offered human beings had—in his opinion—a very noble concept indeed of their God. The Indian fasts, mortifications of the body, sacrifices of animals and men, were clearly superior to the sacrifices of the ancient peoples. Under the horrible and bloody aspects of these rites Las Casas discerned a commendable spirit of religious devotion which could be directed to higher ends and enlisted in the service of the only true God.

Las Casas was deeply convinced of the importance of education and therefore was particularly impressed by the meticulous attention paid by the Mexican Indians to the education of their children in the ways of chastity, honesty, fortitude, obedience, and sobriety. He cried:

> Did Plato, Socrates, Pythagoras, or even Aristotle leave us better or more natural or more necessary exhortations to the virtuous life then these barbarians delivered to their children? Does the Christian religion teach us more, save the faith and what it teaches us of invisible and supernatural matters? Therefore, no one may deny that these people are fully capable of governing themselves and of living like men of good intelligence and that they are more than others well ordered, sensible, prudent, and rational.

Las Casas believed firmly in the capacity of all people for civilization; he emphatically rejected a static and hopeless barbarism. "All the peoples of the world are men," he insisted, and declared that God would not allow any nation to exist, "no matter how barbarous, fierce, or depraved its customs" which might not be "persuaded and brought to a good order and way of life?" Provided the persuasion was peaceful. To practical conquistadores and administrators, men aiming at immediate worldly goals and faced with different kinds of Indians, and perhaps to the Crown as well, jealous of all royal prerogatives, Las Casas' reiteration that the only justification for the presence of Spaniards in the New World was the Christianization of Indians by peaceful means alone must have seemed dangerous nonsense. One can imagine with what contempt and horror his announcement was received that Spain ought to abandon America, with all its Indians un-Christianized, rather than to bring them into the fold by forcible and—to him—profoundly un-Christian methods. The important fact to us today is that Sepúlveda's doctrine did not triumph at Valladolid in 1550 and that his treatise was not approved for publication until late in the eighteenth century.

Since the Valladolid debate the problem of how to treat peoples unlike ourselves in color, race, religion, or customs has given rise in every century to the most diverse and inflammatory opinions. In general the idea of the inferiority of natives to Europeans appeared in whatever far corners of the world Europeans reached. In the English colonies, for example, only Roger Williams had any respect for Indian culture and small attention was given the theories about Indians.

The battle waged by Las Casas and all the other Spaniards of his opinion to win recognition of the humanity of the Indians and to understand their culture is far from won. But today those who believe that "all the peoples of the world are men" have powerful allies. Anthropologists have gone on record that "the basic principles of opportunity and equality before the law are compatible with all that is known of human biology. All races posses the abilities needed to participate fully in the demo-cratic way of life and in modern technological civilization." The United Nations Universal Declaration of Human Rights, adopted four centuries after the Valladolid controversy, announced: "All human beings are born free and equal in dignity and rights. They are endowed with reason and conscience and should act towards one another in a spirit of brotherhood." The Ecumenical Council, now in session at the Vatican, with members "from every nation under heaven" expressed the thought even more succinctly in its Message to Humanity: "We proclaim that all men are brothers, irrespective of the race or nation to which they belong."

Only a partisan in the "war of the myths" would dare to claim that the ideals announced by the Spanish crown were generally followed in the American territory under Spanish rule. Nor should anyone claim that the Spaniards fully accomplished their purpose; to incorporate the mass of New World Indians into a Christian and a European world.

For we know in the twentieth century that the Spaniards faced impossible prob-lems: the clash of cultures complicated by the great area in which they operated, the tremendous diversity of the Indians encountered, and the small number of Spaniards available for conversion and education of the millions of Indians. One important doctrinal question remains. Why did Negroes never receive the same solicitous attention as Indians, and why did the conscience of Spaniard twinge so much more easily for Indians than for Negroes?

The Jesuit Alonso de Sandoval did indeed write a treatise in the seventeenth cen-tury on the culture of the different tribes of Negroes brought to Cartagena and may therefore be called the first Africanist in America. But neither Sandoval nor his dis-ciple Pedro Claver ever denounced Negro slavery as an un-Christian institution, and the moral conscience of Europe was first roused in modern times by the plight of the Indians of America. The difference between the Spanish attitude toward Indians and Negroes has not yet been satisfactorily explained, and remains an important problem for investigation.

Is it not remarkable enough, however, that some sixteenth-century Spaniards studied Indian cultures and that a whole school of powerful and articulate members of this intensely nationalistic people fought stoutly for the rights of the Indians? During the early years of expansion which eventually carried European ideas and goods to almost every corner of the earth, Spain produced, it is true, an aggressive advocate of Aristotle's doctrine of natural slavery. But she also produced the pow-erful champion of Indians as men, whose voice along with many other Spanish voic-es proclaimed the dawn of conscience in America. No matter how far rockets may reach into outer space, will any more significant problems be discovered than those which agitated many Spaniards during the conquest of America? When the story is told of man's attempts in history to grapple with this most difficult problem—how to relate to other men of unfamiliar cultures—will not this become clear: that when the Spanish Crown and Council of the Indies refrained from stigmatizing the natives of the New World as natural slaves they placed an important milestone on the long road, still under construction, which winds all too slowly toward civilizations which respect the dignity of man, that is to say of all men?

SECTION V

The Introduction of African Slavery in Spanish America

THE INFLUENCE OF AFRICA

Africans were present from the earliest days of the "discovery" of America. Two of the men in Columbus's crew are thought to have been black. Africans accompanied Vasco Núñez de Balboa in Panama and the Pizarro brothers in Peru, and, as Peter Gerhard's study of Juan Garrido reveals, they took part in the conquest of Mexico (Reading 3). But the overwhelming majority of those who arrived in the New World were brought as unwilling migrants from their African homelands to labor in the colonies of Spain, Portugal, England, and France. Philip Curtin, a historian at Johns Hopkins University, has estimated that from 1518, when Charles I granted an *asiento*, or license, to ship slaves from Africa directly to America, until 1850, when the trade was finally abolished, more than 9.6 million men and women had been seized against their will in Africa and transported across the Atlantic. Of this total, approximately 1.5 million went to Spanish America and 3.6 million to Brazil.[1] Black slavery undergirded nearly every economic activity performed in the New World, but as Ann Pescatello points out in the introduction to *The African in Latin America,* along with the tradition of servitude, Africans brought with them "a rich heritage of art and religion, advanced cultural methods, technology and sophisticated political and social organization. . . .The story of black men and women in an alien environment is one of both human endurance and the survival of cultures."[2]

THE ATLANTIC SLAVE TRADE

The Atlantic slave trade persisted for nearly three hundred and fifty years, and

1. Philip D. Curtin, *The Atlantic Slave Trade. A Census* (Madison: University of Wisconsin Press, 1969), p. 268. The British and French Caribbean took in over 3.2 million while 399,000 went to British North America.
2. Ann M. Pescatello, ed., *The African in Latin America* (New York: Alfred A. Knopf, 1975), p. 3.

Spaniards Mistreating their Black Slaves in Peru (Reading 4). Despite humanitarian laws and the efforts of the Catholic Church, slavery in Spanish America was inherently cruel. The caption on this drawing from an early seventeenth century manuscript states, "Consider how the masters mistreat their male and female black slaves and the good slaves bear it with patience for the love of God and they do not give them anything to wear or to eat and do not think about the fact that God made them and died for them as well as the Spanish." The illustration is one of many that accompanied a 1,200 page report sent by an acculturated Peruvian Indian, Felipe Guaman Poma de Ayala, to the King of Spain to expose the abuses of the colonial regime. The complete manuscript, first published in Paris in 1936 under the title Nueva Corónica y buen gobierno, *is one of the most valuable indigenous sources from colonial Peru.*

involved all the great powers in Europe. The Portuguese were the first to sail along the African coast, seeking commerce and a route to Asia, and the papal bull of 1493 ratified by the Treaty of Tordesillas a year later ensured their access to that continent. As a result, the Spanish were purchasers rather than suppliers of slaves. First the Portuguese and later the Dutch, French, and English vied with one another to win the *asiento,* which, along with the exclusive right to transport slaves to the Spanish colonies, offered unparalleled opportunities to smuggle in contraband goods as well. As Reading 1 suggests, the impact of this trade on Africa was far-reaching, and regardless of the nations involved in slave trafficking, the horrors of the Middle Passage were constant: "A classic example of man's inhumanity to man, of commercial transactions based entirely on the estimated value of a pound of flesh."[3]

Why didn't the Spanish clergy denounce African slavery when they so vigorously defended the Indians? For one reason, black slavery already existed in Spain; it was tolerated by the Catholic Church and regulated according to civil law. Secondly, the Indians had owned the New World before the Spanish came, and after the conquest were regarded as vassals of the King; the blacks had no such claim, being citizens of African nations who had been sold into slavery by their own rulers. Thirdly, Spanish humanitarians were moved by the plight of the Indians when their numbers were decimated by epidemic disease, while the blacks who survived the Atlantic voyage seemed stronger, having previously acquired resistance to diseases brought by the whites to America. Finally, since all slaves were baptized in Africa before beginning their journey, the clergy could rationalize their bondage by affirming that no matter how difficult their lives were in the present world, their souls would find salvation in the world that was to come.

Nevertheless, some voices were raised. Las Casas himself, who once recommended African slavery in the hope of saving his beloved Indians, later recanted and declared that it was as unjust to enslave blacks as Indians, "and for the same reasons." Another Dominican, Tomás de Mercado, condemned the West African slave trade in his *Tratos y Contratos* (1569), and a Portuguese Jesuit argued in 1608 that the law against Amerindian slavery should be extended to include blacks; yet nothing changed. The most informed critic was the Spanish Jesuit, Alonso de Sandoval, who denounced the slave trade in his treatise *De instaurande Aethiopum* (Seville, 1627) (Reading 2). As Professor Charles R. Boxer states:

Sandoval, though with obvious reluctance, admitted the validity of Negro slavery under the conditions stipulated by canon and civil law. He also admitted that the Amerindian in his natural state was born free, and consequently

3. Ibid., p. 33.

felt himself to be such, whereas the Negro was used to servitude in his native habitat. Having said this, he then proceeded to denounce the Negro slave-trade even more violently than had Tomás de Mercado. He argued that Negros were just as human as were any of the other races of mankind, although they were more shamefully abused than any, and that in the eyes of God a Negro's soul was worth just as much as that of a white man. Far from finding them bestial and unruly savages, as many slave-owners and dealers claimed that they were, he praises their candid and tractable character, providing his points with a wealth of anecdote from his own experience as rector of the Jesuit college at Cartagena de Indias.

Sandoval denounced the sophistries and abuses of the slave traders, even going so far as to advise that they should be refused the sacraments, if they do not mend their ways. He points out that internecine tribal wars in Africa had greatly increased as a result of the European demand for slaves, and that the slaves obtained in this way could not be regarded as having been taken in a "just war." Contrary to what many modern apologists for the slave system assert, he states emphatically that most slave-owners made no efforts to look after their slaves, or to treat them as valuable property which was difficult to replace; but on the contrary the owners and planters treated their Negroes with callous and calculated brutality, careless, if they died as a result of it.[4]

SLAVERY IN SPANISH AMERICA

Since the publication of Frank Tannenbaum's provocative little book *Slave and Citizen: The Negro in the Americas in 1947,* scholars have hotly debated the character of slavery in Spanish America. The first case studies based on archival sources appeared to support Tannenbaum's thesis that slavery was less harsh in Latin America, because of such factors as medieval Iberian law, which recognized the unnaturalness of slavery, the efforts of the Catholic Church to protect the slave family, and the elaborate body of Spanish law defining the rights of slaves.[5] More recently, historians have tended to reject this interpretation as wishful thinking, by pointing out that the protective legislation was often ignored and that "economic rather than cultural factors determined the specific differences between slave soci-

---

4. Charles R. Boxer, *Salvador de Sá and the Struggle for Brazil and Angola, 1602–1686* (London: Athlone Press, University of London, 1952), pp. 237–38.

5. See for example Herbert Klein, *Slavery in the Americas: A Comparative Study of Virginia and Cuba* (Chicago: University of Chicago Press, 1967); Stanley M. Elkins, *Slavery: A Problem in American Institutional and Intellectual Life* (Chicago: University of Chicago Press, 1959).

eties.["6] One of the most comprehensive investigations into the lives of black slaves in sixteenth-century Peru forms a chapter in James Lockhart's important book, *Spanish Peru 1532–1560: A Colonial Society* (Madison: University of Wisconsin Press, 1968) (Reading 4). Although plantations had yet to be formed in Peru, Lockhart shows that already by the second generation blacks were "an organic part of the enterprise of occupying Peru," and were "in a hundred ways the agents and auxiliaries of the Spaniards."

SLAVE RESISTANCE

African resistance to slavery took many forms. On occasion spontaneous reactions to cruel treatment or excessive work escalated into open rebellion. Slave unrest in Panama by the mid-sixteenth century was so serious that the crown temporarily banned further importation of blacks. In Mexico between 1569 and 1580, slave insurrections covered nearly the entire settled area of the colony outside Mexico City (Reading 5). Venezuela was the scene of two unsuccessful revolts in the eighteenth century; one plot was foiled in 1749 when a conspirator was captured and forced to confess the plans under torture; another rebellion actually broke out in Coro in 1795 but was quickly suppressed. Though greatly feared by slave-owners everywhere, such massive revolts were rare.

A more common method of protest has been called "passive resistance." Slaves routinely pretended to be too stupid to follow orders, broke tools, deliberately killed livestock, and in other ways sought to sabotage the plantations. As Frederick Bowser has commented, in these ways slaves could vent their frustrations "without quite crossing the thin line between perceived indolence and insolence. The former was grudgingly tolerated by the white master as a racial characteristic impossible, or difficult, to correct; but the latter received the tender mercies of the whip or worse."[7]

Perhaps the most successful ploy was simply to run away. Over the centuries, thousands of slaves fled to remote areas beyond the reach of Spanish authorities.

6. Benjamin Keen, *A History of Latin America*, 4th ed. (Boston: Houghton Mifflin, 1992), p. 114. One of the first to reject the Tannenbaum thesis was Marvin Harris, *Patterns of Race in the Americas* (New York: Walker and Company, 1964). Other major works on Spanish American slavery include Colin A. Palmer, *Slaves of the White God, Blacks in Mexico, 1570–1650* (Cambridge: Harvard University Press, 1976); Frederick P. Bowser, *The African Slave in Colonial Peru 1524–1650* (Stanford: Stanford University Press, 1974); and William F. Sharp, *Slavery on the Spanish Frontier: The Colombian Chocó, 1680–1810* (Norman: University of Oklahoma Press, 1976).

7. Frederick P. Bowser, "Africans in Spanish American Colonial Society," *Cambridge History of Latin America*, ed. Leslie Bethell, 7 vols. (Cambridge: Cambridge University Press, 1984–91), 2: 374.

Known as *cimarrones,* or maroons, they formed free communities called *palenques* in Spanish America and *quilombos* in Brazil. An account of Palmares, the largest *quilombo* in Brazil, can be found in Section VI. In Spanish America, one of the most successful *palenques* began in 1570 in Esmeraldas, Ecuador, when a cargo of West African slaves en route from Panama to Peru was wrecked off the northern coast. The newly freed slaves took possession of the wilderness, killing the local Indian men and taking the women as wives. Isolated from Spanish authorities in Quito by high mountains, the *zambo* society flourished, blending Indian and African traits into a unique culture. The population had reached five thousand in 1597 when the *audiencia* decided to negotiate a peace treaty with its leaders, rather than to send an expedition to try to subdue them. In 1599 three *caciques* came to Quito. They agreed to swear allegiance to the Spanish King as long as the Spanish made no attempt to enforce their overlordship, to collect tribute, or to demand labor. The *caciques* did permit Catholic missionaries to enter their region, but the Dominicans never arrived in sufficient numbers to carry out intensive indoctrination. Taking pains not to antagonize the Spaniards, the *palenque* at Esmeraldas preserved its independence into the nineteenth century. Even today the region remains one in which African influence predominates.[8]

8. John L. Phelan, *The Kingdom of Quito* (Madison: Univeristy of Wisconsin Press, 1967), pp. 8–10.

THE ATLANTIC SLAVE TRADE

1. "The Greatest Involuntary Migration in Western History"

ANN M. PESCATELLO

Ann M. Pescatello received her Ph.D. from the University of California, Los Angeles, specializing in social history. As a professor at Florida International University, she was one of the first scholars to publish anthologies on women and blacks in Latin American history. Her book *Female and Male in Latin America* (Pittsburgh: University of Pittsburgh, Press, 1973) is still an important source of information, as is *The African in Latin America* (New York: Knopf, 1975), from which the following selections discussing aspects of the Atlantic slave trade have been taken.

AN AFRICAN HERITAGE

Early African history is the record of small groups of state-forming conquerors merging with more numerous conquered populations. With the formation of states from the eleventh century on, slavery and slave trading had developed to meet the demands of an expanding foreign trade. A "slave economy" was established by at least the fourteenth century in western and central Sudan, and by the fifteenth century it had spread to the Senegal and Lower Guinea coasts. Once Europeans entered the trading arena, West African rulers and merchants "reacted to the demand with economic reasoning and used it to strengthen streams of economic and political development that were already current before the Atlantic slave trade began."

The area from Senegal to Sierra Leone was the dominant slave-exporting region during the fifteenth century. An area of small states, its population was divided into groups with differing degrees of power and wealth, a significant fact in light of increasing warfare there and the consequent despoilation of the masses. In the six-

From *The African in Latin America*, ed. with intro. by Ann M. Pescatello (New York: Knopf, 1975), pp. 3–10, 49–57, passim. Reprinted by permission.

teenth century Europeans acquired labor supplies from the Senegambia-Guinea-Bissau-Sierra Leone areas and from regions south of the mouth of the Congo River. The Wolof Empire, which had dominated the region between Senegal and Gambia, eventually disintegrated into several separate kingdoms. This resulted in protracted warfare, which provided an abundance of prisoners of war for sale as slaves.

In the areas around the Congo, African political feuds and penetration by the Portuguese also influenced the course of slavery. Under Portuguese influence, São Tomé became the slave entrepôt for the entire Lower Guinea coast and also for the Congo, where struggles between African chiefs for political succession and economic control had provided another supply of prisoners of war. By the last quarter of the sixteenth century, the "kingdom of Kongo" was little more than a giant slave warehouse. Mulatto offspring of Africans and Portuguese served as agents in its slave trade, establishing a pattern that endured until the 1640s. During this period the Portuguese province of Angola also increased in importance as a source of human labor. The first three centuries of Angolan history (ca. 1550–1850) were, in fact, a patchwork of small wars, expeditions, and commerce in human beings.

Coeval with increasing European involvement in African commercial activities were the massive political, technological, and social changes occurring within West Africa, all of which had a profound impact on slavery in America. By the early seventeenth century West Africa was an organization of highly developed states and empires. Professional armies guarded its lucrative trade routes, causing frequent and destructive wars and thus swelling markets with prisoners of war. Troubles with political and commercial alliances along long-distance trade routes and in the western Sudan also affected trade, as did new commercial links forged between West African and European politics. With the arrival of European ships, Africans, particularly along the Guinea coast, could now purchase commodities from traders directly at shore. The source of supply for goods was thereby shifted from North Africa to West Africa, eliminating costly middlemen along the land routes.

This new local economic partnership changed throughout the seventeenth century from one of transactions in raw materials and manufactures to overseas trade in prisoners of war. From the 1450s until the 1650s African slaves either "were persons who had lost their civic rights, in the state that sold them, by sentence of the courts, or they were citizens of another state who had lost their rights through capture in war," a situation similar to that of medieval Europe. The shift to reliance on slaves as the chief commodity for trade occurred partly because of the disintegration of old empires in Africa and partly because European-African commercial opportunities increased with the extension southward to the coast of old trade routes.

THE SOUTH ATLANTIC SYSTEM

The Atlantic slave trade, already underway, changes and acquired momentum during the second quarter of the seventeenth century. Old patterns of servitude and traditional sources of supply persisted in Africa, on the one hand because of the changes that had occurred in Afro-European relations, on the other because plantation systems had already taken root in America. European colonists succeeded in obtaining millions of African workers because "in the master-servant organization which operated in many states and societies. . . Western African chiefs and kings regularly turned war captives and certain classes of law breakers into slaves." This servitude is best characterized as one in which certain peoples had fewer rights and more obligations relative to the general populace.

By the late seventeenth century expanding trade had engendered new coastal markets and power centers, controlled by Africans acting as middlemen between European sea merchants and African inland merchants. Prosperous city-states developed in the Niger Delta and along the Dahomey coast, while in the Guinea-Gold Coast-Senegal-Gambia area commerce underwent tremendous expansion. The eighteenth century also witnessed the proliferation of slaving along the western coast of Senegambia to Angola, and from central Africa around the Cape of Good Hope to Mozambique. The acquisition of firearms, the reinforcement of slavery as an institution in Africa itself, European encouragement of hostilities between African peoples and the development of slave-trading organizations among Africans and Europeans, all assured the continued growth of slavery. Some states, such as Ashanti and Dahomey, emerged solely in response to demand for slaves. These states depended on European guns to maintain armies for continuous warfare and slave raiding This important chapter in African history is one of almost continuous warfare, of the growth of complex states that depended on war and indigenous socioreligious institutions (such as the Ibo oracle) to support their slave-based economy.

The South Atlantic system, established by the beginning of the seventeenth century, was based on a plantation system of export agriculture. Its primary commercial crop was sugar. This required massive supplies of labor that the Africans were called upon to provide. Slave-trading operations had three phases: the slave was captured in Africa, he or she was transported to an African coastal trading point and attractively displayed to European buyers, and then he or she was shipped to America. The growth of plantation slavery in the Americas had coincided with a revolution in European maritime technology which gave Europe a naval hegemony almost everywhere in the world. With this also came a sharp change in transport costs: ships could carry more cargo, more swiftly and over longer distances, for less money.

American planters generally preferred male workers to female; the feeling was that the economic value of women slaves was greatly reduced by the eventuality of motherhood. Curtin states that slavers normally imported two men for each woman. Since birth rates depend directly on the number of women of child-bearing age in a population, this meant an automatic reduction of 30 percent in potential birth rate among slaves. Also, since planters regarded female slaves essentially as labor units, they did not encourage their female slaves to bear children, and the women themselves used abortive and contraceptive techniques. The key, then, to the continuation of the Atlantic slave trade was the failure on the part of American slave owners to foster a self-sustaining slave population.

The Atlantic slave trade represented the greatest involuntary migration in Western history. Not only was it of demographic importance To Africa and the Americas, but it also was at the core of an economic system in which Africa supplied the labor, Europe the entrepreneurial expertise, North America the food and transport, and South America the precious metals and other raw materials. . . .

THE MIDDLE PASSAGE

The "middle passage" was a euphemism for the horrors endured by the captured African before he ever set a chained foot on American soil. To transport slaves, small ships of 40 to 400 tons were often used. During the eighteenth century the most common slave ship in use was square-sterned 140 tonner, 47 feet long, with 9-foot holds and only 5 feet of space between decks. The larger frigates (200 to 400 tons) were 77 feet long and 20 feet wide, with separate quarters for men, women, and children. The hands and feet of male slaves were usually shackled during their voyage. There was little fresh air in the holds, which were often intolerably hot. Sanitary conditions were primitive, water was a scarce commodity, and the food was barely edible. The passage from West Africa to America lasted from six to ten weeks, while that from East Africa often took up to four months. Under such conditions disease was rampant and mortality rates were high, even among the ships' crews. Ships' doctors on these voyages often reported finding dead cargo chained to the living!

Without qualifying the misery of the slaves in transit, it should be noted that extreme hardships were borne by almost all workers, slave or free, in this capitalistic and exploitative enterprise. Such miserable conditions could be expected to exist given European attitudes, class relationships, and travel facilities at the time. Philip Curtin demonstrates that the death rate per voyage among ships' crews was even higher than that among slaves. The reading of novels, memoirs, and other accounts of sixteenth to nineteenth century naval life and ship travel—for example, *Mutiny on the Bounty, Two Years Before the Mast,* and *Damn the Defiant*—will put the horrors of a transoceanic crossing into the better perspective.

The main narrative that follows is by an Ibo, Olaudah Equiano, who was kid-napped as a boy from his home in Benin, Nigeria. Olaudah worked first as a slave for other Africans: eventually, he was taken to America, where he was sold as a slave in the United States and then in the West Indies. He later served with Quakers, earned his freedom, and became involved in the antislavery movement. His memoirs, published in 1789, represent a unique account by an African of the process into and out of enslavement.

EQUIANO: A SLAVE NARRATIVE

. . . When I was carried on board I was immediately handled, and tossed up, to see if I were sound, by some of the crew; and I was now persuaded that I had got into a world of bad spirits and that they were going to kill me. . . . When I looked round the ship too, and saw a large furnace or copper boiling, and a multitude of black people of every description chained together, every one of their countenances expressing dejection and sorrow, I no longer doubted of my fate; and quite over-powered with horror and anguish, I fell motionless on the deck and fainted. When I recovered a little, I found some black people about me, who I believed were some of those who brought me on board and had been receiving their pay; they talked to me in order to cheer me, but all in vain. I asked them if we were not to be eaten by those white men with horrible looks, red faces, and long hair. They told me I was not; and one of the crew brought me a small portion of spirituous liquor in a wine-glass; but, being afraid of him, I would not take it out of his hand. One of the blacks therefore took it from him, and gave it to me, and I took a little down my palate, which, instead of reviving me, as they thought it would, threw me into the greatest consternation at the strange feeling it produced having never tasted any such liquor before. Soon after this, the blacks who brought me on board went off, and left me abandoned to despair. I now saw myself deprived of all chance of returning to my native country, or even the least glimpse of hope of gaining the shore, which I now considered as friendly; and I even wished for my former slavery, in preference to my present situation, was filled with horrors of every kind, still heightened by my igno-rance of what I was to undergo, I was not long suffered to indulge my grief; I was soon put down under the decks, and there I received such a salutation in my nostrils as I had never experienced in my life; so that, with the loathsomeness of the stench, and crying together, I became so sick and low that I was not able to eat, nor had I the least desire to taste any thing. I now wished for the last friend, death, to relieve

The narrative sequence "Equiano" is from Robert I. Rotberg. *A Political History of Tropical Africa* (New York: Harcourt, Brace & World, 1965), pp. 143–53, passim. Reprinted by permission.

me; but soon, to my grief, two of the white men offered me eatables; and, on my refusing to eat, one of them held me fast by the hands and laid me across, I think, the windlass, and tied my feet while the other flogged me severely. I had never experienced any thing of this kind before; and, although not being used to the water, I naturally feared that element the first time I saw it; yet, nevertheless, could I have got over the nettings, I would have jumped over the side; but I could not; and, besides, the crew used to watch us very closely who were not chained down to the decks, lest we should leap into the water: and I have seen some of these poor African prisoners most severely cut for attempting to do so, and hourly whipped for not eating. This indeed was often the case with myself. In a little time after, amongst the poor chained men, I found some of my own nation, which in a small degree gave ease to my mind. I inquired of them what was to be done with us? They gave me to understand we were to be carried to these white people's country to work for them. I then was a little revived, and thought, if it were no worse than working, my situation was not so desperate: but still I feared I should be put to death, the white people looked and acted, as I thought, in so savage a manner; for I had never seen among any people such instances of brutal cruelty; and this was not only shown towards us blacks, but also to some of the whites themselves. One white man in particular I saw when we were permitted to be on deck, flogged so unmercifully with a large rope near the foremast, that he died in consequence of it; and they tossed him over the side as they would have done a brute. This made me fear these people the more. . . .

. . . The stench of the hold while we were on the coast was so intolerably loathsome, that it was dangerous to remain there for any time, and some of us had been permitted to stay on the deck for the fresh air; but now that the whole ship's cargo were confined together, it became absolutely pestilential. The closeness of the place, and the heat of the climate, added to the number in the ship, which was so crowded that each had scarcely room to turn himself, almost suffocated us. This produced copious perspirations, so that the air soon became unfit for respiration, from a variety of loathsome smells and brought on a sickness amongst the slaves, of which many died, thus falling victims to the improvident avarice, as I may call it, of their purchasers. This wretched situation was again aggravated by the galling of the chains, now become insupportable; and the filth of the necessary tubs, into which the children often fell, and were almost suffocated. The shrieks of the women, and the groans of the dying, rendered the whole a scene of horror almost inconceivable. Happily perhaps for myself I was soon reduced so low here that it was thought necessary to keep me almost always on deck; and from my extreme youth I was not put in fetters. In this situation I expected every hour to share the fate of my companions, some of whom were almost daily brought upon deck at the point of death, which I began to hope would soon put an end to my miseries. Often did I think many of the inhabitants of the deep much more happy than myself; I envied them the freedom they enjoyed, and as often wished I could change my condition for theirs. Every circumstance I met with served only to render my state more painful, and heighten my apprehensions and my opinion of the cruelty of the whites. One day they had taken a number of fishes; and when they had killed and satisfied themselves with as many as they thought fit, to our astonishment who were on the deck, rather then give any of them to us to eat, as we expected, they tossed the remaining fish into the sea again, although we begged and prayed for some as well as we could, but in vain; and some of my countrymen, being pressed by hunger, took an opportunity, when they thought no one saw them, of trying to get a little privately; but they were discovered, and the attempt procured them some very severe floggings.

One day, when we had a smooth sea, and moderate wind, two of my wearied countrymen, who were chained together (I was near them at the time), preferring death to such a life of misery, somehow made through the nettings, and jumped into the sea; immediately another quite dejected fellow who, on account of his illness, was suffered to be out of irons, also followed their example; and I believe many more would very soon have done the same, if they had not been prevented by the ship's crew, who were instantly alarmed. Those of us that were the most active were in a moment put down under the deck; and there was such a noise and confusion amongst the people of the ship as I never heard before, to stop her, and get the boat out to go after the slaves. However, two of the wretches were drowned, but they got the other, and afterwards flogged him unmercifully, for this attempting to prefer death to slavery. In this manner we continued to undergo more hardships than I can now relate; hardships which are inseparable from this accursed trade. Many a time we were near suffocation, from the want of fresh air, which we were often without for whole days together. This, and the stench of the necessary tubs, carried off many

. . . .

[Once in the Americas they were again oiled and shaved and displayed for sale.]

It was the practice . . . to open the sale on shipboard, the males being arranged in one part of the ship, and the females in another. . . [Crowds of people went on board, and began so disgraceful a scramble. . .]

[In other parts of the New World slaves were sold on shore.]

. . . [O] n a given signal . . . the buyers rush at once into the yard where the slaves are confined, and make choice of that parcel they like best. . . . In this manner, without scruple, are relations and friends separated, most of them never to see each other again. . . . O, ye nominal Christians! Might not an African ask you, learned you this from your God? . . . surely this is a new refinement in cruelty, which, . . . adds fresh horrors to the wretchedness of slavery.

2. Alonso de Sandoval, the First Advocate of Black Studies in America

NORMAN MEIKLEJOHN

Reverend Norman Meiklejohn, A.A., of Assumption College in Worcester, Massachusetts, prepared his doctoral dissertation at Columbia University on Negro slavery in Nueva Granada. The following selection comes from this dissertation. Someday we should have an English translation of Sandoval's notable treatise. It is full of unusual detail; Professor Boxer states: "Sandoval gives a very interesting description of the tribal markings of the Guinea and Angola slaves, so that the tribes and districts from which they came could be better identified. I believe this to be the first time that such a classification was attempted, or at any rate printed."* But enough is known now to salute Sandoval for his recognition of the cultural diversity of the Negroes and the need to study their languages and customs so as to better evangelize them.

Later on, another Spanish Jesuit in Peru, Diego de Avendaño, became convinced that Negro slavery was just as wrong as Indian slavery and in his two-volume *Thesaurus Indicus* (Amberes, 1668) called for another royal investigation similar to that which provoked the disputation in 1550 between Sepulveda and Las Casas, whose doctrine Avendaño largely was following. Nothing happened. The Spanish crown did establish in Spain in 1683 a royal commission to examine the legitimacy of African Negro enslavements and of the slave trade. The commission, on the basis of age-old custom, the toleration of these practices by the papacy and the clergy, and the economic advantage to the crown from Negro slavery, concluded that the king should entertain no scruples concerning legitimacy.

Alonso de Sandoval, the remarkable apostle to the Negroes, was born in 1576 in Seville, while his parents were en route to the Indies. Educated by the Jesuits in Lima, Peru, he entered the Jesuit Order in 1593 and was ordained a priest circa 1600. In 1604, he volunteered for service in the newly established Jesuit vice-province of Nueva Granada, and in 1605 he began to work in the Jesuit college in Cartagena. His duties there, like those of the other members of the college commu-

*Charles R. Boxer, *Salvador de Sá and the Struggle for Brazil and Angola, 1602–1656* (London: Athlone Press, University of London, 1952), p. 238, note 35.

From "The Observance of Negro Slave Legislation in Colonial Nueva Granada," by Norman Meiklejohn (Ph.D. dissertation, Columbia University, 1968), pp. 264–84, passim. Printed by permission of the author.

nity, were wide-ranging. They included teaching, ministering to the spiritual needs of the white, Negro and Indian populations, and making missionary field trips to outlying settlements along the Caribbean coast and inland. For a number of years. Sandoval served as procurator of the Cartagena community, and from 1624 to 1627 he held the posts of rector of the college. Dynamic, energetic, and aggressive, Sandoval could be sharp in tongue and harsh in manner. As an administrator, his unorthodox methods earned him a rebuke from his Superior General and made him ineligible to receive the highest honors which the Order bestowed upon its most outstanding members.

Like his fellow Jesuits on the staff of the college, Sandoval ministered to the Negro slaves. But unlike them, he experienced a strong sense of mission to Christianize them. A possible explanation for this sense of mission to the Negro may be Sandoval's background in Lima.

In 1607, Martin de Funes, Procurator of the Jesuits in Nueva Granada, presented a report on the Negro slaves to the Superior General, Father Aquaviva. In this report, the physical and spiritual situation of the Negro slaves in Nueva Granada was described as utterly miserable, and the Jesuits there requested permission to assume the responsibility of serving as their *doctrineros*. Shortly afterward, the General entrusted the major responsibility for the Negro ministry of Cartagena to Sandoval. On the strength of this assignment, Sandoval later took pride in calling himself the Father of the Slaves.

Already, in 1610, the Negro slave population of Cartagena numbered in the thousands. There were more than 5,000 residing on the surrounding estancias alone. To these numbers must be added the yearly transient population of 2,000 to 4,000 slaves who arrived fresh from Africa and who remained in Cartagena while waiting to be sold locally or to be shipped to other ports. If the spiritual destitution of the Negro slaves of Cartagena had sparked the zeal of Sandoval, the utter misery of the Negro slave cargoes set him ablaze. Many were ill with contagious diseases; some were on the point of death. All were hungry, thirsty, exhausted, and practically naked. Many entertained fantastic fears as to the dire fate which awaited them.

Sandoval made it a practice, on receiving news of the arrival of a slave ship, to hasten to the port and board the ship. There he proffered drinking water (especially to the infants), and then sought out the dying to prepare them for their final journey. Once the slave cargo had been unloaded and deposited in warehouses. Sandoval went among the slaves offering them a measure of relief and consolation, and trying to identify them as to language and tribe. Then, having called those of his Cartagena slave acquaintances who had knowledge of the languages of the newly arrived slaves to serve as interpreters, he set about examining the new arrivals in order to verify their baptism. Those who had been baptized he helped to prepare to receive the sacraments. Those who had not been baptized, or whose baptism seemed doubtfully valid, he catechized and then baptized. To all he gave words of encouragement regarding their future as slaves.

The preoccupation of Sandoval with the baptism of slaves was not merely juridicial; i.e., seeing to it that all African immigrants had been baptized in accordance with the law. Rather it was apostolic. As a minister of the gospel, he considered baptism a matter of paramount importance. On their baptism depended the slaves' eternal salvation or their eternal perdition. Until Sandoval began to look into the matter of slave baptisms, the presumption had been that all Negro slaves arriving in Cartagena had been baptized in Africa. No one in Cartagena had checked into the matter any more than had any of the priests and masters in various parts of Spanish America among whom the slaves spent the remainder of their days.

What was Sandoval's dismay when his inquiries began to reveal that many of the slaves had never been baptized, and that the baptism of an even greater number had been invalidly performed? This meant that many slaves were going through life being treated as Catholics and receiving the sacraments when in reality they were pagan. Those slaves who had to continue their voyage by land or sea were in danger of loss of life. If by chance they had not been baptized, or their baptism was invalid, those who died were, in the mind of the sixteenth-century Catholic, doomed to hell fire.

Proceeding cautiously and methodically, Sandoval looked more closely into the matter. He continued to question arriving slaves concerning the details of their baptism. He questioned the masters of slave ships, asking them what they knew of baptismal procedures at the African ports; he also wrote to priests stationed in African slave ports. His most pessimistic suspicious were verified. He found that, although some efforts had been made to correct abuses in Luanda, many baptisms were invalidly performed there, and even more so at Cabo Verde and the river ports in Guinea. The sacrament was being given mechanically and without concern for those circumstances necessary for an adult baptism to be valid. That is, the receiver of the sacrament had to know what the sacrament meant. He had to want to receive it. And the water had to touch his scalp. Sandoval learned that before sailing to America the slaves were assembled on the docks to hear a priest give a short harangue in Portuguese. Then, without making any further attempt to explain to the slaves the significance of what he was about to do, or to ask them if they wished to receive baptism, the priest sprinkled them with water and pronounced the words of baptism. . . .

Deeply concerned over this neglect in such an important matter as baptism, Sandoval submitted his findings to the Archbishop of Seville. Seville was the only Spanish port trading with both Africa and America, and many slave traders and investors resided there. It was also the port of entry for African slaves into Spain and contained a large Negro population. The prelate had his Negro faithful examined by a committee of theologians. Their conclusions agreed with those of Sandoval. Thereupon, besides sending a report to the Holy See, which apparently took no action, the Archbishop decreed that in his diocese the entire Negro population of 30,000 should be assiduously examined with regard to the validity of their baptism. The procedure which he ordered for this examination was the one proposed by Sandoval.

The work undertaken by Sandoval to examine the baptismal credentials of every slave who arrived in Cartagena was monumental. It meant that Sandoval and his assistants would have to examine the entire slave and free Negro population of Cartagena and its surroundings, as well as the many Indians whose baptism had been equally invalid because of lack of understanding and consent on their part. It meant that they would have to examine individually the thousands of Negro slaves arriving in Cartagena annually. Since, in Sandoval's estimation, any one of seventy different languages and dialects were apt to be spoken by the incoming slaves, he had to secure interpreters for all those languages. This entailed first of all identifying the slave's tribe according to his physical appearance, traits, scarifications. Then he had to identify a slave's language. After this had been done, he had to check his list of interpreters, find the proper ones, and obtain the loan of their services from their masters. It also meant working for hours on end through interpreters who were often tired, and who found the work distasteful because many of the slaves were diseased. Some time after the publication of his treatise, Sandoval's superiors were persuaded to buy seven slaves whose principal role was to serve as interpreters for Father Sandoval and his principal assistant, Father Peter Claver.

Once the interpreter was on hand, Sandoval proceeded to pose all sorts of technical questions regarding their baptism to men and women who were of an entirely different culture and at a very different level of sophistication. All this was done in the tropical heat of Cartagena, amid the human stench of the slave ships or slave depots. Once the unbaptized, the doubtfully baptized, and the invalidly baptized had been identified and set apart, there followed a lengthy instruction on the basic teachings of the church and on the meaning of baptism. . . .

In spite of his noble intentions, and the correctness of his methods. Sandoval met with criticism and resistance. Some clerics resented the intervention of a friar into what they considered their exclusive preserve. This of course was only one of many instances of clashes in the colonies between order priests and the diocesan clergy. The latter had official jurisdiction over the faithful, whereas order priests could minister to them only as a result of privileges extended to them by the Holy See and approved by the Crown. The diocesan clergy were scandalized that Sandoval should baptize slaves in a warehouse; they insisted that, according to regulations, the ceremony should be performed in church with all the customary solemnity. To this objection, Sandoval responded that there was no way of knowing who among the slaves would stay long enough in Cartagena to be able to receive baptism in the church. Rather than risk the possibility of their departure before being baptized, it was safer to perform the rite as quickly as possible. Besides, he added, clergymen did not permit the invasion of their churches by filthy naked slaves. On the contrary, they considered it an affront to the house of God and to the dignity of the sacrament being administered. The objection regarding jurisdiction was more serious since it was made by the Bishop's Council and added the further charge that the Jesuits were deriving financial profit from their endeavor. The matter was taken to court and a legal suit followed between the Jesuits on one hand and the Archbishop of Cartagena and his council on the other. The Jesuits not only won their case in court; they also won the administration of the plaintiffs as well. They did this by having the clerics accompany them for a routine day of work among the shipboard and warehouse slaves.

A further source of resistance was the slaves themselves. Many had been living as Catholics; to admit that they might have been pagans all along was a humiliation they could not bear. Thus, some of them did not cooperate with the examining priests who sought to ascertain if their baptism had been valid or not. Others suspected that their baptism had not been valid, but postponed admitting it to the priests out of shame. Another difficulty arose when the slaves who had been baptized on the ships and in the warehouses discovered that there was a more solemn form of baptism. Envious of those slaves who had been solemnly baptized in the church, they tended to conclude that their original baptism had not been valid and they sought to be baptized anew in a church ceremony.

For Sandoval it was not enough that the Negro slaves were baptized. He also wanted them to share fully with their masters the privileges of the Christian life. To this end he strove to persuade them to confess their sins and receive Holy Communion a few times a year. . . .

Success in his undertaking to have slaves share in the fullness of the Church's sacramental life depended to a great extent on the master's cooperation in facilitating the slave's recourse to the confessional and to Communion. While admitting that some masters cooperated in this, Sandoval complained gloomily that others took all sorts of devious means to impede the further catechesis of their slaves and especially their reception of the sacraments other than baptism.

Some motives for this reticence were mentioned at the beginning of this chapter. An additional motive, which might have been a pretext on the part of some, was the contention that Negroes, like Indians, were incapable of comprehending the Christian religion. As we have seen, many priests completely neglected their spiritual ministry to the Negroes, allegedly for that reason. No arguments, nor papal bulls could eradicate their prejudices. The priests, even the missionaries, tended to attribute to the stupidity of the Negroes what was really poor pedagogy on their part.

Besides entertaining the notion that they could evangelize Indians or Negroes in a language that these latter could barely understand, if at all, they explained Christian doctrine in scholastic terms. They made little or no effort to adapt their teaching to the native capacity, the culture, and the language patterns of the Negroes. Furthermore, the priests were more comfortable with their prejudices, for the serious and thorough Christianization of the slaves would have required considerable work. The conviction that the Negroes were incapable of anything beyond baptism freed them from any obligation to further ministry.

If this reluctance was true of confessions and Communion, it was even more true of the sacrament of Extreme Unction, the ministering of which would often have entailed going about at night, bringing the viaticum and the holy oils to dying slaves in squalid and repugnant surroundings. In the same spirit, masters who were convinced of their slaves' limited capacity for Christian living did not bother to call the priest when their slaves were dying. Even if the priest came, Sandoval tells us, some masters pretended that none of their slaves was ill. Sandoval was forced to rely on doctors to inform him when slaves were in serious danger of death.

It is no wonder that, faced with the monumental task we have just described, Sandoval required assistance. Apparently he was never given more than one assistant at a time; the one who assisted him longest was Peter Claver. Less dynamic than Sandoval, Peter Claver was a humble lover and servant of the poor. Sandoval exhausted himself for the spiritual profit of the slaves. Yet he was never able to forget the slaves' crudeness, their ignorance, their dirtiness, and their smell. Throughout his treatise his disdain for the Negro slaves shows through. In his later years he even admitted to Claver that news of an arriving slave ship made him break into a cold sweat, so revolting to his nature were the conditions under which he would once against exercise his apostolic ministry. At opposite poles was Claver, who had the advantage of a mild temperament, a profound humility, an authentic affection and love for the poor, and an acquired indifference to filth and stench and festering sores. Different as they were, these two Jesuits, in a period of fifty years, affected the lives of 300,000 Negro slaves who either passed through the port of Cartagena or lived in that city, its surroundings, and in settlements along the coast and inland. There is no calculating the untold thousands of Negro slaves who received better treatment as a result of the heroic example of Sandoval and Claver.

But Sandoval was not content with the work he was doing directly with the bozales in the Port of Cartagena. He dreamed of making authentic Christians of all the Negro slaves in the Spanish empire. This he would do by writing a treatise on the subject and addressing it to the members of the Company of Ignatius Loyola. His treatise would be both a clarion call to all Jesuits to bring Christ to the most abandoned of God's children, the Negro slaves, and a handbook on methods appropriate to that end. The treatise, which was finished by 1620, represented the fruit of fifteen years of experience as well as of extensive research. Though Sandoval was successful in having it published in 1627, he continued to improve it and the first volume of an expanded second edition was published in 1647. The second volume of the expanded edition never appeared.

One finds in Sandoval's treatise much material of considerable interest, not only on the subject of Negro slaves and the Church, but on the seventeenth-century mind and on the state of knowledge of geography, anthropology, and natural science in that century. Sandoval's geography is imperfect; his anthropology is a compendium of information on Africans and Asians that could be found in contemporary sources, enriched by first-hand observation of Negroes in Cartagena. The treatise also speculates on the causes of monsters, of Negroid characteristics, and of the incidence of albinos.

In Part One of his treatise Sandoval examined Negro peoples and their customs, and various aspects of the slave trade. He considered the various groups of Negroid peoples and described their location, social organization, religions, customs, and practices. Because the Negroes living in the area between Cabo Verde and Angola constituted the bulk of the Negro population brought to Nueva Granada, Sandoval described their coloring, physical characteristics, tatoos and scarifications, natural disposition, and religious attitudes.

On the basis of a study of contemporary theologians and his own investigations, Sandoval was convinced that much of the slave trade was immoral, but he accepted the opinion of the Jesuit school that purchasers in America could buy slaves in perfect good faith The important thing for Sandoval, however, was not to complain of slavery but rather to labor to improve the lot of the slaves. He described the slaves' departure from Africa, the "middle passage," their condition as they arrived in Cartagena, and the treatment they received in the depots and slave market.

Part Two of the treatise contains descriptions of the life of slaves in Nueva Granada and of the ministry to Negro slaves. The Negro slaves suffered greatly at the hands of their masters. Indeed, some masters treated their animals better than they treated their slaves. Nevertheless, Sandoval conceded, some masters did treat their slaves well. Slaves were also made to suffer spiritually as their masters neglected their spiritual needs and opposed their full participation in church life. As a result, Sandoval claimed, slaves lived like brutes and appeared incapable of living like civilized Christians, Sandoval further accused masters of favoring concubinage and prostitution, and of seeking to prevent marriages, of making the conjugal state undesirable by restricting a married slave's movements and by separating children from their parents. Nonetheless, Sandoval encouraged the slaves to obey their masters in the spirit of the gospels. He also encouraged masters to treat their slaves with paternal care, giving them what they needed, correcting them with charity, and bearing with them patiently.

In concluding Part Two Sandoval told his Jesuit readers that the Negro ministry was an excellent school for the acquisition of holiness through the practice of all the virtues. It offered numberless occasions for exercising the corporal and spiritual works of mercy.

In the third part of his treatise, Sandoval presented his method for evangelizing the Negro slaves. This method, which we considered earlier, can be summarized in a few phrases. The missioner should always take the initiative in seeking out slaves. He should prepare and use wisely his own corps of interpreter, and use simple language in teaching Christian doctrine. He should always check the validity of the baptism of the slaves he attends, foster frequent reception of sacraments, and the observance of the Church's precepts. . . .

SLAVERY IN SPANISH AMERICA

3. A Black Conquistador in Mexico

PETER GERHARD

Even in the early years of the conquest not all blacks were slaves as Peter Gerhard shows in this intriguing biographical sketch of Juan Garrido, a free black who took part in the defeat of Tenochtitlán and became "the first wheat farmer on the American continent." Mr. Gerhard abandoned a career as an accountant with an American oil firm to become a specialist in the historical geography of colonial Mexico.

While the role played by the people of equatorial Africa in the colonization of Latin America is relatively well-known, it is for the most part an impersonal history that emerges from the contemporary documents: the establishment of a Negro slave trade as a result of the demand for labor to replace the devastated native population; the employment of these black slaves in the more arduous tasks throughout the colonies; and, in most areas, their gradual assimilation through miscegenation with natives (and to a far lesser extent with Europeans). Information about individual blacks is usually confined to a brief statement of age, physical characteristics, and degree of acculturation at the moment of sale or the taking of estate inventories; less frequently, the place of origin of a slave is indicated. Only rarely do we hear about a Negro slave who achieved distinction in some way. Two examples that come to mind are Juan Valiente, the conquistador of Chile, and Yanga, the famed maroon leader in Veracruz.

Although most blacks who came to America in [the] early years were slaves, records of the Casa de Contratación show that a good many black freedmen from Seville and elsewhere found passage on westward-bound ships. Some of them settled in the Caribbean region, and others followed the tide of conquest to Mexico and Peru, identifying themselves no doubt as Catholic subjects of a Spanish king, with much the same privileges and ambitions as white Spaniards. "Benito el Negro" and

From "A Black Conquistador in Mexico," by Peter Gerhard, *Hispanic American Historical Review* 58 (1978): 451–59, passim. Reprinted by permission of Duke University Press.

"Juan el Negro" (the latter's real name seems to have been Juan de Villanueva) were encomenderos in the province of Pánuco and thus they should not have been slaves, but we cannot be sure of their origin. Spaniards might call anyone with a very dark skin "Negro," and indeed the fact that Villanueva was from Granada makes it seem likely that he was a morisco. On the other hand there is record of an African who apparently crossed the Atlantic as a freeman, participated in the siege of Tenochtitlán and, in subsequent conquests and explorations, tried his hand as an entrepreneur (with both Negro and Indian slaves of his own) in the early search for gold, and took his place as a citizen in the Spanish quarter of Mexico City. His name was Juan Garrido, and he was still alive in the late 1540s when he wrote or dictated a short resume of his services to the crown:

> Juan Garrido, black in color . . . says that he, of his own free will, became a Christian in Lisbon, [then] was in Castile for seven years, and crossed to Santo Domingo where he remained an equal length of time. From there he visited other islands, and then went to San Juan de Puerto Rico, where he spent much time, after which he came to New Spain. He was present at the taking of this city of Mexico and in other conquests, and later [went] to the island with the marquis. He was the first to plant and harvest wheat in this land, the source of all that there now is, and he brought many vegetable seeds to New Spain. He is married and has three children, and is very poor with nothing to maintain himself. . . .

The early chronology of this statement is vague, but working backwards from the fall of Tenochtitlán (1521), one can assume that Garrido arrived in America about 1510. It is perhaps more than a coincidence that a Spaniard called Pedro Garrido landed in Santo Domingo with his family and entourage in 1510, and later accompanied Cortés to Mexico. Slaves were often given the surnames of their masters, and while we do not know whether Juan Garrido was ever a slave it seems most probably that he was at least a protégé of a Spaniard at one time. However, this is pure conjecture, and we might also consider the possibility that the subject of this essay was named for his physical appearance (Juan Garrido can be roughly translated as "Handsome John"). In fact, the matter of how and when Garrido got to Mexico, and what part he played in the conquest, are something of a mystery. The *Diccionario Porrúa,* perhaps relying on an inconclusive passage in Bernal Díaz, says that he arrived with Juan Núñez Sedeño, who accompanied Cortés' 1519 expedition in his own ship with a large retinue that included "un Negro"; Manuel Orozco y Berra has him crossing a year later with the army of Pánfilo de Narváez. Magnus Mörner, after claiming that "many" hispanicized and Spanish-speaking blacks took part in the conquest, leaves us without any details, nor does one find any mention of Garrido by name in the various contemporary accounts of the siege and surrender of Tenochtitlán (indeed the same might be said of many Spaniards who were there). His name appears for the first time in the proceedings of Mexico City's cabildo on March 8, 1524, when that body granted a piece of land for the establishment of a smithy on the Tacuba causeway "going out of this city, just past the chapel [hermita] of Juan Garrido." Lucas Alamán identifies this as the church subsequently rebuilt and dedicated to San Hipólito de los Mártires, occupying the site where so many of Cortés' men died as they fled from Tenochtitlán on the Noche Triste. It may have been the brief statement in Alamán that gave rise to a somewhat embellished and much repeated version of which the following is an example:

> *San Hipólito* . . . Historically and sentimentally this is one of the most interesting churches in the city. In front of the spot where it now stands there existed in the year 1520 the second line of defenses on the causeway (now the street occupied by the horse railway to Tacuba) that connected he Aztec city with the main-land westward. At this point was the greatest slaughter of the Spaniards during the retreat of the memorable Noche Triste (July 1, 1520). After the final conquest of the city, one of the survivors of that dismal night, Juan Garrido, having freshly in mind its bloody horrors, built of adobe at this place a little commemorative chapel .

Terry's guide, drawing on the story as told by Orozco y Berra, identifies Garrido as "one of the Conquistadores [who] undertook to recover the bodies of his slaughtered countrymen and to erect a chapel wherein they could be buried with religious rites."

While his role in the Tenochtitlán episode remains obscure, Garrido took part in at least one of the expeditions sent out by Cortés after the conquest of the Triple Alliance to secure control and investigate the economic potential of outlying areas. According to a *relación geográfica* of 1580, "A Negro . . . who called himself Juan Garrido" accompanied Antonio de Caravajal and three other Spaniards to the hot country of Michoacán and the coast of Zacatula, most likely in 1523–1524. This little group was received hospitably by the Tarascans of Zirándaro, after which it proceeded across the Sierra Madre del Sur "on a deserted trail through a cold rugged area with lions and tigers and snakes and other animals. "Zirándaro belonged to the Tarascan empire which in 1522 had accepted Spanish rule practically without resistance, while the more truculent Indians of the coast had recently surrendered to the army of Gonzalo de Sandoval, which may explain how a small force could emerge unscathed from such an expedition. In fact, Caravajal's mission was to introduce Christianity to the natives (although there was no priest in his party) and to make a careful census of the communities visited, noting the mineral wealth and the tribute-paying capacity of each, for the guidance of Cortés in the first distribution of encomiendas. We do not know whether Garrido stayed with the Caravajal throughout the visitation of Michoacán, which lasted about a year; in any event, we find him once again in Mexico City early in August 1524.

It must have been before he went off with the Caravajal party that Garrido became the first wheat farmer on the American continent. The importance to the expatriate Spaniards, both as a matter of taste and as a measure of social status, of having wheat bread rather than cassava or maize tortillas, can hardly be overstressed. According to the conquistador Andrés de Tapia, "after Mexico was taken, and while [Cortés] was in Coyoacán, they brought him a small amount of rice, and in it were three grains of wheat; he ordered a free Negro [un Negro horro] to plant them." The Negro referred to by Tapia is identified in a parallel account by the seventeenth-century chronicle Gil Conzález Dávila as "Juan Garrido, a servant [*criado*] of Hernando Cortés." Both sources agree that the tiny crop harvested by Garrido at this time was the first in New Spain, and that all wheat subsequently grown came from its seed. . . .

4. Africans in Sixteenth-Century Peru

JAMES LOCKHART

Professor James Lockhart of the University of California, Los Angeles, created a social history of early Peru by mining systematically the rich notarial records there. His monograph on *Spanish Peru, 1532–1560* was a pioneering volume that revealed how promptly and how strongly Spaniards developed a stable society in Peru. In the following section he discusses the roles of Africans and Afro-Peruvians in a Spanish colonial society and their influence on Peruvian culture.

Planned or accidental, ethnic diversity was an element of prime importance in determining the Africans' role in Peru. It meant that Africans lived and acted almost entirely within the Spanish context. Most Africans must have had to speak Spanish to each other. Separated from the Indians by race, culture, and mutual hostility, cut off from one another by their diversity, Africans counted in the conquest and occupation of Peru mainly as so many more Spaniards, so many more spreaders of Spanish language and European ways.

The only African traits that could at all assert themselves were the very general patterns that were more universal than language. African-type dancing was one of these, and appeared wherever Africans could congregate. Kingship was another. The few independent communities of renegade Negroes which managed to exist in certain parts of Peru for a few years operated under that African political institution It would be of great interest to know what language the renegades spoke. Probably it was Spanish. Or possibly these communities enjoyed some degree of success because they had been able to concentrate enough people from one or another of the ethnic groups to form a strong nucleus. In any case, ethnic diversity was one effective deterrent to slave rebellions. . . .

For years the Spanish Negroes were the only significant group of non-African Negroes in Peru. Though much is hidden behind the all-inclusive term "creole," it appears that very few Negroes born in other parts of the Indies ever reached Peru. Only isolated examples occur, mainly from the Isthmus and the Antilles. The first

From *Spanish Peru, 1532–1560*, by James Lockhart (Madison: University of Wisconsin Press, © 1968 by the Regents of the University of Wisconsin), pp. 174–98. Reprinted by permission of the University of Wisconsin Press.

major addition to the Negroes born outside Africa came in the mid-1550s, when a generation of Peruvian-born Negroes reached saleable age, according to the criterion of the time. . . .

"Ladino" and "bozal" were two words that did heavy duty in the description of slaves. Buyers wanted to know two things, whether or not a slave was experienced, used to life outside Africa and among Europeans, and whether or not he spoke Spanish. Two sets of terms were really needed to express all this, but, in the peculiar conditions of slavery in the Indies at the time, experience and Spanish speaking so nearly coincided that one set of terms sufficed. "Bozal" basically meant just an inexperienced new arrival from Africa, and "ladino" merely meant Spanish-speaking, but they were used as opposite poles, "bozal" to mean a new slave who therefore knew no Spanish, and "ladino" to mean a Spanish-speaking slave who was therefore experienced. . . .

To express all kinds and degrees of mixtures of Negroes with other races, only one word, "mulatto," was in common use. Mulattoes were not generally thought of as a group distinct from Negroes; a mulatto was a type of a Negro. . . .

Most Negro slaves went through life with no more than a simple Christian name like Pedro, Antón, or Catalina, often qualified by the word Negro. Generally Negroes assumed surnames only when they were freed. . . .

. . . [I]n the period of 1530–60 Negro slaves did not yet ordinarily arrive in Peru by whole boatloads, as they did in the Caribbean. Negroes got to Peru by miscellaneous and various means, as the Spaniards themselves did. Many Negroes came with their permanent owners, or with Spaniards who, as a sideline, were speculating on the sale of two or three slaves. Small private activity may have accounted for as many Negroes as the more or less official trade carried on by large merchants. . . .

The vast majority of Negro slaves changed hands in small transactions, mostly sales of one slave, less often of two or three. Many of these sales can be called primary; that is, they represented the sale of a newly arrived Negro, by the merchant or speculator who imported him, to the person who was going to own him permanently. But many other transactions were part of a constant disturbingly prevalent process of resale. Among various reasons for the frequency of resale, the most basic was the peculiarly insistent demand for Negro slaves. In a general market situation where most prices, despite violent short-term fluctuations, were remarkable stable over the years, and prices of livestock and food staples actually fell, the price of Negro slaves rose steadily, giving owners a constant opportunity to make a profit by reselling. It was very common for a slave to have had two or three previous owners at time of sale. . .

. . . When, as often happened, Negro slaves were sold along with the land they cultivated, the livestock they cared for, or the tools they worked with, the slave was an element of continuity while the masters changed. At times this became a conscious process of capital formation. A Spanish artisan could acquire untrained Negroes, equip and train them, and sell them as a highly valuable independent unit. Some of the largest sales recorded were of gradually accumulated, trained teams of Negro slaves sold together with the other assets of the company that owned them. In these cases the lives of the Negroes and the operations of the companies remained largely unaffected by a changeover at the top.

After an initial period of instability, the price of Negro slaves was constantly on the rise during the period from 1530 to 1560. . . .

Negro slave owning was very widespread in Peru; not every Spaniard owned Negro slaves, but it can be said that there was no stratum of Spanish Peruvian society which did not include owners of slaves. A complete list of slave owners would include artisans of many kinds, priests, lawyers, notaries, merchants, sailors, and free Negroes, as well as captains and encomenderos. Negro slaves were never the monopoly of the great captains. . . .

. . . With practically all encomenderos and artisans owning several slaves, and many other Spaniards, from rich to poor, at least owning personal servants, or slaves to care for land and stock, it is apparent that Negroes were present in very substantial numbers. All in all, it seems probably that on the coast at least, there were as many Negroes as Spaniards. In the first coastal censuses, around 1570, Negroes had overtaken Spaniards, and may have already done so by 1560. . . . Negroes were present in the highlands in substantial numbers, but less numerous than on the coast.

While there is no sure way of knowing who owned the most Negroes, something can be said about the type of ownership represented by the two most prominent groups of owners, encomenderos and artisans. The encomenderos were purely consumers. The artisans were partly consumers, and partly trainers of slaves, and therefore speculators and sellers. When, in 1560, officials attempted to fix the prices of Negro slaves, forty residents of Lima protested. Of the forty, twenty-one are identifiable as artisans, while not a single encomendero joined the protest.

Whatever else they may have been, most Negro slaves in Peru were personal servants. Though the proportion of full-time personal servants to agricultural workers and artisan slaves is not known, slaves in the latter two categories also performed as servants, and certainly were thought of as such. Personal service was the role most closely associated with Negroes in the minds of the Spaniards. Only those slaves who spent or lost their lives in the migrant gangs organized for gold mining completely escaped the category, and such slaves do not seem to have been really numerous except during the Carabaya gold rush in the Cuzco area in 1542 and 1543. Large encomenderos might own a whole houseful of Negro servants. A notary, priest, or merchant would often have only one, preferably female, as general housekeeper.

Negro slaves were in great demand as servants for two main reasons. The first had to do with their utter foreignness. [It was felt that] foreign slaves who were isolated from the populace at large. . . cannot melt into it. . . .

The second reason why Negroes were desired as servants was that they were one essential part of the general pattern of Spanish ambitions. No encomendero felt happy until he owned a large house, land, livestock, and . . . Negro servants. Most Spaniards could not hope to achieve this goal in its entirety, but they aimed at least for two essentials, a house (which could be rented) and Negroes. One of the most important yardsticks for a Spaniard's contribution to any of the various war efforts was the number of Negro servants he brought to the battle with him. . . .

Negro artisan slaves were at the top of the ladder in the slave world, the most highly skilled and the highest priced, with a certain measure of intrinsic freedom. Doubtless they were less numerous than ordinary personal servants and field workers, but there were enough to form the backbone of the skilled labor force working in the shops of Peruvian Spanish artisans. . . .

The category of artisan slaves merged imperceptibly into the category of slaves with less valuable skills who were employed in large teams or gangs. On the borderline between these two types were the Negro muleteers. Of the three main carriers of goods in the highlands—Indian porters, llamas, and mules—trains of mules were the fastest and most reliable, and the most valuable goods were generally entrusted to them. A pack train consisted of a Spanish muleteer, several mules, and some Negroes who cared for and loaded the mules; Negro slaves had a practical monopoly of the function of accompanying pack trains. Most trains were of moderate size, with ten to twenty mules and, ideally, one Negro for every three mules. The merchants who were the chief owners of pack trains often sold them as a unit, mules, tackle, Negroes, and all Negroes in relatively large teams of ten to twenty They were, principally, the carting companies of Lima, the coastal fisheries, and some incipient large cattle owners. The teams were overwhelmingly male, with only one or two Negro women cooks. . . .

Large-scale use of unskilled Negro slaves on plantations was not yet a factor of importance in Peru by 1560. Only one such operation is known to have existed in Nazca, on the southern coast, where a royal official and encomendero ran a sugar plantation and also carried on stock-raising and general agriculture, with the labor of Negro slaves. . . .

The most frequent use of groups of unskilled Negroes was in mining, particularly gold mining. Even this was not of really basic importance; the great silver mines of highland Peru were always worked by Indians, with an exception of two. Gold mining was thought to be appropriate for Negroes because gold mines were mainly in hot, low-lying river areas. Even so, gold mining was far from a Negro monopoly. There were two major gold rushes in Peru within our period, one in Carabaya, a low-altitude area in the jurisdiction of Cuzco, in 1542 and 1543, and the other in the

Quito area in 1545 and 1546. . . . In Carabaya. . . . Spaniards brought in numbers of Negro slave gangs. Less intensive gold mining with Negroes took place intermittently in various parts of Peru. . . .

Small-scale agriculture was one of the main areas of endeavor of Negro slaves, comparable in importance to personal service and artisanry. In Lima as in other towns, the surrounding agricultural land was divided out to encomenderos and others, in quite small parcels, at the city's founding, in this case in 1535. By the early 1540's at latest, the environs of Lima had become an impressive garden spot, full of closely spaced small holdings where Spanish agriculture was practiced, with irrigation, to supply Lima's markets. Almost every one of those holdings, called chácaras or estancias indiscriminately, had one or more Negroes working on it. In Arequipa the situation was much the same, and apparently in Trujillo as well. It is doubtful that nearly as many Negroes did agricultural work in Cuzco and Upper Peru, but the pattern did extend that far, . . .

Outside the immediate environs of the cities, small landholdings devoted mainly to intensive agriculture gave way to larger, more loosely defined properties where stock raising took precedence over agriculture, and, in distant plains, superseded it entirely. . . . whatever they were called, they had Negro slaves working on them. . . .

As large-scale ranching began to develop in the 1550's, whole teams of Negroes worked at cattle herding. Even in the 1540's, there were some good-sized establishments, like the six Negro slave men and women who cared for a herd of cattle and goats in the Lima area in 1547. But most characteristic were the lone Negroes living deep in the country, far from the Spaniards, in charge of several cows, goats, or pigs. Herdsmen were more closely attached to the stock than to the land; whereas field Negroes were sold along with the land they worked, herdsmen were sold together with the herds. . . .

Despite occasional disappointments, Spaniards placed extraordinary trust in their Negro slaves. Agricultural slaves had infinite opportunities to run away. Negro herdsmen not only could run away, but were in complete charge of easily movable property that had an especially high value in a country only in the process of being stocked with European varieties. The degree of independence of Negro master artisan slaves has also already been seen.

Some slaves were allowed to lend and borrow money, and it was common for Negro slaves to be entrusted with merchandise to sell. . . .

When Spaniards knew individual slaves really well, they gave them the kind of absolute confidence they otherwise extended only to close blood relatives. In 1553 a Spanish muleteer fell ill while taking his pack train, loaded with merchandise, from Arequipa to Potosí. He returned to Arequipa for treatment, leaving the senior Negro slave muleteer in charge of the merchandise, the mules, and the other

Negroes, with 30 pesos in silver to spend on food and maintenance. The pack train and the merchandise, worth several thousand pesos, represented the Spanish muleteer's life savings and more.

Why Negro slaves in Peru, presented with such multiple opportunity, did not all run away, may seem a mystery. Part of the explanation is the lack of a place of refuge. Most Spanish settlements were far away from such dense tropical forests as protected runaway slaves in Panama and the Antilles. Runaway Negroes could not hope to be received among the Indians, to whom Negroes were merely another type of intruder. In any case, hiding among the Indians was impossible for Negroes because their distinctive physical appearance made them readily identifiable. In effect, runaways had only one place to go, some other Spanish settlement than the one they were in. Slaves who had a specific fear or grievance could at times find temporary refuge in the Spanish monasteries, but this was hardly running away.

In conditions like these, the recovery of runaway Negro slaves was a relatively easy, even a predictable process. The Spaniards were so confident of recovering runaways that it was not at all uncommon for a runaway slave, while still absent, to be sold without conditions, at a good price, to a new owner. . . .

Since runaway Negroes could not live among the Indians and were quickly detected in the cities, the only way they could hope to maintain themselves was by organizing bands of cimarrons or renegades in the countryside. Geography kept Peru from becoming a land of cimarrons like Panama, but there were usually a few small bands in operation in some part of the country. . . .

The Spaniards felt little or no reluctance to liberate individual Negro slaves. Negroes in Peru started obtaining their freedom very early, by 1536 at the latest, and the movement continued with increasing momentum right through 1560. Most of the Negroes freed had to buy their liberty in one way or another. Charity played an important role, even when freedom was bought, but it came into full operation only when the owner no longer needed the slave, or the slave was not in the prime of life. Spaniards made true grants of freedom in their testaments, or when they left for Spain; also to aged slaves and to infant children of slaves. Such grants were in their sum effect a significant factor, but they cannot be said to represent the ordinary avenue to freedom.

Slaves somehow managed to accumulate the money to free themselves. If there was any legal obligation on the part of masters to liberate slaves for their just price, the masters did not recognize it. Some owners let their slaves go cheaply as an act of charity, others for a good price. Others held out for exorbitant amounts; . . . Either slaves were allowed to earn money on the side, or they received some sort of pay or allowance from their masters. However, they did it, it was a difficult process. . . . Many slaves could not get the money together, and relied on loans, or worked out the equivalent of the price. The loans came from various sources, often from other

Negroes who were already free and solvent. Loans might take the form of an advance in pay from the new freedman's employer.

Along with the flood of the newly freed was a trickle of Negroes who arrived in Peru already free.

Free Negroes were an important class of people. Though it is impossible to estimate their absolute numbers. . . . they were numerous indeed. In Lima they were already considered a problem as early as 1538. As was true of Negro slaves, more free Negroes lived on the coast than in the highlands, but they were to be found in the highlands too.

The freedom that Negroes bought was far from absolute. In all kinds of legal records, Spaniards were careful to see that freedmen were specifically called free Negroes, the only ordinary exceptions being some light mulattoes. Spanish legal authorities, often calling free Negroes simply slaves, continued to claim far reaching jurisdiction over them. Freemen were periodically ordered to register and to take positions with Spanish masters. Once authorities issued a peremptory order for all free Negroes to leave the country; another time all freedmen were to join an unpaid, involuntary street-cleaning force. All such orders and schemes failed partially or completely, because of the social reality. Though Spaniards as a group were disturbed to see the rise of a class of independent Negroes (whose contribution to slave delinquency is undeniable), Spaniards as individuals tolerated them and found them useful. Not a single free Negro left Peru; . . .

Legislation requiring former slaves to take Spanish masters was more serious. First, it had a strong nuisance value, forcing the freedmen into at least ostensible and sporadic compliance. More basically, such ordinances had a certain shaping effect on the lives of free Negroes; they were the legal precipitation of the Spaniards' determination not to let Negroes take over positions and functions that they desired for themselves. Artisans' shops run independently by free Negroes, for example, were in constant jeopardy. With this upper limit, freedom enjoyed the legal privileges of Spaniards (and it should be remembered that even Spaniards were subject to orders to find a job or leave town). A freedman could own and bequeath any kind of property, marry, and carry on litigation.

Since practically all free Negroes had been slaves, there was a close relationship between the occupations of the two groups. The activities of freedmen can be described summarily by saying that they merely did all the same things slaves did, except that they did them as independent operators or as wage earners. Personal service, agriculture, and artisanry were the primary occupations for Negroes, whether free or slave. As in other ages and countries, many freedmen maintained a close relationship with their former masters. Slaves ordinarily took their master's surname at the tie of freedom; many either continued to work for their masters or stayed dependent on them indirectly, living on or near the master's properties. The very word "freedman" (*horro*) could be synonymous with servant. Free Negro servants got a yearly wage. . . which was not much less than the wage of an unskilled Spaniard. . . .

Africans or Negroes as we must call them, since some of them were born in Spain or the Indies, were a factor of absolutely first importance in Peru in the conquest period. They were an organic part of the enterprise of occupying Peru from its inception. The dominance of Spanish language and culture was never threatened, but in terms of ethnic or racial groups, the conquest of Peru was carried out by an equal partnership. Negroes were in a hundred ways the agents and auxiliaries of the Spaniards, in effect, doubling their numbers, making the Spanish occupation a much more thorough affair than it could have been without them. Far from their own roots, apart from the Indians, the Negroes assimilated Spanish culture with amazing speed, and were for the main part the Spaniards' willing allies, in spite of the cimarrons. And this willingness is understandable. Though Negroes were subordinated to Spaniards, they were not exploited in the plantation manner; except for mining gangs, Negroes in Peru counted as individuals.

SLAVE RESISTANCE

5. Negro Slave Control and Resistance in Colonial Mexico

DAVID M. DAVIDSON

In recent years historians have been investigating patterns of slave resistance, flight and rebellion in different parts of Spanish America and the Caribbean. In this essay David M. Davidson shows that slave control was a persistent problem for authorities in sixteenth and seventeenth-century Mexico.

Negro resistance to enslavement was an integral feature of the history of African slavery in the Americas. Studies in the past few decades in the United States and Latin America have successfully refuted if not entirely erased the once accepted notions of Negro docility and acquiescence in slavery. These works have provided a most convincing panorama of slave mutinies, insurrections, clandestine conspiracies, and individual escapes. Repeated evidence of more subtle forms of resistance—for example, suicide and voluntary abortion and infanticide—reveals further the determined refusal of many slaves to accept their position, and their reluctance to bear children in slavery. Such resistance occurred in varying degrees wherever Europeans established Negro slavery in the New World, primarily in the southern United States, the Antilles, the Pacific and Caribbean coasts of Central and South America, and northeastern Brazil. Although most studies have been restricted to these regions, there is a considerable body of evidence to indicate that Negro slave resistance was also present in colonial Mexico.

Recently, and primarily through the efforts of Gonzalo Aguirre Beltrán, we have gained substantial information concerning the number and role of Africans in Mexico. It is now fairly certain that in the period 1519–1650 the area received at least 120,000 slaves, or two-thirds of all the Africans imported into the Spanish pos-

From "Negro Slave Control and Resistance in Colonial Mexico, 1519–1650," by David M. Davidson, *Hispanic American Historical Review* 46 (1966): 235–53, passim. Reprinted by permission.

sessions in America. The early development of Negro slavery in colonial Mexico was a direct response to the serious labor shortage resulting from the startling decline of the Indian population. Demographics studies suggest that the indigenous population of central Mexico alone, which may have been as high as 25,000,000 in 1419, had decreased to around 1,075,000 by 1605. The spread of European diseases, wars, relocations, and the ecological changes wrought by Spanish settlement and control all contributed to the decline. The advance of Spanish mining and particularly, ranching and agriculture (which spread quickly in the sixteenth century to provision Mexico when decreasing indigenous food production threatened starvation) produced a demand for labor which the declining Indian population could not fulfill.

Although the crown soon made concessions to the colonists' demands for workers by sanctioning forced wage labor (the *repartimiento*), and by failing or refusing to thwart the spread of debt peonage, it hoped to fill the need with African slaves. Royal decrees throughout the late sixteenth century prohibited the use of Indians in certain industries considered detrimental to their health, especially sugar processing and cloth production, and ordered their replacement by Negro slaves. African labor was also encouraged for the mines.

The response to these conditions was a constant demand for Negroes, a flourishing slave trade, and a rising Negro population throughout the sixteenth and early seventeenth centuries. As a result, by 1570 Mexico contained over 20,000 Negroes, and by 1650 there were more than 35,000 Negroes and over 100,000 Afromestizos (mulattoes and zambos). Slaves were found throughout the colony, serving in the mines, plantations and ranches, as well as in the urban areas as peddlers, muleteers, craftsman, day laborers, and domestics. . . .

Spanish officials sought to incorporate this large, culturally distinct labor force into the neo-medieval structure of the American colonies. Legislation spanning the 1530s to 1550s, intended for the most part for general application to the Indies, stipulated the privileges and limitations pertaining to the slaves' place within society. Royal intentions derived in general from the profound Hispano-Catholic faith in the organic structure of a divinely imposed social unity, in which each person or group found its privileges and limitations defined according to its role in the hierarchy of inequality. More specifically, as Frank Tannenbaum has noted, this policy was rooted in the Iberian heritage which had long allowed slaves a legal and moral personality.

Yet the current of realism which accompanied and at times contradicted much of Spain's early idealism in America emerged forcefully in the regulation of slavery. The royal concern for slaves as Spanish subjects and Catholic souls was tempered by the need to create a stable and dependable labor force, maintained by consent in a situation where physical control was difficult. Much of the legislation concerning slavery assumed a conciliatory tone, in which certain privileges granted to slaves were intended to reduce or eliminate causes of slave discontent.

Thus royal decrees and Church proclamations provided legal release from bondage by allowing slaves to purchase their freedom and by encouraging voluntary manumission. Such declarations served equally to give substance to the Spanish belief in the essentially transitory nature of slavery and in the humanity of the slave. Some of them, such as the royal cédula of 1536 to Mexico, also suggested that slaves would work with more spirit and be less inclined to revolt. In seeking to make slave life more palatable by guaranteeing family solidarity and marital privileges, the king observed that a protected marital life was not only a Christian obligation but also an essential means of insuring slave tranquility and stability. Both Church and crown were adamant in restricting the disciplinary authority of masters and in encouraging good treatment, for, as Juan de Solórzano commented, such conditions would protect the slaves as well as preserve an important labor base. Finally there was the desire to hispanize Africans in order to bring them into a community of spiritual and cultural brotherhood with their masters. Slaves would receive the benefits of Hispanic culture and religion, and their masters might rest assured that such fraternal bonds would temper resentment. In these respects the dictates of self-interest and religion went hand in hand.

The conciliatory measures appear to have had only a limited effect. Slaves did not achieve much success in purchasing their freedom or in being manumitted, if the few recorded instances of these are true indications such extralegal channels to freedom as intermarriage and miscegenation were relatively more successful. . . .

Slaves also tried to gain freedom by marrying into the free Indian population. Bartolomé de Zarate complained to the emperor in 1537 that Negroes were marrying Indians and declaring themselves freed. Although the *Siete Partidas,* Spain's ancient legal code, had granted liberty to some slaves who married free persons, Charles V nullified this provision, thus emphasizing that if the authorities would condone a trickle of free Negroes, they would not tolerate a substantial loss of their slave labor. Despite the royal desires slaves continued to marry Indians in order that their children might be free. "Indian women are very weak and succumb to Negroes," wrote Viceroy Martín Enríquez in 1574. "Thus Indian women would rather marry Negroes than Indians; and neither more nor less, Negroes prefer to marry Indian women rather than Negresses, so that their children will be born free." Spanish law and custom respected these marriages, which, with common law unions, produced the free zambo population of Mexico

Legislation which sought to cure some of the worst abuses in slave life provided only minimal protection. Whereas both crown and Church hoped to protect the familial stability of slave life, many masters seemed bent on its disruption. Juan de la Peña informed Philip II in 1569 that masters were separating slave families by selling male slaves, "from which results great harm to their wives and children, because they remain in this land with no aid." The Archivo General de la Nación has many examples of masters forcing slaves to marry against their will, separating slave families, and violating wives and daughters. Both crown and Church did on occasion protect slave families, but in general Aguirre Beltrán seems accurate in stating that slave family life was highly unstable and vulnerable to the masters' whims.

The regulation of slave treatment and discipline did not fare much better. . . . Furthermore, neither crown nor Church intervened in situations which modern opinion would consider brutal. . . . Repeated evidence reveals that cruelty and mistreatment were as much a part of slavery in colonial Mexico as they were in most slave regimes in the New World. As the king frankly stated on more than one occasion, slaves in Mexico and the Spanish Indies in general were subject to "scandalous abuses," and mistreated "to such an extreme that some die without confession." The poor slaves are molested and badly cared for."

The hispanization of Mexico's African population sought to ease the transition into slavery. While conversion was certainly one facet of the broader evangelical mission of Spanish expansion, in regard to slave control the policy served three possible functions: it would influence the development of a society where shared religious and cultural values produced a slave regime based on consent; it would provide certain outlets for slave tensions and discontent through religious ritual and social activities; and it sought to offer slaves spiritual equality in the City of God in return for deference and obedience to their masters in this world. Iberian Catholicism was ideally suited to these ends with its many saint's days and fiestas, auxiliary social organizations, and ingrained sense of hierarchy.

Hispanization of Africans was relatively successful, judging from the countless references to creole Negroes in the archives. True religious conversion was somewhat more difficult, although missionaries apparently made notable gains. Evidence of Negro brotherhoods (confradias) in the urban and mining districts suggests that some slaves benefited from the social outlets and religious balm of Christianity. The Church also established hospitals to serve the Negro population, although the charitable intentions and social functions of these institutions probably outweighed their medical efficacy.

That many slaves did adopt the forms and receive the benefits of Hispanic culture and religion, did not make them contented with their servile life. Christian slaves were just as likely to resist or revolt as any others. In fact, in 1523, the first slaves to revolt in the colony erected crosses to celebrate their freedom "and to let it be known that they were Christians."

Unfortunately conciliatory legislation and hispanization failed to eliminate the general causes of slave resistance in Mexico. Unstable familial and marital life, mistreatment, overwork, and the scarcity of effective channels to freedom undoubtedly contributed heavily to slave discontent. Although these conditions certainly varied from one region, master, and economic activity to another, the worst treatment and the most brutal revolts occurred in the mines and sugar plantations of the colony. . . .

Although individual Negroes fled in the early years, the first alleged effort by slaves to organize a large-scale uprising occurred in 1537. On December 10, 1537, Viceroy Antonio de Mendoza informed the emperor of a plot intended to free the slave population of the young colony. "On the twenty-fourth of the month of November past," wrote Mendoza, "I was warned that the Negroes had chosen a king, and had agreed amongst themselves to kill all the Spaniards and rise up to take the land, and that the Indians were also with them." Mendoza sent an agent to corroborate the rumor and soon received the reply that a plot existed which included the capital city and the outlying mines. He swiftly arrested the "king" and his principal lieutenants and, after eliciting confessions, had the leading conspirators drawn and quartered. There is a good possibility that the alleged plot, although it never materialized, was not a figment of the viceroy's imagination, since an independent sixteenth-century source also records the plot and subsequent events. . . .

Continued tension in Mexico City and the occurrence of at least two more revolts in the 1540s prompted Spanish officials to issue a number of decrees restricting Mexico's Negro population. Mendoza's ordinances of 1548 prohibited the sale of arms to Negroes and forbade public gatherings of three or more Negroes when not with their masters. The viceroy also declared a night curfew on Negroes in the capital city. Mendoza's warnings to Luis de Velasco apparently alarmed the new viceroy, for he repeated Mendoza's restrictions in 1551 and wrote in 1553: "This land is so full of Negroes and mestizos who exceed the Spaniards in great quantity, and all desire to purchase their liberty with the lives of their masters." In the same year Velasco also established a civil militia (the *Santa Hermandad)* in the colony, in part to cope with save uprisings.

With restrictive measures barely under way, Mexico experienced its first widespread wave of slave insurrections in the period 1560–1580 as a result of the increased use of Negroes in mines and estates By the 1560s fugitive slaves from the mines of the north were terrorizing the regions from Guadalajara to Zacatecas, allying with the Indians and raiding ranches. . . . The insurrections continued into the 1570s as Martín Enríquez attempted to implement the royal ordinances. Yet neither the cost of 1571–1574 nor the issuance of restrictive legislation in the 1570s and 1580s was of any avail. A viceregal order of 1579 revealed that the contagion of revolt nearly covered the entire settled area of the colony outside of Mexico City, in particular the provinces of Veracruz and Pánuco, the area between Oaxaca and Gualtuco on the Pacific coast, and almost the whole of the *Gran Chichimeca.* Only emergency repressive measures and the continued importation of Africans maintained Mexico's slave labor supply.

During the last decades of the sixteenth century the focus of slave revolts shifted to the eastern sugar regions of the viceroyalty. Isolated uprisings had occurred there since the 1560s, but by the turn of the century the slopes and lowlands between Mt. Orizaba and Veracruz teemed with small maroon settlements and roaming bands of slaves who raided the many plantations and towns in the area.

The geography of the region so favored maroon guerrilla activities that local authorities proved incapable of thwarting their raids or pursuing them to the palenques. [In one famous incident, a Negro leader named Yanga was able in 1609 to negotiate an agreement with Spanish authorities on favorable terms.]

Yanga's maroon movement is a notable example in the history of Negroes in Mexico–the only known example of a fully successful attempt by slaves to secure their freedom *en masse* by revolt and negotiation and to have it sanctioned and guaranteed in law. This experience demonstrates that, under capable leadership, slaves could maintain an active guerrilla campaign, negotiate a truce, and win recognition of their freedom In view of the tenacity displayed by other maroons as well, it is likely that similar incidents occurred which have not been recorded.

The violence of slave insurrections in the eastern slopes and northern mining regions kept Mexico City in a prolonged state of anxiety. By the first decade of the seventeenth century the Negro population of the capital had grown enormously, and there was a general fear that the urban slaves would unite to take the city. The tensions in the metropolis exploded in 1609 and 1612 when rumors circulated that the Negroes had chosen leaders and planned massive uprisings. In both cases elaborate defensive preparations followed brief periods of panic and confusion. Negroes were apprehended and punished, and the plots, if indeed they existed at all, never materialized. Yet whether or not these conspiracies actually existed, the terror which they caused was a reflection of the tensions inherent in multiracial Mexico where insecurity plagued the Spanish and creole population well into the seventeenth century. . . .

It is apparent that officials and slave owners found it extremely difficult to prevent or contain slave resistance. Few in numbers, they were forced to rely on the scarce royal troops in Mexico aided by untrained and undisciplined bands of mestizos and Indians. These haphazard military operations faced serious strategic and tactical problems, especially in campaigns against distant hideaways in the frontier regions. Mexico's rugged terrain compounded the difficulties, for fugitives could establish settlements in the mountains and isolated barrancas which afforded excellent defensive sites. Moreover, Indian cooperation seems to have been instrumental to the success of various revolts and made the job of repression all the more difficult. With such a weak system of control, the flight and insurrection of slaves continued into the eighteenth century, and it was only the abolition of slavery in the early nineteenth century that put an end to slave resistance in Mexico.

In conclusion, some implications of slave control and resistance in colonial Mexico are evident. In the first place, it appears that flight and revolt constituted the most effective avenue to liberty for the slave population, despite the existence of an elaborate (if often ineffective) machinery of control and conciliation. Thus a major consequence of resistance was the development of the free Negro and Afromestizo population of the colony. Second, slave resistance, real or imagined, had a notably disturbing effect on the society of the conquerors. In this respect the anxiety of colonial society differed more in degree than in kind from that of the fear-ridden slavocracies of the Caribbean and southern United States. The same restrictive and precautionary measures, the same false alarms, and similar bands of roaming vigilantes characterized Mexico as well. Moreover, preventive legislation and Spanish fears extended to the free Negro population, and the status of freedom in the colony suffered regardless of their role in slave resistance. Finally, the study of Negro slave activity reveals an area of social life barely perceived by many students of colonial Mexico—the relations within the non-white and mixed peoples in the multiracial societies that developed throughout tropical America. Of particular importance here are Indian-Negro relations, where miscegenation, marital and common-law unions, cooperation in resistance and also mutual antagonisms provide a rewarding field of study of social history. Slave resistance in Mexico is more than just another chapter in the Negroes' long struggle for freedom and justice. In the context of Mexican social history it illustrates the interplay of diverse races and cultures which make that history one of the most complex and fascinating in the New World.

António Vieira and the Crises of Seventeenth-Century Brazil

A PERIOD OF CRISIS AND CHANGE

Seventeenth-century Spanish America has sometimes been characterized as "the forgotten century" or as a period when no spectacular events occurred as in the previous century of conquest or the succeeding century of reform and impending revolution. This may be true, or it may reflect our ignorance of these years when the basic institutions and ways of life were implanted throughout the Spanish empire in America. But it is certain that the seventeenth century in Brazil was a period of crises and change resulting in part from the end of sixty years of joint rule of Portugal and Spain with the restoration of the Portuguese monarchy in 1640, the expulsion of a Dutch colony in northern Brazil in 1654, the continued conquest and conversion of indigenous peoples, and the subjugation of Palmares in 1694, the largest independent state created by escaped African slaves in the New World.

Since Portuguese and Spanish-speaking historians have largely neglected the important period of Spanish rule over Brazil sometimes referred to as "The Babylonian Captivity," it has remained for the American scholar Stuart B. Schwartz to analyze this union from the standpoint of the influence of reforms and policies initiated by the Hapsburgs on Brazilian administration and affairs (Reading 1). The significance of the Dutch period in Brazilian history, on the other hand, has long been studied and debated by historians. A Brazilian revisionist historian argues that the sugar economy began to decline even before the Dutch arrived, and their invasion was a crippling blow that brought no compensating economic advantages.[1] One remarkable contribution by the Dutch was the appointment of Governor-General Johan Maurits, whose cultural activities and enlightened rule, as described by the indefatigable English historian Charles R. Boxer, put Brazil on the map in a way never before accomplished (Reading 2).

---

1. Mircea Buescu, "Invasão honaldesa: perdas da economia açucareira: *Verbum* (Rio de Janeiro) 25 (1968): 397–408.

António Vieira. This Jesuit missionary, man of letters, economist, orator, and diplomat was "one of the most remarkable Portuguese who ever lived." He played a large part in most of the affairs of seventeenth-century Brazil, especially in the effort to protect the Indians.

ANTÓNIO VIEIRA

Antonio Vieira, the Portuguese Jesuit counterpart of the Spanish Dominican Bartolomé de Las Casas, whom Charles Boxer has called the "the most remarkable man in the seventeenth-century Luso-Brazilian world," played an important role in all of these crises save, perhaps, the defeat of Palmares.[2] Born in Lisbon in 1608, he was only six years old when his family moved to Bahia, then the administrative center of the colony under Spanish rule. He attended the local Jesuit school and was soon singled out by his teachers. He was sixteen when the Dutch occupied Bahia in 1624. This terrible experience fortified Vieira's determination to defend his native country and its prized colonies against the Protestant invaders. He was ordained a priest in 1634 and quickly became the most famous preacher in the colony. As such, he took a prominent part in the defense of Bahia against Count Johan Maurits in 1638, and was chosen to preach the victory sermon after the Dutch withdrawal.

While in Lisbon after the restoration of Portugal's independence from Spain, Vieira became the court preacher and an influential adviser to King João IV, who consulted him on matters of state and employed him on secret diplomatic missions to Paris and The Hague. Vieira saw that if Portugal were to survive as an independent state, it would be necessary to protect the sailing route to Brazil and stop the harassment and losses of Portuguese shipping. As a consequence he supported the establishment of the Brazil Company and the inauguration of a protective fleet system which helped to defeat the Dutch in 1654. He also advised toleration of the New Christians, former Portuguese Jews who had been forcibly converted, in the hope that they would invest in the company.

From the beginning of his career, Vieira had been deeply interested in the peaceful conversion of the indigenous peoples. In 1653 he returned to Brazil as superior of the Jesuit missions in the Marañon. Relations between the Jesuits and settlers there were strained by the missionaries' control over the distribution of Indian workers to Europeans, and João IV gave Vieira the additional task of curbing the notorious slaving expeditions the Portuguese were conducting in the Amazon. From his base in São Luis do Maranhão, Vieira sought to improve relations between the Jesuits and the settlers while leading a series of highly successful missionary expeditions in the hinterlands. His "Sermon Condemning Indian Slavery, 1653" (Reading 3) provides an idea of the arguments he offered against native enslavement. Unable to enforce crown legislation protecting the natives, Vieira returned

---

2. C. R. Boxer, *A Great Luso-Brazilian Figure: Padre Antonio Vieira, S. J., 1608–1697* (London: The Hispanic and Luso-Brazilian Councils, 1957). A more recent study of the work of Vieira and the Portuguese Jesuits in Brazil is *The Fire of Tongues: António Vieira and the Missionary Church in Brazil and Portugal* by Thomas M. Cohen (Stanford: Stanford University Press, 1998).

briefly to Portugal in 1655 to present his case against the settlers at court. Soon after he preached his most famous sermon, the "Sermão da Sexagésima," from the pulpit of the royal chapel. (Reading 4).

He returned to Maranhão and achieved a great personal triumph in winning the conversion of the Nheengaíbas in 1659 (Reading 6), but rebellious settlers soon expelled Vieira and his fellow Jesuits from the Amazon in 1661 and sent them back to Lisbon. After the death of Joáo IV in 1656, Vieira was no longer protected from the wrath of the Inquisition, which had long objected to his support of the new Christians. He spent five years in prison and under house arrest, until a change of power in the royal court led to his release in 1668. He then went to Rome to plead the case of the Portuguese Jews, who he hoped might be spared the rigors of the Inquisition.

In 1681 Vieira went back to Brazil where he served again as a Jesuit administrator and edited his sermons for publication until his death in 1697. By this time his influence as a preacher had no parallel in the Iberian world. His *Sermons and Letters* circulated in pamphlet form all over Latin American and Europe. A learned commentary on one of his sermons, done by Sor Juana Inés de la Cruz, was the occasion of a witty exchange of letters between the Mexican nun and the Bishop of Puebla, and his sermons in Italian attracted the attention of the learned Queen Christina of Sweden, who appointed him her confessor. Missionary, preacher, writer, diplomat, Vieira continues to be considered one of the greatest writers in the Portuguese language and a central figure in the religious and political history of the Luso-Brazilian world.

THE AFRICAN THREAT

Although Vieira's second recorded sermon was one preached to African slaves of an engenho or sugar-mill in the Reconcavo[3] in 1633, like Las Casas, he accepted the institution as a necessary evil and did not concern himself greatly with the lot of the black laborers. Only quite late in his career, in a letter addressed to the King of Portugal on April 20, 1657, did Vieira indicate that he was also opposed to the injustice done to the blacks (Reading 5).

By this time the slave trade to Brazil was dwarfing that to Spanish America, spurred on by the development of the sugar industry in the late sixteenth century and a mining boom after 1695. During the sugar industry's expansion in the seventeenth

---

3. The "Reconcavo" is a semitropical area that surrounds the Bay of All Saints in the state of Bahia. In the mid-1500s it was the most densely populated region in Brazil, where sugar and tobacco formed the basis of a slaveholding plantation society.

century, the number of slaves imported averaged about 5,600 per year. By 1750 black slaves constituted approximately seventy percent of the plantation zone's population.[4]

Throughout the colonial period Brazil suffered from the chronic instability of its slave society and the threat of slave resistance. Often this resistance took the form of flight from their masters and the "establishment of runaway communities called *ladeiras, mocambos,* or *quilombos.*" Professor Schwartz has made a study of these relatively small but numerous escapee communities in the captaincy of Bahia, which demonstrates their significance for the understanding of the social and economic history of colonial Brazil.[5] The most important single example was the "Black Republic" of Palmares, a community of over twenty thousand escaped slaves in Alagoas that existed from 1630 until 1697 despite determined efforts of the Dutch and Portuguese to destroy it. Palmares was one of the most powerful manifestations of the strength of African politics and culture in Brazil, and in Reading 7 Raymond Kent concludes that with the defeat of Palmares in 1694, "the greatest threat to the future evolution of the Brazilian power and civilization" was removed.

4. Mark Burkholder and Lyman L. Johnson, *Colonial Latin America,* 3rd ed. (New York: Oxford University Press, 1996), p. 115.

5. Stuart B. Schwartz, "The Mocambo: Slave Resistance in Colonial Bahia," *Journal of Social History* (1970): 313–33. See also his recent collection of essays, *Slaves, Peasants, and Rebels: Reconsidering Brazilian Slavery* (Urbana and Chicago: University of Illinois Press, 1992), which offers revisionist views of some of the most controversial issues related to Brazilian slavery.

THE "BABYLONIAN CAPTIVITY"

1. Brazil Under Spanish Rule, 1580–1640

STUART B. SCHWARTZ

Neither Spanish or Portuguese historians have devoted much attention to the influences Brazil received during the sixty years when it was ruled along with Portugal itself by the Spanish Hapsburgs. It was a period of important and varied development, as Professor Stuart B. Schwartz explains in this informative and interpretive article.

Few epochs in the history of the Portuguese colonial empire have received less attention from historians than the sixty years from 1580–1640 when Portugal and Spain were jointly ruled by the Spanish Hapsburgs, Phillip II, III, IV (or I, II, III by Portuguese reckoning). The union of the crowns in 1580 brought together the two greatest maritime empires of the sixteenth century, yet, curiously, this phenomenon has remained relatively unstudied. Portuguese neglect is based on the premise that the union with Spain was a "Babylonian Captivity" during which the Spanish rulers and their policies destroyed in a half century what had taken the Portuguese two hundred years to build. Nationalism has prompted Portuguese scholars to concentrate on the loss of independence in 1580 or its triumphant restitution in 1640, but although this motivation is still present, a new generation of Portuguese historians has begun to turn from the shibboleths of their nineteenth-century predecessors. Spanish historiography, on the other hand, disdains the topic; hardly surprising since even today to many Spaniards "a Portuguese is a Galician who speaks poorly." Moreover, there is the embarrassing fact that the Portuguese were able to wrest their independence from Spanish rule.

Brazilian historians have also neglected this period of their history and with the exception of a few outstanding monographs and some suggestive essays our knowledge of Hapsburg Brazil remains characterized by hoary and often unfounded gen-

From "Luso-Brazilian Relations in Hapsburg Brazil, 1580–1640" by Stuart B. Schwartz, *The Americas* 25 (1968): 33–48, passim. Reprinted by permission.

eralizations or by crude attempts at revision. The usual claims that the period had no distinctive effects on Brazil, that Brazilians were indifferent about the union, and that Spanish neglect ruined the colony are often repeated. I hope to present some alternative to this line of thought. Considerations of scope and space limit my remarks to Brazil but I wish to emphasize at the outset that Brazil was only one area of a vast, imperial structure, and in 1580 far from the most important region. Linked to the metropolis and the empire of the South Atlantic, Brazilian developments were often determined or influenced by events in other lands.

In the Cortes of Tomar (April, 1581), at which Philip II negotiated the final settlement of his acquisition of the Portuguese throne, no mention was made of Brazil. This fact reflected not only Portuguese lack of interest, but also the motivation of Spanish action. The decision by Philip II to contest the Portuguese succession was primarily influenced by Spanish desires to become an Atlantic power and the need for a base in the coming struggle with England. If in 1580 the Portuguese colonies influenced Spanish actions, it was the spice of India and the slaves of West Africa that attracted Philip II. Although showing signs of growth after 1570, Brazil in 1580 was still the tail end of empire. Its European population lived precariously in the shadow of attack from hostile Indians and European rivals. Scattered along the littoral and concentrated at a few urban nodules the total population of colonists, officials and clergy was probably around 20,000. Unlike Spanish America, Brazil could boast of no printing press, no universities few noble edifices and little apparent mineral wealth. Within the next fifty years, however, Brazil because of its sugar agro-industry and because of Portuguese losses in Asia became the focal point of empire. The change in dynasty in the metropolis was accepted without difficulty in the colony and without dissent. No sympathy was given to Dom António, and the Portuguese Pretender, or to his French allies. The Spanish Hapsburgs, kings of Spain and now of Portugal, easily became rulers of Brazil.

The presence of Spaniards in Brazil during the union is a matter that need not detain us long. There always had been Spaniards in the Brazilian enterprise just as Portuguese had participated in Spain's colonization of America. Hence, Spaniards resident in Brazil from 1580 to 1640 should not be surprising although there was a considerable increase in their numbers during this period. The Portuguese Crown was traditionally lenient about the settlement of foreigners in Brazil and the original grants to the proprietors (*donatarios*) in the 1530's required only that the lands be distributed to Catholics, Italians, Frenchmen, Flemings, and Englishmen who were along with Spaniards among the foreigners who settled in Brazil. Inquisition records of 1591–93 for northern Brazil, however, indicate that Spaniards constituted 37.8%–55% of the foreign community, by far the largest non-Portuguese group. In São Paulo and the south the percentage was probably even higher, and Spaniards were active members of the Paulista expeditions.

The long-standing and well-documented sentiments of distrust and rivalry between Spaniards and Portuguese did arise in Brazil, and colonists there considered the epithet "dirty Galician" a sufficient cause for drawn swords. Most complaints, however, were directed against specific policies and abuses committed by groups of Spaniards rather than against the individual settler. For example, the Spanish contingent in the joint armada that recaptured Bahia from the Dutch in 1625 looted as well as liberated the city, and the local residents complained that the Castilians had left "neither door nor lock unbroken." There was also a steady stream of complaint against the garrisons of Spanish soldiers stationed in Brazil occasioned by the unruly nature of these troops and the taxes levied to support them. There were some in Brazil who considered Bahia an occupied not a defended city.

Despite these colonial reflections of peninsular prejudices, the Spaniards in Brazil seem to have been well-integrated into society and Luso-Spanish personal relations were amiable This was especially true of the nobility which in both countries shared similar attitudes and aspirations and were often directly linked by kinship or marriage to noble families across the frontier. We need go no further than Salvador de Sá, governor of Rio de Janeiro, who was the brother-in-law of Luís de Cespedes, governor of Paraguay. Just how friendly these relations could be was indicated by Fernando de Vargas, a Spanish noble who visited Bahia in 1594. He stated:

> There is in this city of Bahia a gentleman, Governor Francisco de Sousa, who did me such favors that I know not how to exaggerate them, giving me money with as much willingness as if I were his heir. . . . I found many other Portuguese hidalgos who . . . I must praise for they answered my every need; providing whatever I asked and offering me much more. . . ."

Similarities of religion, culture, and attitudes added to the rigors of colonial existence created a condition in Brazil that allowed for the integration of resident Spaniards into the community.

The common acceptance of the individual Spaniard, however, should not obscure determined Portuguese opposition to any concerted Spanish political or economic penetration of he imperial structure. Sevillian merchants were at first more interested in profiting from the West African slave trade than in participating in the Brazilian sugar and dye-wood commerce, but Spanish mercantile interests soon found it convenient to lease monopoly rights to Portuguese contractors in order to secure Negroes for the Spanish American colonies. Portuguese maritime and commercial groups including those in Brazil derived great profit from this arrangement. Subsequent attempts by Seville and the Casa de Contratación to impose strict regulations on the contractors, to wrest control of the slave trade, or to enter the Brazilian trade were met with bitter and determined resistance by the Portuguese. Not only did the Portuguese profit from their connections with Buenos Aires, Catagena de Indias and Cuba, but despite Spanish regulations a considerable contraband trade developed between Brazil and Spain itself. Some of the Brazilian products passed into southern Spain, but a well-developed network arose in northern Spain where Brazilian sugar was traded for Vizcayan iron.

In Brazil, the most significant economic penetration effected by the Spaniards was the contract ceded to a coalition of Vizcayan merchants in 1602 for the hunting of whales in the Bay of All Saints. The project had been suggested by the Portuguese themselves as a means of providing the colony with oil, but the Vizcayans found it more profitable to reship some of the oil to Spain and thus maintain inflated prices for this commodity in Brazil. This situation and the development of a skilled labor force of Negroes and mulattos eventually moved enterprising Portuguese to break the monopoly, and by 1608 the Vizcayans had competitors. The price of oil in that year fell 40% as a result of the increased supply. A lawsuit developed in 1609 and the high Court of Bahia, staffed by Portuguese magistrates, ruled against the Spanish monopoly. The decision of the court was that "it should not be denied to natives. . . that which is conceded to foreigners."

Reforms and policies initiated by the Hapsburgs in Portugal had a direct effect in Brazil, especially in terms of organization and administration. The creation in Portugal of institutions for colonial control such as the merchant guild or *Consulado* in 1591, and the India Council (Conselho da India) in 1604 placed Brazil in a new administrative relationship to the Crown. Most important, the Spanish reform of Portuguese justice begun in 1582 resulted in the publication of the *Phillippine Ordinances (1603)* which remained the basic law of Brazil until the nineteenth century. It was also as a result of this reform that the first High Court of Appeal (Relaçâo) was established in Bahia in 1609. Moreover, during the Hapsburg period the first visits of the Inquisition were made to Brazil (1591–93, 1618), but despite ardent research no direct Spanish influence has been discovered.

Brazil under Hapsburg control was subject in the early years of the seventeenth century to two territorial divisions. The captaincies of the south—Espirito Santo, Rio de Janeiro, and São Vicente—were placed under a separate governor in 1609 and the vast region of Maranhão was created an independent unit in 1621. We know in both cases the ostensible reasons for these divisions; administrative independence to facilitate mining in the former and difficulties of communication with Bahia in the latter, but whether any Spanish plan for territorial or economic aggrandizement was involved has never been investigated. Certainly, there was some Spanish interest in occupying the Amazon basin after 1640, and even during the union Viceroy Montesclaros of Peru had suggested the incorporation of São Paulo in the Spanish Indies. It may be more than coincidence that the first man chosen to be governor of

Maranhão was Diego de Carcamo, a Spaniard, and that the only region of Brazil to display pro-Hapsburg sentiment in 1640 was the town of São Paulo.

Portuguese colonists in Brazil not only realized that they were under Spanish kings, but they sought to derive some benefit from this fact. Spanish forms or policies that suited the colonists and served local interests were often petitioned for by them. A common tactic was pointing to usage in Spanish America and then appealing for similar solutions in Brazil.

The encomienda and Indian slavery provide a case in point. In Spanish America the encomienda as a system for the control and exploitation of groups of Indians had gradually withered in the face of royal control and the opposition of Spanish moralists. By the beginning of the seventeenth century it was quite clear that the Crown had little intention of expanding this institution. Nevertheless, colonists in Brazil, faced with high prices for Negro slaves and royal legislation against enslavement of the Indian, saw the encomienda as an alternate solution to the chronic problem of labor. Thus in 1605 Governor Diego Botelho petitioned for the establishment of the encomienda in Brazil. A more constant advocate of the encomienda was Bento Maciel Parente, Indian fighter and later Captain-major of Maranhão. In a number of memorials to the Crown, usually penned in Spanish, he suggested a division of the Indians of Maranhão in encomiendas "as is done in the Indies of Castile."

When, however, Hapsburg legislation for Brazil was unpopular the argument was turned about. The Spanish Hapsburgs had continued in Brazil the policy initiated by the dynasty of Aviz against enslavement of the Indian. Protective laws of 1587, 1595, and 1605 should have indicated to the colonists the thrust of royal intent. When, however, in 1609 a new and more stringent law was issued for Brazil local reaction was virulent. There were threats of rioting in Rio de Janeiro and in Bahia rioting actually erupted. Most interesting is a letter from the municipal council of Parahiba to Philip IV complaining that the law of 1609 "was made and formulated in the kingdom of Castile and it has little applicability in Brazil." The colonists in this case were able to force a withdrawal of the unpopular legislation.

Brazilian colonists were aware of the desire of the Spanish Hapsburgs to increase the flow of precious metal into the royal coffers. American silver had become the main support of imperial policy and as the production of Potosí crested in the late years of the sixteenth century of the Crown became increasingly concerned with discovering new sources of supply. Portuguese in Brazil were no less anxious to find these riches and here again the example of Peru and Mexico was constantly before them. There is a Peruvian fixation readily discernible in many of the chroniclers of the period and this "edenic complex" stimulated both rumor and expeditions. But the residents of Brazil not only hoped to get rich from the discovery of mines, they desired other benefits in return for their service to the Crown.

Gabriel Soares de Sousa obtained wide-reaching powers from Madrid in return for his promise to exploit mines near the São Francisco River in the late 1580's. It is worth recalling that his famous chronicle was written as a promotional brochure to gain support at the Spanish court. Others followed his example. Dom Francisco de Sousa, Governor of Brazil when Soares de Sousa made his petition, agitated in Madrid for similar privileges. His proposal to exploit mines in southern Brazil was approved, and Francisco de Sousa was made Governor of the Captaincies of the South which were separated to aid his project. Francisco de Sousa placed a great deal of emphasis on Spanish example and Spanish participation in the mines he hoped to exploit. He urged the Crown to send goldminers from Chile, a silver specialist from Potosí, and an iron mining expert from Vizcaya to act as advisors. From Buenos Aires he wished to receive foodstuffs and even llamas (*carneiros de carga*) to carry out the minerals. To regulate the mines he asked for the mining code of Peru, the *Nueva Caderno* and taxation according to the system used in New Spain The labor force would be provided by Indians once again under the law of Peru, or in other words, institution of the *mita* method of corvee labor. Francisco de Sousa wished the Indians brought to service by persuasion or coercion but the Crown ruled out the second method. It was suggested by the Crown, however, that Jesuits go into the bush to coax Indians to the mines and both Dom Francisco and his successors used this expedient.

What, in fact, we may have here is Portuguese use of Hapsburg cupidity to circumvent Hapsburg Indian legislation. Certainly, this was the case in a similar project in Bahia also considered in 1609. The India Council saw through the ruse and warned the king that the petitioners were rich men who wished to "bring Indians in from the sertão and serve themselves of them for personal ends more than to discover mines." The Hapsburg period was an important era in the search for mineral wealth and Brazilians hoped for a variety of benefits from the mineral aspirations of the Spanish.

Even while the search for the elusive mines continued, sugar was providing Brazil with a basis for wealth and development. The colony was fast becoming the keystone in the economy of the Portuguese empire, an empire that had always been a commercial enterprise above all else. At the same time Brazil was becoming increasingly important to Spain but for very different reasons. This divergence between Spain and Portugal over the role of Brazil in imperial theory bespoke a growing difference in imperial concerns which became a major factor in the revolt of Portugal in 1640.

Luso-Spanish relations from 1580 to 1640 fall into two periods. The first from 1580 to 1622 is characterized by considerable Portuguese profit as a result of the union. . . . The year 1622 marks the beginning of a period of loss and disillusionment. . . .

Both Spaniards and Portuguese had long recognized the strategic importance of

Brazil, a consideration of which the Dutch were also aware. Spaniards feared that with a Brazilian port as a base, the Dutch or English could make forays into the Caribbean against the silver fleets, interdict the homeward bound Indiamen, sail into the seas off Chile and Peru, interrupt the slave trade, and most important, attack Peru and its mines by way of the Rio de la Plata. This fear increasingly determined Hapsburg policy toward Brazil and the colony became crucial in Spanish geopolitics. Brazil was to be the first line of defense for Peru and a rampart or the Spanish Indies. Philip IV and the Count-Duke of Olivares considered Peru and its silver, not Brazil and its sugar, as the heart of empire, and all means had to be taken to defend the arteries to and from that heart. For this end Philip IV was willing to violate the agreements of Tomar, sacrifice Brazilian development, and alienate the Portuguese.

After 1630 Dutch capture of Pernambuco brought forth more extreme responses from Spain which in turn increased Portuguese bitterness. In 1631 Philip IV attempted to populate Brazil with Italians and other foreigners as an effective means of securing the coast. Here was an obvious violation of the Tomar agreements. It is wrong, however, to assume that Spain was unwilling to make sacrifices of her own for the Brazilian line of defense. In 1632 Spain offered diplomatically to surrender hard-won Breda to the Dutch along with 200,000 to 300,000 florins in return for their evacuation of Pernambuco.

Spain , however, expected Portugal to bear the costs for the defense of its empire. This had been the justification of the "Union of Arms" sponsored by Olivares in 1626 and was the cause of increased taxation in the 1630's. Each new measure, each new tax produced Portuguese resistance. Spanish councillors could not perceive the cause of this discontent. Why should the Portuguese grumble, they asked, about paying for the defense of Portuguese colonies? After all, had not Spain equipped fleets, provided funds, and sent troops to defend Brazil? Yet, the Portuguese were recalcitrant.

Attempts were made to force all members of the Portuguese military orders to serve in Brazil under the excuse that the war was a religious matter. The Crown set legal experts to the task of finding some clause in the grants to the *donatarios* that would require them to personally defend their areas. In both cases the Portuguese successfully resisted. In Brazil the High Court was abolished and its salaries applied to the garrison in Bahia. Taxes were imposed on the colonists and after 1633 on all the municipalities of Portugal to pay for the war in Brazil. The first major anti-Hapsburg revolt occurred in Evora, a city with little interest in Brazil, because of a new tax to support the conflict in the colony.

Rather than driving the Dutch from Brazil by force and turning Brazil into a bulwark of empire, colonial and continental Portuguese wished to open the old lines of commerce, lines that included trade with Holland. In 1626, the Governors of Portugal put the matter succinctly. They asked the Crown, "if the utility of closing commerce to enemies is worth more than the lack of commerce." Within this commercial definition of empire, Brazil now exercised a dominant influence and its trade was the motive force of the imperial structure. Spanish interest in Brazil was real but defined in strategic terms. The divergence of these two concepts of the role of Brazil was a major factor for the dissatisfaction with Hapsburg rule in both Brazil and Portugal. Brazil, disregarded in 1580, had become by 1640 a determinant of Spanish policy and a reason for rebellion in Portugal.

THE DUTCH IN BRAZIL

2. The Humanist Prince Johan Maurits in Recife, 1637–1644

C. R. BOXER

Some Brazilian historians are inclined to play down the Dutch period as a time when no substantial results were achieved because of the ever-present commercial spirit of the invaders. They emphasize rather the importance of the local Brazilian effort that successfully expelled the Dutch in 1654, and the consequences of that action. The Dutch moved their tools, slaves, and techniques for raising sugar to the West Indies, which, along with their command of shipping, enabled them to maintain a decisive lead in the world's sugar markets. Some Jews fled from Pernambuco to Manhattan and established the first synagogue there. These years also saw the beginning of a deliberate shift in Portuguese imperial policy, during which Portugal became convinced that Brazil was more valuable than were other parts of the far-flung empire such as the island of Ceylon (present-day Sri Lanka) which they relinquished in 1658.*

But an important result of the rule of one Dutch governor, "the humanist prince" Johan Maurits, was that Europe became aware of Brazil through paintings and books made possible by his imaginative support for a group of artists and scholars as described by Professor Boxer.

Johan Maurits has been called "the most remarkable man ever connected with the sugar industry," and an outline of his record as governor-general of Netherlands Brazil shows that this estimate is not an exaggerated one. He was not only a capable general and a first-class administrator, but a ruler who was in many respects far in advance of his time. . . .

During the seven years of his rule he spared neither his own energy nor the Company's money in his efforts to develop the colony. He improved and enlarged the existing city of Recife with new (and paved) streets, roads, and bridges. He laid

* See George D. Winius, *The Fatal History of Portuguese Ceylon* (Cambridge, Mass.: Harvard University Press, 1971).

From *The Dutch in Brazil, 1624–1654* by C. R. Boxer (Oxford: Clarendon Press, 1957), pp. 112–55, passim. Reprinted by permission of the Clarendon Press, Oxford.

out a new town named Mauritia, or Mauritsstad, on the adjoining island of Antonio Vaz, the site of which forms the heart of the modern city of Recife. Here he built two spacious country-seats, one of them complete with a well-stocked aviary and zoological and botanical gardens, where he indulged his taste for growing exotic fruits and transplanting tropical trees on a lavish scale. He also erected the first astronomical observatory and meteorological station in the New World where regular wind and rainfall records were kept. He even envisaged the foundation of a university which would be frequented by Protestant Dutch and Catholic Portuguese, although this particular project never got beyond the paper stage.

During his stay in Brazil Johan Maurits gathered around him a carefully selected entourage of forty-six scholars, scientists, artists, and craftsmen from the Netherlands, all of whom had their own special functions and assignments. Piso studied tropical diseases and their remedies, Marcgraf made scientific collections of the fauna, flora, and geography of Brazil and Angola, in addition to astronomical and meteorological observations; while half a dozen painters, including Frans Post and Albert Eckhout (the latter possibly a pupil of Rembrandt) filled their portfolios with sketches of every aspect of local life and culture. Only a part of the material amassed by these men was published in Johan Maurits's lifetime; but the sumptuous folio volumes of Barlaeus, Marcgraf, and Piso, printed at the count's expense after his return to Holland, are among the finest examples of seventeenth-century book production. For over 150 years they remained the standard works on Brazil in any language. . . .

"La belle, très belle et bellissime maison" of the Mauritshuis at The Hague, well known to all art-lovers and visitors to the Netherlands, was originally built for Johan Maurits to the design (or at least under the supervision) of his friend, the celebrated architect Pieter Post, whose brother Frans had accompanied him to Brazil. This "sugar-house" as the disgruntled directors of the West India Company sarcastically called the new palace, was largely furnished with Brazil-wood sent home by Johan Maurits during his tenure of office, and it was no wonder that his countrymen nicknamed him "Maurits the Brazilian." The museums of Berlin, Copenhagen, and Paris still contain valuable ethnographical and artistic collections which form only a fraction of those which he and his helpers methodically amassed in Brazil. No such systematic and intelligently directed scientific work by white men in the tropics was seen again until the great expeditions of Captain Cook and his successors. With every justification did Johan Maurits choose for his motto the Latin phrase *Qua patet orbis,* "As wide as the world's bounds."

Nor was Johan Maurits less enlightened in his treatment of the local Portuguese. He fully understood the importance of reconciling the planters and the *moradores* to Dutch rule, and his efforts met with a considerable degree of success, at any rate outwardly. A staunch Protestant himself, and in an age when Calvinists and

Catholics regarded each other as inevitably doomed to hell-fire, he deliberately tolerated the local Roman Catholic priests and Friars (the Jesuits alone excepted), despite the opposition of the colonial Calvinist ministers and their supporters at home. In an endeavour to avoid the evils of monoculture and to make the colony self-supporting in foodstuffs, he fostered the cultivation of manioc and other crops besides sugar. He reduced taxation and allowed liberal credit-terms to the planters to help them rebuild their ruined *engenhos* and to buy Angola slaves. He gave them a form of representative local government, through the creation of municipal and rural councils on which both Portuguese and Dutch colonists could serve, although his efforts to induce the two races to co-operate whole-heartedly met with no lasting success.

On leaving the colony in 1644 he observed that the secret of ruling Pernambuco was to remember that the Dutch merchants attached more importance to their money and goods than to their lives, whereas the Portuguese inhabitants valued courtesy and politeness more than property or pelf. . . .

He stressed the unreliability of evidence extorted under torture, even when this was duly sanctioned by law; and he emphasized the importance of maintaining strict discipline among the garrison, while paying them punctually and feeding them well. All in all, it is not surprising to learn from Fr. Manuel Calado, who was a frequent and welcome guest at government-house, that the Pernambuco Portuguese called Johan Maurits their "Santo Antonio" after the most popular saint in their calendar. His departure was sincerely mourned by the whole colony, Calvinist Netherlands, Catholic Portuguese, and cannibal Tapuyas alike. The total production of sugar during his tenure of office was estimated at 218,220 chests valued at 28 million florins, and the sugar industry was well on the way to compete recovery when he left. It was also during his rule that improved methods of cultivating sugar and tobacco were introduced from Pernambuco into the Antilles, thus giving a great impetus to the economic development of the English and French possessions in the Caribbean. . . .

John Maurits was, as a Brazilian historian recently observed, a true *grand seigneur* who only felt at home in a spacious palace or on an extensive estate. He constructed two country-seats on the island of Antonio Vaz, where he laid out the new city of Mauritsstad, one being called by a Dutch name, "Vrijburg," and the other by a Portuguese, "Boa Vista." Fr. Manuel Calado gives us an entertaining account of John Maurits and his princely tastes in the graphic pages of the *Valeroso Lucideno.*

"The Prince-Count of Nassau was so preoccupied with the construction of his new city, that to induce the *moradores* to build houses, he himself went about very carefully plotting the measurements and laying out the streets, so that the town should look more beautiful. And by means of a dike or levee through the middle of it, he brought the water of the river Capivaribe from the entrance of the bar. Canoes, boats and barges entered by this dike for the use of the *moradores*, underneath wooden bridges which crossed over this dike in some paces, as in Holland, so that the island was completely surrounded by water. He also made there a country-seat which cost him many *cruzados*, and in the midst of that sandy and barren waste he planted a garden stocked with every kind of fruit-tree which grows in Brazil, as well as with many others brought from different parts; and by bringing in much other fruitful earth from outside in lighters, together with a great quantity of manure, he made the site as fertile as the most fruitful soil. He planted in this garden two thousand coconut-trees bringing them there from other places, because he asked the *moradores* for them and they sent them to him in carts. He made some log and beautiful avenues of them, like the Alameda of Aranjues, and in other places many trellised vine-arbours and garden-beds of vegetables and flowers, with some summerhouses for gambling and entertainment. Hither came the ladies and his friends to pass the summer holidays, and to enjoy their convivial gatherings, picnics and drinking parties, as is the custom in Holland, to the sound of musical instruments. The Prince like everyone to come and see his rarities, and he himself delighted in showing and explaining them. And in order to live more at his ease, he left the buildings where he stayed originally, and moved to this country-seat with the greater part of his household.

"He also brought thither every kind of bird and animal that he could find; and since the local *moradores* knew his taste and inclination, each one brought him whatever rare bird or beast he could find in the back-lands. There he brought parrots, macaws, *jacijs, canindes,* wading-birds, pheasants, guinea-fowl, ducks, swans, peacocks, turkeys, a great quantity of barnyard-fowls, and so many doves that they could not be counted. There he kept tigers, ounces, *cissuarana,* ant-bears, apes, *quati,* squirrel-monkeys, Indian boars, goats from Cape Verde, sheep from Angola, *cutia, paguu,* tapirs, wild boars, a great multitude of rabbits—and in short there was not a curious thing in Brazil which he did not have, for the *moradores* sent him these with a good will, since they saw that he was kindly and well-disposed towards them. And thus they also helped him to build these two establishments, both the country-seat Vrijburg where he lived, as well as Boa Vista on the bank of the Capivaribe, where he spent many days strolling around and enjoying himself. For some sent him wood, others tiles and bricks, others lime, and in short they all helped him in what they could." . . .

Fr. Manuel Alado did not exaggerate the popularity of Johan Maurits with the Portuguese of Pernambuco, and not for nothing did they term the heretic but humane and humanist prince their Santo Antonio. As indicated above, Johan Maurits's guiding principle in dealing with the *moradores* was his conviction that if they were treated with courtesy and consideration, they would be more amenable and obedient to the company's rule than were the Dutch colonists themselves. . . .

Johan Maurits naturally had an uphill task in defending the Catholics against the zeal of the *predikants,* who continually tried to whittle down the amount of religious freedom which the *moradores* had been formally granted. The consistory could not very well refuse to allow liberty of conscience, since this much was guaranteed by the terms of the Company's charter and was enjoyed by Roman Catholics in the United Netherlands; but liberty of public worship was something which they were ill disposed to tolerate. In 1638, for example, the consistory complained of "the great liberty allowed the papists, even in places which had surrendered unconditionally." The *predikants* pointed out that monks and friars were "allowed to live in their cloisters, draw their incomes and revenues unhindered, and officiate at the marriages of Netherlanders," &c. They petitioned Johan Maurits to stop these practices, as no such liberties were allowed to the Roman Catholics in the Seven Provinces.

Johan Maurits adopted a policy of masterly inactivity towards all these complaints, as he explained in his 'political testimony' of 1644. He gave the *predikants* fair words, and promised to see that all unauthorized Roman Catholic activities were duly curbed; but in fact he deliberately refrained from doing so, and continued to give aid and comfort more or less secretly to Calado and the Capuchins. . . .

Johan Maurits's religious toleration was even extended to include the Jews, although hatred, ridicule, and contempt for Jewry was the one point on which the *predikants* and the friars were united. Fr. Manuel Calado asserts that the Jews publicly congregated for worship in two synagogues at Recife; and the Calvinist consistory remonstrated against the toleration of Jewish religious practices almost as frequently as they did against "Popish idolatry." The preachers complained that the local Jews were allowed to marry with Christians, convert Christians to Judaism, circumcise Christians, employ Christian servants in their houses, and keep Christian women as their concubines. The consistory considered it the bounden duty of Johan Maurits and his council to stop these unauthorized activities which gave great scandal to Protestants and Catholics alike. Only in Pernambuco, they complained, did the Jews enjoy unlimited freedom; being subjected to some sort of restrictions in every other country in the world. Johan Maurits ignored both these and subsequent protests; although when individual Jews occasionally overstepped the mark by publicly criticizing the Christian religion, such offenders were severely dealt with. Jewish appreciation of Johan Maurits's attitude was convincingly expressed in 1642, when their representative informed the Heeren XIX "that if His Excellency could be paid to stay in this land by the purchase of anything in the world, that they would find no price too great to pay, even if it were their own blood, if only they might retain him."

Since the religious beliefs of the Negroes and the Amerindians (such as they were) was likewise left virtually undisturbed by the authorities, it can be asserted that a greater degree of religious freedom was allowed in Netherlands Brazil during the years of Johan Maurits's rule than anywhere else in the Western world. For this alone his name and fame are deserving of lasting remembrance. Unfortunately, he was too far in advance of his time; and although he kept the peace between the warring factions of Christianity for seven years, even he could not permanently heal the breach made by the Reformation between Catholic and Protestant. . . .

Another barrier between Portuguese and Dutch was formed by their widely differing social habits and customs. Take, for example, their respective attitudes to wine and women. Although Portugal was a wine-producing country, the Portuguese were (and still are) noted for their abstemiousness. The chaplain to the English factory at Lisbon in the last quarter of the seventeenth century just observed: "I believe there is no people in Europe less addicted to that most inexcusable vice of drunkenness than they are. . . . the people of this country, persons of quality more especially, and indeed all who have the least regard to their credit, being very shy of drinking wine." Holland, on the contrary, produced no vines, but wine was cheaper, more plentiful, and better appreciated there than in many wine-drinking countries. A famous Dutch colonial governor wrote of his countrymen in the East, "our nation must drink or die", and a much-traveled contemporary of his observed that most of the officials of the West India Company "knew nothing but how to drink themselves drunk." We have seen how Fr. Manuel Calado watched with fascinated horror the drinking-bouts over which Johan Maurits jovially presided, although prowess with the bottle was not the only art which was cultivated in Netherlands Brazil.

As for women, the attitude of the Portuguese towards the fair sex was thought to be unduly jealous and restrictive even by the Spaniards, who, like their neighbours, had perhaps inherited their ideas about the seclusion of women from the centuries of Moorish occupation. On the other hand, women in the United Provinces probably enjoyed more freedom than anywhere else in contemporary Europe. Foreign observers frequently noted that most Dutchmen not only discussed matters of business and of state with their wives in private, but drank freely with them in public. This was, of course, the strongest possible contrast to Portuguese practice. The chronicler Duarte Nunes de Leão assures us in his *Descrição do reino de Portugal* (Lisbon, 1610) that women who drank wine were regarded as being in the same category as those who committed adultery. Johan Maurits and his council wrote in 1638 that the local *moradores* jealously secluded their womenfolk, "thus recognizing that the men of their own race are prone to covet their neighbours' wives." . . .

The fact that Reife was one of the most expensive places in the world naturally made the Heeren XIX resentful of Johan Maurits's lavish expenditure. The "Prince of Nassau" had incontestable merits as a governor, statesman, and general, but none as an economist or a financier. He was a free spender of his own and the Company's money, but he never bothered about casting accounts, and he ostentatiously ignored the members of his financial council with whom he seldom deigned to speak. A princely patron of the arts, a keen amateur architect and landscape-gardener, he gave his inclinations full rein, whether in the erection of his costly seat at Vrijburg, in building the bridge between Recife and Mauritsstad, in sending home valuable timber for the Mauritshuis, and in maintaining a galaxy for artists and scientists around him in Brazil. It is true that part of this expenditure came form his own pocket, but most of it was a charge on the Company in one form or another.

The outstanding name among Johan Maurits's entourage is that of the young German scientist, Georg Marcgraf of Liebstadt (1610–44), who was educated at Rostok and Leiden, and who died form fever in Angola at the age of thirty-four and the height of his powers. A modern American scientist has remarked that if he had lived to publish more of his work he might well have become the greatest naturalist since Aristotle. Much of his work has ben lost, but what survives is impressive enough. Apart form the botanical and zoological collections which he sent to Europe in 1644, and which continued to be studied down to the nineteenth century, some of the copious notes on natural history which he left were edited and published by his friend Johannes de Laet in the *Historia Naturalis Brasiliae* (Amsterdam and Leiden, 1648). This work contains the first truly scientific study of the fauna and flora of Brazil, a description of the geography and meteorology of Pernambuco, including daily wind and rainfall records, and an ethnographical survey of the local Amerindian races. The illustrations include 200 woodcuts of plants and 222 of animals, birds, insects, and fishes, most of which had never been described before.

Another version of this work appeared in 1658, in which Marcgraf's contributions were mostly embodied with the observations of his colleague, Dr. Piso, and suffered somewhat in the process. In compensation, this edition contains a few of Marcgraf's pioneer astronomical observations in the southern hemisphere, including the eclipse of the sun in 1640. It may be added that Johan Maurits helped Marcgraf by building an observatory for him in one of the towers of Vrijburg, and by ordering all ships' captains to take careful observation of solar and lunar eclipses as well as other celestial phenomena. In addition to being a naturalist and astronomer, Marcgraf was also an accomplished mathematician, surveyor, and cartographer, many of the maps in Barlaeus's truly monumental work being based on his own. He was not the only cartographer on Johan Maurits's staff, and the remarkably accurate charts and maps drawn by these men were not wholly displaced until within living memory.

Even more celebrated, although not so outstanding a scientist, was Marcgraf's Dutch medical colleague, Dr. Willem Piso of Leiden (1611–78). A year younger than Marcgraf and educated at Caen, he followed Johan Maurits to Brazil as his personal physician, returning to Holland with him in 1644. Fr. Manuel Calado declares that the two men quarreled and became irreconcilable enemies, but he must be exaggerating if he is not entirely mistaken. At any rate, Piso continued to be the count's physician after his return home, and the doctor's studies were published with Johan Maurits's approval and financial support, as Marcgraf's had been ten years before. Piso contributed a lengthy section "De Medicina Brasiliensi" to the *Historia Naturalis Brasiliae* of 1648, which remained an authoritative work on tropical medicine and hygiene until well into the nineteenth century. We owe to Piso, among other things, the first knowledge of ipecacuanha as a cure for dysentery. Piso's interests were not purely scientific. He was a member of the celebrated "Muidencircle," which comprised the cream of Dutch literary and intellectual society, as well as twice dean of the Collegium Medicum at Amsterdam.

Many of the woodcuts which illustrate the works of Barlaeus, Marcgraf, and Piso are derived from the paintings and sketches of Frans Post and Albert Eckhout. These were two of the six artists whom Johan Maurits maintained in Brazil, as he explained to Louis XIV in 1678, when offering the Roi Soleil some specimens of their work. . . . Albert Eckhout (fl. 1637–64) specialized in depicting men and animals, and the quality of his work can be judged from the sketches reproduced by Thomsen, and from his lifelike (and life-size) portraits in oils which are preserved in the National Museum at Copenhagen. Better known than Eckout is his colleague, the landscape-painter Frans Post of Leiden (1612–80), examples of whose charming paintings of the Brazilian rural scene are to be found in several public and private collections. Both these artists have been the subjects of intensive study within recent years, but nothing has yet been discovered about their four colleagues mentioned in Johan Maurits's letter to Louis XIV.

Johan Maurits was not content with bringing six painters from the Netherlands, but encouraged local talent when he found it. Noticing that a German soldier from Dresden named Zacharias Wagener was a clever draughtsman, he made him his steward and gave him the opportunity of developing his talents. Wagener evidently worked closely with Eckhout, as many of the lively sketches in his *Thierbuch,* or album depicting Brazilian men and beasts, are miniature copies or adaptations of Eckhout's work. Wagener later entered the service of the Dutch East India Company, where he rose to be successively envoy to Canton, chief of the Dutch factory at Nagasaki in Japan, and governor of Cape Colony before his death at Amsterdam in 1668.

It is a thousand pities that Johan Maurits dispersed his magnificent Brazilian collections before his death in 1679. Always a lavish spender and, it must be admitted, avid for titles and other marks of regal or princely favour, he began to dispose of his treasures in 1652, when he handed over a large section to the elector of Brandenburg in exchange for some lands along the Rhine. Two years later he presented several of Eckhout's great pictures and other "curiosities" to the king of Denmark, who acknowledged this gift with the bestowal of the coveted Order of the White Elephant. Finally, a twelvemonth before his death, he offered a large number of pictures to Louis XIV, with the suggestion that they would make excellent designs for a series of Gobelin tapestries. The subjects of these *peintures des Indes,* as they came to be known, included Chilean and Peruvian themes, as well as Brazilian and Angolan. The tapestries, although long in the making, wee so successful when finished that they were repeated at intervals on the same looms for the next 120 years. In addition to the surviving pictures of Post and Eckhout, Johan Maurits originated many other paintings and frescoes inspired by the Brazilian scene, some of which survived until lately in Saxony. Unfortunately, most of them have become war casualties, or were accidentally destroyed by fire, such as those at Christiansborg in Denmark and the interior decorations of the Mauritshuis at The Hague. Perhaps the most interesting picture which perished in this way was Eckhout's life-size portrait of Johan Maurits in the midst of a group of Tapuyas.

Johan Maurits's lasting monument remains the sumptuous folio volumes of Barlaeus, Marcgraf, and Piso, which were published under his auspices and which opened a new world to the European ken. This is not to say that they had no precursors, or that the works of the earlier Spanish savants, such as Hernández de Oviedo, Joseph de Acosta, S.J., and Fr. Francisco Ximenez, O.P., were not in themselves extremely valuable. They were, and the same can be said of some Portuguese contributions, such as Brandão's *Diálogos,* and Fr. Christovão de Lisboa's work on the natural history of the Maranhão, both of which, however, remained unpublished for centuries. But the work of Johan Maurits's scientific and artistic team, conducted and co-ordinated under his personal supervision, was less hampered by Aristotelian preconceptions and was inspired by a more rigorous idea of scientific exactitude. This was expressed by Marcgraf when he wrote, "I will not write about anything which I have not actually seen and observed."

Naturally enough, these books had a great and lasting success. We find King John IV writing to his envoy in Holland for a copy of Barlaeus's work within a few weeks of it publication. On the other side of the Atlantic, the Jesuit chronicler Simão de Vasconcellos, writing at Bahia in 1659, refers repeatedly to the books of Marcgraf and Piso which he calls "hua cousa grande." Two centuries later, Lichtenstein, Maximilian prince of Neuwied, Spix, Martius, and many other savants who made South America their field of study frequently drew attention to the accuracy and importance of the pioneer labours of Marcgraf and Piso. In 1912 the American scientist, Dr. E. W. Gudger, observed that the *Historia Naturalis Brasiliae* of 1648 was "probably the most important work on natural history after the revival of learning, and, until the explorations of the prince of Neuwied were made known, certainly the most important work on Brazil." Nor are modern Brazilian historians and scientists backward in their acknowledgments of the debt which their country owes to Johan Maurits and his collaborators in the first purely scientific researches carried out in the New World. . . .

THE SERMONS AND LETTERS OF ANTÓNIO VIEIRA

3. Sermon Condemning Indian Slavery, 1653

Vieira's missionary efforts on behalf of the Brazilian Indians were both strenuous and continuous throughout his long life. His attempts to curb the colonists as they strove to enslave the Indians in their fields and homes made him extremely unpopular with most of his fellow countrymen in Brazil, including the friars of the Mendicant Order, whom he accused of disregard for the welfare of the natives. As Professor Boxer concluded:

> Vieira was nothing if not a bonny fighter, but he had the defects of his pugnacious temperament. He did not suffer fools—or friars—gladly, although he remarked resignedly on more than one occasion that even Our Lord with all his miracles had never cured anyone of folly. . . Above all, in an age when anti-Semitism raged with a virulence only surpassed in our own day and generation, Vieira's fearless championship of the New Christians marks him out as a truly admirable man. António Vieira may not have been what King John IV called him, "the greatest man in the world," but he is entitled to an honored place not only in the history of Brazil and Portugal but in the story of Western civilization.*

Father Vieira preached this vigorous sermon at a time when many colonists in Brazil were clamoring for royal laws permitting the enslavement of the Indians.

SERMON CONDEMNING INDIAN SLAVERY, 1653

At what a different price the devil today buys souls compared to what he offered for them previously! There is no market in the world where the devil can get them more cheaply than right here in our own land. In the Gospel, he offered all the kingdoms of the world for one soul; in Maranhão the devil does not need to offer one-tenth as much for all the souls. It is not necessary to offer worlds, nor kingdoms; it is not necessary to offer cities, nor towns, nor villages. All he has to do is offer a

*C. R. Boxer, *A Great Luso-Brazilian Figure: Padre António Vieira, S. J., 1608–1697* (London: The Hispanic and Luso-Brazilian Councils, 1957), p. 32.

couple of Tapuya Indians and at once he is adored on both knees. What a cheap market! An Indian for a soul! That Indian will be your slave for the few days that he lives; and your soul will be a slave for eternity, as long as God is God. This is the contract that the devil makes with you. Not only do you accept it but you pay him money on top of it. . . .

Christians, nobles, and people of Maranhão, do you know what God wants of you during this Lent? That you break the chains of injustice and let free those whom you have captive and oppressed. These are the sins of Maranhão; these are what God commanded me to denounce to you. Christians, God commanded me to clarify these matters to you and so I do it. All of you are in mortal sin; all of you live in a state of condemnation; and all of you are going directly to Hell. Indeed, many are there now and you will soon join them if you do not change your life.

Is it possible that an entire people live in sin, that an entire people will go to hell? Who questions thus does not understand the evil of unjust captivity. The sons of Israel went down into Egypt, and after the death of Joseph, the Pharaoh seized them and made slaves of them. God wanted to liberate those miserable people, and He sent Moses there with no other escort than a rod. God knew that in order to free the captives a rod was sufficient, even though He was dealing with a ruler as tyrannical as Pharaoh and with a people as cruel as the Egyptians. When Pharaoh refused to free the captives, the plagues rained down upon him. The land was covered with frogs and the air clouded with mosquitos; the rivers flowed with blood; and the clouds poured forth thunder and lightning. All Egypt was dumbfounded and threatened with death. Do you know what brought those plagues to the earth? Unjust captivity. Who brought to Maranhão the plague of the Dutch? Who brought the smallpox? Who brought hunger and drought? These captives. Moses insisted and pressed the Pharaoh to free the people, and what did Pharaoh respond? He said one thing and he did another. What he said was, I do not know God and I do not have to free the captives. However, it appears to me proper and I do declare them free. Do yo know why you do not give freedom to your illicitly gotten slaves? Because you do not know God. Lack of Faith is the cause of everything. If you possessed true faith, if you believed that there was an eternal Hell, then you would not take so lightly the captivity of a single Tapuya. With what confidence can the devil today say to you: *Si cadens adoraveris me?* With all the confidence of having offered you the world. The devil made this speech: I offer to this man everything; if he is greedy and covetous, he must accept. If he accepts, then he worships me because greed and covetousness are a form of idolatry. It is an idea expressed by St. Paul. Such was the greed of Pharaoh in wanting to keep and not to free the captive sons of Israel, confessing at the same time that he did not know God. This is what he said.

What he did was to take out after the fleeing Israelites with all the power of his kingdom in order to recapture them. And what happened? The Red Sea opened so that the captives could pass on dry land (because God knows how to make miracles in order to free captives). It did not matter that the Hebrews did not merit this. They were worse than the Tapuyas. A few days later they worshiped a golden calf, and of all the six hundred thousand men only two entered into the promised land, but God is so favorable to the cause of liberty that he grants it even to those who do not deserve it. When the Hebrews had reached the other side, Pharaoh entered between the walls of water which were still open, and as he crossed, the waters fell over his army and drowned them all. What impressed me is the way Moses tells this: that the waters enveloped them and the sea drowned them and the earth swallowed them up. Now, if the sea drowned them how could the earth swallow them? Those men, like his, had both a body and a soul. The waters drowned the bodies because they were at the bottom of the sea; the earth swallowed the souls because they descended to Hell. All went to Hell, without a single exception, because where all pursue and all capture, all are condemned. This is an excellent example. Now, let us look at the reasoning.

Any man who deprives others of their freedom and being able to restore that freedom does not do so is condemned. All or nearly all are therefore condemned. You will say to me that even if this were true they did not think about it or know it and that their good faith will save them. I deny that. They did think about it and know it just as you think of it and know it. If they did not think of it nor know it, they ought to have thought of it and to have known it. Some are condemned by their knowledge, others by their doubt, and still others by their ignorance. . . . If only the graves would open and some who died in that unhappy state could appear before you, and in the fire of their misery you could clearly read this truth. Do you know why God does not permit them to appear before you? It is exactly as Abraham said to the rich miser when he asked him to send Lazarus to this world: *Habent Moysen et Prophetas* (Luc. 16.29). It is not necessary for one to appear on earth from Hell to tell you the truth because you already have Moses and the Law, you have the prophets and learned men. My brothers, if there are any among you who doubt this, here are the laws, here are the learned men, question them. There are in this State, three religious orders which have members of great virtue and learning. Ask them. Study the matter and inform yourselves. But it is not necessary to question the religious: go to Turkey, go to Hell, because there is no Turk so Turkish in Turkey nor no devil so devilish in Hell who will tell you that a free man can be a slave. Is there one among you with natural intelligence who can deny it? What do you doubt?

I know what you are going to tell me . . . our people, our country, our government cannot be sustained without Indians. Who will fetch a pail of water for us or carry a load of wood? Who will grind our manioc? Will our wives have to do it? Will our sons? In the first place, this is not the state into which I am placing you as you soon will see. But when necessity and conscience require such a thing, I answer yes and repeat again yes. You, your wives, your sons, all of us are able to sustain ourselves with our own labor. It is better to live from your own sweat than from the blood of others! . . .

You will tell me that your slaves are your very feet and hands. Also, you will say how much you love them because you raised them like children and took care of them as you would your very own. It may be so, but Christ said to his land: *Si oculus tuus scandalizat te, erue eum et si manus, vel pes tuus scandalizat te, amputa eum* (Math. 5.29; Marc. 9.42.44). Christ did not mean to say that we should pull out our eyes nor that we ought to cut off our hands and feet. What he meant was that if that which we loved as our eyes harmed us, or that which was as necessary as our hands and feet harmed us, we should cast away from us that source of harm even if it hurts us as if we had cut it off from us. Who amongst you does not love his arm or his hand but should it become gangrenous would not permit its amputation in order to save his life.

. . . If, in order to quiet your conscience or save your soul, it is necessary to lose everything and remain as miserable as Job, lose everything.

But take heart, my friends, it is not necessary at such a state, far from it. I have studied the matter carefully and in accordance with the most lenient and favorable opinion and have come to a conclusion by which, with only minor worldly losses, all the inhabitants of this state can ease their consciences and build a better future. Give me your attention.

All the Indians of this State are either those who serve as slaves or those who live as free inhabitants in the King's villages, or those who live in the hinterlands in their natural or free condition. These latter are the ones you go upriver to buy or "to rescue" (as they say), giving the pious verb "to rescue" to a sale so involuntary and violent that at times it is made at pistol point. These are held, owned, and bequeathed in bad faith; therefore they will be doing no small task if they forgive you for their past treatment. However, if after you have set them free, they, particularly those domestics whom you raised in your house and treated as your children, spontaneously and voluntarily wish to continue to serve you and remain in your home, no one will or can separate them from your service. And what will happen to those who do not wish to remain in your service? These will be obliged to live in the King's villages where they also will serve you in the manner which I shall mention. Each year you will be able to make your expeditions into the interior during which time you can really rescue those who are prisoners ready to be eaten. Those justly saved from death will remain your slaves. Also, all those captured in just wars will be made slaves. Upon this matter the proper judges will be the Governor of the State, the Chief Justice of the State, the Vicars of Maranhão or of Pará, and the Prelates of the four orders: Carmelite, Franciscan, Mercedarian, and the Company of Jesus. All of these who after judgment are qualified to be true captives, will be returned to the inhabitants. And what will happen to those captured in a war not classified as just? All of them will be placed in new villages or divided among the villages which exist today. There, along with the other village Indians they will be hired out to the inhabitants of this State to work for them for six months of every year alternating two months of hired work with two months devoted to their own labors and families. Thus, in this manner, all the Indians of this State will serve the Portuguese either as legitimate slaves, that is those rescued from death or captured in a just war, or those former slaves who freely and voluntarily wish to serve their old masters, or those from the King's villages who will work half the year for the good and growth of the State. It only remains to set the wages of those village Indians for their labor and service. It is a subject which would make any other nation of the world laugh and only in this land is not appreciated. The money of this land is cloth and cotton, and the ordinary price for which the Indians work and will work each month is seven feet of this cloth which has a market value of about twenty cents. An Indian will work for less than a penny a day. It is an insignificant amount and it is unworthy of a man of reason and of Christian faith not to pay such a slight price to save his soul and to avoid Hell.

Could there be anything more moderate? Could there be anything more reasonable than this? Whoever is dissatisfied or discontent with this proposal either is not a Christian or has no understanding. To conclude this point, let us look at the advantages and disadvantages of this proposal.

The single disadvantage is that some of you will lose a few Indians. I promise you they will be very few. But to you who question this, I ask: Do not some of your Indians die or flee? Many do. Will death do what reason will not? Will chance do what a good conscience will not? If smallpox strikes and carries off your Indians, what will you do? You will have to show patience. Well, is it not better to lose the Indians to the service of God than to lose them by a punishment of God? The answer is obvious.

Let us look at the advantages of which there are four principal ones. The first is that you will have a clear conscience. You will not longer live in a state of mortal sin. You will live like Christians, you will be confessed as Christians, you will die like Christians, you will bequeath your goods as Christians. In short, you will go to Heaven and not to Hell, which would certainly be a tragic ending.

The second advantage is that you will remove this curse from your homes. There is no greater curse on a home or a family than to be unjustly supported by the sweat and blood of others. . . .

The third advantage is that in this way more Indians will be rescued from cannibal practices. . . . It is important to invade the forest to save Indians from being killed and eaten.

The fourth and last advantage is that henceforth your proposals on the labor problem will be worthy of submission to His Majesty, and worthy of His Majesty's approval and confirmation. Whoever asks for the illegal and unjust deserves to have the legal and just denied him, and whoever petitions with justice, reason, and good conscience deserves the fulfillment of his request. You know the proposal which you made? It was a proposal which vassals could not make in good conscience, nor could ministers consult it in good conscience. And even if the King might have permitted it, what good would it have done you? If the King permits me to swear falsely, will it mean that the false oath is no sin? If the King permits me to steal, will the theft be any less a sin? The same thing applies to the Indians. The King can command the slaves to become slaves. If such a request went to Lisbon, the stones of the street would have to rise up against the men of Maranhão. On the other hand, if you submit a just, legal, and Christian request, those very same stones would take your part. . . .

4. Sermon for Sexagesima Sunday, Preached in the Royal Chapel, Lisbon, 1655

Soon after his arrival in Lisbon in 1655, Vieira preached this sermon from the pulpit of the Royal Chapel. In it he attacked the idleness of the clergy in Portugal, particularly that of the Jesuits' rivals, the Dominicans, and argued that work in the overseas missions was the highest service a religious could render to the church. In the section reprinted here he criticizes the homiletic conventions of the day, declaring his dislike of the useless affectations of the Baroque school of preaching and arguing that a sermon should be like "stars, which are seen by all and measured by very few."

FROM THE SERMON FOR SEXAGESIMA SUNDAY,
PREACHED IN THE ROYAL CHAPEL, LISBON,
IN THE YEAR 1655, BY FATHER ANTÓNIO VIEIRA

Might it perchance have to do with the style which is today employed in the pulpits? A style so twisted, so laborious, so affected, a style so antithetical to all art and to all nature? There is reason enough in this as well. Style should always be very simple and very natural. That is why Christ has compared the preacher's task to the task of sowing: *Exiit qui seminat, seminare.* So does Christ compare preaching to sowing, because sowing is a skill less akin to art than it is to nature. With other arts, all is art: with music, all is built upon rhythm; with architecture, all is built to scale; with arithmetic, computation; with geometry, measure. Such is not the way with sowing. It is an artless art: fall where it will. Remember our husbandman from the Gospels and how he sowed. Wheat fell upon thorns and sprouted forth; *Aliud cecidit inter spinas, et simul exortae spinae.* Wheat fell upon stones and sprouted forth; *Aliud cecidit super petram, et ortum.* Wheat fell upon good soil and sprouted forth: *Aliud cecidit in terram bonam, et natum.* Thus the wheat: falling and sprouting forth.

So likewise should it be with preaching. Things should fall and things should sprout forth; as naturally as they go falling, so opportunely will they come sprouting forth. How different the violent and tyrannical style which is employed today.

From *The Borzoi Anthology of Latin American Literature: From the Time of Columbus to the Twentieth Century,* ed. Emir Rodríguez Monegal, 2 vols. (New York: Knopf, 1983), 134–35. Reprinted by permission.

Let us watch the sad steps of the Scriptures, approaching as if invested with martyrdom: some are carted along; some are dragged; some, distended; others, twisted;
and others come broken; only the properly bound together fail to make an appearance. Is there such tyranny then? And in the midst of all this martyrdom, how lofty
seems that previous falling. Substance is not to be uplifted, but must be allowed to
fall: *Cecidit*. Not here an allegory peculiar to our language. The wheat of the sower,
even though it has fallen four times, sprouts forth only three; for the sermon to begin
to sprout forth, it should fall in three fashions. It should fall with the proper effect,
it should fall with the proper inflection, it should fall with the proper feeling. The
effect is with respect to the substance, the inflection is with respect to the words, the
feeling is with respect to the spirit. The effect is for the substance, since it must
come about appropriately and in its place: it must have effect. The inflection is for
the words themselves, since they must be neither scabrous nor dissonant: they must
have the proper inflection. The feeling is for the spirit, since it must be natural and
unaffected enough to seem feeling and not effort: *Cecidit, cecidit, cecidit.*

While I am speaking against modern styles, I wish to adopt for myself the style
of the oldest preacher in the world. And who is that? The oldest preacher in the
world is Heaven itself. *Caeli enarrant gloriam Dei, et opera manuum ejus annunti-
at firmamentum,* says David (Psalm XIX,1). Now if Heaven is to be seen as a
preacher, then Heaven must have sermons and it must have words. And so it has, the
same David tells us (Psalm XIX, 3)—words and sermons and, even more, the power
to be heard: *Non sunt loquellae, nec sermones, quorum non audiantur voces eorum.*
And what are these sermons and these words of heaven? The words are the stars, the
sermons are the composition—the order, course, and harmony—of those stars. See
how the style of Heaven preaching addresses us, with that style which Christ taught
us here on earth? Preaching should be in the manner of him who sows, and not in
the manner of him who lays tile or brick. Ordered, but in the manner of the stars:
Stellae manentes in ordine suo (Judges V, 20). All the stars are in their appropriate
order, but it is an order that impels, not an order that ornaments. God made not heav-
en into a checkerboard of words. If in one part it be white, in another there must be
black; if in one part it be day, in another there must be night; if in one part it say
light, in another there must be darkness; if here it say "descended," in another part
there must be "risen." Does it suffice that we never see two words at peace in a sermon? Must all words always be at odds with their counterparts? We learn from
Heaven itself the style of the spirit, and that of words as well. How should words
be? Like the stars. The stars are quite clear and quite distinct. And yet for all that,
you do not fear for any lowliness of style; the stars are quite distinct and quite clear,
and yet the quintessence of loftiness. Style can be quite as clear and quite as lofty—
so clear that it may be understood by those who do not know, and so lofty that it
may challenge the understanding of those who do know. The rustic finds lessons in

the stars for his husbandry, and the sailor for his navigation, and the mathematician for his observations and judgments. In this way the rustic and the sailor, who have never learned to read or write, understand the stars; and the mathematician who has read as much as has ever been written fails to understand all that is contained therein. Thus let a sermon be stars, which are seen by all and measured by very few.

5. Letter to King Alfonso VI of Portugal, April 20, 1657

In this letter Vieira describes the plight of the natives in Marañon and urges King Alfonso VI to hold firm on laws passed in 1654 outlawing Indian slavery. The letter is also of interest in that Vieira condemns the injustice of the African slave trade.

FROM THE LETTER TO KING ALFONSO VI
OF PORTUGAL FROM FATHER ANTÓNIO VIEIRA,
APRIL 20, 1657

Senhor—Divine Providence, which in its loftiest judgment has placed the scepter of Portugal in the hands of Your Majesty at such a tender age, will bestir itself to comfort and enlighten the soul of Your Majesty with the special support of its spirit and grace, as necessitates the burden of so extensive a kingdom, in such circumstances as the present. And we, the monastic brothers of this Mission of Your Majesty, shall not cease to thus continually beseech God, offering to that end and for the sake of the life and happiness of Your Majesty all our sacrifices, prayers, and labors.

Senhor, kings are the vassals of God, and, if kings fail to castigate their vassals, still God castigates his own. The principal cause of crowns failing to perpetuate themselves in the same nations and families is one of injustice, or rather injustices, as it says in the Holy Scriptures. And among those injustices none clamors so much before Heaven as the taking away of the liberty of those who were born free, or as the failure to pay for the sweat of those who labor; and these are and always have been the two sins of this State, which still claims so many defenders. The loss of the late king Don Sebastião in Africa, and the seventy years of captivity which resulted for the whole kingdom, was expiation (as the scribes of that time noted) for that enslavement which on the coast of that same Africa our first conquistadors began to effect, with so little regard for justice (as can be seen in those same histories). But the injustice and the tyranny which have been inflicted on the natives of the present territory far exceed that which was carried on in Africa. In the space of forty years,

From *The Borzoi Anthology of Latin American Literature: From the Time of Columbus to the Twentieth Century,* ed. Emir Rodriguez Monegal, 2 vols. (New York: Knopf, 1983), pp. 135–38. Reprinted by permission.

along the coast and in the backlands, more than two million Indians have been killed and more than five hundred settlements the size of large cities have been destroyed, and for this no punishment has even been noted. In the year 1655, some two thousand Indians were captured long the Amazon River, many of whom were friends and allies of the Portuguese, and vassals of Your Majesty, all in violation of the provisions of the law which in that same year had been delivered to this State, and this was done at the instigation of those who had the greatest responsibility to enforce that same law—and again there was no punishment. And not only do they demand, before Your Majesty, total impunity for such crimes, but even license to continue them!

It is with a great deal of pain, and a great deal of fear about reminding Your Majesty, that I say what I am about to say; but God wills that I say it. Upon King Pharaoh, because he had consented in his reign to the captivity of the Hebrew people, God wrought great punishments, and one of these was to take from him his firstborn. In the year 1654, on the advice of the trustees of this State, a law was passed conferring such excessive license with respect to the enslavement of the Indians that later, Your Majesty being better informed, it would have been wiser to have revoked it, and it has been noted that in that same year God took the firstborn of sons and the firstborn of daughters from Your Majesty. *Senhor*, if someone asks or counsels Your Majesty to grant greater licenses than that which exists today in this respect, then take him, Your Majesty, for an enemy of the life, the posterity, and the crown of Your Majesty

They will say perchance (and they do say) that upon such enslavement, in the manner in which it has been effected, depend the preservation and the expansion of the State of Maranhão. That, *Senhor,* is heresy. If, in order not to commit even a venial sin, it should be necessary to lose Portugal, lose it. Your Majesty, and consider well chosen such a Christian and glorious loss, but I say it is heresy even politically speaking, because nothing is either secure or permanent when founded upon injustice. And experience has shown just that, in this same State of Maranhão, in which so many governors have acquired great wealth, but none of them has enjoyed it nor was it ever maintained by them. Nor is there anything acquired on this island that ever lasts, as the very inhabitants themselves confess: nothing which moves ahead, no business which succeeds, no ship constructed here which comes to any good end; because everything is tinged with the blood of the poor, who are always crying out to heaven.

If the blood of one innocent raised such an outcry to God, what will be the result of so many more? And Abel, *Senhor*, was saved, and is now in Heaven. And if one soul which is saved calls out for vengeance, then what vengeance will so many thousands and millions of souls, which because of the injustices of this State are burning in Hell—despite its being Portugal's just obligation to guide them to Heaven—

what vengeance will they cry out for to God? And that being so, *Senhor*, yet only those who defend justice are persecuted; only those who are busy saving souls are affronted; only those who have taken seriously this great service to God have all men here set against them. Your Majesty would do well to begin to reflect that as long as such tyrannies have been committed in Maranhão there has been no one, ecclesiastical or secular, to administer healing or salvation to these souls; and whenever someone has finally assumed responsibility for one or another of God's labors, immediately there have been so many zealots who take up arms against such service—a clear indication of all this being the mark, and at the instigation, of the devil, in order to impede the spiritual well-being of every Portuguese as well as Indian—that both the one and the other were doomed to Hell. And it would be a disgrace, terrible to behold, if the ministers of the devil should prevail over those of Christ, in a kingdom as Christian as Portugal. The other kingdoms of Christendom, *Senhor*, must work for the preservation of their vassals, for the sake of their temporal felicity in this world and of eternal felicity in the other, the kingdom of Portugal, in addition to this purpose common to all, has as its own particular aim the propagation and extension of the Catholic faith to the lands of the gentiles, it being for that purpose that God has instituted and exalted this kingdom. And the more Portugal concerns itself to this end, the more certain and secure it may be of its preservation; and the more it strays from that course, the more doubtful and hazardous will be the same.

With the return voyage of Your Majesty's dispatches I hope that Your Majesty will have ordered the implementation of all the recommendations that I sent by last year's ships. And since I can not know what may have happened in the meantime, I shall summarize here once again everything that at present is necessary for the preservation, increase, and tranquility of this Christian State. They are principally the four points which follow:

First: that with respect to the law and regulation of Your Majesty concerning the Indians and the missions, nothing be altered, and to this end nothing be given or granted to petitions to the contrary.

Second: that the governors and provincial captains who come to this State be men of conscience; and, since such men are not accustomed to come here, that they at least be made aware of the fact that they will truly suffer punishment, if in any way they should break said law and regulation.

Third: that the heads of the Religious Orders be men concerned to make their members conform to their discipline and commands, that they do not consent to any contravening of them in public or in private; and if there be any disobedient member of an Order in these regions, that he be sent away from Manranhão.

Fourth: that Your Majesty send here a greater number of Jesuit Fathers to help carry on what we who have been here have already begun, because it is the only way (since there is so much work for so few brothers) that the number of heathen can be reduced by conversion.

And since news has reached us that, against us, missionaries who in this State serve God and Your Majesty, and against the government of the said mission, there have been presented to Your Majesty a number of complaints, we humbly beg Your Majesty that Your Majesty be so good as to send us all such to look at, even if they be ones which concern the State, because we hope to satisfy all complaints in such a way that it will become known, with absolute clarity, how useful the missionaries of the Company of Jesus are, not only with respect to the spiritual betterment of the Portuguese and the Indians, but even with respect to the temporal well-being of all.

To the most high and most powerful person of Your Majesty, God keep, as all of Christendom and the vassals of Your Majesty have need.

Maranhão, April 20, 1657.
António Vieira

6. Report on the Conversion of the Nheengaíbas, Letter to Alfonso VI, November 28, 1659

In this report Vieira offers a glimpse of one of his greatest missionary triumphs in the Amazon area.

. . . The great mouth of the Amazon River is obstructed by an island which is larger than the entire kingdom of Portugal and which is inhabited by many tribes of Indians, who are generally called Nheengaíbas because of the many different and incomprehensible languages they speak. At first these tribes received our conquerors with friendship, but after long experience had shown them that the false words of peace with which the conquerors arrived turned into declarations of captivity, they took up arms in defense of their liberty and began to make war on the Portuguese everywhere. . . .

Past governors, and most recently André Vidal de Negreiros, often tried to rid the State of this very troublesome problem, employing all their forces, both Indian and Portuguese, and their most experienced captains in their campaigns. But the only effect of these wars was to strengthen the conviction that the Nheengaíbas were unconquerable because of their audacity, astuteness, and constancy but most of all because of the impregnable position with which nature itself defended them. . . .

Finally, last year, 1658, governor D. Pedro de Melo arrived with news of the war declared against the Dutch, with whom some of the Nheengaíba nations had long traded because of the nearness of their ports to those of the Northern Cape, where each year they loaded twenty Dutch ships with manatees. The government of Pará realized that if the Nheengaíbas allied themselves with the Dutch, they would become masters of these captaincies, for the State lacked the power to resist them. Accordingly, a private citizen was sent to the Governor to ask for help and for permission to invade the territory of the Nheengaíbas with as large a force as possible before their alliance with the Dutch could render this precaution ineffective and cause the loss of the entire State.

After the justification and necessity for the war had been settled by the vote of all the secular and ecclesiastical dignitaries whose consultation Your Majesty

From *Cartas do Padre António Vieira*, ed. J. Lúcio D'Azevedo (Coimbra: Imprensa da Universidade, 1925), vol. 1, pp. 549–71, passim.

requires, Father António Vieira expressed the opnion that, since the war was being prepared in secret and in order to give it additional justification, peace should first be offered to the Nheengaíbas, but without the soldiers and clash of arms that aroused their suspicions, as had occurred in the time of André Vidal. And since this proposal of peace seemed as hazardous as war because of the ferocity which was ascribed to these people, the same Father volunteered to act as an intermediary. Everyone believed, however, that not only would the Nheengaíbas refuse to consider the peace overtures but that they would reply with arrows to those who bore such a proposal, just as they had done for the twenty years since the outbreak of the war.

On Christmas Day of the same year, 1658, Father Vieira sent two Indian nobles with a letter to all the Nheengaíba tribes in which he assured them that by virtue of Your Majesty's new law, which he had gone to Portugal to seek, unjust captures and all the other injuries done to them by the Portuguese had ended forever. He also said that he would await a message from them so that he might go to their territory and that they were to believe whatever the bearers of the letter said in his name.

The ambassadors, who were themselves of the Nheengaíba nation, set out like persons going to their sacrifice (so great was the horror of the fierceness of these tribes even among those of their own blood). Thus they took their leave, stating that if they had not returned by the end of the next moon, we should conclude that they had been killed or captured. . . .

On Ash Wednesday, when they were no longer expected, the two ambassadors returned, alive and very happy, bringing with them seven Nheengaíba nobles and many other Indians of the same tribes, who were received with the acclamation and demonstrations of joy that were due to such guests. They made a lengthy defense of their conduct, in which they blamed the past war entirely on the Portuguese, as was true, and concluded as follows: "But we gave full credence to the letter of the "Great Father," of which we had already heard and who for love of us and of other people of our skin had risked the waves of the sea and had obtained from the King good things for us. Therefore, having forgotten all the injuries of the Portuguese, we have come here to put ourselves in your hands and in the mouths of your firearms. We are certain, however, that with the protection of the priests, of which we will henceforth call ourselves sons, no one will do us harm.". . .

The Father wished to leave with them for their territory at once, but they replied with surprising courtesy that they had hitherto lived like animals under the trees and asked for permission to move one of the Indian settlements down to the edge of the river. They said that after they had built a house and a church in which to receive the Father, they would return in large numbers so that he would be suitably escorted, stating that this would be at the time of St. John, the expression they use to distinguish between winter and summer. Although the Nheengaíbas were still hardly believed, they fulfilled exactly what they promised. Five days before the feast of St.

John they arrived at the settlements of Pará with seventeen canoes, which, with thirteen of the Combocas tribe, who also inhabit the same island, brought the number to thirty. In the canoes there were as many nobles, accompanied by so many people that the fortress and city secretly armed itself.

The Father was unable to leave at this time because he was gravely ill. But it was God's will that on August 16 he was able to leave. . . in twelve large canoes, accompanied by nobles from all the Christian tribes and by only six Portuguese, including the master-sergeant of the garrison, in order to indicate our trust. On the fifth day of the journey they entered the river of the Mapuaezes, the Nheengaíba tribe that had promised to build a settlement outside the bush in which to receive the priests. Two leagues from the harbor the nobles came out to meet us in a large and well-equipped canoe which was decorated with plumes of various colors. They were playing horns and shouting *procémas*, which are cries of happiness and praise that they utter in unison at intervals and are considered the greatest demonstration of joy among them. All of us responded in the same manner. . . .

After they had finally reached the settlement, the priests disembarked, together with the Portuguese and the Christian nobles, and the Nheengaíbas took them to the church, which they had made of palms, according to the custom of the country, and was very clean and well built. It was then dedicated with the name of the Church of the Holy Christ, and a *Te Deum laudamus* was said in thanksgiving. . . .

Messages were then sent to the various tribes. But since the tribes that lived closest to the settlement did not appear in five days, the devil was not idle. Introducing into the minds of the Christian Indians and also of the Portuguese such distrust, suspicion, and fear that they almost abandoned the enterprise, which would have been lost forever. Father António Vieira settled the matter by saying to them that he thought their reasons well founded and that they should all leave; he would stay behind with his colleague, for it was they whom the Nheengaíbas were expecting and with whom they would deal.

But on the following day the Mamaianázes, of whom there was the greatest distrust because of their fierceness, began to arrive in their canoes. And so great were their demonstrations of festivity, trust, and true peace that the suspicions and fears of our people gradually disappeared, and soon their faces and minds and even their speech took on a different aspect.

After a large number of nobles had arrived and the new state of affairs had been explained to them at length both by the priests and by the Indian converts, an order was given for the oath of obedience and fidelity to be taken; and so that it might be done with due solemnity and outward ceremony (which is very important or these people, who are ruled by their senses), it was arranged in the following manner. On the right side of the church were the nobles of the Christian tribes, wearing their best clothes, but without any weapons other than their swords. On the other side were the pagan nobles, naked and adorned with feathers in the manner of savages, with bows and arrows in their hands. The Portuguese were scattered among them. Father António Vieira then said the mass of the Adoration of the Kings before a richly decorated altar. The Indians heard the mass on bended knee, and it was a great source of consolation to those present to see them beat their breasts and adore the host and chalice with such strong devotion to that very precious blood, which, having been shed for all men, had a more powerful influence on them than on their grandfathers.

After the mass, the Father, still dressed in his sacerdotal vestments, preached a sermon in which he told them through interpreters of the dignity of the place in which they were standing and of their obligation to answer truthfully to all the questions that they would be asked and to faithfully carry out what they promised. Then each of the nobles was asked if he wished to receive the faith of the true God and to be a vassal of the king of Portugal, as were the Portuguese and the Indians of the Christian tribes whose nobles were present. They were also told that vassals were obliged to obey the orders of Your Majesty in everything and to keep perpetual and inviolable peace with all his vassals, being friends to his friends and enemies to his enemies. If they did this, they would enjoy with freedom and security all the possessions and privileges that had been granted to the Indians of this State by Your Majesty in the law of 1655.

They all responded in the affirmative. Only one noble, who was called Piyé and was the most intelligent of all, said that he did not want to make these promises. And since the onlookers were struck by this unexpected reply, he went on to say that "the questions and sermons of the Father should be addressed to the Portuguese and not to the Indians, for they had always been faithful to the King and had always recognized him as their lord from the beginning of the conquest. They had always been friends and servitors of the Portuguese, and if this friendship had been broken, it was the fault of the Portuguese. Therefore, it was the Portuguese who now had to make promises since they had violated them many times, while the Indians had always kept their word."

The reasoning of this savage was greeted with delight, as were the terms which which he qualified his fealty. Then the leading noble came to the altar where the Father was standing and, throwing his bow and arrows to the ground, fell to his knees. With his hands in those of the Father, he swore as follows: "I promise to God and the King of Portugal in my name and in that of all my subjects to have faith in our Lord Jesus Christ and to be the vassal of His Majesty. I also promise to keep perpetual peace with the Portuguese, to be a friend to their friends and an enemy to their enemies, and to fulfill these obligations forever." After this had been said, he kissed the hands of the Father, who gave him his blessing. Then the other nobles did the same in turn.

After the oath-taking had ended, all of them came to embrace the Father, then the

Portuguese, and finally the nobles of the Christian tribes, with whom they had also been at war. And it was an occasion for great thanksgiving to God to see the happiness and true friendship with which these embraces were given and received and to hear the things that were said among them in their fashion.

Finally, they all got to their knees and the priests said a *Te Deum laudamus*. After they had left the church, the Christian nobles picked up their bows and arrows, which had been left outside. In order to make a public demonstration of what had been dome in the church, the Portuguese removed the balls from their harquebuses, threw them into the river, and fired without them. Then all the nobles broke their arrows and also threw them into the river, thereby fulfilling a statement: *Arcum conteret et confringet arma*. All this was done to the accompaniment of trumpets, horns, drums, and other instruments and of the continuous shouting with which the crowd declared its happiness. . . .

The triumph of the faith was sealed with the erection on the same spot of a very handsome cross, which the fathers did not allow to be touched by any Indian of low rank. Accordingly, fifty-three nobles carried it on their shoulders to the great joy of the Christians and of the tribes, all of whom admired it. The tribes of different languages who came here were the Mamaianás, the Aruans and the Anajás, among whom are included Mapuás, Paucacás, Guajarás, Pixipixis, and others. The number of souls cannot be counted with certainty; some say that it is 40,000. Among those who came was a noble of the Tucujús, which is a province on the mainland of the Amazon, opposite the island of the Nheengaíbas, and it is reported that they greatly exceed the latter in number, both groups totalling more than 100,000 souls. . . .

THE AFRICAN THREAT

7. Palmares: An African Threat in Brazil

R. K. KENT

The quilombo of Palmares, located in the interior of Alagoas, was by far the longest-lived and largest fugitive slave community in Brazil. It emerged in 1605 and endured to 1694 in spite of determined attempts to eliminate it by the Dutch and Portuguese colonial governments and by local residents in the neighboring captaincies. It was not a single community but a number of settlements that together may have totaled twenty thousand inhabitants. The following article by Raymond Kent emphasizes that Palmares was an adaptation of African cultural forms to the Brazilian colonial situation and that its existence had significance for African as well as Brazilian history.

. . . Nothing . . . compares in the annals of Brazilian history with the "Negro Republic" of Palmares in Pernambuco. It spanned almost the entire seventeenth century. Between 1672–94, it withstood on the average one Portuguese expedition every fifteen months. In the last *entrada* against Palmares, a force of 6,000 took part in 42 days of siege. The Portuguese Crown sustained a cumulative loss of 400,000 cruzados, or roughly three times the total revenue lease of eight Brazilian Captaincies in 1612. As Brazil's classic *quilombo*, Palmares gained two more distinctions. It opened the study of Negro history in modern Brazil. Minutes of the Brazilian Historical Institute reveal that Palmares caused lively discussions in 1840, and that search for written materials relative to it began in 1851. Important gaps in knowledge persist, but enough primary sources have been found and published to trace the development of Palmares, to examine it as a society and government, and to suggest its significance to both Brazilian and African history.

Early writers attributed the birth of Palmares to Portuguese-Dutch struggles for Pernambuco, from which slaves profited by escaping in groups. They made no reference to Palmares as a quilombo. Southey came across the term in a Minas Gerais

From "Palmares; An African State in Brazil" by R. K. Kent, *Journal of African History* 6 (Cambridge University Press, 1965): 161–75, passim. Reprinted by permission.

decree of 1722. An official letter, sent from Pernambuco to Lisbon in 1692, contains the first and only definition of Palmares as a quilombo in primary sources. The point is worth stressing. The accepted definition of a quilombo as a fugitive slave settlement has been continuously applied to Palmares since the turn of this century, and the problem of interpretation has been more difficult as a result. An early nineteenth-century historian, for example, could easily classify Palmares as the "unusual exception, a real government of escaped Blacks on Brazilian soil." But subsequent identification of the state which was a major historical event with a mere colony of escaped slaves could not provide a framework to fit the problem. . . .

Clearly, quilombo does not appear in the vocabulary of early seventeenth-century Brazil. Instead, the fugitive slave settlement is known as *mocambo,* an appropriate description since mu-kambo in Ambundu means a hideout. Around 1603, *palmares* was simply any area covered by palm trees. There was no connexion between the Itapicuru mocambo south of Sergipe and the Palmares of Pernambuco. Palmares was not regarded as an ordinary mocambo. By 1612, it had a considerable reputation. It was an organization with which the *moradores* could not cope alone. The foundation of Palmares thus appears to have taken place in 1605/06, possibly earlier, but certainly not later. . . .

All of this leads to the only plausible hypothesis about the founders of Palmares. They must have been Bantu-speaking and could not have belonged exclusively to any sub-group. Palmares was a reaction to a slave-holding society entirely out of step with forms of bondage familiar to Africa. As such, it had to cut across ethnic lines and draw upon all those who managed to escape from various plantations and at different times. The Palmares which emerged out of this amalgam may be glimpsed in a little more detail during the second half of the seventeenth century . . . .

Dutch activities concerning Palmares, from 1640 until the Reijmbach expedition of 1645, are known mainly through Barleus and Nieuhof. They begin with a reconnaissance mission by Bartholomeus Lintz, a Dutch scout who brought back the first rudimentary information about Palmares. Lintz discovered that Palmares was not a single enclave, but a combination of many *kleine* and two *groote* units. The smaller ones were clustered on the left bank of the Gurungumba, six leagues form its confluence with the larger Paraiba and twenty leagues from Alagoas. They contained "about 6,000 Negroes living in numerous huts." The two large *palamars* were deeper inland thirty leagues from Santo Amaro, in the mountain region of Barriga, and "harboured some 5,000 Negroes." In January 1643, the West India Company sent its Amerindian interpretor, Roelox Baro, with a force of Tapuyas and several Dutch regulars to "put the large Palmares through 'fire and sword,' devastate and plunder the small Palmares." Baro seems to have returned without his men to report that "100 Negroes of Palmares were killed as against one killed and four wounded

Dutchmen, our force having captured 31 defenders, including 7 Indians and some mulatto children." The four Dutchmen and a handful of Tapuyas were found two months later. There was no one with them.

A second Dutch expedition left Selgado for Palmares on 26 February 1645. It was headed by Jürgens Reijmbach, an army lieutenant who kept a diary for thirty-six consecutive days. His task was to destroy the two *groote* Palmares. On 18 March Reijmbach reached the first and found that it had been abandoned months earlier. "When we arrived the busy growth was so thick that it took much doing to cut a path through." Three days later, his men located the second one. "Our Brasilenses managed to kill two or three Negroes in the bush but most of the people had vanished." Their kind—the few captives told Reijmbach—"knew of the expedition for some time because he had been forewarned from Alagoas." This Palmares, reads the entry of 21 March,

> is equally half a mile long, its street six feet wide and running along a large swamp, tall trees alongside. . . . There are 220 *casas*, amid them a church, four smithies and a huge *casa de consello;* all kinds of artifacts are to be seen. . . . (The) king rules . . . with iron justice, without permitting any *feticeiros* among the inhabitants; when some Negroes attempt to flee he sends *crioulos* after them and once retaken their death is swift and of the kind to instill fear, especially among the Angolan Negroes, the king also has another *casa*, some two miles away, with its own rich fields. . . . We asked the Negroes how many of them live (here) and were told some 500, and from what we saw around us as well we presumed that there were 1,500 inhabitants all told. . . . This is the Palmares *grandes* of which so much is heard in Brazil, with its well-kept lands, all kinds of cereals, beautifully irrigated with streamlets.

In military terms Reijmbach fared no better than his two predecessors. Bartolomeu Bezzerra and Roelox Baro. An undestroyed Palmares, of which "so much is heard in Brazil," remained free of further interference by Pernambucan authorities until 1672. The ensuing two decades can best be described as a period of sustained war which ended in the complete destruction of Palmares in 1694. As is often the case, warfare and more intimate knowledge of the enemy went together, and the growing information about Palmares in the 1670s threw light on its evolution during the twenty-seven years of relative peace. . . .

There was no doubt. . . . that Palmares maintained its "real strength" by providing "food as well as security" for the inhabitants—largely tillers of land who planted "every kind of vegetables" and knew how to store them against "wartime and winter." All the inhabitants of Palmares considered themselves:

subjects of a king who is called *Ganga-Zumba,* which means Great Lord, and he is recognized as such both by those born in Palmares and by those who join them from outside; he has a palatial residence, *casas* for members of his family, and is assisted by guards and officials who have, by custom, *casas* which approach those of royalty He is treated with all respect due a Monarch and all the honours due a Lord. Those who are in his presence kneel on the ground and strike palm leaves with their hands as sign of appreciation of His excellence. They address him as Majesty and obey him with reverence. He lives in the royal enclave called *Macoco,* a name which was begotten from the death of an animal on the site. This is the capital of Palmares; it is fortified with parapets full of caltrops, a big danger even when detected. The enclave itself consists of some 1,500 *casas.* There are keepers of law (and) their office is duplicated elsewhere. And although these barbarians have all but forgotten their subjugation, they have not completely lost allegiance to the church. There is a *capela,* to which they flock whenever time allows, and *imagens* to which they direct their worship. . . . One of the most crafty, whom they venerate as *paroco,* baptizes and marries them. Baptismals are, however, not identical with the form determined by the Church and the marriage is singularly close to laws of nature. . . . The king has three (women), a *mulata* and two *crioulas.* The first has given him many sons, the other two none. All the foregoing applies to the *cidade principal* of Palmares and it is the king who rules it directly; other *cidades* are in the charge of potentates and major chiefs who govern in his name. The second *cidade* in importance is called *Subupuira* is ruled by king's brother (Gana) *Zona.* . . . It has 800 *casas* and occupies a site one square league in size, right along the river *Cachingi.* It is here that Negroes are trained to fight our assaults (and weapons are forged there).

Nearly three decades of peace had a number of important results in the internal evolution of Palmares.

Instead of the two major *palmars* of 1645, there were now ten. There was a very substantial element in the Macoco of those native to Palmares, people unfamiliar with *engenho* slavery. Afro-Brazilians continued to enjoy preferential status, but the distinction between *crioulos* and Angolas does not appear to have been as sharp as it was in 1645. There was a greater degree of religious acculturation. The reference to a population composed mainly of those born in Palmares and those who joined from outside suggests that slaves had become less numerous than free commoners. According to Pitta, the only slaves in Palmares were those captured in razzias. But they had the option of going out on raids to secure freedom by returning with a substitute. This is confirmed by Nieuhof, who wrote that the main "business" of *palmaristas* "is to rob the Portuguese of their slaves who remain in slavery among them, until they have redeemed themselves by stealing another; but such slaves as run over to them, are as free as the rest." . . .

Palmares did not spring from a single social structure. It was, rather, an African political system which came to govern a plural society and thus give continuity to what could have been at best a group of scattered hideouts.

The almost equally long years of peace and war between 1645–94 point to Palmares as a fluctuating "peril." While not necessarily unfair to the merits of a particular event, the Portuguese took it for an article of faith that Palmares was an aggressor state. No written document originating within Palmares has come to light. . . .

Pernambucan authorities did not view Palmares from the perspective of the *moreadores* who were in contact with it. They were too far removed from the general area of Palmares. Reijmbach, for example, had to march at a fast clip for twenty days to reach it from the coast, which the Pernambucan governors—Dutch or Portuguese— seldom left. The governors did, however, respond to *morador* pressure. "*Moradores* of this Captaincy, Your Majesty, are not capable of doing much by themselves in this war. . . . At all hours they complain to me of tyrannies they must suffer from [the Negroes of Palmares]." Among the complaints most frequently heard were loss of field hands and domestic servants, loss of settler lives, kidnapping and rape of white women. Two of the common grievances do not stand up too well. Women were a rarity in Palmares and were actively sought during razzias. But female relatives of the *morador* did not constitute the main target, and those occasionally taken were returned unmolested for ransom. Checking the "rape of Sabines" tales, Edison Carneiro discovered one exception to the ransom rule, reported by a Pernambucan soldier in 1682. Equally, close examination of documents in the Ennes and Camara de Alagoas collections—117 in all—failed to reveal a single substantiated case of a *morador* killed in *palmarista* raids. Settler lives appear to have been lost in numerous and forever unrecorded "little" *entradas* into Palmares. They were carried out by small private armies of plantation owners who sought to recapture lost hands or to acquire new ones without paying for them. Some of the *moradores* had secret commercial compacts with Palmares, usually exchanging firearms for gold and silver taken in the razzias. Evidence of this is not lacking. A gubernatorial proclamation of 26 November 1670 bitterly denounced "those who possess firearms" and pass them on to *palmaristas* "in disregard of God and local laws."

In 1687, the state of Pernambuco empowered a Paulista Colonel-of-Foot to imprison *moradores* merely suspected of relations with Palmares, "irrespective of their station." Town merchants are also known to have carried on an active trade with Palmares, bartering utensils for agricultural produce. More than that, they "were most useful to the Negroes . . . by supplying advance information on expeditions prepared against them (and) for which the Negroes paid dearly." And

Reijmbach's entry of 21 March 1645 makes it clear that this relationship was an old one.

Loss of plantation slaves, through raids as well as escape, emerges as the one solid reason behind the *morador-palmarista* conflict. The price of slaves is known to have increased considerably by the late 1660s. The very growth of Palmares served to increase its fame among the plantation slaves. . . .

Six expeditions went into Palmares between 1680–6. Their total cost must have been large. In 1694, the Overseas Council in Lisbon was advised that Palmares caused a cumulative loss of not less than 1,000,000 cruzados to the "people of Pernambuco." The estimate appears exaggerated unless the 400,000 cruzados contributed directly by the Crown was included. A single municipality did, however, spend 3,000 cruzados (109,800 reis) in the fiscal year 1679/80 to cover the running cost of Palmeres wars, and a tenfold figure for the local and state treasuries would seem modest for the six years. Casualties aside, the results did not justify the cost. Palmares stood undefeated at the end of 1686. It was apparent that the state of Pernambuco could not deal with Palmares out of its own resources. In March 1687, the new governor, Sotto-Maior, informed Lisbon that he had accepted the services of *bandeirantes* from São Paulo, "at small expense to the treasury of Your Majesty." The Paulistas of the time were Portuguese-Amerindian *metis* and transfrontiersmen, renowned in Brazil for special skills in jungle warfare. Their leader, Domingos Jorge Velho, had written to Sotto-Maior in 1685 asking "for commissions as commander-in-chief and captains in order to subdue . . . (Palmares)." Largely because Lisbon could not be convinced that their services would come cheap, the Paulistas did not reach Pernambuco until 1692. In crossing so great a distance, 192 lives were lost in the backlands of Brazil, and 200 men deserted the Paulista ranks, unable to face "hunger, thirst and agony."

The story of Palmares' final destruction has been told in great detail. Two-thirds of the secondary works discuss the Paulistas and the 1690s, some sixty of the ninety-five documents in the Ennes collection refer to little else, and Ennes has published a useful summary in English. The Paulistas had to fight for two years to reduce Palmares to a single fortified site. After twenty days of siege by the Paulistas, the state of Pernambuco had to provide an additional 3,000 men to keep it going for another twenty-two days. The breakthrough occurred during the night of 5–6 February 1694. Some 200 *palmaristas* fell or hurled themselves—the point has been long debated—"from a rock so high that they were broken to pieces." Hand-to-hand combat took another 200 *palmaristas'* lives and over 500 "of both sexes and all ages" were captured and sold outside Pernambuco. Zambi, taken alive and wounded, was decapitated on 20, November 1695. The head was exhibited in public "to kill the legend of his immortality." . . .

The service rendered by the destruction of Palmares, wrote one of Brazil's early

Africanists, is beyond discussion. It removed the "greatest threat to future evolution of the Brazilian people and civilization—a threat which this new Haiti, if victorious, would have planted (forever) in the heart of Brazil." Indeed, Palmares came quite close to altering the subsequent history of Brazil. Had they not experienced the threat of Palmares in the seventeenth century, the Portuguese might well have found themselves hugging the littoral and facing not one, but a number of independent African states dominating the backlands of eighteenth-century Brazil. In spite of hundreds of *mocambos* which tried to come together, Palmares was never duplicated on Brazilian soil. This is ample testimony of its impact on the Portuguese settler and official.

They organized special units, under *capitães-do-mato* or bush-captains, to hunt for *mocambos* and nip them in the bud. And they sought to prevent, at ports of entry, an over-concentration of African slaves from the same ethnic group or ship. This policy was abandoned in the wake of the Napoleonic wars, and the immediate repercussion came by way of the nine Bahian revolts after 1807. The well-established thesis that uninhibited miscegenation and the corporate nature of the Portuguese society in Brazil produced a successful example of social engineering must also take into account the historical role of Palmares.

Palmares was a centralized kingdom with an elected ruler. Ganga-Zumba delegated territorial power and appointed to office. The most important ones went to his relatives. His nephew, Zambi, was the war chief. Ganga-Zona, the king's brother, was in charge of the arsenal. Interregnum problems do not seem to have troubled Palmares, the history of which spans about five generations of rulers. Zambi's palace revolt did not displace the ruling family. Assuming that Loanda was the main embarkation point for Pernambucan slaves, which is confirmed by the linguistic evidence, the model for Palmares could have come from nowhere else but central Africa. Can it be pinpointed? Internal attitudes toward slavery, prostrations before the king, site initiation with animal blood, the placing of the *casa de conselho* in the "main square," or the use of a high rock as part of a man-made fortress lead in no particular direction. The names of *mocambo* chiefs suggest a number of possible candidates. The most likely answer is that the political system did not derive from a particular central African model, but from several. Only a far more detailed study of Palmares through additional sources in the archives of Angola and Torre do Tombo would refine the answer. None the less, the most apparent significance of Palmares to African history is that an African political system could be transferred to a different continent; that it could come to govern not only individuals from a variety of ethnic groups in Africa but also those born in Brazil, pitch black or almost white, latinized or close to Amerindian roots, and that it could endure for almost a full century against two European powers, Holland and Portugal. And this is no small tribute to the vitality of traditional African art in governing men.

Juana Inés de la Cruz, poet and scholar in seventeenth-century Mexico. This famous nun and outstanding poet of the Hispanic world in the seventeenth century is portrayed quietly seated in the only painting that has come down to us. But she was an independent thinker, too, whose life was one great struggle to develop her immense labor and who found inspiration in everyday concerns, for she once remarked that if Aristotle had been a cook and had observed what went on in a kitchen he would have had many more ideas.

SECTION VII

The Development of Society

THE POSITION OF WOMEN

Although the last three decades have seen a growing interest in exploring the history of women in colonial Spanish America, many questions remain to be answered. In her recent survey of the literature, Professor Asunción Lavrin points out that "much of what we know so far about colonial women reflects the life of the upper echelons of society." Still, she argues, "Enough research has been carried out to point to significant similarities and differences in life-styles, attitudes, motivations, and aims among colonial women of all walks of life." Women's history in the colonial period cannot be measured by events or developments of a political character—the marks of distinction of a man-oriented world:

> Women were not personally or institutionally encouraged to assert themselves through actions that were in any way political; yet it cannot be said that their role was totally passive or marginal. They must be approached through the specific institutions of which they formed an intrinsic part, forms of collective behavior, the manners and mores of classes or groups. Change was slow and not deliberate. Certain traditions were preserved at the personal level by unfailing observance; others by legal means. Thus, continuities are more apparent than changes.[1]

In his book *Race Mixture in the History of Latin America*, the Swedish historian, Magnus Mörner, observed that the Spanish conquest of the Americas was in many ways "a conquest of women," for the Spaniards obtained native women both by force and by peaceful means.[2] They considered them as much a part of the booty as

---

1. Asunción Lavrin, "Women in Spanish American Colonial Society," in the *Cambridge History of Latin America*, ed. Leslie Bethell (Cambridge: Cambridge University Press, 1984), 2: 9.
2. Magnus Mörner, *Race Mixture in the History of Latin America* (Boston: Little, Brown and Company, 1967), 23.

gold, and on the "amazing advent of the bearded white men, many gave themselves freely, not only as to the victorious fighting male, but as offerings to beings who were manifestly gods. Chiefs sought to placate the invaders, or to cement alliances with them, by gifts of women which the Spaniards saw no reason to refuse."[3] In Peru Atahualpa gave one of his sisters to Francisco Pizarro, who fathered two sons by her before marrying off the princess to one of his pages. In Mexico Moctezuma gave Cortés one of his daughters, Tecuichpotzin, who was eventually wedded to five husbands—and who in giving birth to children of two prominent conquistadors became a "pioneer of mestizaje" (Reading 1). The Crown's attitude toward such alliances was ambivalent. At first it prohibited marriage with native women, but after 1514 it passed legislation encouraging it as a way to integrate the conquerors and conquered and bring about more effective rule.

While some native women may have improved their social standing through marriage, the vast majority lost the status they had enjoyed in pre-conquest society to become servants to the new masters. For example, some Aztec women in Mexico had been economically independent through careers as weavers or midwives and even as merchants. After the conquest "the general situation of the women deteriorated, so that such activities as were formerly performed by a servant group fell to them, and this often without the social appreciation that the professional groups had enjoyed." The Catholic Church further restrained Indian women's "possibilities of extending their activities and thus their cultural participation beyond the traditional home-sphere."[4]

Notwithstanding the abundance of native women, the Spanish crown considered the presence of European women vital to the creation of a sound colonial society. It encouraged matrimony in every way possible and steadfastly urged women to migrate to establish stable homes. A comprehensive study of the lives of Spanish women in Peru can be found in James Lockhart's pioneering social history, *Spanish Peru 1532–1560: A Colonial Society* (Madison: University of Wisconsin Press, 1968) whose chapter on African slaves in Peru appears in Section V. Lockhart uses evidence from notarial and judicial documents to challenge the myth that Spanish women took little part in the early settlement of Peru. As Reading 2 reveals, women in fact formed a large minority in the colony's population and exerted an even greater cultural influence than their numbers might suggest.

Scholars have only begun to study the role of women in the Portuguese colony

---

3. Stephen Clissold, *Latin America: New World, Third World* (New York: Praeger Publishers, 1972), p. 47.

4. Anna-Britta Hellborn, *La participación cultural de las mumeres: Indias y mestizas en el México precortesiano y postrevolucionario* (Stockholm: The Ethnographical Museum, 1967), pp. 300–301.

of Brazil, but it is generally agreed that Brazilians shared the typical European attitudes of the time "that women were to be protected and secluded from the affairs of the world and expected to be devoted to the life of an obedient daughter, submissive wife, and loving mother. A rigid double standard of female chastity and constancy and male promiscuity was condoned to the point of the law's permitting an offended husband to kill his wife caught in an act of adultery."[5]

Travelers who visited Brazil observed that the ideas of seclusion and chastity, even for upper-class women, were often circumvented, and Stuart Schwartz has shown that in general, the role of women in colonial society was more complex than is usually portrayed. The archival records reveal that on becoming widows or being deserted by their husbands, many women became the heads of their households. Women owned plantations, sugar mills, and urban real estates. Middle and lower class women had even more active economic roles. For example, "The small-scale ambulating retail trade in the colonial cities was almost exclusively in the hands of women of colour, both slave and free."[6]

SOR JUANA INÉS DE LA CRUZ

Most women in Spanish America married or lived in consensual unions, but a small number chose to take the veil as nuns, dedicating their lives to the service of God. With the founding of the convent of Nuestra Señora de la Concepción in Mexico in the decade of the 1540s, nunneries spread quickly throughout the empire since every major city wanted a convent as a sign of urban rank and religiosity. Within the walls of the cloisters women obtained not only protection and religious fulfillment, but a reasonable education for the period. In addition the convents participated actively in the colonies' economic life. They owned urban property both for their own residences and schools, and as sources of income. "Religious life was an alternative choice for those women who did not wish to marry, who had strong religious vocations, or who appreciated the relative independence that the cloisters gave them."[7]

Sor Juana Inés de la Cruz, the most renowned poet of colonial Spanish America, is an example of a woman who spurned marriage for convent life in order to continue her scholarly endeavors. Born Juana de Asbaje y Ramírez de Santillana at the hacienda of San Miguel Nepantla, not far from Mexico City, she was an intellectu-

---

5. Stuart Schwartz, "Colonial Brazil, c. 1580–c. 1750: Plantations and Peripheries," in the *Cambridge History of Latin America*, 2: 496.

6. Ibid., 2: 497.

7. Lavrin, "Women in Colonial Society," p. 343.

al prodigy who reputedly learned Latin in twenty lessons at the age of eight. At six-teen she went to the Viceroy's palace and soon became a favorite of the Vice-Reina, the Marquesa de Mancera. Her beauty and her brilliant poetry made her the belle of the court, but when faced with the options of marriage or the church, she chose the latter, entering the Convent of the Discalced (Barefoot) Carmelites shortly before her sixteenth birthday. After the daily regime of this order proved too strict, Sor Juana withdrew to enter the convent of San Jerónimo, a far less rigid order located in the heart of Mexico City. In this sheltered community she remained a kind of poet laureate of the viceregal court. She continued to write poetry and to pursue her scholarly studies, until under intense pressure of the Bishop of Puebla, Don Manuel Fernández de Santa Cruz, who urged her to devote her talents to more spiritual pur-suits, she renounced her literary life. In 1693 Sor Juana sold her library of some four thousand books and her musical and scientific instruments, and gave the money to the poor. Devoting her remaining two years of life to the most severe forms of reli-gious penance, she died in the convent in 1695 while nursing her sister nuns during a devastating plague (Reading 3).

THE TEXTURE OF URBAN LIFE

Spaniards have long been noted for their devotion to town and city life, and in America they paid great attention to establishing and administering many centers of population. The royal ordinances of 1573 for laying out new towns reflected this concern and were incorporated into the Laws of the Indies. But a Renaissance spir-it was also present. Spanish-American towns followed a regular and unvarying grid-iron plan of broad, straight streets intersecting one another at right angles to form rectangular blocks and open squares. They radically departed from the system employed in Spain, whereas in Brazil, the Portuguese tended to rely on medieval and traditional forms that sometimes repeated the specific town plans of Portugal.

Through three centuries, colonial life, particularly in Spanish America, was def-initely urban and multiracial. The process of mestizaje produced a unique caste soci-ety that assigned different social values to the respective races and mixtures. The Spanish officials Jorge Juan and Antonio de Ulloa provide an excellent picture of the complicated structure of class and caste that had emerged in the Andean city of Quito by the eighteenth century (Reading 4), while Lewis Hanke's account of the booming mining camp at the Villa Imperial de Potosí in modern-day Bolivia exem-plifies in gaudy colors the passion for wealth that drew many Spaniards to the New World (Reading 5).

Brazilian cities were much less the focus of activity than were their counterparts in Spanish America. The Brazilian scholar José Arthur Rios states that their charac-ter throughout the colonial period was "marginal," but it is clear that important centers of population developed in Brazil, even though economic and political power was usually concentrated to a considerable extent in the hands of the great land-holding *senhores*. The boom and bust nature of the Brazilian economy resulted in drastic changes in the lives of towns as their economies fluctuated violently under the influence of international commerce:

> Thus we had cities of sugar, cotton, tobacco, and later, coffee. When the international market shifted, the cultures died and the cities also died. Brazil is full of these dead cities—houses in ruins, silent bell towers, streets over-grown with grass. They declined with the same rapidity with which they had grown.[8]

One town, Bahia, the "Bay of All Saints," was the capital of Brazil for most of the colonial period and remained important until 1808, when the Portuguese Prince Regent Dom João VI brought his court to Rio de Janeiro, which ensured its dominance. Professor Charles R. Boxer gives a lively picture of this ancient city in Northeast Brazil noted both for its sanctity and for its sinfulness (Reading 6).

8. José Arthur Rios, "The Cities of Brazil," in *Brazil: Portrait of Half a Continent*, ed. T. Lynn Smith and Alexander Marchant (New York: Dryden Press, 1951), pp. 198–99.

THE POSITION OF WOMEN

1. Isabel Moctezuma: Pioneer of Mestizaje

DONALD CHIPMAN

Native women were not necessarily passive victims of Spanish rapacity. In the social process of amalgamating cultures, many sacrificed the "psychic comforts of life among people of their own kind for the chance to achieve greater security and a higher standard of living for themselves, an improved status and greater economic opportunity for their children, and some access to people in the seats of power." The story of Isabel Moctezuma, as related by Professor Donald Chipman of North Texas State University, suggests that this young Aztec noblewoman was a "spirited historical actor, motivated by personal ambition, by an instinct for the preservation of self and family, and in some instances by love itself."*

In 1502 the Aztecs of Central Mexico observed the death of the Emperor Ahuitzotl with a solemn state funeral of four days' duration. Ahuitzotl had been the last of three successive brothers to rule the empire, a fact that complicated the selection of a new sovereign. After some maneuvering, the late emperor's nephew Xocoyotzin prevailed over several of his brothers and cousins, and in 1503 at the age of perhaps thirty-five he assumed power as Moctezuma II. At the new ruler's side was his legitimate wife, Teotlalco, who had been distinguished from a host of concubines by virtue of a formal marriage ceremony.

The marriage of young Aztec noble persons was contracted between the families of the two parties and celebrated with a nuptial dance followed by a feast. When the young couple retired to the wedding bed, the parents symbolically tied the skirt of the bride to a blanket covering the groom. For three days the newlyweds remained

*David Sweet and Gary B. Nash, eds., *Struggle & Survival in Colonial America* (Berkeley and Los Angeles: University of California Press, 1981), 212–13.

From "Isabel Moctezuma: Pioneer of Mestizaje," by Donald Chipman, in *Struggle & Survival in Colonial America,* ed. David Sweet and Gary Nash (Berkeley and Los Angeles: University of California Press, 1981), 214–25. © Copyright by the Regents of the University of California. Reprinted by permission.

in a closed bedroom, attended only by a female servant who periodically brought them food and took care of their needs. Without this ceremony a couple was not properly united, and without it no children could claim legitimacy or inheritance. If one may believe chroniclers of the Spanish conquest, by 1519 Moctezuma II had fathered 150 children, of whom fifty or more were sons; at one point the emperor is believed to have had fifty women in various stages of pregnancy. Whatever the actual numbers, it is clear that only a few of his offspring were legitimate heirs by Aztec standards. In 1509 or 1510 the first-born child of Moctezuma and Teotlalco was a female named Tecuichpotzin, meaning perhaps "little royal maiden." When Moctezuma consulted his daughter's horoscope in the Aztec book of fate, he found to his amazement that she would have many husbands. How this could be possible within the confines of Aztec custom was beyond his comprehension. After the birth of Tecuichpotzin, Teotlalco also bore the Aztec emperor an undetermined number of legitimate sons.

By 1520 the Aztec emperor and his family had unwillingly fallen captive in his capital of Tenochtitlan to a small force of Spaniards and Indian allies led by the conqueror Fernando Cortés. Following an ill-advised and fearful slaughter of Aztec nobility by the impetuous Pedro de Alvarado, the populace of Tenochtitlan rose in massive rebellion. Moctezuma, in collaboration with the Spaniards, attempted unsuccessfully to quell the uprising. Shortly thereafter the emperor died under circumstances that have never been resolved. Before his death, Moctezuma had asked Cortés to assume custody and care of his one legitimate and several illegitimate daughters. They included Tecuichpotzin, later known to the Spaniards as doña Isabel, and her three half-sister, known as doñas Ana, Maria, and Mariana. The conqueror also had in his power several sons of Moctezuma II.

The rebellion in Tenochtitlan, far from being quieted by the entreaties of Moctezuma, intensified in late June 1520, ultimately forcing Cortés to retreat from the Aztec capital via the Tacuba causeway on the night of June 30. This *noche triste,* as it is known in Spanish sources, was also the final night for some four hundred Spanish soldiers. Lost on the causeway were doña Ana and perhaps a legitimate son of Moctezuma. According to Cortés, two other legitimate sons were captured by the Aztecs, of whom one was crazy and the other a paralytic. What is certain is that doñas Isabel, Maria, and Mariana were reunited with their people, for all were captured from the fleeing and panicky Spaniards by the temporarily victorious Aztecs.

For Tecuichpotzin this was the beginning of a matrimonial odyssey that was to deliver her to five husbands—two Indians and three Spaniards—as well as to an extramarital liaison with Cortés. The Aztec princess was first wed to her uncle, Cuitláhuac, brother of Moctezuma II, who had been elevated to emperor by the rebellion of 1520. Within sixty days Cuitláhuac had fallen victim to smallpox, a disease carried into Mexico by the Spaniards that would contribute substantially to their conquest. Because Tecuichpotzin was no more than eleven years of age at this time, it is generally assumed that her first marriage was unconsummated. Soon after Cuitláhuac's death, however, she was claimed as the bride of her cousin Cuauhtémoc, the last Aztec emperor. According to testimony given years later by her fifth husband, Juan Cano, it appears that Tecuichpotzin was married to Cuauhtémoc in the ceremony of tied blanket and skirt. Cano also maintained that Cuauhtémoc had ruthlessly consolidated his power by imprisoning and later killing Asupacací, the last legitimate son of Moctezuma II and the brother of his bride.

For approximately one year Tecuichpotzin remained with Cuauhtémoc, enduring the vengeful siege and destruction of Tenochtitlan perpetrated by Cortés and his captains. When the Aztec capital fell on August 13, 1521, Cuauhtémoc made a desperate attempt to escape across the water of Lake Texcoco in a large canoe accompanied by his young wife. Pursued and overtaken by the fastest Spanish brigantine, Cuauhtémoc is alleged to have said, "I am your prisoner and I ask no favor other than that you treat my queen, my wife, and her ladies-in-waiting with the respect they deserve due to their sex and condition." Taking doña Isabel's hand, Cuauhtémoc then stepped aboard the brigantine. With the emperor taken prisoner, the Aztecs in boats on the lake made no further attempt to escape, choosing to share the fate of their leader.

For Tecuichpotzin, soon christened Isabel, life continued for three decades, during which she figured as the most prominent Indian woman in colonial Mexico and as a pioneer of *mestizaje*. Cuauhtémoc's days, unfortunately, were numbered. He was separated from his wife, subjected to horrible torture in the Spaniards' quest for treasure they believed was buried in the rubble of Tenochtitlan, and then forced to accompany Cortés on the arduous Honduran expedition from 1524 to 1526. En route to Honduras, Cuauhtémoc was tried, convicted, and hanged by Cortés for allegedly plotting an insurrection. Cuauhtémoc has been remembered as a martyr of Mexico and a symbol of its Indian heritage. Doña Isabel's career was less dramatic, but her procedure for coping with the Spanish conquerors undoubtedly had greater impact on the forging of the Mexican nation.

It was not until the late spring of 1526, when Cortés returned to Mexico, that doña Isabel learned of her husband's tragic fate; she was then sixteen or seventeen years old. Marriage to another Aztec nobleman was out of the question, since the Spaniards had eliminated most of those who had been of the appropriate rank and would in any event have been unwilling to allow the establishment of a new family with pretensions to the Aztec throne. Another consideration was that Moctezuma's daughter was a symbol of great legal and sociological importance to the Hispanization and Christianization of Mexico. This was not lost on the shrewd conqueror.

On June 26, 1526, Cortés granted to doña Isabel and her descendants the revenues and income from the important town of Tacuba, as well as from the several smaller villages that were subject to Tacuba. It was a rich inheritance by the standards of the newly established colonial society, although paltry in comparison with the patrimony that might have been due doña Isabel from her father. Altogether this grant of *encomienda*, pending approval by the crown, included twelve *estancias* and the pueblo of Tacuba for a grand total of 1,240 houses and several thousand Indian vassals. Significantly, Tacuba was a "perpetual" grant, similar to the Marquesado del Valle bestowed on Cortés in the late 1520s. Exempted from the restrictive laws that curtailed *encomienda* in the sixteenth century, Tacuba accompanied Isabel through each of her Christian marriages and provided her family with a handsome yearly income. The advantages of a perpetual grant are borne out by the fact that Tacuba, which had ranked ninth in size of tributary units in the immediate post-conquest era, was the largest *encomienda* in the Valley of Mexico by 1566. Each of the eight larger *encomiendas* originally awarded to Spaniards had escheated to the crown by the 1560s.

In awarding the *encomienda* of Tacuba to doña Isabel, Cortés was at pains to establish that Moctezuma II had served as a willing and valuable collaborator in furthering the work and realms of the king of Spain. Making no mention of the times that Moctezuma had tried to ambush his army on its march to Tenochtitlán, he stressed only that the emperor had placed himself under obedience to the king and that he had lost his life in a vain attempt to restore the fidelity of his misguided subjects. The "señor de Tenochtitlán" had been a "defender of Spaniards," and "a sympathizer of the Catholic Faith," and as such must be viewed as having been the legitimate ruler of his lands. In making doña Isabel the *encomendera* of Tacuba, Cortés claimed to be discharging his conscience as well as the king's for having appropriated lands that by right belonged to Moctezuma. It was an argument worthy of a Renaissance diplomat. The crown quickly approved of Isabel's grant and of others bestowed by Cortés on the surviving children of Moctezuma. By awarding these *encomiendas*, the crown hoped to forestall the possibility that the emperor's heirs would later lay claim to much greater inheritances—as in fact they attempted to do. The crown also established by this means the important legal principle that Spanish law took precedence over any natural rights of Indian inheritance.

Cortés had at least one other object in mind when he made this grant of *encomienda* to doña Isabel. It would provide her with a suitable dowry for the marriage he was about to arrange, which he foresaw would be of great significance to the evangelization of Mexico. On June 27, 1526, just one day after his grant of *encomienda* to Isabel Moctezuma, Cortés appointed an old friend and associate to the post of visitor general of Indians. The appointee, Alonso de Grado, was specifically charged with the responsibility of investigating any mistreatment of the Indians and of instituting legal proceedings to punish the guilty. Grado, an

Extremaduran like many of the conquistadors, had come to the New World at an early age. He had been an *encomendero* on the island of Española in 1514 and a charter member of the Cortés expedition to Mexico in 1519. Then, having accompanied the army of the conqueror on its march inland until its first pitched battle with the fierce Tlaxcalans, he had been frightened by the smallness of the Spanish force when compared with the seemingly endless horde of hostiles and had agitated for a retreat to Veracruz where they might be reinforced with troops sent by the governor of Cuba. But Cortés had repudiated the governor's sponsorship and destroyed his own fleet at Veracruz, thereby committing himself to victory. Grado was sent back to the coast for the duration of the conquest and established there a record for exploiting the Indians, demanding payments from them in foodstuffs, jewels, and pretty Indian women. He was also guilty of disloyalty to Cortés by meeting secretly with adherents of the governor of Cuba. After the occupation of Tenochtitlán in late 1519, Cortés ordered Grado arrested and brought to the capital in chains. He then dismissed the charges against him, and from that point on Grado remained on solid terms with the conqueror. Cortés when awarding doña Isabel as a bride in 1526, extolled Grado's lineage and character. Bernal Diaz, of more honest pen, portrayed don Alonso as a sharpster, clever with words both spoken and written.

As the wife of a prominent conquistador, doña Isabel would become a model of Hispanicized Indian womanhood whom Cortés expected others to emulate. The mixture of races in New Spain was to be founded in principle on the legitimate grounds of holy matrimony, providing a solid matrix for a new society. Perhaps even more important, it was to be expected that the daughter of the Aztec emperor, whose namesake had been the most Catholic queen of Spain, once thoroughly converted to the Faith would also by her example hasten the evangelization of the country. Years later there was little doubt in the mind of doña Isabel's fifth husband, Juan Cano, that his wife had indeed served this lofty purpose:

Although born in our Spain [Mexico], there is no person who is better educated or indoctrinated in the Faith. . . . and it is no small benefit or advantage to the tranquility and contentment of the natives of this land, because she is the gentlewoman of all things and a friend of Christians, and because of respect and her example quiet and repose are implanted in the souls of the Mexicans.

Doña Isabel remained married to Alonso de Grado for less than two years. By 1528 don Alonso was dead of unknown causes, whereupon the solicitous Cortés moved the young and childless nineteen-year-old widow under his own roof to join the ranks of his Indian mistresses. She was, according to several eyewitnesses, a comely young lady (Bernal Diaz found her "a very pretty woman for being an Indian"). In a short time the Aztec princess was pregnant with the conqueror's child, and although Cortés himself had no intention of taking her as his wife, he did begin arrangements for her second Christian marriage.

This time the choice fell on one Pedro Gallego de Andrade. Don Pedro had arrived in Mexico shortly after the conquest was completed in 1521. An Extremaduran from the province of Badajoz, he had served in the conquests of Pánuco, Michoacán, and Colima. In compensation for these efforts he had received an *encomienda* town with the sonorous name of Izquiyuquitlapilco and a high-born but pregnant bride. Some four or five months after Gallego's marriage to doña Isabel, a daughter sired by Cortés was born in his household. She was christened doña Leonor Cortés Moctezuma and was the first of seven children to be born to the Aztec princess. Soon afterward the infant was placed in the home of Licentiate Juan Altamirano, a cousin of Cortés by marriage and subsequently chief administrator of the conqueror's vast estates in New Spain. There doña Leonor lived as a ward until the occasion of her marriage.

In 1530 doña Isabel bore Pedro Gallego a son named Juan (Gallego) de Andrade Moctezuma. The celebration in Tacuba of don Juan's birth was a gala event marked by fiestas and banquets with honored guests in attendance. The sacrament of baptism for the infant was administered by none other than His Excellency Juan de Zumárraga, first bishop of New Spain. For Pedro Gallego it was a proud moment. His aristrocratic Indian wife had given him a son; the revenues of Tacuba and his own *encomienda* made him a wealthy man; he was on good terms with the governors in Mexico city, he moved in the highest social circles; and the bishop himself had sprinkled holy water on his first born. But the moment was short-lived. Within two months Gallego was dead—like Grado of undetermined causes—and at twenty-one doña Isabel had been widowed for a fourth time. None of her husbands had survived for more than a few years, her first, Cuitláhuac, for only sixty days. With such a record she might well have assumed that potential suitors would not tempt fate by rushing her to the altar. But such was not the case. In the spring of 1532 the wealthy doña Isabel was married for a fifth time to Juan Cano de Saavedra. This marriage, as it turned out, would prosper for nearly two decades.

About Juan Cano we know quite a lot, more because of his marriage to Isabel Moctezuma than for his own accomplishments. He too was an Extremaduran, the son of a commander of the royal fortifications in Cáceres. The Cano family had been distinguished for its service to the Catholic monarchs during the final phases of the Spanish reconquest. The grandfathers of Juan Cano had fought in Granada; an uncle had been a member of the retinue of the ill-fated prince Juan, the only son of Ferdinand and Isabella. Cano was born near the turn of the sixteenth century, journeyed to the New World at eighteen, and was a member of the Panfilo de Narváez expedition to Mexico in 1520. After the defeat of Narváez by Cortés, Cano became an adherent of the conqueror, participated in several conquests, and received a rather poor *encomienda* in compensation for his services.

When Juan Cano married doña Isabel, his fortunes changed for the better. He shared the lucrative revenues from Tacuba, and with this as a base he threw himself into a series of legal appeals designed to increase his wife's inheritance as a descendant of Moctezuma II. For Isabel, life with her fifth husband provided the first years of tranquility since early adolescence. She bore five children within ten years of marriage; Gonzalo, Pedro, Juan, Isabel, and Catalina. A sixth child in her household was Juan de Andrade Moctezuma, the product of her marriage to Juan Gallego. He days were spend acquiring personal effects and instructing her daughters in the Catholic faith; she attended to her favorite charities; and she perhaps served as an example to the natives of Tacuba of a devout Catholic and Hispanicized woman who had bridged the worlds of Spaniard and Indian. When the governors of Mexico were brought to trial in the 1530s for their conduct in office, doña Isabel was the only Indian woman to be subpoenaed as a witness against them. She testified that the officials had extorted a bed from her home and had made illegal demands for special tribute form the Indians of Tacuba.

In 1542, shortly after the birth of his fifth child, Juan Cano traveled to Spain for a sojourn of two years' duration. He visited relatives in Cáceres, transacted business matters, and spent several months in Madrid in his continuing attempt to establish the "natural" rights of doña Isabel to her patrimony. Then on his way back to Mexico in 1544 Cano stopped off briefly in Santo Domingo, where he recounted to the official chronicler of the Indies, Gonzalo Fernández de Oviedo, his wife's claim as the only surviving legitimate heir of Moctezuma II, the fate of her brother at the hands of Cuauhtémoc, and the symbolic importance of her Hispanization and conversion to other Indians of Mexico.

In 1550 doña Isabel drew up her last will and testament. Among the executors of her estate was Juan Altamirano, the guardian of Leonor Cortés Moctezuma. In her will doña Isabel stated that she had possessed neither furniture nor jewels at the time she wed Juan Cano, a somewhat surprising declaration in view of her previous marriages to Grado and Gallego. But she maintained that only after her marriage to Cano had they acquired personal effects of considerable value, such as tapestries, carpets, cushions, embossed leather, pillows, and bedding. She specifically requested that these items be given to her daughters, doñas Isabel and Catalina. The single most important clause in the will was the disposition of Tacuba and its lucrative rents.

After doña Isabel's death in 1550, Tacuba would become a center of litigation that occupied courts in Mexico and Spain for years to come, it would set children against the surviving parent and brothers and sisters against each other, embittering relations beyond repair. It was the intent of doña Isabel that the bulk of Tacuba become the inheritance of her eldest son, Juan de Andrade, and that a much smaller portion go to Gonzalo Cano, her eldest son by Juan Cano. In the event that these two died without heirs (which did not happen), their inheritance was to pass to her third son, Pedro Cano, and his heirs. The remainder of doña Isabel's estate, less one-fifth for burial expenses, was to be divided equally among her six legitimate children. She did not mention her illegitimate daughter by Cortés, nor did she provide for her husband, who had property in Spain. As a gesture of compassion for "Indians natives of this land," the slaves held by doña Isabel and Juan Cano were to be freed of services and obligations and permitted to live as *personas libres*. The great lady's body was to rest in the church and monastery of San Agustin in Mexico City, which had for some time been a favorite charity. Not long after doña Isabel's death, the executors of the estate provided token recognition of Leonor Cortés Moctezuma as an heir and set aside a small legacy for her.

It is apparent from doña Isabel's will that she still held hope that the Spanish crown would restore her patrimony as heir to Moctezuma II's vast lands and that this expanded inheritance might also be divided equally among her six legitimate children. Perhaps it was this possibility that persuaded Juan Cano to leave Mexico and return to Seville, where he resided until his death some twenty years later. In Spain he remained active in the courts, contesting the disposition of Tacuba in his wife's will and maintaining a steady barrage of petitions to the crown asserting doña Isabel's natural rights as the heir of the Emperor Moctezuma II.

*   *   *

What became of Isabel Moctezuma's seven children? A brief summary of their lives is a suitable epilogue to her story. Doña Leonor remained under the custody of Juan Altamirano until the early 1550s, when she was wed to the wealthy Juan de Tolosa, a man more than twenty years her senior and discoverer of the silver mines of Zacatecas. Leonor bore Tolosa a son who took religious vows and became vicar of Zacatecas, a daughter who married Juan de Oñate, future colonizer and governor of New Mexico, and a second daughter who married into the Zaldivar family, prominent in the history of the mining frontier and New Mexico.

By 1551 Juan de Andrade Moctezuma had married Maria de Castañeda, the daughter of a conquistador. As the principal heir to Tacuba, he had become alienated from his stepfather and half-brothers, who had instituted a lawsuit designed to divest him of his inheritance. After almost twenty years of bitter litigation, the Cano family won a decision in the case that stripped Andrade of all but a sixth of Tacuba's revenues, with the remainder going in equal parts to each of Juan Cano's and doña Isabel's five children. While his estate was tied up in lawsuits, Juan de Andrade and his family resettled in Seville. There he tried his hand at business, a distasteful but necessary alternative to living off rents. However, his commercial venture was a failure, and he spent two years in prison for unpaid debts. Andrade died in Seville in 1576 or 1577, leaving five children as heirs. His descendants eventually became titled nobility as the Counts of Miravalle

Gonzalo and Pedro Cano de Moctezuma, the first two sons of Juan Cano and doña Isabel, married and spent their lives in Mexico, where they and their children formed with some distinction a part of the colonial nobility. Their descendants include the families of Audelo Cano Moctezuma and Raza Cano Moctezuma, a few of whom were admitted to the Order of Santiago. The youngest son, Juan, was rather more successful. It appears that he accompanied his father to Spain in the early 1550s and married a woman of Cáceres, the seat of his father's property. There he built the Moctezuma Palace, which still stands, and set up an entailed estate, which passed on his death in 1579 to his own eldest son, don Juan. From this branch of the family also came titled nobility, the Count of Enjarada, the Dukes of Abrantes and Linares, and the families of Toledo Moctezuma, Cavajal and Vivero, several of whom were also admitted to military orders.

Isabel and Catalina, the daughters of Juan Cano and doña Isabel, became novices of the convent of La Concepción in Mexico City shortly after the death of their mother. La Concepción was the oldest nunnery in the capital and housed the daughters of several prominent conquistadors. Its novices were normally the legitimate children of Spaniards more than thirteen years of age, blessed with good health, an ability to read, write, and handle figures and a 4,000-peso dowry. Doñas Isabel and Catalina were mestizas, but of sufficient "quality" and means that the rules of La Concepción might be relaxed to accommodate them. Once admitted to the order, they took their vows of poverty so seriously as to renounce the share of the revenues of Tacuba that was adjudicated to them in the 1560s, and to arrange to have it bestowed in perpetuity on their father and surviving brothers.

In 1590, after half a century of litigation, a landmark decision regarding the heirs of Isabel Moctezuma was reached in the court of Philip II. In exchange for a permanent renunciation of their natural rights as heirs of Moctezuma II, a general settlement was made with the several grandchildren and great grandchildren of the emperor that granted them revenues from vacant *encomiendas* in Mexico for themselves and their heirs in perpetuity.

The 1590 settlement formalized the legal obligations of the Spanish crown to the many heirs of the Aztec princess Tecuichpotzin. It also vindicated doña Isabel's decision, made more than half a century before, to link her destiny with that of the Spanish conquerors who had destroyed her nation and to contribute to the establishment of a new society on Mexican soil.

2. Spanish Women of the Second Generation in Peru

JAMES LOCKHART

In this essay Professor Lockhart shows that it was the Spanish women in Peru who were responsible for the existence of a second Spanish generation by providing the surroundings in which a generation of mestizos grew up to be primarily Spanish in language and culture.

Spanish women constituted a large minority of the settlers in Peru in the conquest period, and their significance was even greater than their numbers, for although women from home were not numerous enough to give every Spaniard a wife, they sufficed to keep Spanish Peru from being truly a society without women. The analysis Gilberto Freyre made of Brazilian society, that in the absence of European women, Indian women largely determined early Brazilian culture insofar as it had to do with the household, cannot be applied to Peru. While Indian influence was important, both immediately and over time, Peru even in the first generation had enough Spanish women to preclude the simple loss of any important culture elements.

Nevertheless, assessing the role of Spanish women in conquest Peru is a delicate task. In view of the old tradition among historians of ignoring them, the cultural and biological contribution of Spanish women were commonly present at almost all times and places during the early occupation of Peru, and therefore cannot be considered a rarity. On the other hand, there can be no doubt that in Spanish Peruvian society, as in any new community, women were greatly outnumbered by men. Tabulations for the Indies as a whole, based on the *Pasajeros a Indias,* have indicated a ratio of about ten to one. As suggested by Richard Konetzke, however, the actual proportion of women in the Indies must have been higher than it had been at emigration, because of the higher mortality among men. For Peru this was a factor of more than usual significance, with the major Indian rebellion, twenty years of civil wars, and innumerable expeditions of discovery into surrounding jungle areas.

From *Spanish Peru. 1532–1560* by James Lockhart (Madison: University of Wisconsin Press, © copyright 1968 by the Regents of the University of Wisconsin), pp. 150–169, passim. Reprinted by permission.

A list of Spanish and apparently Spanish women in Peru during the period of 1532–60, assembled from all sources used for the present study, reached a total of 550, but this figure is even more ambiguous raw material for arriving at an overall estimate than was the similar list of artisans, since women had little occasion to appear in notarial and official records. Therefore it is reasonable to think that the list of 550 women, brought together for the same archival sources as the more than 800 artisans, is a much smaller fraction of the total than in the latter case; but there is no firm basis for even the rudest approximation of a statistical estimate.

A second element of uncertainty in the listing is the quite broad interpretation Spaniards were willing to give to the concept of a Spanish woman. Women were identified in legal records only as to their marital status, but Spanish women were recognizable as not being specifically called Negro, Indian or mestizo. The Spanish secretaries were very consistent in specifying Negro and Indian women; with mestizo women, particularly daughters of prominent Spaniards, they were somewhat less so, but this group did not become important until the late 1550's. There was, however, hesitance and inconsistency, both in fact and in the matter of their explicit identification and in documents, when it came to two groups who were in the process of being absorbed among the ordinary Castilian women: the *moriscas* and certain light-skinned, Spanish-speaking mulatto women. The moriscas, slave women of Muslim descent, were for the most part Caucasian, Spanish-born, and converted to Christianity, and they spoke Spanish as a native language. Fully acculturated mulatto women were also usually born in Spain or an older colony. Slave-mistresses of both types often obtained their freedom, and married Spaniards or in other ways took their places among the ranks of Spanish women, which they might well do, considering their birthplace. It is particularly hard to find reasons to deny full status as Spanish women to the moriscas who were simply undergoing a process familiar for centuries in Spain's Christian reconquest.

At any rate, one must keep in mind that Spanish women included a minority of moriscas and mulatto women with, after 1555, the addition of some mestizo women. To define the size of the minority is statistically impossible, but it can hardly have been more than a tenth of all ostensibly Spanish women. To make a rough commonsense estimate, then, of the statistical importance of Spanish women, including the women from ethnic minority groups who were accepted as Spanish, and taking into consideration the *Pasajeros a Indias,* Konetzke, and the implications of the list made for the present study, it appears probable that from the early 1540's on, Peru had one Spanish woman for every seven or eight men, in absolute numbers perhaps three or four hundred women by 1543 and a thousand by 1555.

Few Spanish women, except moriscas, took part in the actual conquest of Peru in the years 1532–35, but followed close behind the fighting. . . . The number of Spanish women would seem to have grown quite steadily until 1548, when, with the end of the great Gonzalo Pizarro rebellion, they came into the country at a much faster rate than before. By 1548 enough time had elapsed so that a very large number of Spanish Peruvians had roots in the country, were sure they wanted to stay, and sent for female relatives, such a summons being the principal mechanism for the entry of Spanish women.

As the relatives of the male Spanish Peruvians, the women shared the social and regional origins of the rest of the population. A sampling of the regional origins of Spanish women showed all the principal regions in their usual order, and close to their usual proportions of the total. Andalusia was at the head of the list, as was to be expected, but Andalusian women had already lost the overwhelming numerical superiority they apparently had in the Caribbean area in the early years of the sixteenth century. . . . .

The social quality of Spanish women in Peru was as varied as that of the men, ranging from the sisters of fishermen to the daughters of counts. Just as with men, there took place over the years a rise in average social status on the Spanish scale, as the wealth of Peru attracted people from an ever broader spectrum of Spanish society. It would be hard to say whether social origin had more or less importance among the men than among the women. On the one hand, a woman who could buy fine clothes and learn to imitate polite behavior could make herself more nearly the equal of high society than could a man, who faced the barrier of literacy. For while some ladies could read and write and play keyboard instruments, such accomplishments were far from universal even at the highest level. On the other hand, the use of the "doña" drew a sharp line down the middle of the female population, based on Spanish peninsular distinctions. . . .

Many of the encomenderos' wives in the 1550's, having been married in Spain before their husband became rich, or picked from the generally plebeian women already in the Indies at that time, did not boast the title "doña." After the 1540's, the encomenderos married practically only doñas, and the older ladies' lack of title was sorely felt, but no change was possible. It could happen that their younger sisters, brought to Peru to share the family's good fortune and to make advantageous matches, would be allowed to assume the "doña" which was denied the rich and powerful patronesses. For the second generation, the "doña" was standard for the legitimate daughter of any encomendero, where the mother bore the title or not, and was commonly allowed to the daughters of any prominent and wealthy man. . . .

Family and regional ties were even more important for women than for men. The great majority of women either arrived as part of a family, or were sent for by male relatives already in Peru. The motive was usually to seek marriage or join a husband. If the husband died, as could happen without a moment's notice in tumultuous Peru, the woman would be thrown completely on family and compatriots, for unless she was wealthy, a widow or single woman could sustain herself only with difficulty or loss of honor.

Probably nine-tenths of all adult Spanish women were married. Previous chapters have indicated how marriage was, though nor universal, the rule among encomenderos and established artisans; it was common for lawyers, doctors, notaries, and shipmasters, and not unknown among merchants. All this added up to a formidable demand for marriageable women. The natural desire to form matches was given urgency among the Spaniards by their particularly strong drive to perpetuate and enhance their lineage, and by the importance of an honorable, legitimate wife in the Spanish ideal of life. The official threat to deport all those who, having wives in Spain, failed to have them brought to the Indies, cannot be considered a major factor. Most of the time, and for most people, it was a dead letter, though governors could rid themselves of troublesome individuals by invoking it, and the royal officials could use it to extort money

There was only one area where official policy had a strong effect in encouraging marriage, though there it was admittedly of utmost importance. While an encomendero could hope to avoid the various royal ordinances threatening to take away the encomiendas of those who did not marry, he had no chance of passing his encomienda on to his heirs unless he married and had legitimate children. At this point official policy became a serious matter, for the deadly competition to secure encomiendas would allow nothing else. Many encomenderos had their mestizo sons legitimated to inherit their property, but legitimation was never allowed to include the right to succeed in the father's encomienda, except for the children of Francisco Pizarro and one other noted captain. The encomendero's incentives to marry were increased even more by the prospect, then still very much alive, that the encomienda could be converted into a perpetual fief and family possession. With these motivations, some encomenderos began to marry or bring their wives to Peru as soon as, or even before, the first phase of the conquest was ended. Ten years after the conquest, a large minority, perhaps a third, had their wives with them; in certain more settled areas like Lima, Trujillo, and Piura the proportion was no doubt greater. By the early 1550's two-thirds of the encomenderos of highland Cuzco were married; and in 1563 there were only thirty-two encomenderos left unmarried in all Peru, of almost five hundred.

Certain aspects of marriage were the same whether the man was an encomendero or an artisan, the wife wellborn or plebeian. Practically all marriages were strategic alliances arranged with a view to improving the partners' wealth or social standing; if a few Spaniards married for love, they were exceptions not indicative of any trend for the nature of marriage to change in the Indies. Both partners were seeking the greatest wealth and the highest lineage possible in the other party; but the classic type of match in the Indies was that in which the man had acquired wealth or power and now wanted to gain matching social prestige by marrying a woman of higher birth, though often poor. In these cases the man contributed a large dowry, perhaps many thousands of pesos, reversing the traditional process. Almost always the fiction was maintained that the dowry originated with the wife or her relatives, but occasionally the man alleging the "custom of the Indies," would grant the sum openly, in consideration of the lady's virginity and high birth. However, if the high lineage was on the man's side, the dowry reverted to its traditional form. Some encomenderos paid princely dowries, of 20,000 pesos and over, to have their sisters or daughters marry a member of the Spanish high nobility or a magistrate of the Audiencia.

The dowry had other uses as well. At times it simply represented the total property and money which a widow or wealthy spinster brought into a marriage, and meant to keep under her control. A dowry could also be a hedge against future indebtedness; sometimes husbands acknowledged receipt of a fictional dowry far in excess of the total worth of man and wife, so that if in the future the husband's property were seized for debts, or if claims heaped up after his death, the wife could always retain this large amount in the family as dowry goods.

Spanish Peru, as has been seen elsewhere, was not a place where social mobility was easy, but there were ways a man could, within certain limits, raise his position through his own activity in war or commerce. For a woman, on the other hand, there was hardly anything she could do independently to enhance her position, and much that she could do to lower it. Women took their original status from their family, and it could be altered only through marriage. Practically the only chance for a woman of humble birth to reach the top rank of Peruvian society was to marry an obscure man who later became an encomendero. After the 1530's this was a rare occurrence.

Except for the minority who had married in Spain before leaving, encomenderos chose their wives primarily from among the female relatives of prominent people, other encomenderos or churchmen, in their own Peruvian community. Marriage in the upper levels of society was the first area of life where a new Peruvian regionalism superseded the Spanish regionalism to which the settlers remained generally faithful when choosing friends and associates. Though it would not be unheard of for an encomendero of Cuzco to seek out a bride from his home town, he would be more likely to choose a sister or cousin of the richest and most powerful of his Cuzco colleagues who would deign to consider a match, regardless of the two men's regional origin in Spain. (Such marriages were often arranged while the brides were still in Spain.) In this way, the encomendero class in each Spanish Peruvian town had by 1560 become a closely interrelated group.

Other encomenderos made matches with the wellborn, and allegedly wellborn, ladies who were imported for that purpose almost as a speculative business venture. An impecunious father with three or four marriageable daughters and some claim to hidalgo status would set out from Spain to Peru with no other assets than the prospective marriages and, in some cases, royal cédulas recommending that the Peruvian governors show favor to whomever the daughters might marry.

The encomenderos' wives were the most important and influential women in Peru, their position as central in its way as that of their husbands. They were the heads of large households of dependents, servants, and slaves. (Alone of all the women in the country, some of them had the luxury of a Spanish woman head servant.) Aside from their household responsibilities, they were often left in charge of their husbands' encomiendas and general affairs. In this broader function they were not thought to perform well; there was general agreement that the most heartless, avaricious, and destructive tribute collectors were Spanish women.

Nevertheless, the encomenderos' wives, always maintaining their homes even when the encomenderos were absent at war, were an important force for social and economic continuity, a continuity which was not broken with the death of the encomendero. The mortality rate in the civil wars among prominent men was high, and one woman might retain the same house, servant staff, encomienda, and landed property through as many as three or four husbands. Because of the pressures of custom, the governors, and the dissatisfied pretenders, no woman who inherited an encomienda could stay unmarried. She might have a limited choice as to her next husband, but had to remarry almost immediately. Some governors merely implored and hinted at reprisal if compliance was not forthcoming, while others straightforwardly informed the ladies concerned that they had arranged their marriage; but all were adamant. The record for noncompliance was set by Maria de Escobar, a woman of immense wealth, seniority, and political power, who managed to place a three-year interval between her second and third husbands. In cases like these, the encomienda was juridically and in fact more the woman's than the man's. . . .

The wives of men who were not encomenderos, among whom artisans' wives were the largest group, could not live with as much magnificence as women in the upper rank, but they came nearer to that ideal than might be imagined. In a singular fashion, Spanish Peru preserved most of the social distinctions of the Peninsula, and even invented new ones based on seniority and the possession of encomiendas, yet at the same time, because of the fabulous wealth available to the intruders, and the presence of a large servile population, even those Spaniards who were thought of as poor and plebeian could afford things that in Spain were the perquisites of wealth. Most Spanish women dressed in fine stuffs; none were without servants. An artisan's wife could be expected to have a considerable staff, who would call her "señora" and relieve her of most of the burden of daily housekeeping. In Lima in 1546, the wife of one far from prosperous artisan was waited upon by a Negro woman slave, a freed Indian woman of Nicaragua, and a Peruvian Indian servant, aside from two slaves who aided her husband in his work. In the main, artisans' wives and encomenderos' wives lived in different circles, choosing their confidantes, *comadres* and dining companions from among their equals. Yet there were points of contact; often a humble woman stood in a kind of client relationship to an encomendero's wife, and it could happen that the wife of an encomendero would serve as sponsor at the wedding of an artisan.

Independent economic activities of women, carried on either by married women from the base of their dowry goods, to which they retained rights, or by widows and spinsters who had to gain a living, were channeled into certain areas defined by convention. Women owned a great deal of city real estate, both for their own residences and for the purpose of renting out, but were not too often seen as the owners of agricultural land or livestock. A large proportion of Negro slave house servants were the personal property of women, and much speculative buying and selling took place. Like all other elements of Spanish Peruvian society, women who had achieved solvency invested as silent partners in merchandise and loaned money.

There were single women in Lima who over the years acquired great wealth and a solid position, though not much social prestige, through such enterprise. It was not that any stigma attached to these activities in themselves, being practices by the most patrician of ladies, but if a woman was of humble origin, or had a less than honorable start, such facts were not subsequently forgotten.

Other fields open to women were more in the nature of feminine specialties, and had strongly lower class connotations. The baking of bread and biscuit, both for ordinary city consumption and for the provision of ships and armies, was carried out largely under the supervision of women. Spaniards spoke of the *panaderas* as if male bakers did not exist, which was not quite true, but there is no doubt that the business was mainly shared by Spanish women and free mulatto and Negro women, the bulk of the work in either case being done by Negro slaves and Indians. Women naturally monopolized the occupation of midwifery, which they combined with the general healing of ailments. Poor women, doing as they have always done, sewed and took in boarders. Hospitality by the rich was the principal method of housing and feeding transients in Peru, but some of the women who accepted boarders for a fee began, by the late 1540's and the 1550's, to evolve into regular innkeepers (who also sold odds and ends to the public), not only in Lima but as far into the highlands as La Paz. . . .

For their self-protection and for their honor, it was prudent for women who kept inns to marry, and those who could find willing husbands did so. In 1547 la Valenciana married an Antonio de Toledo, who thenceforth helped in the operation of her house. She became deeply committed to Toledo in more than a formal sense, giving him free management of her properties and supporting his relatives. But the relationship came to an end because of a difficulty that plagued marriage in the Indies. Toledo was a bigamist. Presumably la Valenciana's husband in Spain had died before the new match, but Toledo's first wife was still alive. He had succumbed to the temptation that overcame more than one Spaniard in Peru, that of forgetting a poor, distant wife in Spain for a new one who was rich and present. After a year the validity of the marriage was challenged in the ecclesiastical courts, only to be confirmed, until finally around 1554 Toledo's previous marriage was established beyond doubt, he was exiled from Peru, and his marriage with la Valenciana was invalidated.

There is no particular reason to think that la Valenciana's place was ever more than a boarding house. But it is possible; not all adventurers in the Indies were male. Already in 1537 Bishop Berlanga of Panama complained of the presence of too many single women of bad morals. There were always a certain number of women, not necessarily of the very lowest origin but certainly of low repute, who served the Spaniards as prostitutes, camp followers, and mistresses.

Full-fledged prostitutes definitely existed in Lima, the center of all amenities, and in rich Potosi, but there were not enough such women to be organized by the houseful. Nor was there anything like mass demand for the physical woman. Spanish men found Indian women attractive, and any Spaniard could have as many as he wanted. Spanish prostitutes catered more to the need of Spaniards to be near a woman who shared their language and culture. As much as anything else there were entertainers, who might, like Maria de Ledesma in Potosí, have a fine vihuela or guitar and know how to play and sing well. Jokingly, half in derision, these women were commonly called "doña" by their clients, and this usage has found its way into the chronicles of the civil wars; but they were not so termed in any serious context.

Far more common than true prostitutes were adventuresses who were prepared to form loose relationships, either temporary or quite permanent, with any man who would support them well. They were not averse to an advantageous marriage, but could expect marriage only under unusual circumstances. Often such a woman served in effect as interim or replacement wife for a man whose real wife was still in Spain, or, even more characteristically, for a man who was single and desired female companionship, but did not want to marry until he was in a position to make a match with a wealthy or wellborn lady who could do honor to his lineage. When that time came, if the relationship had been a meaningful one and the man was generous, he might give his former mistress a dowry and marry her to another, less ambitious Spaniard. . . .

At the opposite pole from the concubines were the feminine devotees of the church. Peru was slow to develop true convents of nuns, and the ones that began to be organized, as 1560 neared, already belonged to a new era. But they were preceded, in the late 1540's and 1550's, by the *beatas*. Beatas, a specifically Spanish phenomenon, were women living in pious retirement, sometimes individually and sometimes in groups, who wore the habit of an order with which they had some, usually formal, connection.

The Dominican beatas seem to have been the first to organize themselves; in 1548 the Dominican beata Mari Hernández de Pereda donated her house for the purpose, though she soon added the clause that a rival, Leonor del Aguilar, should not be allowed entry. Later the Dominican friars persuaded her to revoke the clause, and the formerly excluded Leonor, who had lived in her own small house with a mulatto slave girl and a mestizo child she cared for, came there to live. Discipline, one can see, was not what might be expected from regular nuns, but the Dominican effort was serious and sustained. Leonor del Aguilar remained a beata for at least ten years, the Dominican house was still in existence in 1557, and even had affiliated members in the coastal valley of Chincha, where the Dominican friars maintained a monastery.

The Dominican beatas were women of modest circumstances; another establishment started under Augustinian sponsorship around 1557 drew from a different stratum of society, its membership being prominent widows and daughters of encomenderos, all of them doñas. After some years the beatas became regular nuns and founded a convent of the same order.

Rich and poor, concubine and beata, Spanish women made their most basic contribution to the development of the country by educating those around them in the ways of the homeland. In their houses Spanish was spoken and learned. They taught their Negro and Indian maids to make beds, sew European clothes, and prepare Spanish foods in Spanish fashion. As irregular as some of their own private lives may have been, they taught religion to their slaves and servants, and encouraged them to form steady unions and marry.

But above all, this influence extended to the second generation, for whose upbringing the Spanish women were responsible, a generation which included not only their own fully Spanish children, but large numbers of mestizo children, fathered by Spanish settlers who were not content to see their offspring raised as Indians. The demand for people to care for such children was large, and any Spanish woman, whether she had children of her own or not, could expect to be importuned to raise mestizos and orphans. Once the children were taken in, personal attachment grew, whatever the original agreement had been. . . .

When it came to the wives of encomenderos, their collections of children were truly imposing. Isabel de Ovalle, twice married but childless, raised two orphaned Spanish girls, a mestizo girl who had been befriended by her first husband, and two more mestizo girls she had taken in on her own initiative (not to speak of two Negro slave orphans she meant to free). She planned to give them all substantial dowries. Childlessness was not, of course, the rule among encomenderos' wives, many of whom were notably fertile. Doña Francisca Jiménez had, by 1548, ten children alive and with her; two by her first husband, three by her second, and five by her third.

She was also raising the mestizo daughter of her second husband, who acted as her maid. This was the fate of many mestizo children who were raised in Spanish homes; they received sustenance, education, and affection, but were seen in the light of servants.

There was, then, growing up in Peru during the 1540's and 1550's, a new generation whose cultural heritage was strongly Spanish, whether they were of pure Spanish blood or mestizo. For the future character of the colony, this group was of immense importance; but in the period before 1560 they remained little more than a potentiality. Hardly any representative of the second generation, either Spanish or mestizo, appeared in any kind of independent role during the whole thirty years from the time the conquering expedition set out for Peru, not even in the humbler fields of endeavor such as artisanry.

Mestizos and Spanish children were born in Peru from 1533 on, but the second generation had its true beginnings only after the Indian rebellion ended in 1537. By 1560 only a small minority of the second generation were over twenty years of age. The new generation also had to contend with the general Spanish reluctance to entrust anything important to the very young; in the Spanish legal tradition, very much in force in Peru, both men and women were minors and required guardians until their twenty-fifth birthday. Emerging into independence was rendered yet more difficult by the crushing prestige of the first generation of settlers, which kept them in command in all walks of life for an abnormally long time. . . .

There was in conquest Peru no one standard treatment or fixed social evaluation of the thousands of mestizo children born of Spanish fathers and Indian mothers. Many, never recognized, grew up with their mothers as Indians and were reabsorbed into the indigenous population. In other cases, Spaniards went to great lengths to provide for mestizo offspring. Some Spanish fathers sent for their mestizo children to join them from as far away as Mexico and Nicaragua. Many made plans to send mestizo sons and daughters to Spain, to be raised at home by their own families, and though this did not come to fruition as often as intended, it was no idle thought.

For those who were in one way or another received among the Spanish Peruvians, their condition as mestizos was a handicap, but depending on other factors, did not preclude acceptance at a fairly high level. It is hard to separate the Spaniards' feelings about racial mixture, as it affected the mestizos, from their position on illegitimacy, for ninety-five per cent of the first generation of mestizos were illegitimate. To judge by the treatment accorded the few legitimate mestizos, who were accepted fully as equals, the Spanish may have considered illegitimacy to be a more serious blemish than mixture with Indians. Legitimate mestizos could and did inherit encomiendas, and one was considered for an appointment to the city council of Lima. Moreover, there were cases of Spaniards who had both Spanish and mestizo sons out of wedlock and gave them all equal treatment. . . .

The path was easier for the girls of this class, who could hope to marry within Spanish Peruvian society, perhaps not to their fathers' equals, but to substantial Spaniards of lower degree. To a Spaniard, such a marriage offered the advantages of an alliance with the girl's father, and a large dowry, which might be enough for him to live on. If the father was exceptionally rich and powerful, his mestizo daughter might be able to marry well by any standards. A daughter of the famous captain Lorenzo de Aldana married a large encomendero of Charcas. Diego Maldonado, called the Rich, married his daughter to a Spanish don, with a dowry of 20,000 pesos. Ordinarily, however, such girls married men from the second rank: majordomos, merchants, entrepreneurs, or gentlemen pretenders without encomiendas.

The pattern seen among the mestizo children of encomenderos repeated itself at the lower levels, but with alteration. Above all, the frequent presence on the scene of the Indian mother reduced the intensity of Hispanization. Ordinary Spaniards often succeeded in marrying their daughters to juniors or inferiors; a shipmaster to one of his sailors, or a merchant to his factor. But the point was soon reached at which the size of the dowry and the prestige of the father did not suffice to attract suitors. Many Spaniards fulfilled their duty to their mestizo children (both boys and girls) by making them a "donation." If the donation was large, perhaps a thousand pesos in value, the child could be assured of a future, but usually it was much less: two or three hundred pesos, or a mare with a colt, or a few goats. A child so endowed would probably succeed in being raised by some Spanish family, but the amount was not enough for a dowry or a start in life.

By the 1550's, therefore, a major problem in Peru was what to do with the many mestizo girls who were growing up Spanish, but were not wealthy enough to find Spanish husbands. It became a favorite form of charity to donate dowries to mestizo orphans. In Cuzco and Lima, philanthropic citizens established houses to shelter them. (Hardly ever did it occur to the charitable to arrange a marriage between two mestizos, partly, no doubt, because men did not marry as young as women, and few mestizo men had come of age). Philanthropy could not, of course, take care of all the Hispanized mestizo girls; apparently very many ended in purely servile positions, or took to loose living, or were abandoned entirely. . . .

All in all, the Spaniards must be judged to have shown an unusual amount of interest in the fate of their mestizo offspring. Even if many, possibly most, mestizo children suffered neglect, there were many hundreds who were protected, and grew up inside Spanish Peruvian society.

In order to explain the relatively good treatment of mestizos it is not necessary to imagine any unusually strong parental tenderness on the part of the Spaniards, though some had such feelings (they were often struck, it appears, by how much their mestizo children resembled them). Most important was the strong Spanish feeling for lineage, which emphasized solidarity with all one's relatives near and distant, as well as the necessity of carrying on the family name. Another factor was the strict Spanish machinery for legal guardianship. Finally, there was the special sense of responsibility which the Spaniards, in the Arab tradition, felt for the protection of females. At all levels, more care was lavished on mestizo girls than boys, with the probable result that a higher proportion of them were absorbed into the Spanish population, and indeed, with men more numerous in that population than women, they were more needed.

To sum up the substance of the chapter, there were among the settlers of Peru a large minority of Spanish women who, living in the cities, often as heads of the large households of encomenderos, were able to exert a cultural influence on the urban population out of proportion to their numbers. Even humble women had mixed servant staffs to whom they taught Spanish ways. The household of one almost indigent Spanish woman of Lima could stand as a paradigm of Spanish Peru: herself, her Negro slave, her Indian servant, and a mestizo orphan girl. Above all, Spanish women were responsible for the existence of a second Spanish generation who were to inherit the encomiendas and other wealth of the first, and they provided the surroundings in which a generation of mestizos grew up to be primarily Spanish in language and culture.

SOR JUANA INÉS DE LA CRUZ

3. Sor Juana Inés de la Cruz: "The Supreme Poet of Her Time in Castilian"

IRVING A. LEONARD

Professor Leonard, who was the Domingo Faustino Sarmiento Professor at the University of Michigan at the time of his retirement in 1965, made an outstanding contribution in what might be best called the cultural history of colonial Latin America. His many studies were always marked by a grace of style and detailed research that explain their readability and their permanent value. One of his best known books is *Baroque Times in Old Mexico* (1959), from which the essay that follows on Sor Juana de la Cruz has been reprinted.

The late Pedro Henríquez Ureña, probably the most distinguished Latin American literary critic of this century, termed Sor Juana's life "a prodigious tale of devotion and knowledge."* He emphasized the obstacles she faced, "the many censors who doubted the wisdom of so much learning in a woman who even succeeded once in inducing a mother superior—'a very saintly and very foolish woman'—to forbid her the reading of books."

This prohibition lasted only three months: she faithfully gave up books, but this did not prevent her from thinking, and so, she wrote, "Though I did not study in books, I studied in all the things God created." This meant pondering on the many individual differences between people, even though they were of the same species. The geometrical figure of objects interested her: "She observes two girls playing with a spinning top and decides to find out what kind of curve it draws while it spins—she sprinkles flour on the floor and discovers that the curve is a spiral. In the kitchen, she remarks on the properties of sugar or eggs and adds: 'If Aristotle had known how to cook, he would have written even more than he did.'"

Henríquez Ureña also pointed out that her poetry reflects the conditions of her life in seventeenth-century Mexico:

> In a superb sonnet to the rose she draws from its brief life the traditional lesson—"thy life deceives and thy death teaches"—but in another sonnet she

*All quotations in this headnote come from Pedro Henríquez Ureña, *Literary Currents in Latin America* (Cambridge, Mass.: Harvard University Press, 1945), pp. 75–82.

From *Baroque Times in Old Mexico: Seventeenth-Century Persons, Places, and Practice* by Irving A. Leonard (Ann Arbor: University of Michigan Press, 1959), pp. 172–191, passim. © copyright 1959 by the University of Michigan. Reprinted by permission.

approves the rose's life—"happy it is to die while young and fair and not endure the insult of old age." This is an expression of her persistent fighting spirit, which led her to write the defiant lines: "If my displeasure from my pleasure comes, may heaven give me pleasure at the cost of displeasure"—lines strikingly coincident with a number of folk songs and proverbs in Mexico.

Sor Juana needed all the persistence and courage that she had. Archbishop Francisco Aguiar y Seixas (1632–1698), who was in power during the last years of Sor Juana's life, helps us to appreciate the spirit of some of the dominant forces of the age. Professor Leonard discreetly terms him "misogynistic," but his hatred of women led him to shun all contact with them. He even refused to make the ceremonial visit on the Viceroy required by protocol, because he would meet the Vicequeen at the same time. He was a pious and hardworking prelate withal; he visited all parts of his enormous archbishopric and founded a seminary and a colegio as well as a "House for Demented Females" and a "House for Women Abandoned by Their Husbands."

Even though the times were against Sor Juana, she wrote on a subject always dangerous for women to take up: men. "Her best known poem is the one in defense of women; . . . it is her thesis that men are irrational in blaming women for their imperfection, since men constantly strive to make women imperfect. It is not great poetry, but it is a polemical masterpiece."

One August day of 1667 in Mexico City an attractive, talented girl, still some months short of her sixteenth birthday, entered the sternly ascetic Order of Discalced Carmelites as a chorister. The convent that received her was the one that had been the dream of those earnest nuns, Sister Inés de la Cruz and Sister Mariana Encarnación when they plied the fickle Archbishop García Guerra so assiduously earlier in the century with sweetmeats and seductive music. Though immediate success had eluded these efforts, it will be recalled, patience was triumphant in 1616, and the new religious community came into being. The young lady who, a half century afterwards, gained admittance to its holy precincts was Doña Juana Inés de Asbaje y Ramírez de Santillana, better known as Sister Juana Inés de la Cruz, . . . famed as the "last great lyric poet of Spain and the first great poet of America." Also musically gifted, her ecclesiastical name was possibly adopted in veneration of the instrument-playing hostess of Fray García Guerra and cofounder of the Carmelite convent, of which she was now a temporary inmate.

In an age when matrimony and religious reclusion were the sole careers open to respectable females, the act of taking the veil was a commonplace event in Mexican society. In most sisterhoods the discipline was not severe, and within the cloistered walls many comforts and amenities of secular life could be enjoyed, including the services of personal slaves. Indeed for daughters whose matrimonial prospects were not bright, an immured existence of this sort seemed a desirable alternative, and a young woman whose parents or relatives could provide the requisite dowry was regarded as fortunate. But the case of the adolescent Doña Juana Inés de Asbaje y Ramírez de Santillana seemed exceptional, and strangely obscure the reasons for her decision. Here was a maiden "that was far more beautiful than any nun should be," the darling of the viceregal court, and the favorite maid-in-waiting of the vicereine. Her personal attractiveness, her nimble wit in penning verse for any occasion, and her amazing knowledge of books, were all very nearly the talk of the town. In fact, the admiring Viceroy himself, on one occasion, had arranged that a group of the leading professors at the University of Mexico should examine the precocious girl in various branches of learning, and when she emerged triumphant from this ordeal, the learned gentlemen marveled at the erudition and composure of a maiden who hardly seemed more than a child.

Her rise and renown in the courtly circle of the capital had been truly phenomenal. A village lass, born in 1651 in a tiny hamlet called Napantla, "the land in between," that looked up to the snow-crested volcanoes Popocatepetl and Ixtacihuatl, she had begun to read at the age of three, after devouring the small library of her grandfather. When eight years old she went to Mexico City to live with relatives. Soon this pretty child prodigy caught the eye of the vicereine who brought her to reside amidst the luxury and splendor of the viceregal Palace. In this sophisticated environment the young girl rapidly acquired a maturity that quite belied her years, and in the Court she soon found herself envied for her wit by the women and desired for her physical charms by the men.

Social success of this sort in such aristocratic circles was all the more extraordinary in the light of her illegitimate birth, though this circumstance was, perhaps, undisclosed to anyone save her confessor. Her mother, it was later revealed, had had two separate trios of children by as many men, and neither of these unions the Church had hallowed. It was not an uncommon situation at the time, even in families of some distinction, but it was hardly a genealogical asset for any one of patrician pretensions. That this lowly origin influenced the resolve of Juana Inés de Asbaje y Ramírez de Santillana, who thus bore the surnames of her progenitors, to become a nun is likely but, as the sole explanation of her choice, it is unlikely. Her deep passion for study, her stated "total disinclination to marriage," and the promptings of her zealous confessor, the Jesuit *calificador* of the Inquisition, Antonio Núñez de Miranda, had undoubtedly made a life of reclusion seem attractive to her troubled spirit, and finally moved her to abandon the pomp and glitter of the palace social whirl, of which she was so conspicuously a part.

That this determination was attended by doubts, misgivings, and inner conflict appears evident in the fact that illness caused her to withdraw from the Carmelite order within three months. The transition from a worldly court to the harsh confinement of a convent proved too abrupt and severe. Early the following year, however, she took her first vows in the Jeronymite community, the milder discipline of which was better suited to the sensitive temperament and scholarly aspirations of the poetess. The remainder of her forty-three years of life she spent chiefly within the book-lined walls of her cell, to which she retreated as often as her conventual duties permitted. There she pored over her accumulating volumes, attended to an extensive correspondence within and outside of the broad realm of Old Mexico, and wrote the verses so widely known in her time and that have since won enduring fame.

Her poetry is varied in meter and theme, including love lyrics that occasionally border on the erotic, tender Christmas carols, morality plays, allegorical pieces, and even secular three-act comedies like those performed in the public theaters of Spain and Spanish America. Much of this metrical expression abounded in literary conceits and was clothed in the ornate, florid, and obscure style of prevailing Baroque fashion. Unlike most verse of her contemporaries, however, subtle meaning and profound feeling often lay hidden in the intricate foliage of words and clever figures of speech. . . . Yet many of her sonnets and shorter lyric poems have an almost limpid clarity and an exquisite beauty that mark her as the supreme poet of her time in Castilian.

As time passes the appeal of this Creole nun-poetess increases and the circle of her admirers enlarges. It is not merely the esthetic merit of so much of her verse which brings her this homage—though she is often regarded . . . as among the greatest poets in the speech of Spain—but, perhaps even more, the complex personality refracted in many of her writings. Her more intimate and spontaneous expression offers glimpses so fleeting and elusive of the inner life of an extraordinary woman that they serve to pique the reader's curiosity rather than to satisfy it. In certain lines her intention seems illumined for a bare moment, like a flash of lightning in the night, only to be followed by an obscurity more impenetrable than before. Thus it is that the enigmatic quality of Sister Juana's verses, even more than the technical perfection of the best of them, inspires a veritable cult and wins for her an expanding audience. . . .

In the multiplying criticism of the life and work of the Mexican nun-poetess there is increasing agreement that her intellectual distinction exceeds her eminence as a poet, and that her preoccupation with ideas was greater than with artistic creation. Without minimizing the deeply emotional and feminine nature of Sister Juana, she was basically a rationalist with a passion for knowledge, and the processes of analysis were stronger and more obsessive than any other of her psyche. Her extraordinary gift as a lyric poet was ancillary to her acutely rational mentality, and her supreme aspiration was the freedom of her mind to roam untrammeled and unimpeded through every realm of thought. To read, to study, to experiment ". . . just to see if, by studying, I might grow less ignorant. . ." Was the consuming desire of her existence. Since earliest childhood she had experienced this powerful yearning and later she had begged her mother to permit her to attend the university of Mexico disguised in male clothing. "What is indeed the truth," she wrote in her famous *Reply to Sister Philotea,* a letter of much autobiographical significance, "and which I do not deny (in the first place because it is well known to everyone, and in the second place because, though it may be to my detriment, Heaven has bestowed upon me the blessing of a very great love of truth), is that, ever since the first glimmer of reason struck me, this inclination to learning has been so urgent and powerful. . . ." In her young innocence she had desisted from eating cheese in the belief that such food would make her unpolished and uncouth, hence " . . . the desire to know was stronger in me than the desire to eat, even though the latter is so strong in children. . . ." This "inclination" triumphed over every other urge, including the sexual—for marriage she had a "total negation" she had declared—and she candidly confesses that her decision to take the veil—her only other choice —was largely influenced by the relatively freer opportunity it promised for study. The more solitary practices of the Carmelites had induced her; perhaps, to select that Order first. She had thought to escape the tyranny of what almost seemed a vice by dedicating herself as a bride of Christ, but ". . . poor, wretched me? I merely brought myself with me, together with my worst enemy, this inclination!" Instead of extinguishing this passion for reading and cogitation she found that, once subjected to her vows, this thirst for learning ". . . exploded like a charge of powder." . . .

In the medieval atmosphere of seventeenth century Mexico where women could not dream of independent lives, where it was axiomatic that they possessed inferior intelligence, and where they were scarcely more than chattels of their fathers, brothers, and husbands, intellectual curiosity in Sister Juana's sex was not only indecorous but sinful. It might, indeed, be the working of the Evil One and, therefore, imperil one's salvation, as her superiors in the convent more than once assured her. Though there were learned women in history, any emulation of them by a nun was not without an attendant sense of guilt. Sister Juana herself had not escaped this feeling, for she wrote: "I have prayed God to subdue the light of my intelligence, leaving me only enough to keep His law, for anything more (according to some persons) is superfluous in a woman." But, even in these despairing words, one seems to detect in a parenthetical phrase, in which the masculine form is used, a veiled rancor against the man-made world of her time. But her obvious intellectual distinction also aroused the jealousy and antipathy of her companions in the convent, and over the year as this hostility developed in her a persecution complex. Her brilliant, inquiring mind seemed always a source of vexation. "If my intelligence is my own," she wrote in one of her poems, "why must I always find it so dull for my ease and so sharp for my hurt?"

This avid curiosity and desire for knowledge so at odds with her time, place, and sex, seemed only to bring down upon her head the criticism and censure of those about her:

Why, people, do you persecute me so?
In what do I offend, when but inclined
with wordily beauties to adorn my mind,
and not my mind on beauty to bestow?

I value not a treasure trove, nor wealth;
the greater measure of content I find
in placing riches only in my mind,
than setting all my intellect on wealth.

And I esteem not beauty, for, when past
it is the spoils of age's cruelty;
nor faithless riches carefully amassed.

Far better nibble, it seems to me,
at all life's vanities unto the last
than to consume my life in vanity.[1]

And again in one of her ballads she asks bitterly why her fondness for truth must always bring her punishment. "If this fondness I have is licit and even an obligation, why should they chastise me because I do what I must?"

These protests, indicating a sensitiveness to sharp disapproval around her, recur so frequently as to suggest a more disturbed state of mind than would result from eminence in the accepted forms of learning of her time, even after due allowance is made for the fact that such pursuits were deemed unsuitable for a woman, and particularly one bound by vows of perpetual submission. This exaggerated feeling of persecution was possibly generated in part by a growing sense of guilt engendered by the *kind* of methods that she was using to acquire it. In short, her learning might appear more secular than ecclesiastical—"What a pity it is that so rich a mind should so debase itself in the petty matters of this world!" the Bishop of Puebla was to chide her—and her procedures more experimental or scientific in the modern way than scholastic and philosophic. Even more reprehensible than mundane knowledge were the unorthodox means of seeking it. "Experimentation tugged at Sister Juana from earliest childhood," comments a student of her life. Here, then, is the possibility of a conflict, intellectual in origin which, given her environment, profession, and sex, would inevitably be spiritual and emotional as well. This inner discord, with its concomitant overtones of heresy and disobedience, could well produce a brooding

---

1. Translated by Pauline Cook in *The Pathless Crook* (Prairie City, Ill.: Decher Press, 1951). Reprinted by permission [Ed.].

conviction of guilt and thus, through anxiety, accentuate a feeling of persecution. . . .

It was Sister Juana's fate to have her being in this age when, even in Old Mexico, though ever so slightly, the long accepted and sole approach to truth was beginning to be threatened by a new way, a new method. Almost imperceptibly the traditional scholastic and authoritarian concepts of revealed knowledge were yielding to the more sensate procedures of scientific observation and analysis. In the Mexico City of her time there was greater awareness of this intellectual revolution than commonly believed, and the capital had a tiny group of savants who were abreast of contemporary thought, even that of non-Catholic Europe. The comparatively free circulation of nontheological books during the sixteenth and seventeenth centuries, the frequent presence in the viceroyalty of transient men of learning from the Old World, and the personal correspondence of local scholars with thinkers abroad, had all contributed to a more vital mental climate in the New World centers than the contemporary dominance of a medieval Church was thought to permit. A small number of Creole *sabios* were already familiar with the ideas and writing of Erasmus, Copernicus, Kepler, and particularly Descartes, whose philosophies they discussed among themselves in comparative freedom and even cited in their published writings.

Most conspicuous of this intelligentsia of new Spain was Don Carlos de Sigüenza y Góngora. He was a professor or mathematics in the University of Mexico, renowned for his studies of astronomy, archaeology, history and natural philosophy, and also an intimate friend of Sister Juana. Living at the Hospital del Amor de Dios where he served as chaplain, he was a frequent visitor at the Jeronymite convent a few blocks away where the nun-poetess had her cell. It appears that these two intellectually gifted and lonely people enjoyed long discussions together in the locutory of the convent. Sigüenza, a very minor poet, was encouraged in these exercises by Sister Juana, while she in turn received his stimulation and training in scientific disciplines. It is likely that she acquired the mathematical instruments and some of the books said to have furnished her cell as a result of this association. Indeed, the attainments of these two figures working together have moved a discerning critic to comment that they were ". . . the first ones (in Mexico) in whom the modern spirit appears or manifests itself." It was Sigüenza who most often brought visiting savants to her convent, including the great mission-founder of the American Southwest, Father Eusebio Francisco Kino. And it was he who initiated the exceedingly intelligent nun into the new methodology propounded by Descartes, of which there are faint indications in her verse. Doubtless it was he who understood her enthusiasm for, and encouraged her in, the performance of such simple experiments in physics as she mentions in her *Reply to Sister Philotea.* And it was he who shared her love for the dawning Age of Enlightenment of which they both were unconscious precursors in Mexico.

The inherent critical capacity of Sister Juana, coupled with omnivorous reading, moved her to welcome a more pragmatic approach to truth. Latent in her mind was a healthy skepticism regarding the effectiveness of purely verbal rationalization, and her eager curiosity was insidiously drawn to experimentation and direct observation. A scrutiny of Sister Juana's verse and prose tends to support the conviction that she felt an instinctive distrust of the scholasticism dominating the intellectual life of viceregal Mexico. Her deeper regard for observation and a more scientific analysis seems apparent when, in the *Reply*, she emphasizes the importance of varied studies and methods in throwing light on speculative learning, particularly theology, and her underlying preference is revealed when she adds: ". . . and when the expositors are like an open hand and the ecclesiastics like a closed fist." Her reactions to the specious learning and rhetorical ratiocination around her, characterized chiefly by polemical disquisitions with ostentatious displays of classical quotations and cloudy verbosity, emerge clearly in the ballad beginning with the pathetic verse "Let us pretend that I am happy." The wordy debates of bookish pedants and charlatans of the so-called inteligentsia filling the air about her with their din move her to exclaim metrically: "Everything is opinions and of such varied counsels that what one proves is black, the other proves is white." . . .

In the *Reply* she comments, with veiled scorn, on the affectation that passed as learning in the excessive number of quotations from authorities: ". . . and I add that their education is perfected (if nonsense is perfection) by having studied a little Philosophy and Theology and by having a smattering of languages, by which means one may be stupid in numerous subjects and languages because the mother tongue alone is not room enough for a really big fool." Mindful, likewise, of the self delusion facilitated by the verbalism of scholasticism, Sister Juana believed that everyone should keep within his own mental limitations. If this were so, she tartly exclaims: "How many warped intelligence wandering about there would not be!"

Perhaps the most penetrating stanza of this same ballad is the one in which she puts her finger on the core of true wisdom, the development of sound judgment: "To know how to make varied and subtle discourses is not knowledge; rather, knowledge simply consists of making the soundest choices." . . .

Thus it appears that Sister Juana found herself not only torn between "reason" and "passion," but also between *two methodologies of reason:* the time-honored dialectics and syllogisms of scholasticism were still entrenched as the accepted means of rationalization in the Church of Christ which held her in its protective arms and to which she was irrevocably bound by vows. This great institution sheltered and loved her, and obedience to its authority and ways was to her ineludible obligation yet, deep within, she could not reciprocate its love. Instead, she seemed possessed by a way of thinking that threatened to undermine the assumptions on which the Faith rested. On the true object of her affections, the new concept of experimentalism relying on the senses rather than on authority, her benevolent guardian, the Church, severely frowned. Such intellectual exercise might well be inimical to the divine science of theology, and it was potentially, if not actually; heretical. Adherence to such thinking could seriously jeopardize her eternal salvation, which was infinitely precious to her. In her religious play, *The Divine Narcissus,* she wrote: "Behold that what I yearn for I am powerless to enjoy, and in my anxious longing to possess it, I suffer mortal pangs." . . . But convent-bound in the medieval atmosphere of the ecclesiastical society of Mexico City she could only feel at war with it and with herself. The love and kindliness implicit in the Church's paternalism claimed her gratitude and, of course, her vows compelled obedience to it. Yet the persistent longing for a freer expression of her intuition and for another and more open avenue to truth and to God prevented complete reciprocation and submission. . . .

As the dawn of April 17, 1695 was casting a wan light over the troubled City of Mexico the wracked and broken spirit of Sister Juana quietly claimed its longed-for release from the prison of her aloneness. "See how death eludes me because I desire it," she had exclaimed in one of her poems, "for even death, when it is in demand," she had added, "will rise in price." Over the long years of her short life she had struggled against the viselike prejudices and incomprehension of her time and place. She had dreamed of a liberation from shackles of static traditions and stultifying conventions. She had dared to rebuke the men of her society for their double standard of morality and had thus struck a first glow for women's rights.

> Which has the greater sin when burned
> by the same lawless fever:
> She who is amorously deceived,
> or he, the sly deceiver?
>
> Or which deserves the sterner blame,
> though each will be a sinner.
> She who becomes a whore for pay,
> Or he who pays to win her?[2]

But more than all else she had struggled for a freedom of thought for all. "There is nothing freer than the human mind," she had proclaimed to a world that could not comprehend these words, or could only hear them as subversive of a God-given

---

2. Robert Graves, trans. "Against the Inconsequences of Men's Desires . . ." *Encounter* no. 3 (December 1953). Reprinted by permission of Robert Graves [Ed.].

truth. Against her the odds were too great and their relentless pressure brought at last a total renunciation of all effort and a complete submission of her intellect. The passionate woman in her capitulated to the devout nun and this surrender left her bereft of life. Physically she survived herself briefly.

To the unhappy nun-poetess during the last four or five years of her existence the world outside must have seemed a projection of her own inner turmoil and affliction. A series of disasters and phenomena were then plaguing the city and its environs, bringing suffering, fear and violence. Heavy rains in 1691 brought successively ruinous floods, crop destruction, famine, and pestilence, while a total eclipse of the sun stirred panic fear. Sullen discontent and mounting tensions erupted into mass riots that nearly toppled Spanish authority in the land. As these sinister events darkened the world without, the storm, so long brewing within Sister Juana Inés, broke.

In 1690 she inadvertently brought to a head the disapproval and hostility of her religious associates slowly gathering over the years. In some way she was induced to write a successful rebuttal of certain views set forth long before in a sermon by a famous Portuguese Jesuit Father Vieira. Her skill in manipulating the methods of neo-scholasticism evidently pleased the Bishop of Puebla who took it upon himself to publish her paper. At the same time, in the guise of "Sister Philotea," he wrote her a letter chiding her alleged neglect of religious literature and her fondness for profane letters. "You have spent a lot of time studying (secular) philosophers and poets, and now it would seem reasonable to apply yourself to better things and to better books." Clearly, this was a reproof from a superior high in the hierarchy and it could not fail to distress a nun tormented by guilt feelings. Through months of declining health she brooded on a reply to the Bishop's censure. Finally, under date of March 1, 1691, it took form in her famous *Reply* in which, with many autobiographical details and with alternate humility and boldness, she defended herself from the prelate's strictures.

Obscure complications followed this epistolary exchange, chief of which was the withdrawal of her confessor, Father Antonio Núñez de Miranda, who had influenced her decision to enter the convent and had counseled her over the years. Vainly he had urged her to turn from what he considered worldly matters and apply her great talents to things eternal. All her devoted supporters, it seemed to her, were falling away through absence, desertion, or death. And she had never enjoyed the favor of the misogynistic Archbishop Aguiar y Seijas, who had involved her in his frenzied almsgiving. In 1693, as if to remind everyone of her worldliness, a second edition of a volume of her poems, which the vicereine, her friend and patroness, had extracted from her, appeared in Spain, and copies doubtless reached Mexico City soon after. This intended kindness may have hastened her final surrender. On February 8, 1694, using blood from her veins as ink, she indited an abject reaffirmation of her faith and renewed her vows, which she signed: "I, Sister Juana Inés de la Cruz, the worst in the world." She renounced all her possessions, the gifts and trinkets of her admirers, the mathematical and musical instruments that she had so long studied and used, and—the most painful wrench of all—those silent and precious companions of her cell, her beloved books. All were sold and the proceeds given to charity. With this bitter deprivation, she gave herself to excessive acts of penance, self-flagellation, and mortification of the flesh. The coveted death of the body came at last during her tireless ministrations to sisters of her community decimated by a pestilence sweeping the city. . . .

THE TEXTURE OF URBAN LIFE

4. Class and Caste in Eighteenth-Century Quito

JORGE JUAN AND ANTONIO DE ULLOA

In 1734 King Philip V assigned Spanish officials Jorge Juan and Antonio de Ulloa to assist a French scientific expedition in South America. Between 1735 and 1744 they traveled around the northern portion of the continent visiting Cartagena, Porto Bello, Panama, Guayaquil, Quito, Lima, and Concepción, Chile. Returning to Spain they published a five-volume account of their experiences, *A Voyage to South America*, in 1748. Modern historians have found the work an invaluable source for information about the customs, habits, and morals of Spanish colonial life as well as more technical speculations on geology, geography, flora, and fauna. In this excerpt Juan and Ulloa describe the complicated structure of class and caste in Quito.

This city is very populous, and has, among its inhabitants, some families of high rank and distinction; though their number is but small considering its extent, the poorer class bearing here too great a proportion. The former are the descendants either of the original conquerors, or of presidents, auditors, or other persons of character, who at different times came over from Spain invested with some lucrative post, and have still preserved their lustre, both of wealth and descent, by intermarriages, without intermixing with meaner families though famous for their riches.

The commonalty may be divided into four classes; Spaniards or Whites, Mestizos, Indians or Natives, and Negroes, with their progeny. These last are not proportionally so numerous as in the other parts of the Indies, occasioned by it being something inconvenient to bring Negroes to Quito, and the different kinds of agriculture being generally performed by Indians.

The name of Spaniard here has a different meaning from that of Chapitone or European, as properly signifying a person descended from a Spaniard without a mixture of blood. Many Mestizos, from the advantage of a fresh complexion, appear to be Spaniards more than those who are so in reality; and from only this fortuitous advantage are accounted as such. The Whites, according to this construction of the word, may be considered as one sixth part of the inhabitants.

The Mestizos are the descendants of Spaniards and Indians, and are to be considered here in the same different degrees between the Negros and Whites, as before at Carthagena; but with this difference, that at Quito the degrees of Mestizos are not carried so far back; for, even in the second or third generations, when they acquire the European colour, they are considered as Spaniards. The complexion of the Mestizos is swarthy and reddish, but not of that red common in the fair Mulattos. This is the first degree, or the immediate issue of a Spaniard and Indian. Some are, however, equally tawny with the Indians themselves, though they are distinguished from them by their beards: while others, on the contrary, have so fine a complexion that they might pass for Whites, were it not for some signs which betray them, when viewed attentively. Among these, the most remarkable is the lowness of the forehead, which often leaves but a small space between their hair and eye-brows; at the same time the hair grows remarkably forward on the temples, extending to the lower part of the ear. Besides, the hair itself is harsh, lank, coarse, and very black; their nose very small, thin, and has a little rising on the middle, from whence it forms a small curve, terminating in a point, bending towards the upper lip. These marks besides some dark spots on the body, are so constant and invariable, as to make it very difficult to conceal the fallacy of their complexion. The Mestizos may be reckoned a third part of the inhabitants.

The next class is the Indians, who form about another third; and the others, who are about one sixth, are the Casts. These four classes, according to the most authentic accounts taken from the parish register, amount to between 50 and 60,000 persons, of all ages, sexes, and ranks. If among these classes the Spaniards, as is natural to think, are the most eminent for riches, rank, and power, it must at the same time be owned, however melancholy the truth may appear, they are in proportion the most poor, miserable and distressed; for they refuse to apply themselves to any mechanic business, considering it as a disgrace to that quality they so highly value themselves upon, which consists in not being black, brown, or of a copper-colour. The Mestizos, whose pride is regulated by prudence, readily apply themselves to arts and trades, but chuse those of the greatest repute, as painting, sculpture, and the like, leaving the meaner sort to the Indians. They are observed to excel in all, particularly painting and sculpture; in the former a Mestizo, called Miguel de Santiago, acquired great reputation, some of his works being still preserved and highly valued, while others were carried even to Rome, where they were honoured with the unanimous applauses of the virtuosi. They are remarkably ready and excellent at imitation, copying being indeed best adapted to their phlegmatic genius. And what renders their exquisite performances still more admirable is, that they are destitute of many of the instruments and tools requisite to perform them with any tolerable degree of accuracy. But, with these talents, they are so excessively indolent and slothful, that, instead of working, they often loiter about the streets during the whole day. The Indians, who are generally shoemakers, bricklayers, weavers, and the like, are not more industrious. Of these the most active and tractable are the barbers and phlebotomists, who, in their respective callings, are equal to the most expert hands in Europe. The shoemakers, on the other hand, distinguish themselves by such supineness and sloth, that very often you have no other way left to obtain the shoes you have bespoke, than to procure materials, seize on the Indian, and lock him up till they are finished. This is indeed partly owing to a wrong custom of paying for the work before it is done, and when the Indian has once got the money, he spends it all in chicha,* so that while it lasts he is never sober; and it is natural to think that it will not be easy afterwards to prevail on him to work for what he has spent.

The dress here differs from that used in Spain, but less so with the men than of the women. The former, who wear a black cloak, have under it a long coat, reaching down to their knees, with a close sleeve, open at the sides, without folds, and along the seams of the body, as well as those of the sleeves, are button-holes, and two rows of buttons for ornament. In every other particular, people of fortune affect great magnificence in their dress, wearing very commonly the finest gold and silver tissues.

The Mestizos in general wear blue cloth, manufactured in this country. And though the lowest class of Spaniards are very ambitious of distinguishing themselves from them either by the colour or fashion of the clothes, little difference is to be observed.

The most singular dress, with regard to its meanness, is that of the Indians, which consists only of white cotton drawers, made either from the stuffs of the country, or from others brought from Europe. They come down to the calf of the leg, where they hang loose, and are edged with a lace suitable to the stuff. The use of a shirt is supplied by a black cotton frock, woven, by the natives. It is made in the form of a sack, with three openings at the bottom, one in the middle for the head, and the others at the corners for the arms, and thus cover their naked bodies down to the knees. Over this is a capisayo, a kind of serge cloak, having a hole in the middle for putting the head through, and a hat, made by the natives. This is their general dress, and which they never lay aside, not even while they sleep. And use has so inured them to the weather, that, without any additional clothing or covering for their legs or feet, they travel in the coldest parts with the same readiness as in the warmest.

The Indians who have acquired some fortune, particularly the barbers and phlebotomists, are very careful to distinguish themselves from their countrymen, both

* A kind of beer or ale made of maize, and very intoxicating.

by the fineness of their drawers, and also by wearing a shirt, though without sleeves. Round the neck of the shirt they wear a lace four or five fingers in breadth, hanging entirely round like a kind of ruff or band. One favourite piece of finery is silver or gold buckles for their shoes; but they wear no stockings or other coverings on their legs. Instead of the mean capisayo, they wear a cloak of fine cloth, and often adorned with gold or silver lace.

The dress of the ladies of the first rank consists of a petticoat already described in our account of Guayaquil. On the upper parts of their body they wear a shift, on that a loose jacket laced, and over all a kind of bays,* but made into no form, being worn just as cut from the piece. Every part of their dress is, as it were, covered with lace; and those which they wear on days of ceremony are always of the richest stuffs, with a profusion of ornaments. Their hair is generally made up in tresses, which they form into a kind of cross on the nape of the neck; tying a rich ribband, called balaca, twice round their heads, and with the ends form a kind of rose at their temples. These roses are elegantly intermixed with diamonds and flowers. When they go to church, they sometimes wear a full petticoat, but the most usual dress on these occasions is the veil.

The Mestizo women affect to dress in the same manner as the Spanish, though they cannot equal them in richness of their stuffs. The meaner sort go bare-footed. Two kinds of dresses are worn by the Indian women, but both of them made in the same plain manner with those worn by the men; the whole consisting of a short petticoat, and a veil of American bays. The dress of the lowest class of Indian women is in effect only a bag of the same make and stuff as the frocks of the men, and called amaco. This they fasten on the shoulders with two large pins called tupu, or topo The only particular in which it differs from the frock is, that it is something longer, reaching down to the calf of the leg, and fastened round the waist with a kind of girdle. Instead of a veil, they wear about their neck a piece of the same coarse stuff dyed black, and called Lliella; but their arms and legs are wholly naked. Such is the habit with which the lower class of Indian women are contented.

The caciquesses, or Indian women, who are married to the alcaldes majors, governors, and others, are careful to distinguish themselves form the common people by their habits, which is a mixture of the two former, being a petticoat of bays adorned with ribbands, over this, instead of the anaco, they wear a kind of black manteau, called acso. It is wholly open on one side, plaited from top to bottom, and generally fastened round the waist with a girdle. Instead of the scanty Lliella which the common Indian women wear hanging from their shoulders, these appear in one much fuller, and all over plaited, hanging down from the back part of their head almost to the bottom of the petticoat. This they fasten before with a large silver bod-

---

* bays—a course woolen or cotton fabric napped to imitate felt. (baize)

kin, called also tupu, like those used in the anaco. Their head-dress is a piece of fine linen curiously plaited, and the end hanging down behind: this they call colla, and is worn both for distinction and ornament, and to preserve them from the heat of the sun; and these ladies that their superiority may not be called in question, never appear abroad without shoes. This dress, together with that universally worn by Indians, men and women is the same with that used in the time of the Yncas, for the propriety of distinguishing the several classes. The Caciques at present use no other than that of the more wealthy Mestizos namely, the cloak and hat; but the shoes are what chiefly distinguish them from the common Indians.

5. The Imperial City of Potosí, Boom Town Supreme

LEWIS HANKE

The history of the mining city of Potosí in colonial Peru, now part of Bolivia, might be reduced to a series of graphs recording the amount of silver produced each year. Such a statistical report would tell the economic story of Potosí, and someday, when the archives have been more thoroughly searched, a chart of rising and falling production to indicate the curves of prosperity and decline in Potosí's history will surely be made. The following sketch, however, emphasizes the human aspects of the vicissitudes of this legendary silver city.

No city in all of the vast territory of America won for the King of Spain—save perhaps Mexico City—has had a more interesting or more important history than Potosí, located in the Viceroyalty of Peru. The colorful story of this great mountain of silver began when the Inca Emperor Huayna Capac started digging almost a century before the Spaniards arrived. He was halted—so legend has it—by a terrible noise and a mysterious voice which commanded, in the Quechua Indian language: "Take no silver from this hill. It is destined for other owners." The *conquistadores* heard no such prohibitory voice in 1545 when they were told of the rich silver ore by Indians who had accidentally discovered it, and indeed, if they had, would doubtless have considered themselves the rightful owners. They immediately began to develop Potosí, which was to become one of the most famous mines in the history of the world.

Treasure seekers flocked from Spain and many other parts of the world to this bleak and uninviting spot high up in the Andes, to exploit the silver in the *Cerro*, or sugar-loaf mountain, which rises majestically over the plateau to a height of almost 16,000 feet above sea level. The first census, taken by Viceroy Francisco de Toledo about twenty-five years after the news of the lode first burst upon the world, showed the unbelievable total of 120,000 inhabitants. By 1650 the population had risen— we are told—to 160,000 and Potosí was incomparably the largest city in South America. At a time when Virginia and the Massachusetts Bay Colony were puling

From *The Imperial City of Potosí: An Unwritten Chapter in the History of Spanish America* by Lewis Hanke (The Hague: Martinus Nijhoff, 1956), pp. 1–42, passim. Reprinted by permission of the publisher.

infant colonies, unsure of their next harvest, Potosí had produced such quantities of silver that its very name had become so common a symbol for untold wealth that Don Quijote quoted to it Sancho Panza. *Vale un Potosí,* the Spaniards expressed it. The phrase "as rich as Potosí" became current in English literature as well, for within a generation of its discovery the astronomical quantities of silver mined there had become known to Spain's enemies and to others in far corners of the world. Potosí was soon marked on maps by the Portuguese, always the vigilant rivals of Spain, and even on the Chinese world map of Father Ricci, where it was placed in its correct position and called Mount *Pei-tu-hsi.*

The flush times of Potosí lasted for almost two centuries, and during this period the Imperial City (as it was officially designated by the Emperor Charles V) developed a wealthy and disorderly society. The vice, the piety, the crimes, the *fiestas* of these Potosinos, all were on a vast scale. In 1556, for example, eleven years after the founding of the city, the inhabitants celebrated the accession of Philip II to the throne of Spain with a party which lasted twenty-four days and cost eight million pesos. In 1577 three million pesos were spent on water works, an improvement which ushered in a period of even greater prosperity. By the end of the sixteenth century, miners in search of recreation could choose among the fourteen dance halls, the thirty-six gambling houses, and the one theater, the price of admission to which ranged from forty to fifty pesos. Later, one of the governors organized a "grandiosa fiesta," to celebrate an ecclesiastical event, which included the establishment in one plaza of a circus "with as many different kinds of animals as in Noah's Ark, as well as fountains simultaneously spouting wine, water, and the native drink *chicha*." The seventeenth-century ecclesiastical chronicler Antonio de la Calancha declared: "In Potosí the signs of Libra and Venus predominate, and thus most of those who live there incline to be covetous, friends of music and festivities, zealous in the pursuit of riches, and somewhat given to venery." The scanty literature now available emphasizes about equally the carnal pleasures obtainable in the silver-rich mining camp, and the curious, awe-inspiring, and stupendous events of its uproarious history. Our knowledge of Potosí may be said to be still in the folklore stage.

For many years Potosí was boom town supreme and full of turbulence. Treachery, assassination, and civil war flourished as the natural result of the gambling, the intrigues, the antagonism between Peninsular Spaniards and American born Creoles, and the rivalries for the favor of women. Fighting became a pastime, a recognized social activity. Even the members of the town council came to their meetings armed with swords and pistols, and wearing coats of mail. The Dominican friar Rodrigo de Loaysa described the "accurséd hill of Potosí" as a sink of iniquity, but the Viceroy García Hurtado de Mendoza declared that the mine was the *nervio principal en aquel reino,* "the principal support of that realm."

At one time, in the early part of the seventeenth century, there were some 700 or

800 professional gamblers in the city and 120 prostitutes, among them the redoubtable courtesan Doña Clara, whose wealth and beauty, the chroniclers assure us, were unrivalled. The most extravagant woman in Potosí, she was able to fill her home with the luxuries of Europe and the Orient, for her salon was frequented by the richest miners, who competed enthusiastically for her favors. Vagabonds abounded, and royal officials indignantly reported that there ne'er-do-wells did nothing but dress extravagantly and eat and drink to excess. So high were the stakes that one Juan Fernández dared to start a revolution in 1583, by which he hoped to make himself king of Potosí. He and his brothers planned to seize the city and, "despite the fact that he was a married man, Fernández had selected a widow, María Alvarez, to share the throne of his kingdom-to-be." The government learned of this plot and captured Fernández before his revolution could erupt, but this was not the last time that the wealth of Potosí engendered a fever of boundless hope and all-consuming desire among the bold spirits attracted to that cold and windy city.

A thick volume could be compiled on the plots that were hatched. One was the conspiracy led by Gonzalo Luis de Cabrera and the *relator* of the Audiencia de La Plata named Juan Díaz Ortiz. They caused royal officials much trouble in 1599 because they tried to smuggle in hundreds of Englishmen through the port of Buenos Aires to help them with their plans to take over Potosí.

When other mines were discovered, particularly after 1640, production began to slacken at Potosí. It continued to decline steadily throughout the eighteenth century, despite frantic efforts to improve the methods by which the silver was exploited, and at last the glory departed. The War for Independence was a decisive influence in the final decline of Potosí under Spanish rule. During this agitated period the Indians practically stopped working in the mine, and it was difficult to obtain materials needed for its operation. Up to 1816 Potosí was lost and won by the opposing forces three times. After 1816 Upper Peru was wholly occupied by royalist forces despatched by the Viceroy in Lima, and continuous guerrilla warfare was the rule. . . .

The citizens of Potosí early felt the growing pains of greatness and from the earliest years demanded royal recognition of their city's value to the crown. The Emperor Charles V bestowed upon Potosí the title Imperial City, and placed upon its first coat of arms the words: "I am rich Potosí, the treasure of the world, and the envy of kings." His prudent son Phillip II devised the scarcely less modest legend on the shield he sent them, which is used to the present day: "For the powerful Emperor, for the wise King, this lofty mountain of silver could conquer the whole world." Here was a slightly veiled royal hint that it took money to make the wheels of empire turn around. Besides the royal cut of one-fifth of all silver mined there was also the possibility of "gifts" or "loans" by individual Potosinos to a succession of ever necessitous kings whose coffers held too little for their needs. A number of documents in the archives attest to the fact that Potosinos did assist the crown in this way.

The Potosinos naturally expected some return for their assistance. As the old Spanish proverb has it: "You trim my whiskers and I'll do your topknot." Therefore the Villa Imperial regularly sent representatives to the court thousands of miles away to make known their desires. Potosí early became irked at the fact that the City of La Plata, some 150 miles away, held jurisdiction over it. The miners at Potosí struggled to throw off this yoke and by 1561 had gained their independence.

The *cabildos* or municipal councils in America were relatively weak creatures in the Spanish colonies, but not so the group that ran the affairs of rich Potosí. Their representatives enjoyed real bargaining power, and they presented their demands in well-executed and detailed documents. Antonio de León Pinelo, one of the most outstanding administrators, lawyers, and bibliographers of the seventeenth century, drew up briefs and petitions on behalf of Potosí. Sebastián de Sandoval y Guzmán was particularly active, and his *Pretensiones de la Villa Imperial de Potosí,* printed in excellent fashion in Madrid in 1634, was typical of a whole literature which might be labeled "Pretensiones de Potosí."

What did the miners want? A steady supply of Indians for the *mita,* mercury at a low price, and freedom from bureaucratic interference by royal officials were some of the demands; and loud and insistent complaints of the miners on these and other problems fill many volumes in the archives. They resisted the drawing off of miners to fight as soldiers in Chile or other threatened parts of the empire. They felt that the regulation of Viceroy Toledo, establishing that miners should never be imprisoned for debt or their property sold to satisfy debts, was a wise law which should never be revoked, because it assured a steady production upon which depended the economic health of Potosí and consequently a steady revenue to the crown. The Real Bianco de San Carlos was designed to help the miners, too, and the history of this bank will doubtless provide a valuable chapter in the fiscal history of Potosí.

The Potosinos agitated for an exemption from the *alcabala,* or sales tax, and also urged the crown to see to it that merchants in Panama and Peru sent sufficient merchandise to the ever-thirsty markets of Potosí. Above all, the Potosinos wanted the royal share of silver mined cut down from one fifth to one tenth of production.

All these and other privileges and exemptions were clamored for by a city conscious of its power and aware of the king's constant need for funds. Sometimes these requests were granted in part and for limited periods, but the Potosinos were never completely satisfied. As late as 1783 we find the king decorating the Villa Imperial with the title of "Fidelísma" or "Most Faithful," in another royal attempt to assuage some of their feelings with fine words. The struggle between a succession of hardpressed monarchs and Potosí was in fact a continuous seesaw, ending only with the successful revolution against Spain.

The wealth of Potosí drew to this Andean mining center Indians from many parts of Peru, a forced migration movement of great proportions that had never before been seen in the land, for under Inca rule only Indians on royal business had moved along the Inca highways. Negroes were also brought to Potosí, despite the doubts concerning their usefulness in the cold, rarefied atmosphere of Potosí. Spaniards from most parts of the peninsula and from all walks of life participated in the rush to explore the mine, and it does not seem strange to learn that one of the miners was a descendant of Columbus.

Foreigners were so numerous that the crown became alarmed at the dangers of their presence. A document dated 1581 lists the foreigners then in the city, and many other censuses of foreigners and reports on what they were doing, and whether their presence was "inconvenient" or not, were prepared by the hard-working representatives of the crown. The Inquisition documents provide information on suspected heretics and also on various Portuguese, who seem to have prospered in Potosí.

Another concern of the crown was the large number of vagabonds and ne'er-do-wells that flourished in the city. Not only did these lazy fellows not produce silver, but they might even be potentially dangerous, as a rebel group. Orders were despatched regularly for the "vagabonds that infest the city" to be punished and summarily ejected. These measures failing, the crown suggested that they be discreetly encouraged to engage in new discoveries and colonization attempts. If not killed in the frontier battles, at least they would be drawn away from Potosí and established far away, perhaps never to return!

The whole round of social life in this ebullient community has a sort of wild-west atmosphere. It was a vast melting pot, even more so than some other parts of the empire, for few white women could stand the climate; childbirth was particularly difficult because of the altitude. By 1586 enough *mestizos* or mixed bloods were present to provoke a riot, and the history of Potosí is well laced with disturbances which probably derived, in part at least, from the tremendous mixing of peoples that went on steadily. One little-known rebellion was attempted in 1599 with the help of the English.

The mixing of racial strains produced some interesting results. From time to time legal documents are found in the archives concerning the action of an individual who wishes to be recognized legally as a *mestizo,* because otherwise he would be forced to work in the mines as an Indian. And at least one legal process relates to a person who stated that he was an Indian and did not want to be considered a *mestizo.*

Tailors went berserk in 1604 over an election of their guild officers and even Augustinian friars once had to be reproved by the government for resisting the law with swords. Some ecclesiastics engaged in commerce or led loose lives, the crown interested itself in sending married men back to their wives in Spain or in other parts of the empire, excess ostentation in funerals had to be reproved, bull fights held in holy years were frowned upon, Indians who had fancy merchandise forced upon them against their will protested, priests quarrelled about preferential places in processions, and the descendants of Diego Huallpa, the discoverer of the mountain of silver, claimed special rights and privileges they considered due them. The detail on the social life of Potosí is rich, copious, and unexploited. . . .

Even if all the thousands of pages of manuscripts on Potosí were to be organized and made available for study, and even if monographs were prepared on all the topics listed above, problems of interpretation would still remain.

One great pitfall to be avoided is that of exaggerating everything connected with the mine. Historians writing on Potosí have not infrequently fallen victims of the boom spirit so typical of the city itself. . . Américo Castro reaffirms the belief in the overriding importance of American treasure in the history of Spain in Europe, and Victor Andrés Belaunde has remarked that the entire colonial epoch in Peru might be designated as a "vast religious and political organization for the exploitation of the mines." The Cerro was the most noted of these mines and just as the Portuguese classic seventeenth-century historian Francisco Manoel de Melo referred to that "inestimable Potosí," other writers old and new, Spanish and foreigner, beat the drum on behalf of Potosí. The belief in the opulence of Peru generally began when Atahualpa in 1532 paid over to Francisco Pizarro a roomful of gold and two more of silver. And even after New Spain began in the seventeenth century to produce more silver than Peru, the Viceroy of Peru still received a higher salary than the Viceroy of New Spain, whose position was considered an inferior one. Was this due, in part at least, to the influence of Potosí and the general belief in its supposedly inexhaustible wealth? Myths about Potosí still influence the historians who study its past.

We know that Charles V and Philip II were usually hard pressed for cash, but did Potosí really provide funds for running the empire, in the splendid way it is supposed to have done? Or were the undramatic and mundane factories in the Low Countries the solid economic base for Spain, as R. H. Tawney stated years ago? If so, was not the revenue from Potosí still a fairly steady flow which permitted the Spanish crown to act more independently than if it had to rely on Spanish revenue alone?

Did Potosí also affect the economy of the other parts of Europe? Did its cheaply produced silver cause the collapse of such mining centers as those directed by the Fuggers in Tyrol? We know, from the classic study of Earl J. Hamilton, of the influence of American treasure on prices in Spain. G. N. Clark is even more emphatic and has this to say, in commenting on the discovery of Potosí and the fact that in a few years silver was flowing to Europe in quantities that had never been imagined before: "This might in other conditions have affected silversmiths and ladies more than anyone else; but coming at this time it played a part, and perhaps a very great part, in changing the hunger for the precious metals as money into a surfeit of them. All over Europe metallic money became easier to get; in other words there was a great rise in prices, which is called 'the price revolution.' . . . Some men became suddenly rich. All those who were entitled to fixed sums, whether as rents or as taxes or dues, could buy less with these sums than before; all those who were free to demand what prices they could exact had new and rising opportunities. So broadly speaking, the old world of landlords and peasants found it harder to carry on; the traders and bankers found it easier, and capitalism advanced."

What was the influence of Potosí in America itself? Did mining play a progressive role, as Bailey W. Diffie believes, through which "an urban civilization came into existence, a middle class was created, the buying power of the people increased . . . and in general America was able to grow? Or did Potosí help to fasten upon the Viceroyalty of Peru a pernicious economic and social system which exacted quick profits from the mines, and kept agriculture in such a secondary place that its growth was dangerously retarded and a feudal society prolonged for centuries? If the answer is "yes" to this last question, can one escape the conclusion that some of the present desperate problems of Bolivia constitute, in part at least, a heritage from Potosi? Or, perhaps did the mountain of silver rather help to develop a Bolivian nationality by establishing an economic, governmental, and social nucleus around which a nation could be organized, as that energetic historian of La Paz, Humberto Vásquez Machicado, has suggested? Or is it possible that each proposition contains some measure of truth?. . .

One final observation must be made which affects all the problems of interpretation raise above. Potosí was a part, albeit a particularly important and flamboyant part, of a vast empire and functioned within the structure which Spain established in America. Its history, therefore, must be written with one eye on the rest of the empire. Potosí was necessarily influenced by the legislation, policies, and foreign entanglements of Spain just as the mountain of silver exerted an influence on other parts of America and the mother country as well. The history of Potosí is a broad and complicated story, and therefore a tale which cannot be told adequately from the vantage point of the Cerro alone. If its historians are to avoid myopia, they must always remember that Potosí, although physically isolated from most of the other New World possessions of Spain, was in fact an integral part of lands governed by the crown of Spain from its capital thousands of miles away. Potosí was unusual, of course, in some ways. The rapidity of its growth, for example, sets Potosí apart from Mexico City, whose population grew rather slowly until recent years, and from Lima, which never suffered the spectacular decline that came upon Potosí in the eighteenth century.

The truly unique aspects of Potosí, however, were its size and dramatic history.

Other mining centers existed in the empire and developed somewhat similar societies and sets of institutions. But Potosí came to exhibit those common characteristics of all mining societies in such a theatrical way that it became symbolic of the process that was going on everywhere. Perhaps herein lies the real justification for assigning to Potosí a long and significant chapter in the history of Spain in America. Just as the vociferous and learned Dominican Bartolomé de Las Casas, although not the only defender of the Indians, most persistently captured the imagination of his contemporaries and later generations as The Defender, so Potosí exemplified, in the gaudiest and most memorable colors, the passion for wealth that drew many Spaniards to the New World. Bernal Díaz del Castillo, the famous and articulate foot-soldier of Cortez, exhibited the remarkable combination of *Gott und Gewinn* which characterized the Spanish conquest of America when he exclaimed: "We came here to serve God, and also to get rich." As the mountain of Potosí towers above the surrounding peaks, so will this mine, once its story is adequately told, stand as the towering symbol for the spirit of all Spaniards who came to the New World to get rich.

6. The Bay of All Saints

CHARLES R. BOXER

It would be difficult if not impossible to give an adequate course on the history of Brazil without drawing heavily on the writings of that prolific historian, Professor Charles R. Boxer, whose publications are as noted for their excellence as for their number. Here he presents a vivid description of Bahia, the single most important city in colonial Brazil.

The famous Brazilian sociologist, Gilberto Freyre, is the author of a small work on Bahia which is humorously entitled, "Bay of All Saints and of nearly all the sins," and in truth the city's reputation for both sanctity and sinfulness was not undeserved. As is the way with mankind the world over, sinners rather than saints predominated in the capital of colonial Brazil; but colorful manifestations of both the sacred and the profane in the daily life of the city are recorded by many observant travelers. On the one hand were the numerous and richly decorated churches—popularly if erroneously supposed to number three hundred and sixty-five, one for every day in the year—crowded with worshippers, whose real or apparent devotion impressed even prejudiced Protestant visitors. On the other hand were the daily—or rather, nightly—deaths by murder most foul, and the sexual license typified by the richly dressed mulatta prostitutes. The multitude of Negro slaves, on whom the life of the city and the cultivation of the neighboring sugar and tobacco plantations depended, formed a perpetual reminder that Brazil had an African soul.

The City of the Savior (*Cidade do Salvador*) was the capital of Brazil from 1549, when it was founded on the southeastern shore of the Bay of all Saints (*Bahia de Todos los Santos*), until 1763, when the seat of the colonial government was moved to Rio de Janiero. Though Salvador was the name of the city, the looser designation of Bahia was usually employed instead, even in official correspondence. The term Bahia was also applied to the vast captaincy of that name, which confined roughly with the river São Francisco on the north and west, and with the captaincies of

From *The Golden Age of Brazil, 1695–1750* by C. R. Boxer (Berkeley and Los Angeles: University of California Press, 1962), pp. 126–61, passim. Copyright © 1967 by the Regents of the University of California. Reprinted by permission.

Ilheus and Minas Gerais on the south. Since bay, city, and captaincy alike were indiscriminately termed "Bahia" for centuries, it will, I hope, be apparent from the context to which one I am referring hereafter. . . .

Bahia had long since outstripped "Golden Goa" to become the second city in the Portuguese empire, being surpassed only by Lisbon in population and in importance. An Italian visitor in 1699 estimated the population of the city and its environs at 700,000 souls. This is certainly a great exaggeration, and about 100,000 would seem a more reasonable figure, although we have insufficient data for anything more than very rough estimates. It was the seat of the governors-general and viceroys, and, from 1675 onward, of the only archbishopric in Portuguese America. It was a thriving entrepôt of trade with Portugal and West Africa, the chief whaling station in the South Atlantic, and boasted a shipbuilding yard of some importance. It was also the seat of a *Relação* or High Court; and if it did not possess a university, as did several cities in Spanish America, this was because the citizens' petition that the local Jesuit College should be raised to that status was rejected by the Crown on the advice of the University of Coimbra.

The city was built, like Lisbon and Porto in the mother country, or like Luanda in Angola, Macao in China, and Rio de Janeiro and Olinda in Brazil, on very uneven and hilly ground, running steeply into the sea. The commanding heights were occupied by churches, convents, public buildings, and the town houses of the gentry. The long narrow waterfront contained the commercial quarter with warehouses, stores, shops, and the like. There was thus an upper and a lower city, connected by narrow, tortuous, and steep streets and alleys, which made wheeled traffic virtually impossible. Slaves and (to a lesser degree) pack horses or mules were used for the transport of goods, and litters were employed by the gentry and merchants instead of coaches or carriages. In other words, it was a typical Portuguese city, medieval in its lack of planning and in its haphazard growth, forming a strong contrast to the methodically laid out Spanish-American towns.

One of the best descriptions of Bahia at the end of the seventeenth century is that by William Dampier, who stayed there in April and May, 1699. His description is worth reproducing in full, although he does not mention the great windlass which was used for hauling heavy goods between the upper and lower towns, and which was the forerunner of the electric elevator that is such a prominent feature of the city today. His description of the streets is evidently rather flattering; but the general accuracy of his observations is attested by comparison with those of Ramponi and others who were there about the same time.

> The town itself consists of about 2,000 houses; the major part of which cannot be seen from the harbour; but so many as appear in sight with a great mixture of trees between them, and all placed on a rising hill, make a very

pleasant prospect. . . . here lives an Archbishop who has a fine palace in the town; and the governor's palace is a fair stone building, and looks handsome to the sea, though but indifferently furnished within. Both Spaniards and Portuguese in their plantations abroad, as I have generally observed, affecting to have large houses; but are little curious about furniture, except pictures some of them. The houses of the town are two or three stories high, the walls thick and strong, being built with stone, with a covering of pantile; and may of them have balconies. The principal streets are large, and all of them paved or pitched with small stones. There are also parades on the most eminent places of the town, and many gardens, as well within the town as in the out-parts of it, wherein are fruit trees, herbs, salladings and flowers in great variety, but ordered with no great care nor art.

Nearly all visitors to eighteenth-century Bahia were deeply impressed by the number and magnificence of its convents and churches. Even Mrs. Nathaniel Edward Kindersley, who felt that "no Protestant ever saw a monastery, without reflecting as I do now, on the indolence and inutility of a monastic life, and the folly of its mortifications," felt constrained to admit that the convents at Bahia were "handsome buildings." She was still more complimentary about the churches. "Some of them are large and superb," she wrote, "and by being unencumbered with pews, the double rows of pillars have a very fine effect, and give the whole choir an open airy appearance which our churches can never have: they are kept in the greatest order, and adorned, particularly the altars, with carving, paintings, and gilding; with candlesticks and ornaments of gold and silver to a vast experience." . . .

The frequent complaints of the misdemeanors of many of the colonial clergy did not alter the fact that as a body they were most powerful and influential, being held in awesome regard by the majority of the laity. The Portuguese had a deep-rooted tradition of respect (amounting to veneration) for the Cloth, though some contemporaries claimed that it was less noticeable in Brazil than in the mother country and in Portuguese Asia. Be this as it may; it was a common theme in classical Portuguese literature that the worst priest was superior to the best layman. Nuno Marques Pereira, who is not sparing in his criticisms of the Luso-Brazilian clergy, explains that nevertheless the Roman Catholic priesthood is superior to all other human callings, and even to that of the angels. "With five words they can bring God Himself down into their hands; and with another five they can open the gates of heaven to a sinner and close those of hell: the first five words being those of consecration, and the second five those of absolution." . . .

However much Protestant observers might deplore the all-pervading prevalence of "Popery" at Bahia, they could not deny the devotional fervor displayed by all classes of the population. No respectable man was to be seen in the streets without a sword at his side and a rosary in his hand, and with another, as often as not, round his neck. At the sound of the Angelus bell, passersby knelt down in the street and said their prayers. The churches were thronged with worshipers of all classes, and even the censorious Mrs. Kindersley felt bound to commend "the warm and steady devotion of the common people here." She was particularly impressed by the piety of the converted Negro slaves. "They are all made Christians as soon as bought, and it is amazing to see the effect the pageantry of the Roman Catholic religion has upon their uninformed minds; they are as devout as the common people in our cities are profane; constant at their worship, obedient to their preceptors without scruple, and inspired with all the enthusiasm of devotion; the gilded pomp, the solemnity of processions, the mysterious rites, the fear as well as the admiration of their ghostly fathers, all conspire to render them so."

The religious processions which took place on many of the feast days of the Church were indeed a striking feature of life at Bahia, blending the sacred and the profane together in the most intriguing way. Portuguese Catholicism has always tended to concentrate on the external manifestations of the Christian cult, and the large African element at Bahia undoubtedly strengthened this tendency. Popular amusements were few, and the gaily dressed and richly decorated religious processions, with their masqueraders, musicians, and dancers, served social needs, which are nowadays supplied by the dance-hall, the theater, and the cinema. They afforded the sole opportunity for the mingling of all classes on terms approaching equality, even if they sometimes ended in rioting and disorder. A French voyager in 1718 was astonished to see the elderly and dignified viceroy dancing before the high altar in honor of São Gonçalo D'Amarante, just as if he had been a choirboy in Seville Cathedral on the Feast of Corpus Christi. Le Gentil de la Barbinais added that a Brazilian Portuguese was quite capable of spending his whole year's income on celebrating his patron saint's feast day, "Si on ôtoit aux portuguais leurs Saints et leurs Maitresses," he concluded, "ils deviendront trop riches."

These colorful religious processions were organized by the lay brotherhoods or confraternities (*Irmandades*), which were voluntary associations of the faithful for charitable and pious ends. Much of the social work that would be done nowadays (if at all) by the government or by the Church, was then performed by the brotherhoods. The principal Religious Orders each had their own affiliations of such laymen, and there was often considerable rivalry between them. Their social status varied from those restricted to pure whites of good family to others whose members were composed solely of Negro slaves. As a rule their composition was on racial lines, whites, mulattoes, and Negroes each having their own *Irmandade;* but a few made no distinctions of class or color, or between bond and free. Some brotherhoods were devoted to purely pious ends; others had a guild character, their membership being limited to a particular trade or calling; and others combined social and religious activities in about equal proportions.

The first half of the eighteenth century saw the full flowering of these brotherhoods in Brazil, where some of them amassed very considerable wealth. Childless members, who had made their money in mining mercantile, or other pursuits, often bequeathed their entire fortune to their brotherhood. The palatial hospice for respectable women attached to the Misericordia at Bahia was built with a legacy of 80,000 *cruzados* left by João de Mattos. Even those with family responsibilities often bequeathed a considerable sum, and smaller legacies were an almost daily occurrence.

Membership of these brotherhoods was naturally confined to men, but women were at least allowed to watch their processions, which was one of the very few diversions permitted them in colonial days. Even the Spaniards made fun of the jealous seclusions in which the Portuguese of all classes kept—or strove to keep—their wives and daughters. The Portuguese themselves were not ashamed of this, save for a few eccentrics like Thomé Pinheiro da Veiga, whose *Fastigimia,* written in the early seventeenth century, is full of mordant criticism of his compatriots' habit of secluding their women. The more general attitude was exemplified by the proverb that a really virtuous woman left her house only thrice during her lifetime: for her christening, for her marriage, and for her funeral. The harem-like seclusion in which nearly all upper-class women were kept, inevitable gave their menfolk an unenviable reputation as husband abroad. A Portuguese envoy in London, Dr. António de Sousa de Macedo, observed in 1642: "The English women are so convinced of the subjection in which Portuguese women are kept, that it would be very difficult for a Portuguese man to find anyone willing to marry him here," although he slyly added, "there are women who would like them as lovers." All travelers in the Portuguese empire were equally uncomplimentary about the rigorous seclusion of Portuguese women, from Huighen van Linschoten in sixteenth-century Goa to Maria Graham in nineteenth-century Bahia.

The misogynistic attitude is attributed by some authorities to the influence of the long Moorish occupation during the Middle Ages, and by others to the Roman Catholic Church. Admittedly this latter body was certainly no advocate of the equality of the sexes, but Luso-Brazilian custom went too far even for those prelates who took a Pauline view of women. We find the Archbishop of Bahia complaining in 1751 that the local girls could not be induced to attend the lessons given in the Ursuline Convent, owing to the opposition of their parents. These latter, "despite the continual complaints of prelates, missionaries, confessors, and preachers, kept their daughters in such strict seclusion that they rarely let them go out to hear Mass, much less for any other reason." The Archbishop added that this practice was not confined to white women, but was imitated by colored girls, "and by any others who can make confession at home." This attitude did not help to enliven family life in colonial Brazil, which the great Brazilian historian. Capistrano de Abreu, characterized as "taciturn father, obedient wife, cowed children."

However tedious the lives of the Bahian ladies may have been, their lot was in most ways more enviable than that of their slaves. . . . A royal dispatch of March 1, 1700, denouncing the barbarity with which many slaveowners of both sexes treated their slaves, stated that these atrocities originated on plantations in the interior, but had lately spread to the cities and towns. The Crown condemned as particularly shameful the practice of lady owners living on the immoral earnings of their female slaves, who were not merely encouraged but forced into a life of prostitution. This practice was a reprehensible extension of the more common habit whereby women slaves were allowed to work on their own account as cooks, seamstresses, or street hawkers, provided they paid their owners a fixed sum out of their daily or weekly earnings. Similarly, male slaves who were skilled laborers were often allowed to work as journeymen, on condition that they paid their masters an agreed proportion of their wages. . . .

One of the matters which had been left to the decision of the Brazilian viceroys or governors-general by a decree of 1693 was the creation of new townships in the interior, provided that the expense of erecting a council house, jail, and municipal buildings was borne by the local inhabitants. The more capable and energetic administrators, such as Dom João de Lencastre, the Marquis of Angeja, and the Count of Sabugosa made full use of their powers. They were rightly convinced that the erection of such townships was the best means of civilizing and developing the rough settlements of the *sertão*. When the Overseas Councillors claimed prior consultation on this matter, the Marquis of Angeja tartly observed that if the viceroy of Bahia was not competent to make such decisions on his own responsibility then the king should not have chosen him to govern Brazil. This reproach seems to have had the desired effect, at any rate for a time.

The Count of Sabugosa was particularly active in founding townships in the *Reconcavo*. On erecting that of Maragogipe in 1724, he pointed with pride to the precedent of Jacobina. No fewer than 532 persons had been murdered with firearms in that unruly mining camp between 1710 and 1721, when he promoted it to a municipality, complete with a town council, magistrate, and militia. In the three years which had elapsed since that date, only three murders had been recorded, and these were unpremeditated affairs with knives and swords. Similarly, Maragogipe, which was described as a "den of thieves" (*covil de ladrões*) in 1716, became a model municipality in 1724, when the grateful townsmen offered the viceroy an annual contribution of 2,000 *alqueires* of manioc flour for the Bahia garrison's basic ration. . . .

Brazilian historians differ on whether the municipal councils were genuine representatives of the people, or merely of a self-perpetuating and selfish oligarchy.

They also argue over whether the councils were largely autonomous or were merely rubber stamps for governors and viceroys. The answer, I think, depends largely on the time and the place. The distant *Camara* of SãoPaulo (which has been the most publicized, since its history is the best documented in print) was in a much stronger position regarding the central authority at Bahia before 1720, than was the Senate of Salvador in the shadow of the viceroy's palace. A senior Crown official in Minas Gerais in the late 1730's, accused the town councillors of that captaincy of acting as if they were "seditious parliamentarians" in England, adding that they were openly hostile to any extension of the authority of the Crown. Such a truculent attitude was not possible at Bahia. But even the Bahia council had a will of its own during the period with which we are dealing, and its members not infrequently differed from so powerful a personality as the count of Sabugosa.

The sugar planters of the *Reconcavo* had their representatives on the council but they did not necessarily dominate it. On the other hand, planters, council and viceroy sometimes made common cause against the Crown. A royal edict of 1687 forbade the council to fix the prices of sugar and ordered that this commodity should be sold freely. Ten years later this policy was reversed, and the Crown ordained that the annual sugar prices should be fixed by agreement between two representatives of the planters and two of the local merchants, under the supervision of the municipal council of Salvador. All sugar chests were to be inspected, graded, and weighed in accordance with certain specifications before they were shipped to Portugal. Planters who adulterated their sugars were to be fined and exiled from Bahia for two years. Another edict of 1698 fixed the maximum weight of a loaded sugar chest at forty *arrobas*, "including the wood." Experience had shown that the Lisbon stevedores could not cope with heavier chests, "with the result that many of them left their jobs and absented themselves for fear of imperiling their life and health with a weight which was more than they could bear." With the connivance of the *Camara* and of successive governors, the Bahia planters systematically evaded compliance with these edicts for more than thirty years and the Crown was only able to call them to order in 1732.

Since sugar was for so long the mainstay of the Brazilian economy, the *senhores de engenho* (as planters were termed) came to be recognized as the rural aristocracy and were awarded corresponding privileges and immunities. Gubernatorial and royal decrees exempted their sugar mills, technical equipment, and slaves from being seized or distrained for outstanding debts. Their creditors were only allowed to take a portion of the cane ground at harvest time. These privileges were later extended to the *lavradores* or copyholders who cultivated small fields and had their cane ground by the planters. The production of sugar in the *Reconcavo* varied greatly in the first half of the eighteenth century owning to the fluctuating demand in Europe and to periods of unseasonable weather in Brazil. A good harvest, such as that of 1725–1726, produced between 12,000 and 13,000 chests for export to Portugal, which may be compared with the corresponding figure of 14,000 chests in Antonil's day. . . .

As is apparent from this chapter, it was gold, sugar, and tobacco that occupied the minds of educated laymen at Bahia rather than literature, art, or music. Nevertheless these latter manifestations of the spirit were not neglected, even if they did not normally reach very high standards. The chief focus of culture was inevitably the local Jesuit College, where instruction was not confined to actual or potential members of the Society, and whose library contained in 1694 some 3,000 volumes "by every kind of writer who could be desired." The Jesuits had many lay brothers and priests who were professional painters, sculptors, woodcarver, and metalworkers. Though much of their work has disappeared, enough survives to show that in woodwork particularly they often attained more than a merely mechanical skill. There were also numerous goldsmiths and silversmiths in Bahia, but such of their works as survived do not indicate that they possessed more than mediocre abilities. The local school of military engineering (*aula de fortificação*) produced some competent practitioners; but the intellectual caliber of the officers of the Bahia garrison does not seem to have attained the standard reached by their colleagues at Rio de Janeiro under the patronage of Gomes Freire de Andrada.

Poets and poetasters abounded at Bahia, as everywhere and always in the Portuguese-speaking world; but the only one of outstanding merit, the satirist Gregorio de Mattos, died in 1696 just when our concern with Bahia begins. His verses were too pungently critical to be printed in his lifetime and for long afterwards, but they circulated in manuscript during this period. . . .

Historical studies received an impulse when the Count of Sabugosa was commanded by the king to collect information that might be useful for the Royal Academy of History. This body had been founded at Lisbon in 1720 and was entrusted with the task of compiling a history of the Portuguese empire in all its aspects. The royal order stimulated the viceroy to found an academy at Bahia, whose members decided, with what was obviously mock modesty, to call themselves. "The Forgotten" at their inaugural session in March 1724. The "Academia dos Esquecidos" only flourished for a short time, during which period the forty-four members limited themselves to exchanging poetical effusions, laudatory speeches, and dissertations on trivial themes in the manner of similar literary academies which waxed and waned in Portugal Sabugosa's initiative was not entirely wasted, however. The corresponding members of the Academy included Pedro Leonel Mariz, who spent most of his life in the turbulent mining camps of the Bahia *sertão*, and this indicates that some of the graces of life may have penetrated there. The only production of a Bahian academician that achieved the dignity of print during its author's lifetime was Sebastião da Rocha Pitta's *Historia da America Portuguesa,* published at Lisbon in 1730. Though scornfully dismissed by Robert Southey as being "a meagre and inaccurate work which has been accounted valuable, merely because there is no other," the *Historia* does not deserve this censure. For all its Gongoric turgidity, it contains some valuable and authentic information, being on some points more fair-minded and accurate than Southey's better written but more prejudiced work.

The indefatigable count of Sabugosa was also responsible for the establishment of the first secular theater in Bahia, with the object of "acting comedies on occasions celebrating royal festivities." This theater was built at his own expense as an adjunct of the municipal hall, but it was pulled down in 1733 by order of his pet aversion, the Royal Judge, Dr. Joseph dos Santos Varjão, which led to an acrimonious correspondence between those concerned. During the few years it lasted, this comedy theater may have provided a welcome change from the Jesuit tragicomedies or religious operas which they staged on occasional high days and holy days. Early eighteenth-century Bahia also witnessed the flowering of the *modinha,* which was later transplanted to Portugal and described by William Beckford in glowing terms. "Those who had never heard this original sort of music, must and will remain ignorant of the most bewitching melodies that ever existed since the days of the Sybarites." But despite the popularity of the *modinha*, the introduction of African musical influences through the slaves, and the initiative of the Count of Sabugosa, the culture of the educated élite at Bahia remained preponderantly a clerical one....

José Gabriel Condorcanqui Tupac Amaru, Marqués de Oropesa and cacique de Tungasuca, Surimana y Pampamarca. Like the seventeenth centuey Inca Garcilaso de las Vega, Tupac Amaru was a mestizo who moved uneasily between two very different worlds. Wealthy and well-educated in a Spanish colegio, he had thoroughly absorbed the values of Spanish culture as this portrait by the Peruvian painter Augusto Díaz suggests, but on his mother's side he was a direct descendant of the last Inca emperor, Tupac Amaru, who was executed by the Spanish in 1572. Condorcanqui became acutely aware of the abuses suffered by the indigenous people while serving as the cacique of Tungasuca. When his efforts to bring about peaceful reforms came to naught, he adopted the name Tupac Amaru II and along with his Spanish wife, Michaela, embarked on an open rebellion which would become the most serious native challenge to three hundred years of Spanish rule (Readings 1, 2, and 3).

Crisis and Climax in the Eighteenth Century

THE BOURBON REFORMS

The century before the Portuguese and Spanish colonies in America won their independence brought considerable cultural, economic and political change. Tensions between the mother countries and the New World increased, despite or perhaps because of the many improvements in the lot of the overseas colonists. The Iberian empires were no longer so isolated from the world, and the increasingly determined attempts of Spain and Portugal to keep their American citizens more efficiently under peninsular control led to resistance rather than acquiescence. Portugal administered a shock to Brazil when she expelled the Jesuits in 1759, even before Spain took the same decisive step a few years later. The causes for what many considered a harsh and wrong attack in both Brazil and Spanish America upon this powerful order were many and complicated, as Professor Magnus Mörner has ably shown in a volume on this controversial event.[1]

During the eighteenth century Spain made a remarkable recovery from the state of abject weakness into which it had fallen, thanks to the efforts of three princes of the House of Bourbon: Philip V (1700–1746) and his two sons, Ferdinand VI (1746–1759) and Charles III (1759–1788). The Bourbon kings introduced the French concept of a centralized government and gradually replaced outmoded Hapsburg institutions. Throughout the century they reorganized the governmental structure, the economic system, the relations between church and state, and modified the intellectual orientation of Spain and its empire. These reforms sought not greater autonomy for the colonies but a more profitable system for the mother country. Nor did the Bourbons encourage greater participation of American-born colonists in the government. As a result, enmity between Spaniards and creoles grew stronger as the century neared its end.

1. Magnus Mörner, *The Expulsion of the Jesuits from Latin America* (New York: Knopf, 1965).

Although the government was interested in furthering education, medicine, and the fine arts, the reforms never addressed the basic social inequalities of colonial life. Society remained hierarchically divided into many socioracial groups, and suggestions to soften or eliminate these cleavages went unheeded. The Indians and *castas*, although forming the majority of the population, continued to bear the burden and the social stigma of personal taxes and continued to be excluded from governmental posts and other privileged occupations. The intolerable conditions of the common people led to major revolutionary outbreaks in Peru, Bolivia, and Colombia (1780–83) that were sternly suppressed by Spanish arms.

THE REVOLT OF TUPAC AMARU IN PERU

Eighteenth-century Peru was the locale of probably the most significant indigenous rebellion in the whole colonial period. Led by the mestizo José Gabriel Tupac Amaru, Marquis of Oropesa, a descendent of the Inca leader Tupac Amaru who had been beheaded by Viceroy Francisco de Toledo in 1572, its history "is intricate and obscure."[2] Was the revolt primarily aimed at ending the oppression of the Indians, as many have asserted, or was it an attempt to throw off the Spanish yoke completely and achieve an independent Peruvian Indian state? (Reading 1) Whatever the true causes, and research is still going forward, the rebellion of 1780–81 failed despite widespread support of Indians and the aid of the leader's intelligent and vigorous wife (Reading 2). In a recent assessment, Ward Stavig asserts that although the "situation was ripe for rebellion," it was the "strength of the relationships between Tupac Amaru and other curacas and the Indian peoples over whom they ruled that won adherence to the movement" (Reading 3). That the bloody affair shook Spanish officialdom is demonstrated by the fact that in 1787 an audiencia was established in Cuzco which was designed to afford greater protection for the Indians against exploitation by their Spanish governors and Indian curacas alike.

MEXICO

In Mexico a different set of circumstances created another kind of problem. Spain decided to organize a colonial militia to protect the land from foreign incursion, such as Havana and Manila had both suffered in 1762 at the hands of the British. The well-born young men in Mexico displayed no great enthusiasm for military service until granted the *fuero militar*, which conceded such privileges and

2. George Kubler, "The Quechua in the Colonial World," *Handbook of South American Indians*, ed. Julian H. Steward (Washington, D.C.: Smithsonian Institution, 1946), 2: 331–410.

immunities as to create an officer class largely exempt from civil responsibility. Thus came into being a significant inequality that laid the basis for the nineteenth-century military dictators (Reading 4). Yet relatively speaking, Mexico appeared to be advanced. Alexander von Humboldt, in his classic overview of Mexico about 1800, lauded Mexico City: "No new city of the new continent, without even excepting those of the United States, can display such great and solid scientific achievements as the capital of Mexico." He added, however: "Mexico is the country of inequality. Nowhere does there exist such a fearful difference in the distribution of fortune, civilization, cultivation of the soil, and population" (Reading 5).

THE REVOLT OF TUPAC AMARU IN PERU

1. The Last Incan Rebellion

LUIS MARTÍN

Luis Martín is a professor of history at the Southern Methodist University. Born in Spain, he was educated there and in the United States. He has lived and taught in Peru and is the author of several books about that country including a pathbreaking study of colonial women entitled *Daughters of the Conquistadores: Women of the Viceroyalty of Peru* (Albuquerque: University of New Mexico Press, 1983). The selection reprinted below is from his one-volume survey of Peruvian history, *The Kingdom of the Sun*. In it he discusses how the changes wrought by Bourbon rule in the eighteenth century increased social tensions, and he provides a concise overview of Tupac Amaru's revolt.

THE BIRTH OF A NEW NATION

The intellectual, political, and economic changes that affected Peru in the eighteenth century were not the only forewarnings of an impending new era. The different social and racial groups comprising the population of Peru reached such a degree of mutual alienation after 1700 that hopes of maintaining a peaceful, stable colonial society all but vanished by the end of the century. The census conducted in 1793 by Viceroy Gil y Taboada y Lemos reported a population of 1,076,122 persons within the boundaries of the viceroyalty. According to the computations of the German scientist Humboldt, the population of Peru had reached 1,400,000 inhabitants by the opening years of the nineteenth century. Indians comprised 56 percent of that population or about 784,000 persons, and only 139,000 or 13 percent of the total population were white Europeans. The remaining 31 percent were made up of black slaves and *castas* (mixed-blood mestizos and mulattoes). Even in the eighteenth century the Indians were brutally exploited under the mita and the corregi-

From *The Kingdom of the Sun: A Short History of Peru* by Luis Martín (New York: Charles Scribner's Sons, 1974), pp. 158–60, 165–69, passim. Reprinted by permission.

dores. The white minority, still considering themselves lords of the land, monopolized the economy and all the important positions in the royal administration and the Church. The mixed-bloods were painfully torn between the cultural worlds of the Indian and the Spaniard, unable to find a permanent refuge in either. The eighteenth century, with the increase and improvements in communications and trade and with freer and more abundant dissemination of ideas, began to shape a new awareness and a new mentality among these different social groups. The Indians abandoned the meek passivity of previous centuries and, invoking the names of Atahualpa and Tupac Amaru, revolted against their oppressors. The restlessness of the mestizos also erupted in violence and rebellion. Bands of runaway slaves took refuge in the hills, harassed travelers on the roads, and came at times to the outskirts of cities and towns searching for food.

The social tensions and clashes of the eighteenth century did not even spare the white, Spanish minority of the population. The members of this class, although identical in racial origin and cultural background, had split into two irreconcilable groups by the middle of the century. The *peninsulares* (or "natives of the Iberian peninsula") constituted only 5 percent of the white population of the Spanish empire, the rest being creoles. In Lima, which had a population of 52,527 in 1791, 16,809 persons were classified as white Spaniards: 2,626 peninsulares and 14,183 creoles. The roots of the alienation between peninsulares and creoles sank back into the sixteenth century. The peninsulares had arrived in Peru with airs of superiority and had monopolized the best royal and ecclesiastical offices; even the poorest and least educated of them thought that it was their birthright to become lords and masters in Peru. They despised the creoles and considered them somehow degenerated by the climate and luxuries of the colonies. The creoles, in turn, hated the haughty newcomers, who held the most profitable offices and thought of Peru only as an appendage of the mother country to be exploited for the benefit of Spain. During the seventeenth century violent clashes between peninsulares and creoles occurred in, of all places, the colonial convents and religious communities. Creole friars confronted the peninsulares in conventual elections, each group supporting opposing candidates for office, and the confrontations often led to violence.

By the eighteenth century the alienation between the two groups had spread throughout the social body of Peru and was so intense that many European visitors perceived it as unsurmountable. Some wrote in their diaries and memoirs of the strong nationalism and social awareness of the creoles, who saw themselves as "children of the land," different from and opposed to the hated peninsulares. The Peruvian creoles of the eighteenth century resented being called "Spaniards" and identified themselves rather as "Americans." They spoke Castilian with a distinctive "Peruvian" accent and introduced into the language words and idioms unknown in Spain that were imposed by the realities of life in the environment of Peru. The new modalities of the language not only set them apart from the Spaniards of Iberia, but they had also begun to shape their minds and souls into a new psychological profile. Their writings showed a pride in, and a love for, Peru as the fatherland and not as a mere appendage to an imperial, colonial structure. They resented the political and economic interference of metropolitan authorities, looked down on Spain and its cultural accomplishments, and had an almost worshiping admiration for England, France, and Germany as originators of the Enlightenment and modern technology.

In the eighteenth century Indians, mestizos, and creoles were ready to strike and dismantle the Spanish colonial administration of Peru. During the century riots, revolts, and revolutions rocked the foundations of Spanish Peru with alarming periodicity, and to many observers they were the deep rumblings of the earth warning of the imminent collapse of the Spanish empire.

THE LAST INCAN REBELLION

José Gabriel was born in 1740 of a noble Indian family that claimed the last Incan emperor, Tupac Amaru, as its ancestor. The child received his early education from a village priest, and as the son of a prominent cacique he was later sent to the Colegio de Caciques of San Borja in Cuzco where he received a Jesuit education. He learned Castilian and some Latin, the basic principles of public administration, and the institutional and administrative system of the viceroyalty As a future cacique the Indian youngster learned at San Borja the legal and moral responsibilities toward his own people, whom he was supposed to guide and protect. José Gabriel eventually became a cacique of Tungasuca in the province of Tinta and in this position was the royal official closest to the common Indians. As cacique he had to execute the orders of the corregidor, gather the Indians obliged to the mita, supervise the collection of taxes, and force the Indians to accept the goods offered by the corregidor in the periodical repartos. José Gabriel could not have been in a better position from which to gather insight into the wretched plight of the Indians and the brutal exploitation they suffered at the hands of the corregidores. The young cacique of Tungasuca tried to alleviate the condition of the Indians by all legal means at his disposal. In 1776, he journeyed to Lima to plead their case with the highest authorities of the viceroyalty. He argued that the mita of Potosí was depopulating the region and that his Indians should be exempt from this forced labor in the silver mines. There was at the time a royal inspector in Peru who dismissed the case and ordered José Gabriel to keep silent on the question of the mita. An appeal to the audiencia of Lima also failed; in 1778 the audiencia upheld the visitor's decision, and the cacique of Tungasuca found himself powerless to help his people within the framework of the law. The high court had also failed to rule favorably on a personal matter of great importance to the cacique. José Gabriel had presented to the audiencia legal documents showing that he was a direct descendant of Emperor Tupac Amaru and was therefore entitled to use the noble title of Marqués de Oropesa granted by Phillip III to the Incan royal family in 1616. The audiencia recognized the justice of this claim and the authenticity of the documents presented, but it did not grant official recognition of the title.

His visit to Lima convinced José Gabriel of the futility of seeking a peaceful solution, and by 1780 he had decided on rebellion. On 4 November he seized the corregidor of the province of Tinta and held him captive in Tungasuca. José Gabriel now began acting under the royal name of Tupac Amaru. He summoned the people of the province to the town of Tungasuca, and on 10 November he executed the corregidor as punishment for his crimes against the Indians. The new Tupac Amaru drove the multitude to a frenzy when he claimed to have the king's approval to abolish the mita, the repartos, and the Indian taxes and also to execute all the corregidores of Peru. The Indian multitudes stood solidly behind him, ready to strike regardless of the consequences. Within a week the forces of Tupac Amaru, more a mob than an army, had burned to the ground the obrajes of the region, where hundreds of Indians had been forced to work as slaves. On 18 November they took the town of Sangarara and surprised the royal forces that had taken refuge in the village church. The Indians attacked; when the fight was over, the church was destroyed and almost six hundred persons had been massacred. As the news spread quickly through the Andean regions, revolts broke out in many remote Indian villages from Quito in the north to Tucumán in the south. Although the rebels invoked the name of Tupac Amaru, the cacique of Tungasuca could not control or direct these popular uprisings. In the province of Chayanta, in the northern fringes of the new viceroyalty of Buenos Aires, the Cataris brothers led a rebellion that became even more violent than that of Tupac Amaru. The Indians slew one thousand persons in the village of San Pedro, whose church was also desecrated and destroyed. The population of Palca was exterminated without sparing priests, women, or children. In their violent outburst of hatred for Europeans, the Indians made no distinction between creoles and peninsulares and went through the entire province in an orgy of burning, looting, and killing.

Although some of his followers dreamed of a restoration of the Indian empire of the Incas, Tupac Amaru recognized the irreversibly mixed character of Peruvian society in the closing decades of he eighteenth century. He appealed to mestizos and creoles to join the revolt against the Spaniards who exploited the children of the land. He was aware of the vital power of the creoles and mestizos, whose rights to form part of the new order were for him equal to the rights of the Indians. Perhaps for this reason, Tupac Amaru never clearly demanded complete autonomy from the Spanish king and went out of his way to declare his loyalty to the Christian faith. The creoles were for Tupac Amaru "my beloved creoles," and they were earnestly invited to help the Indians in building a just Andean society that would be rid of the abuses of the peninsulares. Unfortunately, his appeals were in vain. Many influential creoles were horrified by the Indian mobs who burned obrajes, sacked haciendas, killed village officials, blocked the flow of laborers to the mines, and disrupted the trading routes of the viceroyalty. The massacres of Sangarara and San Pedro and the burning of churches must have convinced many of the true nature of the rebellion. It was not a movement of political emancipation, but a social uprising in which the oppressed class had begun to use violence to destroy the yoke of oppression. Many creoles were landowners and wealthy merchants who enjoyed social prestige and occupied important positions in the audiencias, the cabildos, and the Church. They were men of law and order, and in the midst of social and economic rebellion they had no choice other than to take the side of the Spaniards and oppose the Indians. The creoles had deep grievances against peninsulares, but those grievances could not be redressed by freeing the slaves, abolishing the mita, and making the Indians their equals.

Cuzco, the ancient capital of the Incas, became the center of resistance to Tupac Amaru. The bishop of Cuzco, a creole, was among the most active organizers of the movement; by excommunicating the rebel, he placed all the moral authority of the Church on the side of the Spanish authorities. The bishop exhorted his clerics to organize the faithful of their parishes into a militia, and priests and members of the religious orders were allowed to join the improvised army. Many Indians and mestizos, deeply attached to the symbols of religion and fearful of divine punishment, followed their priests and prepared to fight against their racial brothers. Merchants and landowners enthusiastically supported the efforts of the bishop and clergy, and Cuzco became an armed camp ready to resist the attack of Tupac Amaru. On 18 December 1780 the unorganized and poorly armed Indian mob of Tupac Amaru reached the hills surrounding Cuzco. The Indian leader expected an uprising of Indians and mestizos from within the city; when it did not materialize, he hesitated and lost precious time by vainly trying to negotiate the surrender of the city. On 8 January 1781 the defenders of Cuzco, aided by reinforcements from Lima, by the corregidores of neighboring provinces, and by local caciques, marched out of the city and attacked Tupac Amaru on the hills of Picchu. The rebel army was defeated, however, not so much by the attacks of the defenders as by its own lack of discipline. By 10 January the siege of Cuzco was over, and the city had been spared the horrors of Sangarara, San Pedro, and Palca. When new reinforcements of men, weapons, and munitions arrived from Lima in February, the royal forces took the offensive. An army of more than seventeen thousand men left Cuzco to corner the rebel Indian in the mountains of Tinta. On 6 April 1781 Tupac Amaru was captured, with the help of the betrayal of a mestizo, and sent to Cuzco under guard. The Spanish authorities imposed on the great rebel a brutal sentence unworthy of a civilized nation: he was forced to watch the execution of his wife and son; his tongue was cut off and he was tied to four horses that ran in four different directions, tearing him to pieces.

The death of Tupac Amaru did not end the last Incan rebellion. His half brother Diego and his son Mariano assumed the leadership of the rebellion that continued to rock the Andes for two more years. The movement acquired a more radical and violent character in this second stage. Indians attacked and killed all white people, and no pretense was made of befriending the creoles. Churches and priests were not respected, and religious properties, parishes, and convents were destroyed with the same hate as secular buildings. The new leaders sought to ally themselves with the fierce Cataris, who were still drenching the province of Shayanta in blood. All Indian males between the ages of seven and seventy were ordered to take weapons and undergo military training; war to the death was preached all through the Indian communities of the Andes. Not only small villages but even important towns like Puno fell to the rebels, who at one time controlled most of the Peruvian altiplano. La Paz underwent a brutal siege of six months, and only superior reinforcements from Buenos Aires saved the city. Lack of supplies, discipline, and efficient leadership on the part of the Indians and the combined forces of the viceroys of Peru and Buenos Aires finally brought the Indian rebellion to an end in the middle of 1783. The rebellion ended in a victory for the Spanish colonial system, which would endure in Peru for a few more decades. If José Gabriel Tupac Amaru could have found a common ground to unite the Indians and the Peruvian creoles, he could have become the liberator of Peru, but he failed; Peru had to wait forty more years for its independence. When independence finally came, it was brought about by an international crisis and by the efforts of two creoles, San Martín and Bolívar. The two liberators of Peru were born and raised far from the Peruvian Andes, and their movements of liberation had little in common with the violent social and economic rebellions led by the Cataris and the Tupac Amarus.

2. Documents from the Revolt of Tupac Amaru

BENJAMIN KEEN

For more than forty years Benjamin Keen's textbooks and anthologies of translated readings in original sources of Latin American history have been an indispensable source for college courses. Professor emeritus at Northern Illinois University where he taught from 1965 to 1981, Professor Keen is also the author of *The Aztec Image in Western Thought* (New Brunswick, N.J.: Rutgers University Press, 1971) and a specialist in intellectual and cultural history of colonial Spanish America. In the section reprinted below, he presents three documents from the revolt of Tupac Amaru: A) an analysis of the event written by the prosecuting attorney of the viceroyalty of Buenos Aires dated January 15, 1781; B) a letter dated December 6, 1780 written to Tupac Amaru by his wife, Micaela Bastidas, rebuking him for failing to capture Cuzco, and C) a contemporary account describing the execution of Tupac Amaru and other leaders of the rebellion on May 18, 1781. The sections in italics are Keen's introductions to the documents.

A. THE PLAN OF TUPAC-AMARU

The general causes of the great revolt in Peru are sufficiently clear. More obscure are the precise aims that the rebel leader, Tupac-Amaru, set for himself. It is difficult to believe that the well-educated José Gabriel, who had had years of experience in dealing with Spanish officialdom, seriously believed that he could obtain sweeping reforms from the crown by negotiation, even from positions of strength, especially after his execution of the corregidor, Arriaga. More plausible is the view that his professions of loyalty to Spain represented a mask by means of which he hoped to utilize the still strong faith of the Indians in the mythical benevolence of the Spanish king and perhaps to soften his punishment in case of defeat. If this view is correct, it follows that his true object was the establishment of an independent Peruvian state, with himself as king or Inca. Such a state would have been essentially Spanish in religion and in political and social organization. The fiscal, or

From *Readings in Latin American Civilization: 1492 to the Present*, ed. Benjamin Keen (2nd ed. Boston: Houghton Mifflin, 1967), pp. 173–76. Reprinted by permission of the author.

prosecuting attorney, of the viceroyalty of Buenos Aires offers a shrewd and convincing argument in favor of the thesis that the rebel leader aimed at independence.[1]

What is worthy of attention in this affair is not so much the pitiful death of the corregidor Don Antonio de Arriaga, the theft of his fortune, the seizure of the arms that he had in his house, or the outrages committed by the perfidious Tupac-Amaru, as the astuteness, the painstaking care, and the deceptions with which he managed to perform them and to subvert that and other provinces, preparing them to carry out his reprehensible secret designs.

It appears that in order to seize the corregidor Arriaga, in his own house, he arranged a banquet for his victim. In order to summon the military chiefs, caciques, and Indians of the province, he compelled the unhappy corregidor to issue or sign orders to that effect. In order to drag him to the gallows in the presence of the multitude with no disturbance, he published a decree, pretending that he acted on His Majesty's orders. On the same pretext, after his horrible deed, he departed for the neighboring province of Quispicanchi, in order to perpetrate similar atrocities on the corregidor and as many Spaniards as he could find, and as soon as he had returned to his town of Tungasuca issued orders to the caciques of neighboring provinces to imitate his example.

And although in the provinces of Azangaro and Carabaya, which belonged to this viceroyalty of Buenos Aires, his wicked designs failed to bear fruit, thanks to the loyalty with which his commissioner Don Diego Chuquiguanca (the cacique and governor of the town of Azangaro) and his sons turned over the dispatches of which copies are found in the file on this case, the fact is that the province of Quispicachi, since the flight of Don Fernando Cabrera, its present corregidor, is under the sway of the rebel Tupac-Amaru; and he himself asserts in one of the papers written at Chuquiguanca that four more provinces obey his orders. And, knowing as he did the natives' great respect for the orders of the king and their hatred of the corregidores and their European associates, he probably did not find it difficult to incite them to execute the supposed orders of the king.

But the essence of the careful planning and perfidy of the traitor Tupac-Amaru consists in this, that after speaking so often of the royal orders which authorized him to proceed against the corregidores and other Europeans, in his orders, letters, and messages, and in the edicts which he dispatched to Don Diego Chuquiguanca, in order to revolutionize that province and Carabaya, he now says nothing about the orders of the king, and proceeds as the most distinguished Indian of the royal blood

1. "Vista del fiscal del virreinato de Buenos Aires, enero 15 de 1781," in Manuel de Odriozola, ed., *Documentos históricos del Peru* (Lima, 1863), pp. 132–33. (Excerpt translated by Benjamin Keen.)

and principal line of the Incas to liberate his countryman from the injuries, injustices, and slavery which the European corregidores had inflicted on them, while the superior courts turned a deaf ear to their complaints. From which it follows that he repeatedly used the name of the king—in a vague way, not specifying our present ruler, Charles III—only to secure the acquiescence of the natives of those provinces in the violence done to Arriaga and to induce them to do the same to other corregidors. And considering these aims partially achieved, he transforms himself from a royal commissioner into a redeemer from injustices and burdens, moved only by pity for his compatriots, preparing the way for them to acclaim him as king, or at least to support their benefactor with arms, until they have raised him to the defunct throne of the tyrannical pagan kings of Peru, which is doubtless the goal of his contrivings.

Actually he has already succeeded in assembling a large number of Indians, as noted by Colonel Don Pedro la Vallina (who was his prisoner) in a letter contained in the file on this case—and with their aid, it is stated, he defeated and slew some 300 men who came out to halt his advance in Cuzco, and took their weapons to arm the rebels who follow him. He took these first successful steps in his titanic enterprise after certain other things had occurred: the rising that took place in Arequipa as a result of the establishment of a customs house: the rioting that with less cause broke out in the city of La Paz; the disturbances that occurred in the provinces of Chayanta for the same reason: and the rumors that the natives in other provinces were somewhat restless. When one considers that the rebel Tupac-Amaru, informed of these events, offers the natives freedom, not only from customs-house duties but from sales taxes, tributes, and forced labor in the mines, it must be admitted that he offers them a powerful inducement to follow him, and that there is imminent danger that the party of rebellion will progressively increase unless the most energetic effort is made to slay this insolent rebel, the prime mover of this conspiracy, so that others may be deterred from joining the rebellion and abandoning their loyalty to their legitimate monarch and natural lord, to the detriment of themselves and the commonwealth.

B. A HEROINE OF THE REVOLT

Micaela, the wife of Tupac-Amaru, played a leading role in the great revolt. From the first she was the rebel leader's principal adviser, and in his absence assumed full direction of the movement. After the initial victory over the small Spanish force sent from Cuzco she strongly advised an immediate march on the city, to take advantage of the chaos and panic that reigned there. The capture of Cuzco, ancient capital of the Inca Empire and center of Spanish power in the highlands, would have been a stroke of the greatest moral and military significance. Tupac-Amaru decided instead

*to invade the provinces to the south, promising to return immediately and advance
on Cuzco—a promise he failed to keep. By the time he returned, reinforcements had
reached Cuzco from Lima, and the golden opportunity had vanished. The bitterness
of Micaela's letter to José Gabriel reflects her appreciation of the immensity of his
blunder. Despite these harsh reproaches, her letters to Tupac-Amaru contain "notes
of profound and laconic tenderness." ("Chepe" was an affectionate nickname for
her husband.)[2]*

DEAR CHEPE:

You are causing me mortal concern. While you saunter through the villages,
wasting two days in Yauri, showing no sense of urgency, our soldiers are rightly
becoming bored, and are leaving for their homes.

I simply cannot endure all this any longer, and I am ready to give myself up to
the Spaniards and let them take my life when I see how lightly you regard this serious matter that threatens the lives of all of us. We are surrounded by enemies and
constantly insecure; and on your account the lives of all my sons, and of all our people, are in danger.

I have warned you again and again not to dally in those villages, where there is
nothing to do—but you continue to saunter, ignoring the fact that the soldiers are
running short of food. They are receiving their pay, but the money will not last forever. Then they will all depart, leaving us to pay with our lives, because you must
have learned by this time that they came only for reasons of self-interest, and to get
all they could out of us. They are already beginning to desert; they are frightened by
the rumor spread by Vargas and Oré that the Spaniards of Lampa, united with those
of other provinces and Arequipa, are going to surround you, and so they want to get
away, fearing the punishment that might befall them. Thus we will lose all the people that I have gotten together for the descent on Cuzco, and the forces at Cuzco will
unite with the soldiers from Lima, who have been on the march for many days.

I must tell you all this, though it pains me. If you want to ruin us, continue to
sleep and commit such follies as that of passing alone through the streets of Yauri,
and even climbing to the church tower—actions certainly out of place at this time,
and that only dishonor you and gain you disrespect.

I believed that you were occupied day and night with arranging these affairs
instead of showing an unconcern that robs me of my life. I am already a shadow of
myself and beside myself with anxiety, and so I beg you to get on with this business.

You made me a promise, but henceforth I shall not heed your promises, for you
did not keep your word.

2. Micaela Bastidas to José Gabriel Tupac Amaru, Dec. 6, 1780, in Francisco A. Loáyza,
ed., *Martíres y heroinas* (Lima, 1945), pp. 48–51. (Excerpt translated by Benjamin Keen.)

I do not care for my life, but for the lives of my poor children, who need all my help. If the enemy comes from Paruro, as I suggested in my last letter, I am prepared to march to meet them, leaving Fernando in a secure place, for the Indians are not capable of acting by themselves in these perilous times.

I gave you plenty of warnings to march immediately on Cuzco, but you took them all lightly, giving the Spaniards time to prepare as they have done, placing cannon on Picchu Mountain, and devising other measures so dangerous that you are no longer in a position to attack them. God keep you many years. Tungasuca, December 6, 1780.

I must also tell you that the Indians of Quispicanchi are tired of serving as guards so long a time. In fine, God must want me to suffer for my sins. Your wife.

After I had finished this letter, a messenger arrived with the definite news that the enemy from Paruro is in Acos; I am going forward to attack them, even if it costs me my life.

C. THE DEATH OF TUPAC-AMARU

The rebel attack on Cuzco came too late. The strong resistance of the reinforced Spanish defenders and their Indian auxiliaries (the majority of combatants on both sides were natives), the superiority of the Spanish armaments, the constant desertions from Tupac-Amaru's undisciplined host, and the treason of the captured Spaniard who commanded the rebel artillery and systematically misdirected the fire of his pieces were among the reasons for its failure. In January, 1781, Tupac-Amaru suddenly abandoned the siege and began a rapid withdrawal toward his base in the province of Tinta. The Spaniards soon launched a powerful offensive. The insurgent forces were defeated in fierce battles, and Tupac-Amaru evacuated Tinta, fleeing southward with the apparent intention of organizing a new resistance in the highlands around Lake Titicaca. During the disorderly retreat he, his wife, his sons, and a number of his captains were seized by treachery and handed over to the Spaniards. After a summary trial, on May 15, 1781, the visitador Areche handed down sentences whose ferocity revealed how thin was the veneer of Enlightenment over the medieval mentality of Bourbon Spain. A contemporary account describes the death of Tupac-Amaru and other leaders of the rebellion.[3]

On Friday, May 18, 1781, the militia of Cuzco, armed with spears and some firearms, surrounded the public square, and the corps of mulattoes and Indians from Huamanga district, with fixed bayonets, surrounded the four-sided gallows. Then

3. Odriozola, *Documentos históricos del Perú*, pp. 161–62. (Excerpt translated by Benjamin Keen.)

the following persons were brought forth: José Berdejo, Andres Castelu, and *zambo* Antonio Oblitas (the executioner of the corregidor Arriaga). Antonio Bastidas, Francisco Tupac-Amaru, Tomasa Condemaita, the woman cacique of Acos, Hipólito Tupac-Amaru, son of the traitor, his wife Micaela Bastidas, and the rebel leader himself. They were all brought out together in chains, in baskets of the kind they use to bring yerba maté leaves from Paraguay, and dragged along behind a harnessed horse. Accompanied by their guards and by priests who offered them spiritual consolation, they were brought to the foot of the scaffold, and there the executioners meted out the following deaths to them:

Berdejo, Castelu, the zambo, and Bastidas were simply hanged. Francisco Tupac-Amaru, the rebel's uncle, and his son Hipólito had their tongues cut out before they were thrown down the steps of the gallows. The Indian woman Concemaita was strangled on a little scaffold provided with an iron screw made for this purpose, the first ever seen here. The Indian and his wife witnessed all these punishments, even that of their son Hipólito, who was the last to go to the gallows. Then Micaela went up to the scaffold, where, in the presence of her husband her tongue was cut out and she was garroted, suffering infinite agony all the while, because since her neck was very slender the screw could not strangle her, and the executioners had to dispatch her by tying ropes around her neck, each pulling in a different direction, and kicking her in the stomach and breast. Last to die was the rebel leader, José Gabriel. He was brought into the middle of the square, and there the executioner cut out his tongue. Then they took off his chains and laid him on the ground. They tied four ropes to his hands and feet and attached the ropes to the girths of four horses, which four mestizos drove in four different directions. Cuzco had never before seen a spectacle of this kind. Either because the horses were not very strong or because the Indian was really made of iron, they simply could not tear him apart, although they tugged at him for a long time, while he dangled in the air like a spider. Finally the visitador Areche, moved by compassion, decided to end his sufferings and sent an order from the Jesuit college, from whose windows he was watching these punishments, that the executioner should cut off his head, and so it was done. Then they laid his body under the gallows and cut off his arms and legs, They did the same to the women, and the heads of the others were cut off and sent to be displayed in various towns. The bodies of the Indian and his wife were borne to Picchu, where a great bonfire was made, into which they were thrown and reduced to ashes, which were thrown into the air and into the little river that runs through there. Such was the end of José Gabriel Tupac-Amaru and Micaela Bastidas, whose pride and arrogance reached such a pitch that they called themselves Kings of Peru, Chile, Quito, Tucuman, and other parts, even including the Grand Paititi, with other followers of the same kind.

A considerable number of people gathered on this day, but no one gave a cry or even spoke; many, and I among them, noted that there were no Indians in that multitude, at least not in their customary dress; if there were any there, they must have ben disguised in cloaks or ponchos. Sometimes things happen as if the Devil had planned them to confirm these Indians in their abuses and superstitions.

I say this because, although the weather had been very fine and dry, that day dawned with the sky heavily overcast, and at twelve o'clock, when the horses were tugging at the Indian, there arose a gust of wind followed by a downpour that forced all the people and even the guards to run for shelter. This has caused the Indians to say that the heavens and the elements were mourning the death of their Inca, whom the inhuman or impious Spaniards were putting to death with such cruelty.

3. A Modern Interpretation

WARD STAVIG

In this analysis of the Tupac Amaru revolt based upon his Ph.D. dissertation written in 1988, Professor Ward Stavig of the University of South Florida concludes that despite long provocations, the majority of Indians in rural Cuzco did not involve themselves in the 1781 rebellion and that only those in partidos or sections ruled directly by Tupac Amaru supported his insurrection, which was initially instigated in the name of the king.

In recent years there has been renewed scholarly interest as to the causes and significance of the Thupa Amaro rebellion that exploded on the colonial landscape of rural Cuzco in 1780 and quickly spread through much of the southern Andes. This interest was spurred by the Peruvian military government's use of Thupa Amaro as a symbol of its commitment to social change after it took power in 1968 and by the flurry of publications and events surrounding the bicentenary of the rebellion in 1980. While most of the writings have focused on the leadership of the movement and the colonial demands imposed on the native peoples, or *naturales,* recent research has begun to shift attention ever closer to the Indians themselves, as scholars try to understand the roots of change and social violence. However, due to its complexity and scope, no single analysis adequately explains the Thupa Amaro rebellion. An analysis that seems convincing at the level of the state loses much of its explanatory power when events are seen from the perspective of the Indian community, or ayllu. Strong emphasis on economic conditions has deepened historical understanding of the movement, however, the lives of the Indians in the region where the rebellion broke out were shaped by a complex set of factors. While material conditions were important, they alone did not determine Indian behavior. In order to better understand this behavior and get closer to the perceptions of the native people, I propose to discuss the interplay between material conditions, culture, and the structures that shaped Indians' lives in rural Cuzco on the eve of the Thupa Amaro rebellion.

From "Ethnic Conflict, Moral Economy, and Population in Rural Cuzco on the Eve of the Thupa Amaro II Rebellion," by Ward Stavig, *Hispanic American Historical Review* 68:4 (November 1988): 737–70, passim. Reprinted by permission of the Duke University Press.

This study focuses on the native people in two provinces or *partidos* of rural Cuzco, Quispicanchis and Canas y Canchis (Tinta), in the decades preceding the 1780 rebellion. These two *partidos* were selected because their population remained heavily Indian in character, their forastero* population was not large, and they were at the center of the Thupa Amaro rebellion. By examining a region with strong Indian heritage, where *originarios* dominated and where the European and mixed population was small, I believe that we can better understand the actions of the Indians in colonial society, which were quite different in this case as compared to regions where European and mixed populations had more significant roles in daily life.

The article also looks at efforts of the native people to maintain the basic framework of the social, economic, and political order that governed their lives under the effects of increasing colonial demands, long-term structural changes, and population pressures. I give special attention to the small localized revolts that broke out in the years preceding the Thupa Amaro rebellion and to inter-Indian conflicts. The revolts, unlike the very different and larger-scale rebellions, can best be seen as efforts to restore or preserve the existing order. Yet, the tensions that threatened the Indians' way of life also led to conflicts among Indians and weakened their internal cohesion. These inter-Indian conflicts, while reflecting immediate problems, often stemmed from more ancient divisions between Indian communities. Such ethnic divisions served sometimes to prevent sometimes to delay and sometimes to weaken conflict with the state. . . .

CONTRADICTIONS AND CONJUNCTURES

In the late eighteenth century, the world view of the Indians of Quispicanchis and Canas y Canchis was both compex and contradictory. Population pressure eroded their resource base at the same time that state economic demands pressed them ever more. By 1780, Spanish colonial policy that for more than two centuries had functioned to reduce ethnic identity, and which in the process exacerbated local and internal divisions within Indian society, had been so effective that the native people began to question their ability to maintain their way of life, given the intrusion of

---

*Indians who moved from their community of origin to another community were known as forasteros. Their descendants maintained this designation. Forasteros were exempt from certain obligations such as service in the Potosí mita and part or all of the tribute payment. Exemption from obligation was a major reason for Indians becoming forasteros. They were not full legal members of the communities in which they lived and did not have a legal right to community lands. Indians who remained in their communities of origin and met the obligations imposed on them by the community and the state, and who received the rights that came with this compliance, were known as *originarios*.

outside forces and the erosion of internal community relations. When mid-eigh-teenth-century changes in political administration and economic policy were added to longer term and structural changes, a conjuncture was produced in which the rela-tions and assumptions that collectively formed the moral economy began to come under doubt, and compliance with its norms no longer seemed to assure the social reproduction of the Indian communities.

To be sure, the same circumstances could produce opposite tendencies. Demands of the colonial state created Indian solidarity at the same time that they caused inter-nal tensions As we have seen, some Indians turned the state's labor demands for the Potosí mita into a force for maintaining community solidarity. The mita, disliked by virtually all Indians, produced an interclass united front of protest and antagonism, and in the long journey to and from Potosí, as well as during their stay in the min-ing center, *naturales* more fully comprehended the burden Andean Indians shared. In the same manner, population pressure in conjunction with state demands led to conflicts between communities, while also contributing to antistate antagonism. As native people found it harder to meet their obligations, friction with neighboring Indian groups became more common, but so did revolts and claims of official abus-es and excesses. These protests were often directed against specific individuals, yet the cumulative impact was a growing questioning of the legitimacy of the colonial system.

Likewise, while some curacas became more "European," and state representa-tives appointed caciques who would promote imperial interests, other curacas react-ed to the changes and pressures of the period by harking back to the Inca heritage. This identification with the Inca past was not a new phenomenon, but it became stronger in the eighteenth century. Throughout the colonial period there had existed myths of Gran Paititi, an Inca society in the jungle where the survivors of Cuzco had fled after the Spanish conquest. Another myth, that of Inkarri, developed around the idea of an Inca who would bring order to the world. These myths provided a basis for a limited degree of cultural identity, although Alberto Flores Galindo cautions that one should not see in them "a mechanical response to colonial domination," and he notes that while by the eighteenth century such ideas were widespread they were not continuous and are probably best thought of as "small islands and archipelagos." These myths in any case, accompanied by such changes as the adoption of Inca dress by curacas (at least when having their portraits painted) and an increased read-ing of the *Royal Commentaries* of Garcilaso de la Vega (El Inca) by the Indian elite, form part of what John Rowe referred to as Inca nationalism. For those who would see in Inca revivalism a growing class or caste consciousness. Rowe cautions that it is necessary "to maintain a clear distinction between the mass of the tributary pop-ulation and the aristocracy of the caciques: both groups conserved part of the old tradition, but a different part." However, even if this concern with Inca heritage was not "the unifying factor" for caste or class consciousness, it clearly contributed to the larger awareness that evolved among the Indian population in the complex and contradictory years just before the 1780 rebellion.

This larger awareness or consciousness had limited implications for collective action as long as Indians responded to certain colonial pressures along lines of ethnic division, rather than against the state. Some inter-Indian conflicts were created by colonial demands, others, with roots in "time immemorial," were enhanced by these demands. Either way, they made identification or concerted action with Indians of neighboring communities, let alone more distant Indian groups, difficult. Added to such contradictions was the strong desire of the native peoples to maintain their traditional way of life, based in part on reciprocal relations with the state, even as changes in the world around them threatened that life. These factors combined to raise the collective boiling point of Indian society appreciably.

Nevertheless, by 1780 long-term structural changes and conflicts, economic tensions, and population fluctuations that developed in the eighteenth century, as well as more immediate problems specific to Quispicanchis or Canas y Canchis, combined to create a conjuncture that made the existing order vulnerable. It was in these circumstances that the lid the Spanish had successfully kept over the simmering tensions of Indian society blew off. The desire of the Indians to maintain their way of life, together with the divisions (many of which stemmed from colonial demands) that fractured Indian society, had made rebellion unlikely until the moral economy that helped preserve this way of life was severely threatened and the legitimacy of the state questioned. Even then, the majority of the Indians in rural Cuzco did not rupture their relationship to the state and involve themselves in the rebellion. The only *partidos* in rural Cuzco that provided strong support to the rebellion were Quispicanchis and Canas y Canchis, the home territory of Thupa Amaro. There, Thupa Amaro organized the rebellion by claiming descent from the Inca and by relying, in typical Andean fashion, on his network of family and associates. Among these Indian and non-Indian associates were most of the local curacas, whose support was instrumental in mobilizing the Indian peoples, since the Indians of Canas y Canchis and Qispicanchis with only a couple of exceptions followed the lead of their curacas in joining or not joining the rebellion. The situation was ripe for rebellion, but it was the strength of the relationships between Thupa Amaro and other curacas and the Indian people over whom they ruled that won adherence to the movement. This support stemmed from their traditional authority and from the strength of their personal, face-to-face relations with the Indian peoples in the ayllus and communities. Even so, the rebellion, initially, was instigated in the name of the king.

MEXICO

4. The Reorganization of the Army

LYLE N. McALISTER

Professor Lyle N. McAlister of the University of Florida has analyzed the development of society in the eighteenth century in a sophisticated and stimulating fashion. Besides the present selection, which explains how the privileged colonial militia officer class of eighteenth century Mexico eventually produced in the following century such military dictators as Agustín de Iturbide and Antonio López de Santa Anna, he has also written a valuable essay, "Social Structure and Social Change in New Spain,"* in which he develops a theoretical approach.

The military situation in New Spain was fairly representative of Spanish America as a whole. The armed forces of the colonies were strong enough to maintain internal security and defense against the hostile Indians or sudden raids by enemy forces. They were completely inadequate, however, to repulse a strong, well-organized expeditionary force. Their deficiencies were emphatically demonstrated by the loss of Habana and Manila to the English in 1762.

As a result of the lessons learned during the Seven Years War, a secret committee for imperial defense was organized in Madrid consisting of the principal ministers of the crown. This body met once a week to discuss measures for a defense of the Spanish Indies and early in 1764, presented the outlines of a general plan. To provide a first line of defense, the fortifications of the important American ports were to be strengthened, but the fate of Habana had illustrated the folly of too much dependence on fixed defenses. Fortifications, therefore, were to be supplemented by the creation of colonial armies. The nuclei of these armies were to be regular troops of two classes: First, *fijo* units, that is, regiments and battalions which were raised

* *Hispanic American Historical Review* 43 (1963): 349–70.

From "The Reorganization of the Army of New Spain, 1763–1766," by Lyle N. McAlister, *Hispanic American Historical Review* 33 (February 1953): 8–32, passim. Reprinted by permission of the Duke University Press.

and stationed permanently in the colonies, and second, peninsular units which would rotate in overseas service. Considerations of economy, however, made it impossible to maintain enough regular units in America to bear the burden of defense alone. The mass of the armies would have to consist of colonial militia, greatly augmented in numbers and organized on a disciplined footing like the provincials of Spain.

The execution of the new military program in New Spain was entrusted to Lieutenant-General Juan de Villalba y Angulo, then captain-general of Andalusia and an officer of firmness and energy. As an indication of the importance the crown attached to his mission, Villalba was given authority and discretionary powers of an extent generally denied even to the viceroys. In matters relating to the reorganization of the army his authority was supreme and even the viceroy could not veto his plans or decisions. To provide him with the rank and title commensurate with his jurisdiction, he was named "commandante general de las armas de Nueva España" and inspector-general of all the regular and militia troops of the kingdom. On the other hand, with its customary reluctance to give a clear cut definition of authority to any of its officers, the Spanish government ordered Villalba to recognize the authority of the viceroy as captain general. This ambiguity left some doubt as to just who was the supreme military commander in New Spain. . . .

In addition to the administrative problems involved in forming a disciplined provincial militia, there were certain political considerations that had to be taken into account. The program could succeed only with public support, and military service was not popular in New Spain The experiences of [Viceroy] Cruillas during the mobilization of 1762 had clearly illustrated this point. In spite of the danger of an English attack on Veracruz the inhabitants of the kingdom were extremely reluctant to enlist in the militia, and the most arbitrary methods had to be used to fill the companies. In addition to popular opposition and apathy, Cruillas had to contend with lack of coöperation from the *justicias* themselves. These officials, by regulation responsible for providing men, procrastinated, made excuses, and sometimes openly refused to coöperate with the viceroy and his lieutenants. In the procurement of personnel, therefore, Villalba was ordered to use the most diplomatic methods possible. His instructions contained the following admonition:

It will be your inalterable maxim and that of the *mariscales de campo* who accompany you, to establish your labor principally in the hearts of the inhabitants of New Spain, treating them in all matters as my true and loving vassals, making them understand with more or less firmness according to your prudent observations, that the changing times require different policies than those followed up to now; that the security of their families and homes make it necessary to take steps to repulse the enemies of their liberty and possessions; and finally you will make use of every idea and method which will make this service mild and agreeable to them, since the maintenance and development of this program will depend on a solid and favorable impression at the beginning.

The crown emphasized that the regular officers and noncommissioned officers assigned to militia duty must maintain good relations with the provincial troops and ordered that any regular who, in an excess of soldierly zeal, treated a militiaman with unnecessary harshness, be returned to Spain immediately and there be punished with the severity that his offense deserved.

The crown hoped to gain the support of the upper classes for the military program by appealing to the creole love of titles and honors. Commissions as senior officers were to be offered to members of the nobility or of the best families of the kingdom, while company grade officers were to be chosen from among the most distinguished and worthy *vecinos* of the communities in which the companies were raised. Thus the leading citizens of New Spain would be flattered by a recognition of their position and merit. An additional attraction was to be provided by granting the *fuero militar* and other privileges and exemptions to the provincial officers. By these appeals to the vanity and self-interest of upper class creoles, it was hoped to build a loyal and enthusiastic officer corps which would have a personal interest in the success of the militia program.

A problem which did not exist in the mother country but which assumed serious proportions in New Spain, where racial mixture had been in progress for over two centuries, was how to combine whites, mestizos, mulattoes and all the other shadings of color and caste in the formation of the militia. Here, again, Villalba was allowed to use his discretion. The crown suggested that with the exceptions of Negroes and Indians, it might be practical to recruit indiscriminately, or at least allow one-third of each company to be made up of castes if, however, combining castes and whites in the same unit was repugnant to the latter or for some other reason was impractical, the inspector-general was authorized to raise separate units of each group. . . .

Unfortunately for the success of the militia program, the inspector-general disregarded both the letter and spirit of his commission. His instructions emphasized the importance of treating the people of New Spain with the utmost consideration. Instead, he and his officers acted in the most arbitrary and high-handed manner . . . . Villalba's lieutenants intervened in the selection of men by ignoring the classifications and exemptions established by law, dispensing with the *sorteo* [or drawing of lots to determine who would serve] and arbitrarily drafting recruits regardless of their age, marital status, physical condition or occupation. Whites and castes were mixed indiscriminately in the companies and, in the selection of officers, the suggestions of the *ayuntamientos* were ignored and the viceroy was not consulted. Villalba had his side of the case to present, however. The *ayuntamientos,* he complained, were lax in their responsibilities; they procrastinated in conducting censuses, in classifying personnel, and in conducting the *sorteos.* The members of the upper class refused to apply for commissions, and the common people tried every means to avoid military service. The inspector-general was a professional military man accustomed to issuing orders and obtaining results. He had been directed to raise an army in New Spain and proposed to do so with or without the coöperation of the civil authorities.

Regardless of where the blame lay, the military program produced unrest and resentment throughout the kingdom. In Pátzcuaro, a mob forcibly liberated a body of draftees from a recruiting detail of regular troops and stoned the party out of the city. Puebla experienced riots in connection with the enlistment of the provincials, and in that city the *ayuntamiento* abruptly voted to dispose of 15,000 *pesos* in the municipal treasury so that the money could not be used for the purchase of uniforms for the militia. In the capital mobs stoned and jeered detachments of regular troops.

In order to popularize militia service, Viceroy Cruillas, on May 3, published a declaration conceding extensive privileges and exemptions to the provincials. By this instrument the officers of the provincial units were granted the complete *fuero militar,* that is, military jurisdiction in all their legal affairs civil and criminal, except when they were claimants, accusers, or if they were prosecutors, and except for offenses specified by law or regulations. Chief among these special offenses were smuggling and frauds against the royal treasury. Enlisted personnel, when not on active service, were granted the protection of the *fuero* only in criminal cases, but when their unit was mobilized they also enjoyed the complete *fuero.* In addition to these general concessions, there were certain additions and exceptions. . . .

The publication of the privileges and exemptions to be enjoyed by the provincials carried significant implications for the future welfare of the kingdom. It had, however, no immediate effect on the popular attitude toward the new military program. Resistance to the enlistment of militia continued and, to add to the unrest, the regular troops stationed in Mexico, Veracruz, and Puebla experienced a decline in discipline and morale. Desertion became a serious problem, and other military offenses were common. Confronted by a hostile population, the regulars committed crimes and excesses against civilians, and often these offenses were not properly punished because of the protection of the *fuero militar.* The viceroy reported that the situation was so serious that a general uprising was not unlikely. If the English should invade, he predicted, they would find more partisans than enemies. . . .

The difficulties expressed and implied above were inherent in the character of the population, in the social structure, in the economic circumstances, and in the political organization of new Spain. The fact that Inspector-General Villalba was unable to overcome them does not detract from the significance of his mission. Although successive viceroys and inspectors reorganized he army on several occasions, the basic structure of the armed forces of New Spain was established in the instructions issued to the inspector-general, and basic procedures were introduced during the period when he was in charge of the military program.

Aside from its military aspects, the formation of a standing army of regular troops and a large corps of militia had far-reaching social, economic, and political results. The impact of the new military establishment was felt by all sections of society. Members of the upper classes provided the officer corps, lower-class families furnished their sons and husbands for the ranks, merchants and landowners contributed in money for military expenses. As the army increased in size during the remainder of the century, officials of the kingdom from the viceroy down to the *alcaldes* became more and more pre-occupied with military affairs, while military expenses absorbed a larger and larger share of the national income. Before the Seven Years War the obligations of a military service were largely theoretical except in infrequent crises. After the organization of the new militia and regular formations the common people of the kingdom faced the ever-present prospect of being forcibly enlisted in one of the regiments of the army. Perhaps the most significant feature of the military program was the *fuero militar* with its associated privileges and immunities. As the army increased in numbers and importance, this concession, with subsequent amplifications, tended to create a military class exempt from civil responsibility and liability. This situation was particularly dangerous in the case of officers. Although the declaration of Viceroy Cruillas produced no immediate rush to the colors, as time passed the advantages of the *fuero* became more obvious. This attraction and the lure of honors and prestige connected with military service moved the sons of the best families in New Spain to accept commissions in the militia or regular regiments. Thereafter, their primary interest lay outside constructive spheres. "In military service," as Lesley Byrd Simpson has so aptly put it, "with its immediate satisfactions in the form of honors and brilliant uniforms, the young men of New Spain found their true calling." It was this class which was to produce an Agustín de Iturbide and an Antonio López de Santa Anna.

5. Problems and Progress in Mexico

ALEXANDER VON HUMBOLDT

The first non-Spaniard of stature to be allowed to visit the empire in the last years of Spanish rule was the German scientist Alexander von Humboldt who, accompanied by French botanist Aimé Bonpland, traveled through Central and South America between 1799 and 1804 recording geographical measurements, collecting mineral, botanical, and zoological samples, visiting centers of education, and befriending the local learned creoles. His accounts of his experiences published in numerous books and essays are an important source of information about Spanish America on the eve of independence. This excerpt from his *Political Essay on the Kingdom of New Spain* offers an honest and informative view of the economic, political, and social life in Mexico at the beginning of the nineteenth century.

Mexico is the country of inequality. Nowhere does there exist such a fearful difference in the distribution of fortune, civilization, cultivation of the soil, and population. The interior of the country contains four cities, which are not more than one or two days' journey distant from one another, and possess a population of 35,000, 67,000, 70,000, and 135,000. The central table-land from la Puebla to Mexico, and from thence to Salamanca and Zelaya, is covered with villages and hamlets like the most cultivated part of Lombardy. To the east and west of this narrow strip succeed tracts of uncultivated ground, on which cannot be found ten or twelve persons to the square league. The capital and several other cities have scientific establishments, which will bear a comparison with those of Europe. The architecture of the public and private edifices, the elegance of the furniture, the equipages, the luxury and dress of the women, the tone of society, all announce a refinement to which the nakedness, ignorance, and vulgarity of the lower people form the most striking contrast. This immense inequality of fortune does not only exist among the cast of whites (Europeans or Creoles), it is even discoverable among the Indians.

The Mexican Indians, when we consider them *en masse*, offer a picture of extreme misery. Banished into the most barren districts, and indolent from nature,

From *Political Essay on the Kingdom of New Spain* by Alexander von Humboldt, trans. John Black (London: Longman, Hurst, Rees, Orme, and Brown, 1811), 1: 134–217, passim.

and more still from their political situation, the natives live only from hand to mouth. We should seek almost in vain among them for individuals who enjoy anything like a certain mediocrity of fortune. Instead, however, of a comfortable independency, we find a few families whose fortune appears so much the more colossal, as we least expect it among the lowest class of the people. In the intendancies of Oaxaca and Valladolid, in the valley of Toluca, and especially in the environs of the great city of la Puebla de los Angeles, we find several Indians, who under an appearance of poverty conceal considerable wealth. When I visited the small city of Cholula, an old woman was buried there, who left to her children plantations of *maguey* (agave) worth more than 360,000 francs. These plantations are the vineyards and sole wealth of the country. However, there are no caciques at Cholula; and the Indians there are all tributary, and distinguished for their great sobriety, and their gentle and peaceable manners. The manners of the Cholulans exhibit a singular contrast to those of their neighbors of Tlascala, of whom a great number pretend to be the descendants of the highest titled nobility, and who increase their poverty by a litigious disposition and a restless and turbulent turn of mind. Among the most wealthy Indian families at Cholula are the Axcotlan, the Sarmientos and the Romeros; at Guaxocingo, the Sochipiltecatl; and especially the Tecuanouegues in the village de los Reyes. Each of these families possesses a capital of from 800,000 to 1,000,000 of livres. They enjoy, as we have already stated, great consideration among the tributary Indians; but they generally go barefooted, and covered with a Mexican tunic of coarse texture and a brown colour, approaching to black, in the same way as the very lowest of the Indians are usually dressed.

The Indians are exempted from every sort of indirect impost. They pay no *alcavala*; and the law allows them full liberty for the sale of their productions. The supreme council of finances of Mexico, called the *Junta superior de Real Hacienda,* endeavored from time to time, especially within these last five or six years, to subject the Indians to the alcavala. We must hope that the court of Madrid, which in all times has endeavored to protect this unfortunate race, will preserve to them their immunity so long as they shall continue subject to the direct impost of the *tributos.* This impost is a real capitation tax, paid by the male Indians between the ages of ten and fifty. The tribute is not the same in all the provinces of New Spain; and it has been diminished within the last two hundred years. In 1601, the Indian paid yearly 32 reals of plata of *tributo,* and four reals of *servicio real,* in all nearly 23 francs. It was gradually reduced in some intendancies to 15 and even to five francs. In the bishopric of Mechoacan, and in the greatest part of Mexico, the capitation amounts at present to 11 francs. Besides, the Indians pay a parochial duty (*derechos parroquiales*) of 10 francs for baptism, 20 francs for a certificate of marriage, and 20 francs for interment. We must also add to these 61 francs, which the church levies as an impost on every individual, from 25 to 30 francs for offerings which are called voluntary, and which go under the names of *cargos de cofradias, responsos* and *misas para sacar animas*.

If the legislation of Queen Isabella and the Emperor Charles V appears to favour the Indians with regard to imposts, it has deprived them, on the other hand, of the most important rights enjoyed by the other citizens. In an age when it was formally discussed if the Indians were rational beings, it was conceived granting them a benefit to treat them like minors, to put them under the perpetual tutory of the whites, and to declare null every act signed by a native of the copper-coloured race, and every obligation which he contracted beyond the value of 15 francs. These laws are maintained in full vigour; and they place insurmountable barriers between the Indians and the other casts, with whom all intercourse is almost prohibited. Thousands of inhabitants can enter into no contract which is binding (*no pueden tratar y contratar*); and condemned to a perpetual minority, they become a charge to themselves and the state in which they live. . . .

Amongst the inhabitants of pure origin the whites would occupy the second place, considering them only in the relation of number. They are divided into whites born in Europe, and descendants of Europeans born in the Spanish colonies of America or in the Asiatic islands. The former bear the name of *Chapetones* or *Gachupines,* and the second that of *Criollos*. The natives of the Canary Islands, who go under the general denomination of *Islenos* (islanders), and who are the *gerans* of the plantations, are considered as Europeans. The Spanish laws allow the same rights to all whites; but those who have the execution of the laws endeavour to destroy an equality which shocks the European pride. The government, suspicious of the Creoles, bestows the great places exclusively on the natives of Old Spain. For some years back they have disposed at Madrid even of the most trifling employments in the administration of the customs and the tobacco revenue. At an epoch when everything tended to a uniform relaxation in the springs of the state, the system of venality made an alarming progress. For the most part it was by no means a suspicious and distrustful policy; it was pecuniary interest alone which bestowed all employments on Europeans. The result has been a jealous and perpetual hatred between the Chapetons and the Creoles. The most miserable European, without education, and without intellectual cultivation, thinks himself superior to the whites born in the new continent. He knows that, protected by his countrymen, and favored by chances common enough in a country where fortunes are as rapidly acquired as they are lost, he may one day reach places to which the access is almost interdicted to the natives, even to those of men distinguished for their talents, knowledge and moral qualities. The natives prefer the denomination of *Americans* to that of Creoles. Since the peace of Versailles, and, in particular, since the year 1789, we frequently hear proudly declared, "I am not a *Spaniard,* I am an *American!"* words which betray the workings of a long resentment. In the eye of law every white

Creole is a Spaniard; but the abuse of the laws, the false measures of the colonial government, the example of the United States of America, and the influence of the opinions of the age, have relaxed the ties which formerly united more closely the Spanish Creoles to the European Spaniards. A wise administration may reestablish harmony, calm their passions and resentments, and yet preserve for a long time the union among the members of one and the same great family scattered over Europe and America, from the Patagonian coast to the north of California. . . .

The Spanish laws prohibit all entry into the American possessions to every European not born in the peninsula. The words European and Spaniard are become synonymous in Mexico and Peru. The inhabitants of the remote provinces have therefore a difficulty in conceiving that there can be Europeans who do not speak their language; and they consider this ignorance as a mark of low extraction, because, everywhere around them, all, except the very lowest class of people, speak Spanish. Better acquainted with the history of the sixteenth century than with that of our own times, they imagine that Spain continues to possess a decided preponderance over the rest of Europe. To them the peninsula appears the very centre of European civilization. It is otherwise with the Americans of the capital. Those of them who are acquainted with the French or English literature fall easily into a contrary extreme; and have still a more unfavorable opinion of the mother country than the French had at a time when communication was less frequent between Spain and the rest of Europe. They prefer strangers from other countries to the Spaniards; and they flatter themselves with the idea that intellectual cultivation has made more rapid progress in the colonies than in the peninsula.

This progress is indeed very remarkable at the Havannah, Lima, Santa Fe, Quito, Popayan, and Caraccas. Of all these great cities the Havannah bears the greatest resemblance to those of Europe in customs, refinements of luxury, and the tone of society. At Havannah, the state of politics and their influence on commerce is best understood. However, notwithstanding the efforts of the *patriotic society of the island of Cuba,* which encourages the sciences with the most generous zeal, they prosper very slowly in a country where cultivation and the price of colonial produce engross the whole attention of the inhabitants. The study of the mathematics, chemistry, mineralogy, and botany is more general at Mexico, Santa Fe, and Lima. We everywhere observe a great intellectual activity, and among the youth a wonderful facility of seizing the principles of science. It is said that this facility is still more remarkable among the inhabitants of Quito and Lima than at Mexico and Santa Fe. The former appear to possess more versatility of mind and a more lively imagination; while the Mexicans and the natives of Santa Fe have the reputation of greater perseverance in the studies to which they have once addicted themselves.

No city of the new continent, without even excepting those of the United States, can display such great and solid scientific establishments as the capital of Mexico.

I shall content myself here with naming the School of Mines, directed by the learned Elhuyar, to which we shall return when we come to speak of the mines; the Botanic Garden; and the Academy of Painting and Sculpture. This academy bears the title of *Academia de los Nobles Artes de Mexico*. It owes its existence to the patriotism of several Mexican individuals, and the protection of the minister Galvez. The government assigned it a spacious building, in which there is a much finer and more complete collection of casts than is to be found in any part of Germany. We are astonished on seeing that the Appollo of Belvidere, the group of Laocoon, and still more colossal statues, have been conveyed through mountainous roads at least as narrow as those of St. Gothard; and we are surprised at finding these masterpieces of antiquity collected together under the torrid zone, in a table-land higher than the convent of the great St. Bernard. The collection of casts brought to Mexico cost the king 200,000 francs. The remains of the Mexican sculpture, those colossal statues of basaltes and porphyry, which are covered with Aztec hieroglyphics, and bear some relation to the Egyptian and Hindoo style, ought to be collected together in the edifice of the academy, or rather in one of the courts which belong to it. It would be curious to see these monuments of the first cultivation of our species, the works of a semibarbarous people inhabiting the Mexican Andes, placed beside the beautiful forms produced under the sky of Greece and Italy.

The revenues of the Academy of Fine Arts at Mexico amount to 125,000 francs, of which the government gives 60,000, the body of Mexican miners nearly 25,000, the *consulado*, or association of merchants of the capital, more than 1,500. It is impossible not to perceive the influence of this establishment on the taste of the nation. This influence is particularly visible in the symmetry of the buildings, in the perfection with which the hewing of stone is conducted, and in the ornaments of the capitals and stucco relievos. What a number of beautiful edifices are to be seen at Mexico! Nay, even in provincial towns like Guanaxuato and Queretaro! These monuments, which frequently cost a million and a million and a half of francs, would appear to advantage in the finest streets of Paris, Berlin, and Petersburg. M. Tolsa, professor of sculpture at Mexico, was even able to cast an equestrian statue of King Charles the Fourth; a work which, with the exception of the Marcus Aurelius at Rome, surpasses in beauty and purity of style everything which remains in this way in Europe. Instruction is communicated *gratis* at the Academy of Fine Arts. It is not confined alone to the drawing of landscapes and figures; they have had the good sense to employ other means for exciting the national industry. The academy labours successfully to introduce among the artisans a taste for elegance and beautiful forms. Large rooms, well lighted by Argand's lamps, contain every evening some hundreds of young people, of whom some draw from relievo or living models, while others copy drawings of furniture, chandeliers, or other ornaments in bronze. In this assemblage (and this is very remarkable in the midst of a country where the prejudices of the nobility against the casts are so inveterate) rank, colour, and race is confounded: we see the Indian and the Mestizo sitting beside the white, and the son of a poor artisan in emulation with the children of the great lords of the country. It is a consolation to observe, that under every zone the cultivation of science and art establishes a certain quality among men, and obliterates for a time, at least, all those petty passions of which the effects are so prejudicial to social happiness.

Since the close of the reign of Charles the Third, and under that of Charles the Fourth, the study of the physical sciences has made great progress, not only in Mexico, but in general in all the Spanish colonies. No European government has sacrificed greater sums to advance the knowledge of the vegetable kingdom than the Spanish government. Three *botanical expeditions* in Peru, New Granada and New Spain, under the direction of MM. Ruiz and Pavon, Don Jose Celestino Mutis, and MM. Sesse and Mocino, have cost the state nearly two millions of francs. Moreover, botanical gardens have been established at Manila and the Canary Islands. The commission destined to draw plans of the canal of *los Guines,* was also appointed to examine the vegetable productions of the island of Cuba. All these researches, conducted during twenty years in the most fertile regions of the new continent, have not only enriched science with more than four thousand new species of plants, but have also contributed much to diffuse a taste for natural history among the inhabitants of the country. The city of Mexico exhibits a very interesting botanical garden within the very precincts of the viceroy's palace. Professor Cervantes gives annual courses there, which are very well attended. This *savant* possesses, besides his herbals, a rich collection of Mexican minerals. M. Mocino, whom we just now mentioned as one of the coadjutors of M. Sesse, and who has pushed his laborious excursions from the kingdom of Guatimala to the north-west coast or island of Vancouver and Quadra; and M. Echeveria, a painter of plants and animals, whose works will bear a comparison with the most perfect productions of the kind in Europe, are both of them natives of New Spain. They had both attained a distinguished rank among *savans* and artists before quitting their country

The principles of the new chemistry, which is known in the Spanish colonies by the equivocal appellation of new philosophy (*nueva filosofia),* are more diffused in Mexico than in many parts of the peninsula. A European traveller cannot undoubtedly but be surprised to meet in the interior of the country, on the very borders of California, with young Mexicans who reason on the decomposition of water in the process of amalgamation with free air. The School of Mines possesses a chemical laboratory; a geological collection, arranged according to the system of Werner; a physical cabinet, in which we not only find the valuable instruments of Ramsden, Adams, Le Noir, and Louis Berthoud, but also models executed in the capital, even with the greatest precision, and from the finest wood in the country. The best mineralogical work in the Spanish language was printed at Mexico, I mean the Manual of Oryctognosy, composed by M. del Rio, according to the principles of the school of Freyberg, in which the author was formed. The first Spanish translation of Lavater's *Elements of Chemistry* was also published at Mexico. I cite these isolated facts because they give us the measure of the ardour with which the exact sciences are begun to be studied in the capital of New Spain. This ardour is much greater than that with which they addict themselves to the study of languages and ancient literature.

SECTION IX

Historical Interpretations

The readings in this section have been selected to point to an important aspect of the study of Latin American colonial history—the sharp and apparently irreconcilable disagreement over the true nature of Portuguese and Spanish rule. These contrasting opinions and perspectives on the essential contributions of Portugal and Spain offer students an excellent opportunity to exercise critical judgment on what they read and encourage further meditation on some basic controversies that color much of the writing on Latin American colonial history, which, after all, is one of the principal reasons we study history.

While some Portuguese historians may point with pride at the flowering of their language and culture in the New World, some Brazilian historians have reached dismal conclusions on the nature of Portuguese rule. Caio Prado, Júnior, has written: "The panorama offered by colonial society may be summarized as follows: settlement, scattered and unstable; economy, poor and miserable; mores, dissolute; administration, both lay and ecclesiastical, inept and corrupt." A nineteenth-century Brazilian, Capistrano de Abreu, penned a famous description of the colonial family in Brazil: "Taciturn father, submissive wife, cowed children."[1]

Characteristically there is more written on Spanish America than on Brazil, for the dispute goes back to the earliest part of the Conquest when Bernal Díaz del Castillo, indignant at the pro-Cortés version of the Conquest, wrote his *True History of the Conquest of Spain*, and Bartolomé de Las Casas, determined to protect the Indians from genocide, wrote *A Very Brief Account of the Destruction of the Indies*. Stung by criticisms of their rule launched by Las Casas and political enemies, Spaniards have been sensitive to attacks upon their actions in America, particularly to the allegations that they mistreated the Indians, whom they considered as their wards to be protected and Christianized. One of the most reasoned defenses to be made in Spain was prepared by the eminent seventeenth-century administrator and judge, Juan de Solórzano y Pereyra (Reading 1). Three centuries later Professor Philip W. Powell continues the defense of Spain in his book *Tree of Hate: Propaganda and Prejudices Affecting United States Relations with the Hispanic*

---

1. Caio Prado, Júnior, *The Colonial Background of Modern Brazil* (Berkeley and Los Angeles: University of California Press, 1969), p. 414.

The Pride of Spaniards in America. Historians today looking back on the actions of Spain in the New World see many problems and many crises. But Spaniards were satisfied, even complacent, about their American empire, as may be seen from the official work by Antonio de Herrera entitled "General History of the Deeds of Spaniards in the Islands and Tierra Firma of the Ocean Sea." This title page from an eighteenth-century edition, with representations of all the Inca rulers, illustrates the conviction many Spaniards had that their work of civilizing and converting the Indians and of developing a new society overseas was a worthwhile and even noble accomplishment.

World (Reading 2). In Reading 4, R. A. Humphreys presents an excellent general analysis and description of the fall of the Spanish empire in America, which stretched "in unbroken line from California to Cape Horn." He accepts C. H. Haring's assertion that "at the end of the colonial era most of the American provinces enjoyed greater prosperity and well-being than ever before," but other interpretations flourish, too, as may be seen from an "essay on economic dependence in perspective" (Reading 3) by Stanley J. and Barbara H. Stein in their stimulating volume *The Colonial Heritage of Latin America.*

Today the questions foremost in the minds of many historians relate to the social and economic impact of conquest on the conquered indigenous peoples and enslaved Africans. Comparative history has become a flourishing growth industry among an ever-widening circle of scholars who grapple with problems involving factual, moral, and nationalistic considerations. For example, comparative cruelty and questions of comparative oppression are almost impossible to discuss in such a way as to satisfy many historians, because facts are difficult to obtain and moral indignation is often present. Alexander von Humboldt in his classic work on Mexico at the end of the colonial period believed that the condition of the Indians was not much worse than that of the serfs of the time on the rural estates of the Baltic. Stanley J. and Barbara H. Stein acknowledge that it might be valid to state that the existence of West European peasants, craftsmen, and miners was as wretched as that of the lowest stratum of society in Spanish America in the sixteenth and seventeenth centuries. But they go on to ask: "Were West Europeans forced into mines and kept there in the seventeenth century without surfacing from Monday to Saturday? Was there in operation in western Europe an annual labor draft which forced unwilling laborers to move hundreds of miles to pitheads along with their families, supplies, and pack animals?"[2] One wonders whether anyone can really compare the lives of the wretched, because of the inherent problems and prejudices involved.

Finally, in discussing Spanish American economic ills, we should not forget that there has always existed in Spanish-speaking lands a not unimportant segment of society that maintains that economic matters are of minor significance. Américo Castro has expressed it this way: "Religious faith as a basis for life and the monarchy as social horizon" are the two fundamental facts of Spanish life. "Those who attribute the troubles of Spaniards to the poverty of their land are perpetuating a myth."[3] Another eminent Spanish historian, Claudio Sánchez Albornoz, violently disagrees with Castro on many points, but both are convinced, as were many Spanish writers of Spain's Golden Age in the sixteenth century, that economic

---

2. Stanley J. and Barbara H. Stein, *The Colonial Heritage of Latin America* (New York: Oxford University Press, 1971), p. 79.

3. Américo Castro, "The Spanish People," *Texas Quarterly* 3 (1960).

affairs were only minor determinants in Spanish history. How far Spanish Americans today are moved by these attitudes is a moot question, as is the question as to what extent those countries with large indigenous populations have inherited the noneconomic attitudes of the pre-Columbian peoples.[4] These considerations of values may be debatable, but they cannot be ignored by the historian.

4. For a thoughtful interpretation along this line, see Frederick Pike, *Spanish America 1900–1970: Tradition and Social Innovation* (New York: W. W. Norton, 1973).

1. A Seventeenth-Century Defense of Spanish Treatment of the Indians

JUAN DE SOLÓRZANO Y PEREYRA

Juan de Solórzano y Pereyra was one of Spain's foremost seventeenth-century administrators and jurists. After training in law at the University of Salamanca he served for a number of years as a judge in the important audiencia in Lima, Peru. Then he returned to Spain where he became a member of the prestigious Council of the Indies. He also wrote extensively. His *De jure indiarum* (1629) was a learned defense of Spain's titles to the Indies and government, while his *Politica indiana* (1648), from which this excerpt is taken, became the most widely cited treatise on Spanish administration in America. He also played an important role in the organization of the great law code, *Recopilación de leyes de las indias*, which finally was published in 1681. Solórzano was distinctly a member of the imperial establishment, but an intelligent and knowledgeable one.

Although heretics and other rivals of the glories of our Spanish nation have realized the validity of its titles to the New World and the great increase that the Monarchy has achieved through its conquests and conversions, they try to discredit these titles, saying in the first place that we were impelled more by greed for the gold and silver of its provinces than by zeal for the propagation of the Gospel. They also say that since all things must be judged by their intent or principal end, if this is wicked or erroneous, then it cannot produce a title or effect that can be considered constant and legitimate. . . .

Even if we concede that greed for gold and riches. . . may have prevailed among some, this blemish does not lessen the merit of the many good men who took part so sincerely and apostolically in the conversion of the New World. Nor does it lessen the merit of the zeal and concern repeatedly displayed by our Kings in their sagacious *cédulas* and instructions. . . .

The second charge of our enemies is that this greed was the cause of the slight peacefulness and benevolence which have been shown to the Indians.

. . . They also say that these are the only qualities needed for the conversion of

From *Política indiana* by Juan de Solórzano y Pereyra (Madrid, 1930), vol. 1, pp. 117–27, passim.

the Indians and that gentle and pacific methods can be efficacious, as the example of our Lord Jesus Christ and His Holy Apostles shows and as is proven by many passages of Scripture. They also feel that Christians, even when they take part in just wars should always be as kind and amiable as possible. . . .

At each step they throw in our faces the fact that the Indians have been badly treated and that in many places they have completely disappeared. To prove this they have recourse to the treatise written by the Bishop of Chiapas advancing the same argument, which, to stir up greater hatred for us, has been printed in four languages . . . .

But although I do not wish to excuse completely – not should I – the wars that must have been waged unjustifiably against the Indians in the early days of the conquest, nor the many injuries that have been and are still being done to them. . . . I still make bold to assert that these excesses cannot wipe out all the good that has been accomplished in the conversion and instruction of these non-believers by clerics who were disinterested and punctual in the fulfillment of their mission of preaching the Gospel. Even less can they wipe out the piety and ardent zeal of our Kings, nor the justice of their titles. With great solicitude and care and without taking costs or difficulties of any kind into account, our Kings have tried to provide for the conversion of the Indians in a kind, religious, and Christian manner and have sought the services of persons of all estates, laymen as well as ecclesiastics, in order to repress bad treatment and offenses against the Indians and to carry out the obligations imposed on them by the Holy See. . . .

Thus the principles and regulations governing the conquests and conversions were always laid down with all the vigilance and Christian and human prudence that their high ends demanded, though it is understood that in their execution there may have been some excesses and Indian deaths, as our rivals, heretics, and rumor-mongers charge. However, these flaws cannot prejudice the titles and rights of our Kings, nor diminish the glory and repute of what has been achieved in those remote and extensive provinces by means of their expenditures and conscientious attention in converting so many savage infidels and in reducing them to civil life. This is a fact acknowledged by all the serious and Christian authors, both foreign and Spanish, who have dealt with this matter and have endlessly praised the way in which our conquests were organized and conducted. . . .

Although Nicetas audaciously declared that there is nothing that kings and emperors cannot correct, nor that surpasses their power and authority, much truer is the aphorism of Tacitus that wherever there are human beings there are bound to be vices and sin, especially in provinces so distant from their Kings, where royal commands tend to be ignored or diluted and the residents or governors can regard as licit anything that occurs to them. The temerity of human beings easily leads them to scorn what is very remote. And just as doctors considered the cure of diseased lungs

to be extremely difficult because medicaments must reach them through the stomach, following a long and narrow route, so the distance of the Supreme Power makes
it unlikely that appropriate remedies can succeed in alleviating the ailments of these
provinces.

This state of affairs was even less to be wondered at in the early days of the conquest of the New World, when governors and magistrates were not yet able to protect the Indians nor rigorously execute the laws enacted for this purpose. At that time
everything was ruled by captains, soldiers, and sailors—people driven by ferocity
and greed who did not hesitate to violate the laws of men and, as Lucan Seneca,
Sallust and many other authors point out, were not likely to refrain from transgress-
ing divine laws as well. People of this type regard as just only what fills the depths
of their greed; they do not know how to return their swords to their sheathes without shedding blood nor to restrain themselves from despoiling the vanquished.

For this reason the Marquis of Pescara, Don Fernando Davalos, used to say that
nothing is more difficult in war than to respect Christ and Mars with equal discipline. We will not pause to consider this point at present. . . nor the question of when
and how the misdeeds of servants cast a reflection on their masters, a matter that
various authors have discussed at great length. All agree that when kings do not
order these misdeeds nor know of them nor fail to punish them when they are discovered nor are guilty of negligence in appointing their servants, they are absolved
of all blame. And this is precisely the position of our glorious and Catholic Kings,
as we have shown. . . .

In addition, if this question is considered dispassionately, in many places the
Indians gave cause for their mistreatment or for war to be made against them, either
because of their bestial and savage customs or because of the excesses and treason
that they attempted or committed against our people. . . .

Moreover, it is not the Spaniards who have exterminated them, but their own
vices and drunkenness or the earthquakes and repeated epidemics of smallpox and
other diseases with which God in His mysterious wisdom has seen fit to reduce their
numbers, as Acosta and other eye-witness writers testify.

Everywhere they seem destined to undergo these hardships, for. . . nothing is
ordered or legislated for their health, usefulness, and preservation that does not turn
out to cause greater harm to them, according to what the same authors affirm. All of
this, therefore, should be attributed to the wrath and punishments of God rather than
to the oppression and other offenses that we are said to commit against them.
Perhaps God has acted in this fashion because of their grave sins and persistent and
abominable idolatry, as some historians observe with respect to similar calamities
that befell the cities of Rome and Jerusalem.

In any event, I would like those persons who calumniate us to state frankly
whether they would not have been guilty of greater excesses if it had been their lot

to make our conquests. This is a point made by one of the very authors [Theodorus de Bry] who has depicted our cruelties in print.

Indeed, we have already seen the destruction of the islands and other lands which they have unjustly occupied and sacked with great cruelty and insatiable greed. Nor have they shown that they took any pains to instruct the natives in religion but instead have tried to pervert them with their execrable errors, without establishing bishoprics or building churches, which we have erected in large numbers.

But to put an end to this chapter, I again repeat what I said at the outset: I do not wish to extol past excesses against the Indians and even less those that may occur in the future because the principal wealth we ought to seek from them is their conversion, instruction, and preservation, since it was for this purpose that they were commended to us, and it can be accomplished more effectively with gentleness and piety than with bad treatment and atrocities. . . .

2. The Three Centuries of Spanish Rule in America Should Not Be Characterized as a "Tyranny" or as "Oppressive"

PHILLIP W. POWELL

The late Professor Philip W. Powell of the University of California, Santa Barbara, long defended Spain from what he believed to be unjust attacks on its rule in America and the charge that all of the ills of Spanish America today are colonial legacies. Students who compare his interpretations with that of the Steins (Reading 3) will see how fundamentally professors of history can disagree!

The standard simplistic version of Spanish rule in America as a slavocracy filled with tyranny, looting, bleeding taxation and suffocating obscurantism, does not conform to the facts. Spanish rule through all this period was generally more benign than much or even most Spanish American government has been since separation from Spain. Had this not been so, Spain's rule would not have lasted as long as it did.

One of our leading authorities in such matters, Professor Lesley Byrd Simpson, writes:

It seems to me that the average stature of the viceroys of New Spain [Mexico] was so great that no country to my knowledge was ever more fortunate in its rulers. New Spain had plenty of things the matter with it, . . . but it enjoyed a long life (three hundred years!) of relative peace, stability, and prosperity, in marked contrast to the squabbling nations of Europe. Some of the men who made this possible are worth our knowing.

And an English scholar, Ronald Syme, recently implied something similar, in broader context:

From "Spain in America: The Real and the Unreal," in *Tree of Hate: Propaganda and Prejudices Affecting United States Relations with the Hispanic World,* by Philip Wayne Powell, pp. 23–29. © Basic Books, Inc., New York, 1970. Reprinted by permission.

In spite of the handicaps of geography and of distance, Spain was able to hold her wide dominions for three centuries and set upon them indelibly the stamp of her language, thought and institutions. That achievement deserves more honour than it has commonly earned—and a more searching investigation. . . .

One finds, at times, the curious paradox that taxation overseas was not as onerous as it was in some parts of the mother country. One also finds that American life was often easier, or more prosperous, than in much of the mother country, where poverty was commonplace. In food availability, for example, Spanish Americans, of whatever level, were apt to fare as well or better than their European counterparts, Spanish or otherwise. Even the lower classes of Spanish America were likely to live somewhat better than much of the European peasantry.

There were, of course, many abuses of governmental authority, and all the many and varied evils of a vast bureaucracy, cholesterol of empire. Crimes of all sorts were committed, as one might expect in an empire of such size and long life. But there was also judicial machinery and legislation for punishment of abuses.

The important point is that the norm was legality and law enforcement, just as in other civilized societies. In general, Spaniards did not try to impose upon America something hypocritically foreign or inferior to what they lived with at home. Taxation, municipal practices, university statutes, criminal and civil legislation, judiciary, artistic endeavors, social welfare agencies, commercial practices, etc., were, *mutatis mutandis,* close approximations of Spanish usage and norms in European territories. For example, in governmental and private welfare practices alone, there is abundant testimony to the comparatively advanced concern and practices of Spaniards in the New World. Moreover, this is a subject that merits much more attention and honor than it has received. . . .

The one great innovation was, of necessity, in Indian affairs. Spain's three centuries of tutelage and official concern for the welfare of the American Indian is a record not equaled by other Europeans in overseas government of peoples of lesser, or what were considered lesser, cultures. For all the mistakes, for all the failures, for all the crimes committed, and even allowing for Crown motives of practicality and self-service, in its overall performance Spain, in relation to the American Indian, need offer no apology to any other people or nation.

Spain's Inquisition and her State-Church structure are usually blamed for an oppressive obscurantism that supposedly blighted the three centuries in America and entrenched so many of the ills that today beset Spanish American nations. Anti-Catholic prejudice in our own country makes this myth particularly attractive, and nineteenth- and twentieth-century Latin Americans are fond of reiterating it. But no scholar having acquaintance with Spanish educational and other intellectual achievement in America—e.g., Indian education, encouragement of literature, history, scientific investigations, university instruction—would subscribe to such a judgment. The Spanish record of some twenty-three colleges and universities in America, graduating 150,000 (including the poor, mestizos, and some Negroes) makes, for example, the Dutch in the East Indies in later and supposedly more enlightened times, look like obscurantists indeed. The Portuguese did not establish a single university in colonial Brazil nor in any other overseas possessions. The total of universities established by Belgium, England, Germany, France, and Italy during later Afro-Asian colonial periods assuredly suffers by any fair comparison with the pioneering record of Spain.

In this vein, let us observe a few comments by Professor John Tate Lanning, of Duke University, our leading authority on the subject of Spanish American colonial culture:

> Up until a generation ago the view that all intellectual products of Europe were excluded from America by a zealous monarch and Inquisition went almost without question. No careful scholar would now pronounce upon the availability of books in America upon the exclusive basis of the estimable *Recopilación de Indias* or the *Index of Prohibited Books*. The bibliographical avenue of Enlightenment to Spanish America was at no time so thoroughly barricaded as the statutes and indexes indicate.

Again:

> An effective and relatively unhampered literary contact with the whole world of thought is implicit in the propositions defended in the [Spanish American] universities toward the end of the eighteenth century. The censorship of the Inquisition, well established though it was in law, was even more than many other somnolent colonial institutions, essentially bureaucratic and ineffectual.

He also said:

> A grandiose and tenacious injustice springing from the traditions and emotions of the early national historians [of Spanish America] is the sweeping condemnation of Spanish colonial culture as "three centuries of theocracy, obscurantism, and barbarism!"

Along the way, let us notice also that barely more than one hundred persons were executed in Spanish America as a result of Inquisition action during its some 250 years of formal existence. This would seem, I think, to compare rather favorably, as these things go, with the torture and execution of Roman Catholics in Elizabethan England (130 priests and 60 laymen, or a total of 250 killed by the state if one includes those dying in prison). And estimates of deaths for witchcraft in the German states during the sixteenth and seventeenth centuries run well into the thousands. . . .

The substantial scholarly literature on American institutional development under Spanish rule continues to increase, but this fact usually comes as a surprise to many university students and intellectuals in the United States. It seems incredible to some that achievement worthy of later intellectual consideration could have taken place in an inquisitional Spanish-Catholic environment; but, if one applies a bit of logic to the situation, there should be no such astonishment. Spain, as should be well known, was enjoying a Golden Age during most of the first two centuries of her empire-building in America, and there was no reason for the mother country to withhold this intellectual activity from her colonies. And the answer is that she did not. Spaniards in America, and their progeny, had access to Spain's great intellectual achievements, and what's more, American universities were modeled on that of Salamanca, one of the most famous in Europe. Through the mother country came the intellectual currents of the rest of Europe. This was as true of the eighteenth century as it was of the sixteenth or seventeenth.

Almost all of Spanish and Spanish American history is a testimonial to the fact that people of Spanish descent do not long acquiesce to any tyranny that the majority, or even much of a minority, finds unbearable. Spain ruled in America for more than three centuries without professional soldiery or standing military forces except in a few places where they were needed mainly to repel foreign attack or guard against frontier Indian depredations. And in all that time there was not a single rebellion that indicated widespread dissatisfaction with the Crown's rule. There were, of course, local disturbances, conspiracies, and uprisings, which made some mark on this history; but in virtually every case, except the few strictly Indian rebellions, there were apt to be Peninsulars and Americans on both sides and the circumstances were local, with little or nothing to indicate significant separatist spirit. Even when Napoleon invaded the mother country, usurped the throne, and "shook the tree of independence" by pushing Spanish Americans to extraordinary measures of self-government, most Spanish Americans did not initially aim at separation from Spain; independence from the mother country was a slow-growing idea even in that heady atmosphere of crumbling traditions. Independence was almost an accidental outcome, and there were far more important factors in this achievement than any popular rebellion against Spanish tyranny or obscurantism. The strong anti-Spanish propaganda inspired within relatively limited circles did not achieve wide popularity until years of it and abrasive fighting had crystallized dogmatic hatred into war for independence. The war period and subsequent decades spawned a literature of justification with strong hispanophobic twists.

In summary, the evidence so far presented in scholarly monographs, articles, and in documentary publications, does not allow any fair-minded observer to characterize those three centuries as a "tyranny," as uniquely "oppressive," as purposefully or generally cruel, or as "obscurantist." There is still much to be studied concerning those centuries, but it is already clear that they were too complex to fit such generalized epithets. Above all, it is completely fallacious to consider them as merely a continuation of the initial conquest patterns. . . .

3. "The Pre-eminent Social Legacy of Colonialism was the Degradation of the Labor Force, Indian and Negro, Everywhere in Latin America"

STANLEY J. AND BARBARA H. STEIN

The Steins are one of the few husband-and-wife teams who write on Latin American history. A professor emeritus at Princeton University, Stanley Stein first established his reputation by publishing two outstanding monographs on nineteenth-century Brazilian history, but afterwards he turned to investigating the roles of merchants in Mexico and Spain in the last half century of the colonial period, and with Barbara H. Stein, also trained in history, he has carried on prolonged archival research on this theme. The present selection is taken from their book *The Colonial Heritage of Latin America,* which has a frankly economic and social focus since its purpose is to examine "certain basic institutions, patterns of behavior, and attitudes which have had impressive continuity in Latin America: hacienda, plantation and associated social patterns, mining enclaves, the export syndrome and related trade mechanisms and mentality; elitism and racism; nepotism, clientilism, and a tradition of private right in public office."

Revolution in America occurred in 1810 because the criollo elite finally provided the leadership that the castas and the lower even more oppressed strata of colonial society had long awaited. To those who have examined the process of economic development and social change in a historical context it is clear that social systems appear to have extraordinary powers of cohesion, flexibility, adaptation. The cohesion of Latin American colonial social structures was maintained, if transformed, during three centuries largely because no viable alternative system appeared. Fidelity to Spain, sanctified by religious injunction, cemented the structure of colonial society, economy, and polity. The principle of hierarchy, of superordinate and subordinate social groups tied to the European metropolises, was accepted since it satisfied the interests and aspirations of an elite which, in effect, had the monopoly of force to maintain it.

In deciding to break with metropolitan controls, the colonial elite found natural

From *The Colonial Heritage of Latin America: Essays on Economic Dependence in Perspective* by Stanley J. and Barbara H. Stein, pp. 114–19. Copyright © 1970 by Oxford University Press, Inc. Reprinted by permission of Oxford University Press, Inc.

allies in the mestizos, mulattoes, and castas in general; the Indian masses they handled gingerly. The Indians recognized their exploitation under the colonial system, but their bitterness had never successfully found effective expression. The criollo leaders now feared the masses, who often erupted in urban and rural violence, and they rationalized their repression and exploitation of them with the myth that they were inferiors. Undoubtedly some of the colonial elite believed that the Indian masses might remain inert in case of rebellion or, if mobilized intelligently, could be controlled to aid in the elimination of the handful of Spanish bureaucrats and merchants. Support by the castas strengthened the elite's position and promised assistance in controlling the Indians. With the backing of the castas, who were perhaps even more irked by the Spanish-imposed social hierarchy and by restrictions on "passing" and upon economic activity, some of the colonial elite probably saw the possibility of a rather peaceful transition toward independence. In allying with the castas, they co-opted a small but influential social group whose role was magnified by the expansion and diversification of the eighteenth-century colonial economy and by demographic growth.

Put another way, one detects in eighteenth-century Latin America the transformation of the older bases of colonial hierarchy, estates and corporations, into something approximating economic classes based upon wealth and income. The castas seem to have grown proportionately faster than the other social groups, and the lighter-skinned castas moved upward into the group of what were now called American Spaniards. In a word, "passing" became easier and more widespread. Castas were accepted in the colonial militia where criollo officers predominated. The large and growing intermediate group of mestizos and mulattoes spilled over from the hacienda and the Indian communities to fill the expanding number of occupations a diversifying economy requires. They resented the social stigma a colonial regime fastened upon them because of their "inferior" social origins. They bribed local priests to register their children as Spaniards rather than as light mulattoes or light mestizos, or they later had parish records changed. European officials at the end of the eighteenth century complained of the difficulty of registering people as castas for tax purposes. Nor could castas be kept out of artisan guilds nor even kept from pursuing artisan production outside them. They became weavers who established. their own weaving shops; they became shopkeepers and itinerant merchants; they entered the church in large numbers; they flowed into the lesser bureaucracy. In colonial areas of heavy slave importation in the eighteenth century the number of free Negroes and mulattoes increased proportionately. It is not that racial prejudice declined; it is simply that rigid maintenance of status based upon color and ancestry became too difficult. To some extent the sheer number and diversity of castas tended to create a new basis of hierarchy, wealth, at the end of the colonial period. Those able to break away from the status of slave, those who abandoned the Indian communities or indigenous enclaves of Amerinds, became a middle group which could survive only by ruthless pursuit of self-interest. The hispanized Indian or ladi-no, the mestizo, the free Negro, became in many cases a more ruthless exploiter of his social inferiors than the White elite. This was becoming evident before the wars of independence; it was to become even clearer afterward.

If the major legacy of colonial society was degradation and social conflict, what basis exists then for the often heard view that the Iberians had a policy toward Indians and Negroes which was more humanitarian and more tolerant than that of the non-Catholic west Europeans in America? It is true that there were sensitive, articulate, and hard-headed churchmen in the colonies who perceived the decultur-izing, brutalizing, and exploitative aspects of culture-contact and imperialism in the sixteenth century. Such a man was Las Casas. One must, however, recall that other clerics who left posterity detailed ethnographic accounts of the social, political, and religious history of the conquered peoples of America studied the major institutions and values of dominated peoples in order to make colonial rule enduring. They were applied anthropologists. This, after all, was the aim of Las Casas' clerical contem-poraries, Landa and Sahagun. If they often admired the institutions described, the admiration was given grudgingly.

Iberian colonialism did not exterminate subject peoples. It did accept the people of miscegenation. It did tolerate a degree of slave manumission. Yet the direction of colonial rule was not toward social uplift, toward integration; colonial rule was predicated upon separation, not integration, whether one examines tax systems, access to political or military office, even the church. Limited social integration and racial toleration were by-products of special conditions, in particular, the shortage of free labor available for interstitial occupations, those between field hand and elite. Since few Europeans were available to fill these jobs, the colonial society had to supply them. Hence the number of mestizos and mulattoes accepted at certain levels of society, in certain occupational roles. The fact that access to high status and occupation was rigidly controlled permitted the absorption of some newcomers.

The pre-eminent social legacy of colonialism was the degradation of the labor force, Indian and Negro, everywhere in Latin America. This is the abiding signifi-cance of debt peonage and chattel slavery. That occasionally members of the mixed groups were incorporated into the ruling group during the colonial period or distin-guished themselves in the struggle for independence is not a persuasive argument for the racial integration of either colonial or post-colonial society. To argue in this fashion is to raise random sexual activity to the level of planned parenthood and to consider the growth of a mestizo or mulatto population a reliable index of racial integration and equality. On the contrary, it might be argued that the rigor of the bar-riers to upward social mobility—the barriers of birth, color, and economic depriva-tion in both colonial and post-colonial Latin America—permitted the elite to absorb

an insignificant percentage of the more aggressive mixed groups and thereby to preserve the essence of social stratification. Absorption into the elite meant that newcomers accepted the social values and aspirations of that group, in striving for higher status, they lost contact with the disadvantaged groups which they abandoned and
simultaneously removed themselves as leaders of the struggle for the amelioration
of the lot of the illiterate, impoverished masses of color.

To be sure, social aspects of colonialism cannot be divorced from the economic
matrix, and the heart of that matrix in Latin America remained privilege in the form
of access to property and occupation, to ownership of mines, large farms, cattle
ranches, to trade, and to the bureaucracy. A stratified and hierarchical society meant
that a small group closely interrelated by marriage and kinship controlled wealth
and income. Failure to diversify the colonial economy meant that economic opportunity remained limited. For the masses there was no role other than that of field
hands or urban proletariat. And those who labored as dependents, debt peons or
chattel slaves, were stigmatized as inferior. Rationalization buttressed inferiority.
Indians were ignorant, superstitious, docile, lacking intelligence and initiative, not
because society made them so, but because they were Indians—so thought the elite.
Similarly they rationalized the maintenance of Negro slavery on the grounds that
Christianity saved the Negro from barbarism and tribal warfare. To educate such elements of congenital backwardness was an exercise in futility. The colonial legacy of
social degradation and racial prejudice surfaced in the nineteenth century in the
form of acute racial pessimism, in the belief that only the immigration of European
Whites via colonization could supply the industrious labor force capable of effectively transforming Latin America.

Social realities have a habit, however, of proving rationalizations of the *status
quo* inadequate. We are now beginning to realize that much of the social unrest of
Latin America in the past century was a continuation of conflicts over access to
property and occupation that the lower classes touched off in the eighteenth century, that flared up briefly in the struggles for independence and which the elite suppressed after 1824. It is in the twentieth century that the long struggle for social vin-
dication, rooted in the colonial past, is again re-emerging.

4. The Fall of the Spanish American Empire

R.A. HUMPHREYS

Professor R. A. Humphreys almost single-handed created a school of Latin Americanists in Great Britain after World War II. As a Commonwealth Fellow he became attracted to the field while in the United States, and after his appointment to the first Chair of Latin American History in University College, London, in 1948, he steadily and systematically fostered a sound development of teaching and research. It was largely his influence that led to the establishment of several Latin American centers in British universities, the excellent *Journal of Latin American Studies*, and the Institution of Latin American Studies in London of which he served as Director for many years. His publications on modern Latin American history have been distinguished for their balance and style.

At the time of the Napoleonic invasions of the Spanish peninsula in 1807–8, the Spanish empire in America stretched in unbroken line from California to Cape Horn. From Stockholm to Cape Town is less distant, and within the area ruled by Spain all western Europe from Madrid to Moscow might lie and be lost.

A hundred years earlier, at the beginning of the eighteenth century, Spain had been a major battlefield of Europe. That experience was now to be repeated, and this time foreign invasion spelt imperial destruction. The French Revolution in its Napoleonic aspect was the occasion, if not the cause, of the emancipation of Spanish America. But in the years between the war of the Spanish Succession and the wars of Napoleon, Spain herself had risen with remarkable resilience from the decrepitude into which she had fallen in the seventeenth century. Her economic decline had been first arrested and then reversed, and under Charles III and during the early years of Charles IV she enjoyed what seems in retrospect to have been an Indian summer of prosperity.

What was true of Spain was true also of her empire. Of the empire during the long years of Spain's weakness and decay we know all too little. But of its material and intellectual advance during the so-called century of enlightenment there is abundant evidence. And Spain, like Britain, undertook in the eighteenth century the

From "The Fall of the Spanish American Empire" by R. A. Humphreys, *History* (October 1952), pp. 213–27, passim. Reprinted by permission of the Historical Association.

task of imperial reorganization and reform. At home and in the empire the administrative system was overhauled.

New viceroyalties and captaincies-general were created. The establishment, in the very year of the North American Declaration of Independence, of the viceroyalty of the Rio de la Plata, covering the whole, indeed more than the whole, of what is now Argentina, marked a period in the history of Spanish America. And the attempt to systematize and centralize colonial government by the division of the colonies into intendancies—"to unify the government of the great empires which God has intrusted to me," as Charles III expressed it in the Great Ordinance of Intendants for New Spain—was scarcely less important.

The reforms in the imperial economic system were equally radical. The Spanish system of colonial and commercial monopoly differed not in kind from the colonial policy of other powers, but in the extraordinary rigour with which it was applied. There were special reasons for the severity and minuteness of these economic regulations and special reasons for the quite disastrous consequences that followed. But though the policy of colonial monopoly was never abandoned, it was, in the eighteenth century, liberalized. Slowly and cautiously the natural trade routes of the Indies were opened up. Where once Cádiz and Seville had enjoyed a monopoly within a monopoly, and the fleets and galleons had divided between them the commerce and treasure of Mexico and Perú, step by step the ports of America and the ports of Spain were opened, the age-old restrictions on inter-colonial commerce were lightened, and the tariffs and duties hampering trade revised. The so-called Decree of Free Trade of 1778, by which all the more important ports of Spain and of Central and South America were allowed to trade, if not freely at least directly with one another, was as much a landmark in the economic history of the later empire as was the establishment of the viceroyalty of the Rio de la Plata in its political history.

The reasons for these striking innovations were, in the broadest sense of the word, strategic. Efficiency in administration, the rehabilitation of colonial trade, were not so much ends in themselves as means to an end; and the end was imperial defense, the protection of the empire against foreign aggression, particularly English aggression, the elimination of foreign economic competition, and the restoration of Spanish maritime and military power in Europe. And as in British colonial policy after 1763, so in Spanish, the financial problem was paramount. Defence demanded revenue, "it being necessary," as Charles III instructed his visitor-general to New Spain,

on account of the large sums needed in attending to the obligations of my royal crown, to exhaust all means which may appear conducive to increasing as much as possible the income from the revenues.

This was a dominant consideration both in administrative and in economic reform. And what Britain in part proposed to effect by tightening up the acts of trade, Spain in part proposed to effect by their relaxation.

The results, or the apparent results, were remarkable. The volume of imperial trade notably increased. At Buenos Aires, now the capital of the viceroyalty of Río de la Plata and no longer a dependency of Lima, the economic life of the colony was transformed. Its customs receipts, its exports, its shipping, its population, all alike rapidly increased. At Havana, Cuba, where six vessels had sufficed for the trade of Spain in 1760, two hundred were insufficient in 1778, and more than a thousand, Spanish and foreign, entered in 1801. New Spain, or Mexico, repeats the same story—a larger volume of shipping, swelling revenues, greater exports. In Perú, when the legislation of 1778 first came into effect, "speculations were multiplied to so extraordinary a degree" in the first fervour of novelty that the merchants resorted to the now familiar device of destroying their goods in order to maintain the price level. And even remote Chile experienced a new and vigorous impulse of economic change.

Whatever truth, therefore, there may be in the legend of the stagnation and decay of Spain and of the Spanish American empire in the seventeenth century, it does not hold for the eighteenth. Within Spain's transatlantic dominions the signs of an expanding economy and of a growing prosperity were everywhere, or almost everywhere, writ large. "It is just . . . to observe," wrote a competent British observer, that Perú, during the late eighteenth century

> was not only in a flourishing state both in respect to her mines and to her commerce, but also as referable to the capitals possessed by individuals, to the comparative extent of her manufactures, and to her navigation. Between the years 1790 and 1800 there existed in Lima a *commercial* capital of above 15 millions of dollars; whereas in the present year [1826] it is under one million.

Humboldt, in Venezuela, noted that "everything seemed to announce the increase of population and industry." In New Spain the public revenues increased more than sixfold in the eighteenth century, and so also did the produce of the mines. And though more than half of the world output of the precious metals still flowed from Spanish America, and though there is a lively superstition that the Spanish American colonies were made of gold and silver and nothing else, agriculture as well as mining, as the great Gálvez tells us, were the basis of their prosperity. The value of the gold and silver of the Mexican mines, says Humboldt, was less "by almost a fourth" than that of the agricultural produce. Of Venezuela and Cuba he observes that agriculture "founded more considerable fortunes" than had been accumulated by the working of the mines in Perú, and in southern South America, where the mines were few, but where Buenos Aires and even Montevideo were rapidly rising in importance, the pastoral and agricultural industries, then as now, were the economic staples.

It is reasonable to conclude, with Professor Haring, that as the eighteenth century closed the peoples of Spanish America were probably more prosperous than at any time in their history. True, in a colonial and developing area, there was no considerable growth of manufactures. Nor was there in the English colonies. But domestic manufacturing was in fact more widespread than is commonly supposed. True, also, the whole population of Spanish America was certainly not greater than that of the British isles in 1811. But its increase in the eighteenth century was remarkable. In 1800 Mexico City was the leading city of the western hemisphere, larger than any city of Great Britain and Ireland except London and Dublin. Its rival. Lima, compared with Bristol and was itself outstripped by Havana. Even long-neglected Buenos Aires was as large as New York or Philadelphia in 1790. And the growth and embellishment of the cities (not merely the capital cities) illustrates the same expansionist trend. Here, at least, in public buildings and public display, were the marks of opulence; and it is no accident that here also, at the end of the century, there was an efflorescence of intellectual activity, in the universities and academies, in the growth of a periodical press, in literary societies and in clubs. In Santa Fé, Perú and Mexico, observed an English merchant in 1804, there was not only a greater degree of knowledge and a greater degree of progress in civilization than was commonly supposed in Europe, but, he added, though perhaps with prejudice, "much more than exists in Old Spain."

The disruption of this society by a violent cataclysm which would, within a few years, destroy much of its wealth, would seem, at first sight, an improbable event. The Conde de Aranda, one of the more far-sighted of Spanish statesmen, indeed foresaw it. "We must imagine" he wrote in 1782 "that sooner or later in [Spanish] America there will occur revolutions like those of the English colonies." And Canning's retrospective judgment, on the effect of the American Revolution, that "the operation of that example' was "sooner or later inevitable," is well known. The influences of eighteenth-century rationalism and of the French Revolution were equally powerful dissolvents. The continent, despite the censorship of the Inquisition, was not closed to ideas. Forbidden literature is always the most enticing of literature. A cultivated minority was certainly acquainted with the writings of the *philosophes,* of Rousseau, of Locke, even of Adam Smith. These were to be echoed, along with the Declarations of Independence and the Rights of Man, in the pronouncements and charters of revolutionary leaders and revolutionary governments. Yet despite the activities of an adventurer like Francisco de Miranda, who knew the "brace of Adamses" and had seen the French Revolution at first hand, despite occasional conspiracies and even outright rebellion, there was little specifically revolutionary activity in Spanish America before Spain herself fell a prey to Napoleon. The revolution, when it came, rose like a sudden tide from still, or comparatively still, waters.

Yet Spain's colonies were lost before the revolution began. The Bourbon reforms came too late, they did not go far enough, they were given insufficient time, to save the empire. And politically at least they contained no concession to the newer movement of ideas.

> "Instead of considering its colonies as a place of refuge for the idle, the profligate, and the disaffected, where they might learn to amend their lives, and, if possible, forget their errors," wrote the *Edinburgh Review* in 1806, "the Spanish Crown has watched over its foreign settlements with the solicitude of a duenna, and regulated their government as if they were to be inhabited by Carthusians."

The question, perhaps, is mainly interesting for the light it throws on the value placed on colonies in early nineteenth-century Britain. But it contains a solid grain of truth. The empire, from first to last, was built on paternalist and absolutist lines. It could not, in point of fact, be quite so centralized as theory might imply. The royal will was always limited by circumstance. But the price of paternalism was procrastination and inefficiency, a tradition of legalism and a disrespect for law, a class system which almost, but not quite, became a caste system, and a mounting jealousy between Spaniards born in Spain and Spaniards born in America, between, that is, the governors and the governed. "The most miserable European" wrote Humboldt "without education, and without intellectual cultivation, thinks himself superior to the whites born in the new continent." The creoles, excluded generally from the higher administrative posts, found almost their sole representation in municipal institutions. "Even in the most despotic states" says Robertson in his famous *History* "this feeble spark of liberty is not extinguished." But even here it was the local, not the representative, character of the *cabildos,* or town councils, too often closed corporations, petty oligarchies, which caused them to play so prominent a part in the events of 1808 to 1810.

There was no relaxation of this paternalistic system in the eighteenth century. On the contrary, enlightened despotism sought to rationalize and simplify the machinery of imperial administration both in Spain and in America in the interests of order, uniformity, centralization, efficiency. And though, for a time, a new life was breathed into the imperial system, the political aspirations of the creoles were forgotten, or ignored. In so far as the newly appointed intendants, invariably Spaniards, superseded minor, but creole, officials, and trespassed, moreover, on the functions of the *cabildos*, the Spanish American creoles were, in fact, still further removed from the work of government. "We were left" Bolivar was to say "in a state of permanent childhood."

And, paradoxically enough, the measures designed to secure a still closer integration between Spain and her colonies had precisely the opposite effect. In Spanish America, as in Spain, local and regional loyalties were always strong. Customs, conditions, varied enormously. Cities and squares, law and administration, might be drawn to a pattern, but the life of the colonies flowed in its own individual channels; and at a time when the Bourbon economic reforms gave to the several regions of Spanish America a new economic autonomy, the creation of new viceroyalties and captaincies-general promoted and consolidated a growing sense of regional nationalism. Colonial self consciousness was directly stimulated. It can be no accident that the revolution, when it came, gained its first successes in those areas whose economic and political status had thus been raised. The origins of the new Spanish American nations must properly be sought in the developing life of the eighteenth century.

Apart from a small minority, an intellectual *élite,* it is possible that the rising creole middle class of lawyers, merchants, landowners and soldiers might have reconciled themselves for some time longer to their political inferiority, however much they resented their social inferiority, to the Spaniards. The loyalists, or royalists, were always far more numerous during the Spanish America revolutions than they were during the revolution for North American independence. But whatever the prosperity of Spanish America, whatever the rehabilitation of Spain, in the second half of the eighteenth century, the economic foundations of the empire had been irretrievably undermined. The recovery of Spain had failed to keep pace with the expanding economy of her colonies, and the imperial economic reforms of Charles III were no more than palliatives of a condition imperfectly understood. The trade of the empire was still a closed monopoly of Spain, but the monopoly was imposed by a country which could still not successfully apply it, a country outstripped in financial and technical resources, in facilities and skills, by its greatest colonial rival, Britain. The empire, Professor Whitaker has observed, "fell not so much because of decay within as because of pressure from without"; and from this point of view its fall was no more than a corollary of the commercial expansion of Europe and particularly of England.

What really stimulated the economic expansion of Spanish America in the eighteenth century, perhaps, were not so much the imperial economic reforms as the European search for Latin American markets and the European demand for Latin American products. And for the continued growth of European interest in Spanish America there were, apart from considerations of strategy and politics, three main reasons. First, Spanish America provided dollars, the gold and silver coin and specie which was the lubricant of international trade. The bullion supply was as interesting to the continental as it was to the British and North American merchant. Secondly, Spanish America supplied a number of raw materials, such as drugs and dyewoods, hides and skins, increasingly important for industrial and commercial purposes. Thirdly, it afforded a market for manufactured goods, particularly textiles and hardware. The market, perhaps, was not infinitely extensible as was sometimes imagined, but its potentialities were great, some English and some continental merchants knew it far better than might be supposed, and it was undoubtedly profitable.

There were, also, two ways of tapping the resources and trade of Spanish America. The first was to do so indirectly by way of Cádiz and, still more indirectly, by way of Lisbon and Rio de Janeiro. The second was the direct of contraband trade. Both had long been practiced. At the end of the seventeenth century everybody knew that the fleets and galleons at Cádiz were stocked with foreign, principally French and English, not Spanish goods, that the Spanish merchants were little more than agents or shippers, and that the returns which flowed to Spain immediately flowed out again.

"We owe to Divine Providence," Philip V complained, "the special blessing of vast dominions in America, the centre of abundant precious metals; [yet] the Crown has always seen that . . . this is the kingdom which retains the least."

Or, in Pufendorff's phrase, which Mr. Christelow has recently quoted, "Spain kept the cow and the rest of Europe drank the milk."

Spain, in short, could not supply her colonies herself. But she maintained the pretense of so doing. What was more, she insisted that colonial products should flow only to Spain. Since the tonnage of the galleons fell by three quarters in the seventeenth century, it is obvious that the volume of imperial trade had seriously contracted. Not only this, high duties and restrictive freights combined with the monopolistic interests of the merchant houses in Seville and Cádiz to raise the price level in America to fantastic heights. An increase of two to three hundred per cent above the prices in Spain was not uncommon. And if Spain could not herself supply her colonies with enough or cheap enough goods, neither could Europe obtain from Spain all that she wanted of colonial products. The result was an enormous contraband trade. This was the second method employed by the French, the English and the Dutch, the direct or contraband trade; and the more debilitated Spain became, the greater grew the contraband, the more the contraband, the greater Spain's debility, and the weaker her empire. . . .

The effect on Spain can partly be measured in the continuing decline in the tonnage of the fleets and galleons and in the irregularity of their sailings. When the galleons sailed for the last time in 1737 they were unable to dispose of their goods because the markets were already overstocked. Royal decree after royal decree complained of the presence of foreigners and foreign goods in the Indies. Foreigners must be expelled. Officials who connived at contraband trade should be punished with death. Even their immortal souls would be imperilled, for in 1776 the Church was recommended to teach that contraband was a mortal sin. Finally, of course, the great series of economic and commercial reforms which began in 1740 with the permission given to register ships to sail round Cape Horn and culminated in the legislation of Charles III, reflected the acute anxieties of the crown.

The reforms could alleviate, but they failed to remedy the situation. It is true that they did much to rehabilitate Spanish commerce. Though the old monopolists protested, new and more enterprising Spaniard and Spanish Americans entered trade. Shipping and revenue increased. But the contraband continued. To tap the trade of the Gulf of Mexico and the Spanish Main, the British, in 1766, established free ports in Dominica and Jamaica, extending the system, after 1787, to other strategic points in the West Indies. And there is no doubt that, despite temporary vicissitudes, the free port trade, encouraged in time of peace and specially licensed in time of war, was, as the board of trade found it, when reviewing the Free Port Acts themselves, highly "beneficial." The Spaniards might properly complain. But it was no part of British policy to enforce the Laws of the Indies. And whatever may have been the prospects that the imperial reforms of Charles III could have arrested foreign economic pressure upon the walls of the empire and that Spain herself could have been brought successfully to compete in the swelling volume of international trade, the doom of Spanish hopes was sealed by two events. The first was the death of Charles himself in 1788 and the accession of the incompetent Charles IV. The second was the entry of Spain into the French revolutionary wars.

The war of 1779 to 1783, when Spain had actively promoted the independence of England's colonies, had been costly enough. For the first time in Spanish history the crown was forced to issue paper money, soon to be inflated. The brief war with France, from 1793 to 1795, was a further blow. But when, in 1796, Spain again went to war with England, and, with a brief interval of only two and a half years, remained at war for twelve years more, the result was disaster. This was the crisis of the empire. Spain and her colonies were severed. The Spanish economy was seriously deranged. The Spanish navy was almost destroyed. And the colonies were thrown upon their own and foreign resources.

There had been occasions, in earlier years, when Spain had been compelled to tolerate the trade of friends or neutrals in Spanish America. In 1782, for example, Louisiana had been allowed to trade with France. Cuba, in 1793, was permitted to trade with the United States. In the years after 1789, moreover, the slave trade had been thrown open and foreigners allowed to engage in it. But when, on November 18, 1797, the crown opened the ports of Spanish America to neutral shipping, the measure was one of desperation. The order was indeed revoked in 1799 because it had "redounded entirely," as the decree of revocation complained, to the injury of the state and of the interests of its subjects. But what the law forbade, local regulation continued to tolerate and the crown itself to license; and though the old system was restored at the peace in 1802, with the renewal of the war once again the ports were opened.

The result, or partial result, was the rapid growth of North American trade, from Cuba to Buenos Aires and Buenos Aires to Chile. And more than one American, perhaps, like the young Richard Cleveland of Massachusetts, carried in his cargo a copy of the Federal Constitution and of the Declaration of Independence, conveniently translated into Spanish. But it was not only American trade, legitimate and illegitimate, that grew. So also did British trade. The contraband flourished at the free ports in the West Indies. It flourished at Trinidad, which alone was said to supply the Spanish colonies with goods to the value of one million pounds a year. It flourished at Vera Cruz, as Viceroy Marquina bitterly complained. It flourished at Buenos Aires. And, even on the Pacific coast, where the South Sea whalers were actively engaged in it, it extended and strengthened its hold.

There was still to be fought out in Spanish America the battle between monopoly and free enterprise, between the beneficiaries of an old order and the partisans of a new. But the issue was already resolved. It was impossible to re-enact the Laws of the Indies. The economic emancipation of Spanish America was determined before its political emancipation began.

And so far as political emancipation was concerned, the years from 1796 to 1808 were equally decisive. As Britain had formerly wavered between plundering the Spanish American colonies and trading with them, so now she hesitated between their conquest and their emancipation. In 1797 the governor of Trinidad was specifically instructed to encourage revolution on the Mainland. The invasion of Buenos Aires was prepared, and cancelled, in the same year. And there were other plans, in the mind of the British government as well as in that of Francisco de Miranda, so long plotting in England and America the emancipation of Venezuela. But fundamentally Britain was more interested in trade than territory. Her designs were commercial and strategic rather than imperial, and when, in 1806, Sir Home Popham captured Buenos Aires, it was at his own responsibility. *The Times,* indeed, rejoiced. It knew not, it said, how to express itself in terms adequate to the national advantage obtained. But the government vacillated. It did too little and that little too late. Buenos Aires was recaptured and Montevideo lost. The whole affair, said *The Times,* was "a dirty, sordid enterprise, conceived and executed in a spirit of avarice and plunder," and the chief source of the calamity was the unauthorised beginning of it.

But for Spanish America its end was all important. The viceroy of Rio de la Plata had fled. It was the creoles who defeated the British, deposed the incompetent viceroy and appointed a new one. Spanish America had seen the deposition and imprisonment of the legal representative of the king. It had seen a creole militia defeat a European army. It had seen a colonial port crowded with British ships and flooded with British goods. It was not a revolution that took place at Buenos Aires as a result of the British invasion. But it was a political and economic transformation that contained the seeds of revolution.

Suddenly, however, the situation changed. Napoleon invaded Spain. The crown fell into captivity. A usurper sat upon the throne. From an enemy Britain became, overnight, the ally of Spain, and the army which Wellesley was preparing in Ireland for the liberation of Spanish America sailed, not to emancipate Spanish America from Spain, but to liberate Spain from France.

The news of the fall of the monarchy, and of the invasion of the mother country, stirred the loyalty and moved the indignation of the colonies, and, superficially, the resistance movement in Spain was almost exactly imitated in Spanish America. As juntas sprang up in Spain in the name of Ferdinand VII, so in Spanish America juntas and *cabildos* assumed the powers of viceroys presidents and captains-general, the agents, now, of an authority which had ceased to exist. Extraordinary circumstances called for extraordinary measures. The colonists took thought for their own protection and their own future. Power reverted to the people, though by "the people" nothing more can be meant than a small but active creole minority: the revolutions in Spanish America were the work of the few, not of the many.

But that a movement which began as an assertion of independence from France should have ended as an assertion of independence from Spain was due quite as much to Spain herself as to the creole minority in her colonies whose thwarted aspirations in government and trade were thus fulfilled. For though the monarchy had collapsed, though the Peninsula was overrun, the Spaniards still clung to the principles of imperial monopoly and colonial subordination. Crown, Regency, Cortes, showed themselves equally blind, equally determined. The colonies, declared the Junta Central, in 1809, were an integral part of the Spanish monarchy, and the deduction soon followed that they owed obedience to the extraordinary authorities erected in Spain. That was not the Spanish American view. Nor had it been the Habsburg view. "Estos y esos reinos," "these and those kingdoms," was the famous phrase used to define the royal possessions in Spain and the Indies. The Indies had never belonged to Spain. They were the property of the crown of Castile, united to the kingdoms of Spain merely by a dynastic tie. The Bourbons forgot, or ignored, this Habsburg view; and so did the Spaniards. But the creoles remembered it. Just as the English colonies, in the eighteenth century, refused to accept subordination to the sovereignty of parliament, so the Spanish Americans refused to accept subordination to the people of the Peninsula. And in both cases what reason failed to arrange, force was left to decide.